LATINO COLORADO

LATINO COLORADO

The Struggle for Equality in the Centennial State

Ernesto Sagás

UNIVERSITY PRESS OF COLORADO
Denver

© 2025 by University Press of Colorado

Published by University Press of Colorado
1580 North Logan Street, Suite 660
PMB 39883
Denver, Colorado 80203-1942

All rights reserved
Printed in the United States of America

 The University Press of Colorado is a proud member of
Association of University Presses.

The University Press of Colorado is a cooperative publishing enterprise supported, in part, by Adams State University, Colorado School of Mines, Colorado State University, Fort Lewis College, Metropolitan State University of Denver, University of Alaska Fairbanks, University of Colorado, University of Denver, University of Northern Colorado, University of Wyoming, Utah State University, and Western Colorado University.

∞ This paper meets the requirements of the ANSI/NISO Z39.48-1992 (Permanence of Paper).

ISBN: 978-1-64642-725-3 (hardcover)
ISBN: 978-1-64642-726-0 (ebook)
https://doi.org/10.5876/9781646427260

Library of Congress Cataloging-in-Publication Data

Names: Sagás, Ernesto author
Title: Latino Colorado : the struggle for equality in the Centennial State / Ernesto Sagás.
Other titles: Struggle for equality in the Centennial State
Description: Denver : University Press of Colorado, [2025] | Includes bibliographical references and index.
Identifiers: LCCN 2024056845 (print) | LCCN 2024056846 (ebook) | ISBN 9781646427253 hardcover | ISBN 9781646427260 ebook
Subjects: LCSH: Hispanic Americans—Colorado—History | Hispanic Americans—Colorado—Politics and government | Hispanic Americans—Colorado—Social conditions | Immigrants—Colorado—History | Colorado—Ethnic relations—History
Classification: LCC F785.S75 S35 2025 (print) | LCC F785.S75 (ebook) | DDC 305.868/0730788—dc23/eng/20250424
LC record available at https://lccn.loc.gov/2024056845
LC ebook record available at https://lccn.loc.gov/2024056846

Cover art: "Sierras y Colores" (Mountains and Colors), Mural, San Luis, Colorado, by Carlos Sandoval (Hispanic/Cherokee/Apache), represented by FaraHNHeight Fine Art Gallery in Santa Fe, New Mexico. Courtesy of the artist and the Town of San Luis, Colorado. Photograph by Augustine Romero.

To the people of Colorado, whether they just got here or have been here all along.

CONTENTS

List of Illustrations and Tables ix
Acknowledgments xi

Introduction: Latino Colorado 3

1. The San Luis Valley: Forging a Hispano Homeland 31
2. The Eastern Plains: Sugar Beets and Braceros 69
3. The Front Range: El Movimiento 107
4. The Western Slope: NAFTA's Legacy 152

    Conclusion: Colorado's Latinxs and the New American West 189

Notes 213

References 229

Index 257

About the Author 273

ILLUSTRATIONS AND TABLES

Figures

0.1. "Welcome to Colorful Colorado" road sign located at I-25 and the Wyoming state line   2
0.2. Latinx population of the Front Range (by county), 2020   20
1.1. La Capilla de Todos Los Santos, San Luis, Colorado   32
1.2. Latinx population of the San Luis Valley (percentage Latinx, by county), 1990–2020   64
2.1. Latinx population of the Eastern Plains (percentage Latinx, by county), 2020   103
2.2. "The Hand that Feeds" sculpture, Fort Collins, Colorado   105
3.1. UMAS logo   144
4.1. Anti-Mexican graffiti, Glenwood Springs, Colorado   153
4.2. Latinx population of the Western Slope (by county), 1990–2020   166
4.3. Rate of change of the Latinx population of the Western Slope (by county), 1990–2020   174
4.4. Latinx population of the Western Slope (percentage Latinx, by county), 1990–2020   175
5.1. Chile ristras at the Pueblo Chile & Frijoles Festival, 2019   207

Maps

0.1. Geocultural regions of Colorado   15
0.2. Latinx population of Colorado (percentage Latinx, by county), 2020   19
2.1. Beet sugar factory locations in Colorado, 1899–present   72

Tables

0.1. Latinx population of Colorado, 1910–2020   17
0.2. Selected demographic and socioeconomic indicators for Latinxs in Colorado, 2010–2020   23
4.1. Latinx population of Colorado's Western Slope, 1990–2020   165

ACKNOWLEDGMENTS

When I was a kid, I remember gazing at a postcard showing Devils Tower, a unique rock formation in the US state of Wyoming. It was so beautiful and different from anything in my immediate surroundings, that I promised myself that when I grew up, I would visit it. I believe that on that day I took the first step toward becoming a *Westerner* (as in the American West), and years later, I realized that dream. Not only did I end up visiting Devils Tower, but I also moved west to Colorado and never looked back. As the child and grandchild of immigrants who moved around seeking freedom, dignity, and opportunity, I always felt rootless; that is, until I came to Colorado. Here, I found a welcoming community of people who loved the outdoors and the endless vistas of the American West. I also found a supportive academic environment at Colorado State University (CSU), a thriving Latinx community in the state, and a remarkable quality of life in Fort Collins. Soon, the place started to feel like *home*. In a state full of transplants new to the region, I found fertile soil to grow my own roots. That is the mythical promise of the American West—and that is the story behind this book.

Many individuals contributed to the making of this book, but my first intellectual debt of gratitude is to Dr. Arturo J. Aldama (ethnic studies, University of Colorado Boulder). His book *Enduring Legacies: Ethnic Histories and Cultures of Colorado* (University Press of Colorado, 2011) provided me with valuable insights on how to write about race and ethnicity in Colorado and the American West. Fortunately, once I knew what I wanted to do, I also had the support of great historians of the American West like Dr. Jared Orsi (Colorado State University) and Dr. Brenden W. Rensink (Brigham Young University). Both are inspirational scholars who believed in this work, and I am thankful to them for their support. As I conducted research for this book around the state of Colorado, librarians, community leaders, activists, politicians, academics, government employees, and people from practically all walks of life gave freely of their time and contributed valuable information to this project. In the San Luis Valley, the librarians at Adams State College's Nielsen Library (in Alamosa) helped me find materials about Colorado's first Latinxs and the political evolution of the Valley's Hispano population, while the staff of the San Luis Valley Immigrant Resource Center put me in contact with key Latinx community members. In Pueblo, University Archivist Beverly Allen opened the doors of the Colorado State University Pueblo Library special collections to me, in particular the remarkable Colorado Chicano Movement Archives. In Fort Collins, the diligent staff at CSU's Morgan Library helped me find materials throughout the state and the nation, thanks to its excellent interlibrary loan service. Lorena Fuentes Ibáñez, an outstanding undergraduate student in the Department of Ethnic Studies, helped me obtain materials related to Rodolfo "Corky" Gonzales and the Crusade for Justice from the Denver Public Library's Western History Collection. Betty Aragon-Mitotes, an inspirational community activist who founded and directed the Museo de las Tres Colonias in Fort Collins, exposed me to the world of sugar beets and the travails of the Mexican American/Chicanx community in northern Colorado. In the Western Slope, Dr. Tom Acker, Larry Archibeque, Nicole Bernal Ruiz, Karla Gonzales García, Ricardo Pérez, Danny Quinlan, and Marketa Zubkova provided me with valuable insights on recent migration to the area and contacts for further interviews. They are all to be commended for their selfless commitment to helping the region's Latinx communities.

Generous internal and external donors funded this project. I received three Professional Development Program grants from CSU's College of Liberal Arts that allowed me to do research in the San Luis Valley during the summer of 2012, in the Western Slope in 2014, and in southwestern Colorado in 2015. A Faculty Development Fund Award for Outstanding Research and Creative Activity funded my research at the CSU Pueblo archives during the summer of 2013, and a research grant from the Charles Redd Center for Western Studies (at Brigham Young University) provided additional support for research in the Western Slope in 2015. I also received financial support from the Department of Ethnic Studies in the form of professional development funds. Former CSU Ethnic Studies Chairs Dr. Irene Vernon and Dr. Joon Kim, and current Chair Dr. Sushmita Chatterjee, were instrumental in helping me with matching funds and a little extra whenever I needed it. This book would not have been possible without their leadership, support, and encouragement. Jodi Griffin, our former office manager, and Lynn Stutheit, our former administrative assistant, had to bear with all my questions, requests, and paperwork. I truly appreciate every minute of our conversations, their support, and their sense of humor. Among my outstanding colleagues at CSU's Department of Ethnic Studies, one individual deserves special recognition: Dr. Norberto Valdez. Norberto was my mentor in all things Colorado and a committed reader of my writing. *Compa*, this book is as much yours as it is mine. Finally, the editors and staff at University Press of Colorado, as well as the anonymous experts who reviewed this manuscript, offered valuable suggestions and challenged me to tell a better, richer tale. In particular, Skylar Cooper, Tobin Gold, Darrin Pratt, and Robert Ramaswamy answered multiple queries in a timely fashion, and shepherded this manuscript to publication. The production team, including Laura Furney, Tina Kachele, and Sonya Manes, improved the manuscript's readability and must be credited for its beautiful design. Thank you all for your patience and good advice. Despite the valuable help of all the individuals and organizations listed here, I must make clear that all errors and omissions in this book are entirely mine.

My family has been a pillar of strength while writing this manuscript. My wife, Ailyn, our children, Samuel and Matthew, and my mother-in-law, Rita, bore with me while I spent countless hours glued in front of a computer screen typing away. My adult children, Antonio and Anaís; my mother; and my late father and stepfather are always present in my thoughts when I write, because I also write for them. Further back into the past, the struggles of generations of immigrants in my family from Spain and the Caribbean made it possible for me to be where I am, and their sacrifices, difficult decisions, and commitment set in motion forces that made me who I am. I am thus honored to be a part of their American story. Little did they know that one day I—and my immediate family—would become Coloradans.

LATINO COLORADO

FIGURE 0.1. "Welcome to Colorful Colorado" road sign located at I-25 and the Wyoming state line. Source: The author.

INTRODUCTION

Latino Colorado

They are hard to miss. The "Welcome to Colorful Colorado" iconic road signs are one of the first things that visitors driving into Colorado get to see as they catch their first glimpse of the mountains. These signs are found on every major road that enters the state from neighboring Utah, Wyoming, Nebraska, Kansas, Oklahoma, and New Mexico. Yet, despite their bold claim, the signs themselves are not very colorful—just plain wooden rectangles with white lettering (see figure 0.1). But one may argue that they are a good metaphor for Colorado's colorfulness: It is there, but you have to go find it. A similar argument can be made for the state's racial landscape. At first glance, Colorado may seem plain and lacking "color"—another Anglo-majority Western state. Upon closer inspection, though, the visitor soon realizes that the state is more "colorful" and racially diverse than it seems (Aldama et al. 2011). Colorado may not be a majority-minority state like New Mexico, but neither is it a Western Anglo enclave like Montana nor Wyoming. Just like the driver who crosses the state line into Colorado beckoned by the promise inscribed on the welcoming road sign, one must travel a bit further (and do some inquiring) in order to gauge how truly "colorful" Colorado really is—a development mostly driven by the state's rapidly growing and increasingly influential Latinx population.

At least one out of five Coloradans is Latinx.[1] Dozens of names for counties, rivers, cities, and towns in the state are Spanish in origin. Even the name *Colorado* comes from the Spanish word for the color red, a reference to the silty Colorado River (Colorado State Archives 2023). Yet relatively little has been written about Colorado's Latinx population.[2] Unlike the case of New Mexico, where Hispanics have always been a large segment of the population and with countless books written about (and by) them, a cursory review of the literature shows that comparatively very few books have been written about Colorado's Latinxs, and most of them are dated and out of print. Colorado's Indigenous cultures and archeological ruins, the state's mining history, and even the expansion of the railroad have generated far more works. Also, many of these manuscripts on Colorado's Latinxs deal with Hispanic culture, while topics such as Colorado's Latinx politics, labor force participation, or Latinxs' demographic characteristics have not been covered adequately. It is not that Colorado's Latinxs lack importance; rather, mainstream historians seem to take them for granted, as a mere folkloric footnote in a state with deep roots into its Spanish and Mexican past. Another reason for this academic neglect lies in the still subordinate position that Latinxs occupy in the state's politics and economy. Very few of Colorado's Latinxs have been empowered to tell their own history, while non-Latinx academics have focused their efforts elsewhere. Finally, the lack of coverage also has to do with the fact that most Coloradans are recent transplants to the state, or that their family history in Colorado does not go beyond a generation or two. It still bemuses me to see "Colorado Native" bumper stickers all over the Front Range, plastered on the cars of folks that most Native Americans would see as newcomers. These non-Hispanic residents often see Colorado's Latinxs as part of larger, recent national immigration trends (i.e., as aliens) or as a folkloric remnant reminiscent of times past (i.e., as historic relics). In the words of Western historian Patricia Nelson Limerick (1987, 255):

> contemporary attitudes make it difficult to put Hispanic history in its proper place at the center of Western American history. On the Anglo

side, attitudes have over the last century developed a peculiar split: one attitude toward Spanish borderlands history—conquistadores, missions, and rancheros viewed from a safe distance in time; and another, often very different attitude toward actual Hispanic people, especially people working at the low-paid jobs that were and are a key support of the Southwestern economy.

While the old Spanish roots of Colorado are mythologized in the names of suburban developments and scenic roads (e.g., Los Caminos Antiguos Scenic & Historic Byway in the San Luis Valley of southern Colorado), present-day Latinxs and their everyday contributions to the state remain largely ignored in the best of cases or denigrated by xenophobic nativists in the worst. One way or the other, Latinxs never play much of a role in official narratives or the popular imaginary. Cast as eternal outsiders, Colorado's Latinxs have never seemed to really "belong" in the state of which they are such an integral part. This study seeks to remedy this situation.

Latinxs have been an integral part of Colorado even before it became a state, contributing to its historical development and cultural makeup for close to two centuries. Latinxs make up a substantial percentage of the state's population, play a vital role in its main economic sectors, and are becoming a political force to be reckoned with. Colorado has become a hub of US Latinx life and a case study of the old and the new interacting to fashion a multitiered Latinx community in the Intermountain West. Some of Colorado's Latinxs can trace their roots in the US Southwestern region to Spanish colonial times. Others are arriving as you read this book. Some are rural workers and others are urban dwellers, while an emerging Latinx middle class is quietly expanding into the suburbs of the state's metro areas. This study examines the multifaceted experience of Latinxs in the state of Colorado, from the nineteenth century to the present, from the old Hispano families to the newly arrived immigrants, and from metro Denver to the Western Slope. Its focus is not on one particular region or subgroup but on a statewide phenomenon that is as complex and diverse as Colorado's geography. And it is written from the perspective of a Latinx transplant who has come to live, love, and enjoy the diversity inherent in the Centennial State.[3]

The main premise of this study is that Latinxs in Colorado have been a racialized group whose ethnic identity has been forged historically as a result of their cultural isolation from mainstream American society and reinforced by waves of immigration. Generations of Colorado's Latinxs faced the onslaught of a US military takeover and its aftermath in the nineteenth century, their political and cultural exclusion from Anglo society, and their incorporation into the state's economy as cheap labor—all the while contesting their sociopolitical and economic oppression through strategies of resistance and accommodation. Since the 1960s, however, the Chicano Movement, as well as the state's rapidly changing demographics and incorporation into the national mainstream, has opened spaces for Latinxs in Colorado to promote a vocal subaltern discourse that seeks to achieve equality for all, as well as a new—less local, more national—identity as Latinxs. In other words, we are witnessing a transition from Hispanos to Chicanxs to Latinxs, from outsiders to denizens. In turn, the emergence of Latinxs as a substantial ethnic group in the state has rekindled a debate about nativism, social citizenship, and identity. This study also seeks to examine the ways in which Latinxs—as a racialized, socially ostracized group—have historically interacted with Colorado's Anglo society, resisted their exclusion and subordination, and even helped define the latter, for as much as Anglo society has influenced Latinxs in Colorado, the opposite also rings true. I argue that this cultural gap has many unacknowledged crossovers, which this study will examine.

The long-standing struggle for equality by Latinxs in Colorado has also been characterized by periods of intense political activism (such as during the Chicano Movement of the 1960s–1970s) and by the intersectionality of factors such as race, ethnicity, class, gender, and sexuality, giving rise to fluid and changing identities that challenge mainstream representations. These overarching themes engender related research questions such as: How have Latinxs in Colorado identified themselves vis-à-vis Anglo society, other ethnic groups, and each other—particularly as other Latinxs migrate from neighboring states and foreign countries into the state? What role have Latinxs played in the state's economic development as a mostly subordinate labor force? How have Latinxs in Colorado struggled for political recognition and social equality? The answers to these questions serve to unravel the multiple layers of complexity behind Latinx identity (or identities) in a state where Latinxs have such a long—but academically neglected—historical trajectory. Moreover, this study aims to shed light on a historically marginalized community that is increasingly becoming a major political and economic force in the state, while advancing our understanding of racial and ethnic minorities in the Old and New West.

In conclusion, my study seeks to reexamine the role and perception of Latinxs in Colorado's history and present-day society—a state where Latinxs have always "been" but never "are." In other words, it aims to provide a more nuanced view of the vital, constant (yet often unacknowledged) presence of Latinxs in Colorado. Ramón Gutiérrez's (2000, 107) description of the Spanish conquest and colonization of the Americas sums up the path that lies ahead well: "It is a history of the complex web of interrelations between men and women, young and old, rich and poor, slave and free, Spaniard and Indian [Latinx and Anglo], all of whom fundamentally depended on the other for their own self-definition." Latinxs and Anglos have struggled against each other—and relied on each other—for centuries in Colorado, and out of these interactions a New West and new identities have emerged. The recent heated debate about the role of immigration in American society in general (and Latin American immigration in particular) has reignited this conversation about American identity, and it is bound to generate public conversations as the face of America undergoes rapid demographic changes. When Samuel P. Huntington (2004) rhetorically asked, "Who are we?" he should have preceded that question with "Who are they?" for "they" (i.e., racialized Others) define us as much as we define them. Thus, this project is more than simply about Latinxs in Colorado; it is about all of us in the American West and in the United States of America and how we continue to (re)define each other.

Racializing Latinxs in America

Race is a social construct, dating back to the early colonization of the Americas. More specifically, it dates to the first interactions between European colonists and Amerindians and the subsequent importation of enslaved Africans. In the case of the United States, the Virginia colony served as a laboratory where ideas of race, racial superiority, and whiteness played out as European colonists laid down the foundations of capitalism in a plantation society. "White" meant "free," while "Black" was a synonym for "slave," in a caste-like society based on the exploitation of human beings held in bondage (Zinn 2010). A process of racialization thus began, defined as "the extension of racial meaning to a previously racially unclassified relationship, social practice or group" (Omi and Winant 2015, 111). In the English colonies—as well as in the rest of the Americas and other colonized territories in Africa and Asia—race and class would go hand in hand, giving rise to societies where the color of your skin (one of the features—though not the sole one—of the social construct called "race") would determine not only your status as a free person or an equal under the law but also your economic privilege and social standing. Capitalist exploitation was determined at the time by a race-class nexus, in which whites owned property (including other human beings), whereas persons of color had few economic rights and no political rights. Indigenous persons, Black people—and eventually—Latinxs would become the cheap labor force that mostly white property owners needed, and their black and brown skins served as markers that kept them segregated, isolated, and powerless. The combined oppression of race and class (and gender too, in the case of women of color) meant that by the mid-nineteenth century people of color had few rights and little possessions. White males in the United States owned land and slaves and controlled the legal system that supported this race-based status quo.

The United States was the race-obsessed country that took over the territories of northern Mexico in a war of imperial conquest from 1846 to 1848. Before that, a similar coalition of interests, bent on acquiring land, expanding slavery, and fulfilling the Manifest Destiny of the United States, had declared the independence of Texas in 1836 and annexed the young republic to the United States in 1845.[4] Anglo Texans soon developed stereotypes about Mexicans, based on centuries of systematic exploitation of Indigenous persons and Black people, and refined by their own biased perceptions of the racial, cultural, and religious characteristics of Mexican Tejanos (De León 1983, 1–13). The Texas Revolution was more than just about seceding from Mexico; it was also a racial war that pitted Anglo settlers against the Mexican federal authorities, and it placed Mexican Tejanos supportive of the independence cause in an increasingly awkward position (Horsman 1981, 213). Mexican Tejanos (simply known as "Mexicans" thereafter) came to occupy an interstitial place in Texan society: trapped as low-wage laborers between Anglos, who held political power and most of the land, and enslaved persons, who had nothing. The war with Mexico eventually brought the reach of the United States to the Pacific coast, and with it the nation's racial mores were imposed over new subjects. Just as Texas had been occupied and rendered productive by the Anglo-Saxon race, the same fate would await the new territories. For Hispanics in New Mexico, it would mean the loss of their lands to Anglo speculators and local Nuevomexicano elites, who formed an alliance and political machine known as the Santa Fe Ring. The Santa Fe Ring used its control of the territory's politics, courts, and bureaucracy to seize 80% of New Mexico's land grants in the two decades that followed the end of the Civil War (Acuña 2000, 90–94). This massive land grab left hundreds of Hispanic families dispossessed and fueled migration to the Colorado territory, where they helped settle the San Luis Valley and eventually would provide cheap labor to Anglo entrepreneurs.

The former citizens of Mexico were now occupied by Anglo America, facing a new sociopolitical reality, with US citizenship and other rights in theory but few rights in practice.[5] They would lose their land, their homelands, and in some cases (such as the Californios) they would end up disappearing as a people (Pitt 1998). "Mexicans" would become minorities in an Anglo-dominated world, and subject to the whims of US laws and politics, over which they had little control. Although some light-skinned Hispano elites sided with the Anglo invaders and retained some political power, by and large their reign was over. Eventually, even they would be lumped together with the working masses of Indigenous persons and mestizos and become "Mexicans" to the Anglos. Legal citizenship did not translate into social citizenship and equality for thousands of "Mexicans" throughout the US Southwest. This view of Hispanics in the US Southwest as peoples trying to survive in an occupied territory while pushing back against the Anglo establishment provides a lens through which to examine Anglo-Hispanic relations in the American West for well over a century (from 1848 to the 1960s), and in particular in Colorado (Acuña 2000). Isolated from the mainstream and trying to retain their culture in order to survive as a people, Hispanics were, however, under constant pressure to assimilate, and their apparent "failure" to do so was seen by Anglos as proof evident of their incapacity to become part of the American nation, while serving as additional justification for the hostile takeover of the West. In the particular case of Colorado, Hispanics were politically segmented from their New Mexico homeland by the creation of the Colorado Territory and demographically overwhelmed by the arrival of thousands of Anglo miners, ranchers, pioneers, speculators, and all sorts of entrepreneurs (Gonzales and Sánchez 2018). Under this set of historical circumstances, Hispanics remained as outsiders (i.e., racialized Others) until the social upheaval of the 1960s radically reshaped their standing—and that of other Others—in American society.[6]

Becoming racialized Others meant that Hispanics had to rely on themselves. Mexican Americans formed self-help organizations (known as *mutualistas*), and, in some cases, they retaliated against the Anglo establishment with sporadic acts of violence (e.g., the raids carried out by Las Gorras Blancas in New Mexico). But mostly, they sought accommodation in the face of Anglo dominance. Hispanic organizations throughout the Southwest had an assimilationist orientation to them (e.g., the Order of Sons of America), or at least, a moderate stance (e.g., the League of United Latin American Citizens) (LeMay 2000, 252). As African Americans and other communities of color started mobilizing for civil rights in the 1960s, Mexican Americans followed suit. By then, Latinxs in the Southwest had been part of the United States for over 100 years, and as the country modernized, urbanized, and became more interconnected following World War II, new generations of Mexican Americans had become more familiar with mainstream America and had started challenging Anglo tropes about the "Mexican" presence in the American West (D. Gutiérrez 1993, 527). The community had become larger too, mainly as a result of the Bracero Program, which, beginning in 1942, brought thousands of Mexican workers (and their families) as contract workers into the United States. Thus, the Mexican Americans that came of age in the 1960s were more urban, educated, and connected to the outside world than their parents were. Many of them were the first ones in their families to graduate from high school and attend college. Others served in the Vietnam War and came back radicalized from the experience, while other Mexican Americans fought against deep-seated injustices at home. And as the country was rocked by the antiwar movement and the civil rights struggle, Mexican Americans in the US Southwest began adopting more radical political postures under the Chicano label.[7] The Chicano Movement took the form of a militant ethos that rejected assimilation and emphasized cultural survival and self-help (I. García 1997, 34–35). Chicanxs mobilized for labor rights, land struggles, civil rights, and political power. As a mestizo people with deep roots in the Southwest, they claimed to be the rightful heirs of the land and challenged mainstream perceptions of them as "Mexican" Others. The Chicano Movement brought about an "awakening" of the community that led to major social, political, and economic gains. Chicanxs helped carve out spaces for themselves and others, and the Chicano Movement became a watershed event with repercussions that reach into the present. The radical nature of the Chicano Movement brought about a concerted effort by the authorities to confront it, and the establishment sought to defuse it by granting concessions to the Latinx community—ushering in a new era for Latinxs in the United States.

The Chicano Movement started waning by the late 1970s, but by then, Latinxs were finally being recognized in American society. *Time* magazine featured Hispanics in its October 16, 1978, cover with the suggestive headline "It's Your Turn in the Sun," and politicians, businesses, and the media began trying to figure out what to make of them. By the 1980s, the ascendancy of Latinxs in politics and society continued, and the US Census Bureau officially adopted the term *Hispanic* to count them as separate category, starting with the 1980 decennial census. As US politics became less radical in the 1980s, Latinxs and their organizations paralleled those trends. In a way, Latinx politics in the United States—and in Colorado—has come full circle: from accommodation politics in the nineteenth and twentieth centuries, to radical politics in the 1960s–1970s, to a more moderate approach since the 1980s. These changes in political strategies have reflected the times but also the relative standing of Latinxs in US society. Currently, with Latinxs as the largest demographic minority in the nation and with their numbers rapidly increasing decade after decade, cooperation is preferred over confrontation. In Colorado, where Latinxs make up over a fifth of the population, they are rapidly increasing their share of the electorate. The radical politics of the 1960s–1970s got Latinxs a place at the table; now Latinxs are a force to be reckoned with.

In order to understand the sociopolitical spaces that Latinxs have occupied in Colorado since the war with Mexico, one must understand how they have been racialized in American society. Latinxs still remain a racialized Other—in Colorado as in the nation at large—but they have also made considerable political and economic gains. A solid Latinx middle class has developed; Latinxs have achieved high political office in the state,[8] and the nation; and equal opportunity laws and a culture of political correctness have eliminated most overt practices of racial discrimination. Though serious health disparities and income gaps remain, Latinxs have reached a political tipping point where the radical politics of the past lacks urgency, and working with the establishment seems like the most gainful political strategy. It remains to be seen, however, if the progress achieved by Latinxs in the last few decades will translate into gaining socioeconomic parity with the state's Anglo majority and the shedding of their label as racialized Others.

But being Latinx in Colorado is not only about the group's role vis-à-vis mainstream society. In Colorado, as in the rest of the American West, the setting where these interactions have taken place is a powerful force that shapes the history, meaning, and nuances of the Latinx experience in Colorado. Colorado is—in many ways—unique.

Crossing Borders in the American West

It may not look like it on the map, but it can be argued that Colorado is a "border" state. While not lying on the US-Mexico border itself, southern Colorado historically has been seen as part of the "borderlands," a geocultural area that stretches north from Mexico.[9] Originally on the northern fringes of a claimed (but not entirely settled) Spanish empire in the mainland, and later part of the northern territories of a newly independent Mexico, the borderlands finally emerged as such after the US-Mexican War and the conquest of the Southwest by US military forces from 1846 to 1848. The Colorado Territory (1861–1876) and, after 1876, the state of Colorado, marked the northernmost extension of the borderlands, a homeland for thousands of Hispanos who did not cross the border but who were crossed by the border. In Colorado, the borderlands mainly referred to the San Luis Valley, a natural entry into the territory from neighboring

New Mexico, and the location of the first permanent settlements in the newly acquired US possession. As the territory and state was settled by Anglos coming from the East, Hispanos also moved in from the South, in search of jobs and opportunities, taking the borderlands with them and expanding the geocultural area to cities and towns, mainly on the Front Range. When the Chicano Movement took place in the 1960s–1970s, Chicanxs in Colorado played a significant role in the struggle and its definition. The concept of a Chicano Homeland in the US Southwest took shape in those years and now overlaps and reinforces the concept of the borderlands as a region where peoples and cultures rub edges in a shared landscape. Nowadays, the Colorado borderlands include large cities like Denver and small rural towns like Fort Morgan, both hundreds of miles from the US-Mexico border, but with deep Latinx roots. For these Latinxs, the American West is actually El Norte (The North).[10]

Colorado's borders are not only limited to the Hispanic/Chicano borderlands; Colorado is a border(ing) state in more ways than one. In Colorado, the Great Plains and the Rocky Mountains meet, the Old West and the New West converge, and cowboys and yuppies mingle, creating a sui generis place that defies easy classification. According to William Wyckoff, the West is defined (among other things) by "the unique juxtaposition of peoples who came to live here" (1999, x). Colorado has drawn Native Americans, Latinxs, Europeans, African Americans, Asians, Midwesterners, New Englanders, Californians, and people from all over the world, attracted by its allure and the promise of a fresh start in a visually stunning landscape (Iber and De León 2006, 3–6). Colorado is a dream, a promise, and a state of mind. It has been hunting grounds for Native Americans, farmland for Hispano settlers, prospecting claims for Anglo miners, open prairies for ranchers, boom-and-bust oil and gas deposits for drillers, snowy slopes for the ski resort industry, a postcard-perfect destination for tourists, and home to millions of Baby Boomers (and their children) who have arrived since the 1970s. It is a prominent part of the American West, but it is also a place of its own, uniquely Coloradan in its vibe—and Latinxs have always been a part of it. From the first permanent settlement in the territory to today's ritzy tourism industry, Latinxs have been an inseparable—yet largely unacknowledged—part of the Colorado experience. When the Colorado territory was born, Latinxs were here, and as Colorado has grown into what it is today, Latinxs have been part and parcel of that growth, more often than not providing the labor required to sustain the distinctive Colorado lifestyle. Unfortunately, the dominant narrative, popular mythology, and Colorado's traditional historiography have largely ignored the contributions of non-Anglo groups to the state (Aldama et al. 2011, 2). By and large, the dominant narrative tells a story that begins with Zebulon Pike's expedition, American conquest, and statehood; then salutes the perseverance of Anglo miners and railroad entrepreneurs; extols the virtues of pioneer families; and finally, fast-forwards to a glorious present and a promising future. This historical omission of racialized Others is part of a larger trend that characterized Western history since the US conquest of the territory and that only began to be challenged in the last decades of the twentieth century (Limerick 1987, "Introduction"; Milner 1996).

Its bordering regions and diverse landscapes also connect Colorado—and Latinx Coloradans—to neighboring states, cultural regions, the nation, and the world (see map 0.1). The plains of eastern Colorado (irrigated by the South Platte and Arkansas Rivers) connect Coloradans to the grasslands of the American Heartland (from Texas to the Dakotas) and to lifestyles based on ranching and agriculture. Southern Colorado (watered by the Rio Grande watershed) represents, as mentioned earlier, the northern edge of the borderlands and connects the state to the US Southwest. Western Colorado (defined by the Colorado River) links the state to sparsely populated and isolated areas of Utah, Wyoming, and beyond. Finally, the Front Range (defined by its layout parallel to the Rocky Mountains rather than by rivers) is an urban corridor that connects the over 80% of the state's population that lives there to other parts of the state, the nation, and the world through highways, rail lines, commercial aviation, and high-speed communications technology (Abbott, Leonard, and Noel 2005, 7–8). These diverse natural and human landscapes affect how Latinxs—and others—live and work in Colorado. There is no such a thing as *a* Latinx experience, or *a* Latinx community, in Colorado. Rather, cultural, geographic, economic, and political factors have combined to create a mosaic of Latinx communities and experiences: the Hispano farmer of the San Luis Valley, the sugar beet worker of the Eastern Plains, the chambermaid of Vail, the small business owner of Grand Junction, the college

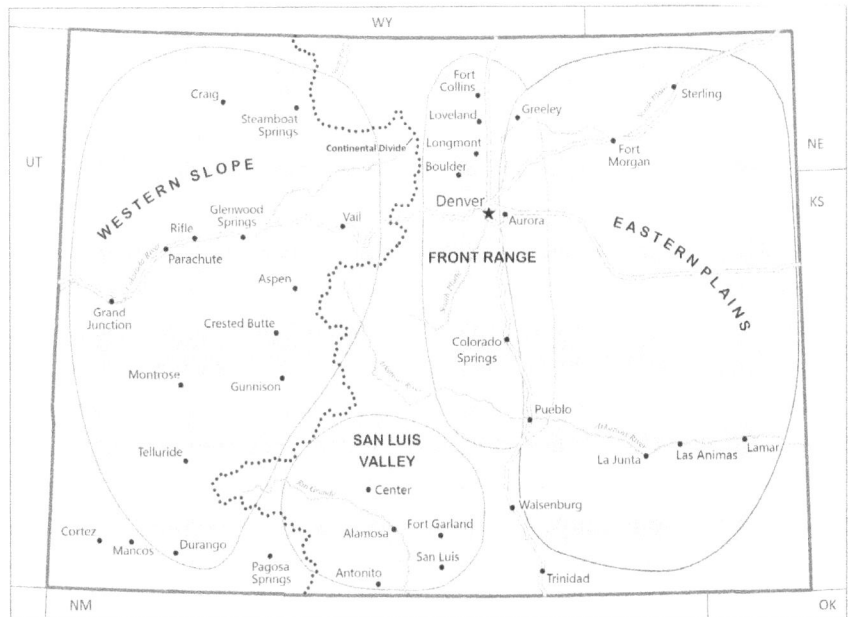

MAP 0.1. Geocultural regions of Colorado. Source: Sophia E. Linn, Geospatial Centroid, Colorado State University.

student of Fort Collins, the yuppie of Denver, and many, many others. Local, national, and transnational social networks and economic links connect these Latinxs to each other, to homelands in Latin America, and to American society at large. As such, borders—whether real or just imaginary social constructs—connect as much as they divide and define Colorado as a unique setting but also as an integral part of the American West.

The Numbers Game

The significant presence of Mexican American, Chicanx, and Latinx populations in most of Colorado's counties by the early twenty-first century reflects decades of rapid internal growth, as well as shifting domestic and international patterns of labor migration. When teaching about Latinxs, I refer to the US Census Bureau as "the birth certificate of demographic minorities." If your group is not recognized and counted as such by the US Census Bureau, it might as well not exist. Numbers mean recognition, resources, and political leverage. In the case of Latinxs, accurate numbers tend to be a problematic issue for several reasons. First, Latinxs tend to be poorer than the average population, and that makes them harder to count. Nontraditional housing arrangements (e.g., living with relatives), lower levels of literacy, unemployment, underemployment, irregular employment, seasonal employment, and other factors combine to make poorer populations harder to track and count than more affluent ones. Second, undocumented Latinxs (or those who are regularizing their status) are understandably reluctant to be counted by government agencies for fear of persecution and deportation. That leaves uncounted not only a large, undetermined number of undocumented Latinxs but also members of their immediate family (e.g., spouses, children) and roommates and tenants living with them. Third, language barriers lead to lower response rates during the decennial census. Non-English-speaking Latinxs are less likely to be counted, even though the US Census Bureau provides forms in several languages and hires bilingual census takers. And fourth, historical trends oftentimes combine with poverty and other factors to create distrust of authorities, including the federal government and its US Census Bureau. For some Latinxs, coming out of the shadows can feel threatening; it is better to lay low. All these reasons combine to make Latinxs particularly hard to count. As a result, most official figures from the US Census Bureau and state authorities usually tend to undercount the number of Latinxs in the United States (C. Rodríguez 2000, 177–181), and Colorado is no exception. The numbers are not entirely accurate, but they are all we researchers have. We are left with no choice but to rely on official statistics, though we must err on the side of caution and assume that there is more than meets the eye. This section relies on those government statistics to paint a profile of Colorado's Latinxs, while remaining cognizant of the aforementioned issues of reliability that may undermine the accuracy of the data.

The 2020 decennial census counted well over a million Latinxs in the state of Colorado (or 21.88% of the state's population). That is a 41.2% increase from 2000–2010, when 735,601 Latinxs (or 17.1% of the state's population) were counted by the US Census Bureau in 2000 (Ennis, Ríos-Vargas, and Albert 2011, 6), and 21.6% growth from 2010–2020 (US Census Bureau 2020). In total, Colorado's Latinx population grew a whopping

TABLE 0.1. Latinx population of Colorado, 1910–2020

Year	State Total	Latinx (n)	Latinx (%)
1910[a]	783,415	3,269	0.42
1920[a]	924,103	14,340	1.55
1930[a]	1,018,793	57,676	5.66
1940[b]	1,123,296	92,549	8.24
1970[b]	2,207,259	255,994	11.60
1980	2,889,964	339,717	11.76
1990	3,294,394	424,302	12.88
2000	4,301,261	735,601	17.10
2010	5,029,196	1,038,687	20.65
2020	5,773,714	1,263,390	21.88

Sources: Ennis, Ríos-Vargas, and Albert (2011, 6); Gibson and Jung (2002, 38); US Census Bureau (1980–2020); Wilmot (2006, 17).

a. In 1930, the US Census Bureau counted "Mexicans" as a separate category (for the first and only time). The figures for 1910 and 1920 are estimates.

b. Estimates based on sample data.

72% from 2000 to 2020, at over twice the rate of the state's 35% overall population growth (UCLA Latino Policy & Politics Institute 2023)! Table 0.1 shows the approximate number of Latinxs in Colorado since 1910, although it was not until 1980 that the US Census Bureau tried to count Hispanics nationwide accurately by employing a "Hispanic origin" category. Before 1980, the bureau used categories such as "Mexican" (1930), "Spanish mother tongue" (1940), and "Spanish surname" or "Spanish language" (1950–1970) to count the Hispanic population of the US Southwest, so the resulting data only provide a guesstimate of Colorado's Latinx population (Wilmot 2006). If the questionable data are used, the percentage of Latinxs in Colorado has ostensibly increased from an official low of 5.6% in 1930 (the "Mexican" category) to today's high of over a fifth of the state's population.

Demographic shifts are behind many of these changes. As of mid-2022, it is estimated that Latinxs (or Hispanics) make up 22.5% of Colorado's population. That is approximately 1.3 million Latinxs out of an estimated population of 5.8 million Coloradans (US Census Bureau 2022). To put it simply, about one out of every four to five Coloradans is a Latinx—and the numbers just keep on rising. Nationally, Colorado has the seventh-largest percentage of Latinxs among US states, and it has the ninth-largest Latinx population in the nation. The growth of the state's Latinx population has also taken place at a rapid pace: 41.2% growth from 2000 to 2010, and 21.6% growth from 2010 to 2020. These state-level percentages are close to the US national trends for those two decades: 43% Latinx growth in the United States from 2000 to 2010, and 23% Latinx growth in the United States from 2010 to 2020 (US Census Bureau 2000–2020). A closer look at some of Colorado's largest metro areas also reflects some interesting patterns. Fort Collins, Colorado Springs, and Greeley had the fastest Latinx growth from 2010 to 2020 (at 41.2%, 38.7%, and 37.4%, respectively), while Denver's Latinx population went slightly down during the same period (by 4%) due to the high cost of living in the state's capital (Alvarez 2021; Frank 2021). As Latinxs left the city of Denver for the suburbs, Adams County joined the growing list of majority-minority counties in Colorado, after the 2020 census confirmed that people of color made up the majority of the county's population (53.9%), which covers the northern and northeastern suburbs of metro Denver (including a small portion of Aurora, the most diverse city in Colorado). Adams County's precipitous demographic change was fueled by the growth of its Latinx population, which by 2020 accounted for about 41% of the county's population (from 29% just a couple of decades before). Most of these Latinxs are of Mexican and Mexican American origin, and like other locals in the Denver metro area, Latinxs have been moving to Adams County in the last few decades to escape Denver's traffic congestion, high crime rates, and the city's steep cost of living. The suburbs of Adams County are quiet and spacious, the schools are good, and real estate prices are more affordable (Foster-Frau 2021).[11]

The spatial distribution of Latinxs in Colorado also shows some interesting patterns. As seen in map 0.2, as of 2020 most of Colorado's Latinxs are clustered in three geographic areas: metro Denver and environs, southern Colorado, and (more recently) the Western I-70 corridor. Metro Denver and the counties that surround it house most of the state's population, and by extension, most of Colorado's Latinxs. The urban/suburban counties of Adams, Arapahoe, and Denver are at least 15%–30% Latinx, as well as more sparsely inhabited rural counties further east into the plains, such as Morgan, Weld, Logan, Phillips, Yuma, and Kit Carson. Denver has

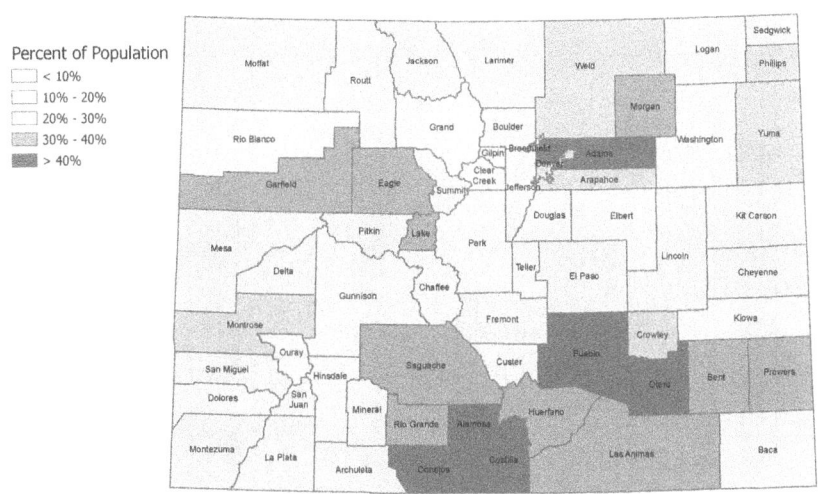

MAP 0.2. Latinx Population of Colorado (percentage Latinx, by county), 2020. Source: State Demography Office 2020.

a significant Latinx population whose growth has paralleled the metro area's rapid development in the last four decades. Its growth spurts now make it hard for the visitor to distinguish between the city proper and surrounding cities (like Aurora) that have been absorbed into the metro area. This urban sprawl created hundreds of jobs that have attracted Latinxs from other parts of the state, the nation, and overseas to metro Denver. Not too far away and connected by highways, the rural counties of the plains have historically provided agricultural jobs for Latinxs, but as some rural areas have been turned into bedroom communities (or exurbs) for commuters to metro Denver and other cities, service and construction jobs have sprung up there too. Change is currently the norm for this part of the state, where farms nowadays coexist uneasily with new, pricey housing developments.

Colorado's Front Range urban corridor not only is home to most of the state's population (84%) but also accounted for 94.8% of its population growth from 2010 to 2020 (Cronin and Loevy 2021a). Not

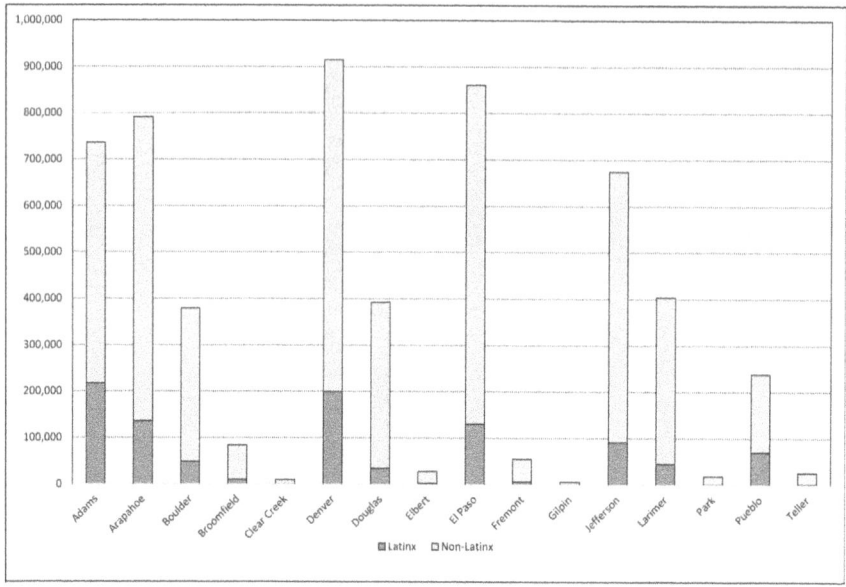

FIGURE 0.2. Latinx population of the Front Range (by county), 2020. Source: US Census Bureau.

surprisingly, Front Range counties are also home to four-fifths of Colorado's Latinxs—about a million Latinxs as of 2020 (US Census Bureau 2020). To a large extent, the Front Range drives the state's demographic dynamics, and Colorado's Latinxs are no exception to that trend. Figure 0.2 displays population data for Latinxs and non-Latinxs in Front Range counties. Two trends are readily apparent. First, Adams, Arapahoe, Denver, El Paso, Jefferson, and Pueblo Counties, which are home to Denver and its suburbs, to Colorado Springs (El Paso County), and to Pueblo, is where most Latinxs in the Front Range (and Colorado) are to be found. Denver and El Paso Counties are the largest counties in Colorado (in terms of their population), so it is not surprising to find plenty of Latinxs where most of the state's population concentrates—and where most of the jobs are. Second, Boulder, Douglas, and Larimer Counties are emerging Latinx enclaves just a short distance from Denver. The growth of their Latinx populations—again—reflects these counties' overall demographic growth and the increased availability of jobs. Thus, Latinxs are both beneficiaries of the state's demographic growth at large, and active drivers in the process. Latinxs not only go where the jobs are (as most people do) but are also local creators of jobs and other economic opportunities that attract new residents.

Southern Colorado is the historical heart of the state's Latinx community (MacAulay 2011). The San Luis Valley was first settled by Hispanics from New Mexico, and from there they spread into the Arkansas River Valley. Cities like Pueblo and Alamosa anchor these communities lying on both sides of the Sangre de Cristo mountain range. At least 30%–40% of the population is Latinx in counties east of the range, such as Las Animas, Otero, and Pueblo, and the percentages are even greater west of the range in counties such as Alamosa, Conejos, Costilla, Rio Grande, and Saguache. With the exception of Pueblo and Alamosa, these are mostly rural communities, and most of the jobs are in agriculture. Some families here have cultivated the land for generations, whereas others are recent arrivals that work as field hands or in the service sector in small towns. These areas truly feel like borderlands—particularly in the San Luis Valley—and the roots of the Latinx community are deep and strong in there.

The Western I-70 corridor is a more recent development tied to Colorado's tourism industry. The construction boom of resort towns like Aspen and Vail in the 1990s–2000s attracted hundreds of Latinxs. Jobs were plentiful not only in construction but also in the service sector in places such as hotels and restaurants and in such occupations as maids, gardeners, and childcare providers in private homes. The construction boom was fueled by a strong economy in which wealthy individuals were buying condos and second (or third) homes and/or investing in businesses in resort towns, and thousands of Latinx immigrants were drawn to an area of the state in which there had never been any major Latinx communities before. These towns are historically white—and now very affluent—and the sudden influx of Latinxs has created significant challenges, as the newcomers are oftentimes first-generation immigrants with low levels of literacy and limited English-language skills. To make things even more complicated, the boom times of the 1990s–2000s drove up real estate prices, making it practically impossible for working-class Latinxs (and even middle-class Anglo families) to live where they work (Park and Pellow 2011). With real estate prices averaging in the millions of dollars for homes in places like Aspen, and with few affordable housing options available in these resort communities, Latinxs have to live in mobile home parks or commute to work from towns far away—often driving two hours to get to work. As of 2020, counties like Eagle, Garfield, and Lake were 30% Latinx or more (US Census Bureau 2020). These Latinx communities are located mostly in towns lying downriver from Vail and Aspen, like Edwards, Gypsum, Basalt, Carbondale, Glenwood Springs, New Castle, Silt, Rifle, Parachute, and Battlement Mesa. Some of these are poor, boom-and-bust rural towns hit hard by the downswing of oil and gas prices; thus, they are affordable, and their location next to I-70 makes for an easier commute. Further west, the cities of Grand Junction and Montrose—and their construction booms—have also attracted Latinx immigrants. Montrose even serves as a bedroom community for those Latinxs who commute to Telluride, another major resort town in the state.

But the growth of Colorado's Latinx population goes beyond the mere redistribution of people from one place to the other lured by the promise of better jobs, housing, and schools in the Centennial State. Overall, Latinxs in Colorado tend to be young, married, and with children, though poorer than average. Most are also native born (75%) and of Mexican origin[12] (74%); 53% speak a language other than English at home (Pew Hispanic Center 2011; UCLA Latino Policy & Politics Institute 2023). "Other" Latinxs make up 16% of this population: a mix of mainly young folks who embrace a pan-ethnic identity (McConnell and Delgado-Romero 2004), and older Hispano families who no longer see themselves as connected to a very remote Mexican ancestry. Puerto Ricans, mostly found in Denver and Colorado Springs (due to the heavy military presence), account for another 3% of Latinxs—making them the second-largest national-origin group among Colorado's Latinxs.

Table 0.2 summarizes the main demographic and socioeconomic indicators for Latinxs (and non-Hispanic whites) in Colorado. As seen in the table, the median age for Latinxs in Colorado is only 28, which is well below the median age for non-Hispanic whites (or Anglos) at 40. However, when the total is broken down by national origin, it is obvious that most of the native-born Latinx population is made up of children and young adults (a median of just twenty), while the foreign-born population is older (with a median age of thirty-six). Essentially, we are looking at two Latinx generations: one of adults in their prime reproductive years, and another one of their children. This demographic phenomenon

TABLE 0.2. Selected demographic and socioeconomic indicators for Latinxs in Colorado, 2010–2020

	Latinxs	Non-Hispanic Whites
Median Age	28	40
Native-born	20	
Foreign-born	36	
Percent Married	47%	53%
Native-born	39%	
Foreign-born	61%	
Annual Personal Earnings (median)	$22,000	$34,200
Percent in Poverty		
17 and younger	31%	9%
18–64	21%	10%
Homeownership Rate	47%	70%
Percent Uninsured	27%	11%
Native-born	17%	
Foreign-born	56%	

Sources: Pew Hispanic Center 2011; UCLA Latino Policy & Politics Institute 2023; US Census Bureau 2020.

is particularly common among immigrant families, which are usually made up of middle-aged adults with children. Other data further reinforce this trend. For example, marriage rates (for persons ages fifteen and older) are higher than average for foreign-born Latinxs (61%), well over the 53% for non-Hispanic whites, who make up the majority of Colorado's population. Moreover, in 2010 Latinxs made up 31% of all the births in the state (Pew Hispanic Center 2011), which was well over their 21% share of the state's population, and nowadays 20% of Colorado's Latinxs are ten years old or younger (UCLA Latino Policy & Politics Institute 2023). Thus, Latinxs in Colorado tend to live in family units with children, and they are younger than their Anglo counterparts.[13]

As in other parts of the United States—though not as pronounced a trend—a generational gap exists between Latinxs and Anglos in Colorado. Latinxs tend to be Gen Xers, Millennials, and increasingly Gen Zs, while Anglos tend to be older Baby Boomers. The gap is not as wide in Colorado, because of the state's younger-than-average population, but it still has major implications for economic status. The older generations tend to be wealthier (having spent more time in the labor market), have greater rates of home ownership, and are on a more secure footing when it comes to access to health care. The fact that race and ethnicity go hand in hand with wealth only compounds the generational gap challenge, giving rise to all sorts of potential future issues as Anglo Baby Boomers age and retire, and younger Latinxs will have to take their place. For example, annual personal earnings for Latinxs in Colorado are only $22,000 (median) versus $34,200 for non-Hispanic whites (a $12,200 gap). Household annual income shows an even greater gap: $53,300 for Latinxs (median) versus $71,500 for whites (Pew Hispanic Center 2011; UCLA Latino Policy & Politics Institute 2023). These gaps are the result not only of age but also other compounding factors, such as education, which are harder to bridge. Only 17.4% of Latinx adults in Colorado have a college degree, versus 51.5% of whites—a massive 34.1% difference! That is the second-largest educational gap in the nation, after California's (at 34.5%), and it presents a major challenge for the state's future as Anglo Baby Boomers start leaving the labor market (Camacho Liu 2011, 9). To make matters worse, "Colorado ranks forty-eight in the nation in state support for higher education" (as of 2010), and "tuition is 29% higher than the national average," making it more difficult for poor students to get a college education (Straayer 2011, 210–211).

    The income and education gaps are clearly reflected in Latinx poverty rates: The poverty rate for Latinx children in Colorado is over three times that of white children, whereas for Latinxs adults it is twice that of whites (see table 0.2). Colorado's minimum wage has increased substantially in the last decade, as Colorado roared out of the 2008 recession, and the state experienced the fifth-highest growth in the nation in real gross domestic product and in per capita income. As of 2021, Colorado's Latinx poverty rate was just 15%—one of the lowest ever recorded (Hindi and Griego 2023). But despite gains in income and falling poverty rates, Latinxs in Colorado still lag far behind non-Hispanic whites. One of the ripple effects of poverty is that it affects your ability to purchase a home (usually the largest source of personal wealth for Americans); only 47% of Latinxs in Colorado own a home, compared to 70% of whites. That places Latinxs at a major disadvantage and reduces the size of their financial safety net. In addition, 27% of Latinxs in Colorado lack health insurance, whereas only 11% of whites are without health coverage. For foreign-born Latinxs, the uninsured rate is an alarming 56%. Lack of health insurance means that some of these families are just one catastrophic illness (or accident) away from financial ruin, and even a common malady can become a major burden on their finances. Moreover, preventive health care is oftentimes beyond the means of the uninsured, which translates into costly trips to the emergency room, which in turn overburdens medical services and increases overall costs for the public. Colorado is one of three states that defy the "Hispanic paradox": the phenomenon by which Latinxs have lower age-adjusted mortality rates than non-Hispanic whites, despite persisting income and educational gaps. In Colorado, higher-than-average rates of liver disease, diabetes, and overdoses among Latinxs help buck this national trend (Wingerter 2024)—a sobering reality check on the status of Latinxs in the otherwise wealthy and healthy Centennial State.

The worst part about these figures is that—in some sectors—Latinxs in Colorado are comparatively worse off now than they were forty or fifty years ago. For example, in 1970, Latinx families earned 72% of white family incomes; by 2010, it was only 50%. Gaps in college graduation rates and home ownership have also widened for Latinxs, even as poverty rates have gone down. Cuts in the provision of social services since the 1980s, combined with a changing economy that saw thousands of manufacturing jobs leave the state, hit Latinxs—and other communities of color—hard and undermined some of the gains made during the civil rights movement (Hubbard and Carnahan 2013). The COVID-19 pandemic also sent many Latinx households into a financial tailspin, hitting them harder than most Anglo families (Bunch 2021). The arrival of hundreds of impoverished asylum seekers from Central and South America has reversed some of the statistical gains made by Latinxs and presents new challenges that the state of Colorado has yet to meet (Rivera and Beaty 2022). Finally, Colorado is being loved to death: Demand for housing—and home prices—hit new heights right during the COVID-19 pandemic as remote workers and investors took advantage of low interest rates and flooded the market, even as the construction of new homes stalled during the 2008 recession and the COVID-19 pandemic (Kwak-Hefferan 2021).

Poor and middle-class Latinx families that had previously aspired to the American Dream of owning a home (Flowers 2022) are being priced out of this red-hot housing market.

In conclusion, Latinxs represent the tip of a generational iceberg in Colorado. They are poised to become a sizable part of the state's population in the near future: 35% of Colorado's total population by 2050, according to estimates based on US census data (Bell Policy Center 2018). And as their numbers increase, Latinxs will figure more prominently in the state's economy and politics. However, major hurdles remain in their path: closing the educational gap, economic inequality, health disparities, access to affordable housing, and legalization of the undocumented—just to name of few. These challenges do not augur well for Colorado. The state needs to invest more in educating and providing services for its poorest residents, yet its hands are tied by a series of budget-balancing and tax-cutting measures enacted over the last three decades (Straayer 2011). It remains to be seen whether Colorado lawmakers will find their way out of this fiscal conundrum and help close the gap between Latinxs and Anglo Coloradans, or if the socioeconomic gains of the 1960s–1970s will be further eroded.

Organization of This Book

This book examines the history and current standing of Latinxs in Colorado in order to raise awareness about the state's largest minority group—and one that keeps on growing. Latinxs in Colorado have been a subordinated part of the population since the arrival of US troops into the territory, and it was not until the 1960s–1970s that the Chicano Movement forced a reassessment of their exclusion from mainstream society. Since then, Latinxs in Colorado have made important strides, yet their future—and that of the state—depends on making decisions now that will prioritize equitable growth for all Coloradans. This book seeks to inform; but, also, to question. It seeks to provide some answers, as well as to generate discussions. I like to think of it as a point of departure.

The format of this book is geohistorical, in more than one sense. As stated earlier, geography is a major determinant factor in Colorado (and throughout the American West). How the territory and state of Colorado was acquired, settled, and developed by the United States was determined to a large extent by geographical factors. Similarly, the role that Latinxs played in that economic history is also influenced by geography. Latinxs went or were attracted to where jobs and opportunities existed for them, and that usually paralleled the state's economic development. Thus, the history of Latinxs in Colorado can be more or less told following a geographic format that takes them from the first Hispano settlements in the San Luis Valley to the latest immigrant arrivals in remote parts of the Western Slope to the ever-changing dynamics of Denver's Latinx community. Each chapter in this book covers a different geographic area of the state, as well as a different period in the history of Latinxs in Colorado. Some overlap is unavoidable, as significant events took place in different parts of the state at the same time, but the geohistorical format of the book aims at helping the reader understand the connection between peoples and places that is so intrinsic to the history of Colorado and the American West.

Chapter 1 starts where it all began: in the San Luis Valley of southern Colorado. There Hispano farmers established the first permanent settlements in the newly acquired territory shortly after the end of the war with Mexico, only to see the land grants that they had obtained a few years before being lost to a new legal and land tenure system that was beyond their control. As American capitalism irrupted into the San Luis Valley, local Hispanos sought ways to shelter themselves from its consequences and held on to their culture for generations—and to this day. As a result, the San Luis Valley became the historical heart of Colorado's Latinx community, and it still remains a major Hispano/Chicanx/Latinx enclave.

Chapter 2 looks at the expansion of the sugar beet industry into the plains of eastern Colorado during the twentieth century and the central role that Latinxs played in it. The development of the sugar beet industry—as well as other crops—attracted hundreds of Latinx workers who extended the cultural borderlands into dozens of rural communities throughout eastern Colorado. Hispanos from the San Luis Valley, New Mexico, and other states, as well as immigrants from northern Mexico, made up the bulk of the agricultural workers who planted, tended, and harvested sugar beets, and did a myriad other jobs. Although nowadays eastern Colorado is the state's most sparsely inhabited region, the migration of hundreds of Latinx workers established deep-rooted communities in the region and served as a springboard for future migrations into other parts of the state.

Chapter 3 examines the widespread sociocultural revolt of the 1960s–1970s that eventually became known as the Chicano Movement. Although El Movimiento played out throughout Colorado (though in different ways depending on location), it was in the urban centers of the Front Range where it found its utmost expression. Not only did large numbers of Latinxs live in cities like Denver and Pueblo, but it was also there that unofficial forms of segregation and discrimination (in jobs, housing, and respect for civil rights) were most rampant and obvious. Moreover, these cities housed the state's largest schools and main postsecondary academic institutions, thrusting students to the forefront of the Chicano Movement. El Movimiento was a watershed event that transformed Colorado's Latinx communities and forced the Anglo establishment to reexamine racial relations in the nation.

Chapter 4 fast-forwards to the 1990s and looks at how international market dynamics have transformed the state and the face of Colorado's Latinx population by focusing on socioeconomic changes in the Western Slope. There, the forces unleashed by trade deals like the North American Free Trade Agreement (NAFTA) brought about an expansion of agricultural markets and a demand for cheap immigrant labor. The expansion of the resort industry would also bring Latinxs to work in upscale locations like Aspen, Telluride, and Vail. Finally, the rapid growth of towns and cities in a formerly underpopulated region created hundreds of jobs in construction and services—jobs that Latinxs would come to fill. In barely two decades, some Western Slope communities underwent significant transformations: from fairly homogenous, Anglo communities, to ethnically diverse towns with growing immigrant populations from Mexico and Central America.

The conclusion revisits the themes presented in the preceding chapters and places Latinx history in Colorado in the context of the American West and the nation. Colorado's Latinxs are more than just another Latinx community in the United States; they represent a unique case study in the northern US-Mexico borderlands and in international migratory circuits. While Colorado's Latinxs share many traits with other Latinx communities across the nation, their particular historical, cultural, demographic, and socioeconomic characteristics, as well as the geohistorical context provided by Colorado's topography and economic development, make of them a case unlike that of neighboring states or elsewhere in the nation.

Latinxs in Colorado are at a tipping point, best exemplified by the race for Colorado's Sixth Congressional District in 2014. A safe Republican district for years, the Sixth historically encompassed the affluent suburbs south and east of Denver. For a decade, it was the political bastion of Representative Tom Tancredo, who ran—unsuccessfully—for the Republican presidential nomination and the governorship of Colorado (twice) on a nativist—if not outright xenophobic—platform. In 2010, redistricting brought major changes to the district, whose boundaries shifted north, losing some of its wealthy suburbs to the south and gaining all of Aurora, a racially diverse city with a large immigrant and refugee population. In 2012, incumbent Mike Coffman, a "birther" who publicly doubted that President Barack Obama was an American (and later apologized for his remarks), narrowly won reelection by less than 7,000 votes (or 2% of the vote). Coffman had also demanded the use of English-only ballots and had voted against the DREAM Act in the past. Shaken by the close outcome and facing a changed district that was now 20% Latinx, Coffman "evolved" in his position. He softened his stance on immigration, began attending Latinx community events, and decided to learn Spanish (Fox 2014). During the 2014 congressional campaign, he even participated in a Spanish-language debate hosted by the local Univisión TV station in Denver. He easily won reelection against a well-known Democratic opponent. Representative Coffman's "evolution" points out to the changing demographics and political landscape of the Centennial State, where Republicans—until recently—stood far to the left of their counterparts in states like Arizona. Representative Coffman saw the writing on the wall and took the appropriate measures to save his political career. Other Republicans, like former Senator Cory Gardner, also modified their positions on immigration in the face of a changing electorate. Flip-flopping politicians are nothing new; what is new is the role of Latinx Coloradans as agents of change. Whereas in the past Latinxs suffered the brunt of decisions made by authorities who did not care much for them or had to resort to protest politics to be heard (as in the 1960s–1970s), nowadays the growing electoral weight of Latinxs is weeding out extremist, reactionary candidates who, like Tancredo, would have been easily elected in safe districts just a decade or two ago. Though the political influence of Latinxs is not even across the state, their influence in some areas translates into a changing political environment statewide, where moderation and compromise in issues like immigration, education, health care, and jobs, is becoming the new normal. In this sense, Latinxs are destined to play a major role in a changing state by fueling change as well as benefiting from it. And in doing so, all Coloradans gain from a more competitive electoral landscape, where political offerings have to appeal to a large and diverse range of voters, and where elected officials can no longer rely on safe districts or comfortable legislative majorities to impose their personal agendas. Change is the only constant for Colorado, and Latinxs represent the tip of the iceberg.

1

THE SAN LUIS VALLEY

Forging a Hispano Homeland

Driving into the San Luis Valley brings into view not only a different geographical landscape, but a cultural one as well. A deep, profound Hispanidad (Spanishness) can be felt—one that contains elements of Spain and Mexico but that is also unique to the region. Like New Mexico (which is, as the saying goes, neither new nor Mexico), Colorado's San Luis Valley is different from other Hispanic/Latinx communities throughout the United States. Its idyll, rural character gives newcomers the impression that time has stood still in the Valley (as locals call it) and people have always lived placid lives on the farms and ranches that dominate the landscape. Situated on a mesa overlooking the small town of San Luis, and against the backdrop of the Sangre de Cristo mountains, La Capilla de Todos Los Santos (The Chapel of All Saints) makes visitors feel as if they had been transported to central Mexico, while its Stations of the Cross sculptures evoke sites of religious pilgrimage in Spain (see figure 1.1). This flight of fancy can be attributed to the fact that centuries ago, this land was claimed as a part of Spain and later of Mexico, and those cultural

FIGURE 1.1. La Capilla de Todos Los Santos, San Luis, Colorado. Source: Smithat88, Wikimedia Commons, https://commons.wikimedia.org/wiki/File:Capilla_de_Todos_Los_Santos_-_San_Luis,_Colorado,_2016.jpg. Note: The original color image was saved in grayscale.

roots still run deep in the San Luis Valley (Gallegos 2011; Gustin 2004). Yet, Colorado's San Luis Valley is an American product too, facilitated and molded by the US military takeover, the interaction between Indigenous peoples, Hispanics, and Anglos, and global modernizing trends that percolate into the Valley as products, ideas, and people come and go. But for Latino Colorado, it is a starting point, a sort of birthplace—because it all began here.

The San Luis Valley of south-central Colorado is also a geographical and historical oddity. A broad, flat, alpine valley ringed by the Sangre de Cristo range on the east and the San Juan mountains on the west, the San Luis Valley extends for 150 miles in a north-south fashion from southern Colorado into northern New Mexico, with a maximum width of 50 miles (Upson 1939, 721). Its high desert environment (at an average elevation of 7,000–8,000 feet throughout the valley, much higher in the surrounding mountains that can reach 14,000 feet) accounts for extreme temperature differences and a short growing season, yet the waters of the

Rio Grande and other tributaries have turned the Valley into one of the most important agricultural communities in Colorado. The San Luis Valley is well known in the state for its production of potatoes, head lettuce, and barley, among other crops. The San Luis Valley is also the birthplace of Colorado (with the small town of San Luis being the oldest permanent settlement in the state) and of the state's oldest Latinx community. Except for an artificial state border that follows a straight line defined by the thirty-seventh parallel, the San Luis Valley is in many ways more like New Mexico than Colorado. Geographically, the river and valley flow south into northern New Mexico (see map 0.1), while a cultural continuum blends the Valley's Hispanic communities with their kinfolk down river (see Beeton, Saenz, and Waddell 2020). The drawing of Colorado's southern border as a straight line for simplicity's sake willfully ignored these realities and was a contentious issue for decades (Everett 2014, chap. 7; Gonzales and Sánchez 2018).

Spanish-Mexican-American Settlement

The Hispanic connection to Colorado dates to the late sixteenth century. In 1598, Spanish conquistador Don Juan de Oñate claimed the New Mexico territory, including the lands drained by the Rio Grande. However, neither Oñate nor his men entered present-day Colorado. Over the next couple of centuries, the Spanish would explore the lands that today make the US Southwest by undertaking several *entradas* (military expeditions) and establishing permanent settlements along the margins of the Rio Grande, as far north as present-day northern New Mexico. The Spanish conquistadors founded cities and towns such as Santa Fe and Taos, bastions of Spanish military power from which they subjugated the local Puebloans while mixing with them, eventually giving rise to a mestizo frontier society in which "the other slavery" (i.e., the widespread "informal" enslavement of Indigenous peoples by the Spanish empire, even in the face of laws that banned the practice) played a key role.[1] In spite of their claimed "pure" bloodlines, the Spanish themselves were the product of centuries of immigration into the Iberian Peninsula by peoples from the circum-Mediterranean, mixed with invading Moors from North Africa who occupied parts of the Iberian Peninsula from 711 to 1492, and Jews who had settled in European cities (Meier and Ribera 1993, 16–18). After the Spanish Crown forced Jews to convert or face expulsion in 1492 and authorized the Inquisition to enforce religious orthodoxy, Sephardic Jews left Spain for the far reaches of the empire, away from the long arm of religious tribunals. Some of them reached northern New Mexico, where their religious practices went underground, and their descendants turned into "crypto-Jews" (Hordes 2008). Through the violent conquest and subjugation of dozens of Indigenous nations in the large Nuevo México territory, the lengthy Spanish imperial presence stirred a racial melting pot of highly diverse societies on the northern fringes of the Viceroyalty of New Spain—as it had done throughout the Americas (Duncan 1988, 49). From Taos, several attempts were made to expand settlements further north, into the San Luis Valley, in a vain effort to settle territories long claimed by the Spanish empire. All of them were to fail in the face of Indigenous resistance, mainly by the Utes (Gallegos 2011, 92–93; Mitchell and Krall 2020, 320). Neither the Spanish colonial government nor the Mexican Republic (after Mexico's independence in 1821) had enough resources or manpower to promote and defend colonial settlements in these northern fringes of Nuevo México, only promises of land for those settlers brave enough to colonize this valley by themselves (Simmons 1999, 78–81).

The US-Mexican War (1846–1848) and the invasion of these frontier territories by US troops broke the impasse. The US Army of the West under Brigadier General Stephen W. Kearny took over Santa Fe in 1846 and placed it under the command of the US government. The change in sovereignty in general and the behavior of US troops in particular caused resentment among the local population, as well as fear over the loss of their lands at the hands of the Americans. On January 19, 1847, Mexican settlers and Pueblo Indians rebelled in Taos, killing territorial governor Charles Bent and other US officials. The insurrection was quickly put down, but bitterness festered among the locals after most of the rebels were tried and hanged for treason, even though they were Mexican citizens engaged in acts of war in a territory occupied by foreign troops (C. Herrera 2000, 32–35). The war ended with Mexico's defeat and the signing of the Treaty of Guadalupe Hidalgo in 1848, which ceded to the United States most of northern Mexico; an enormous tract of land that almost doubled the size of the United States and nowadays includes the territory of the US states of California, Nevada, Utah, New Mexico, most of Arizona and Colorado, and parts of Texas, Oklahoma, Kansas, and Wyoming (Guardino 2017, 1; Sálaz Márquez 2004).

It was not until after the US takeover of New Mexico in 1848 that permanent settlement happened in Colorado's portion of the San Luis Valley. Technically, the first Hispanic settlements in Colorado occurred in New Mexico, not only because the settlement of southern Colorado was part of a spillover effect from northern New Mexico (Simmons 1999, 108) but also the land that these Hispanos settled was then part of the territory of New Mexico until the territory of Colorado was created in 1861 (Schulten 2013, 42). The term *Hispanos*[2] refers specifically to the racially mixed descendants of Spanish and Indigenous peoples in the Southwestern United States who shared a Spanish language and culture, forged over centuries of Spanish colonization in the region. This population, because of its geographic isolation from Spanish authorities and its interaction with local Indigenous peoples and the environment, developed a unique culture, different from that of other Spanish colonies. These colonists often used local and regional terms such as *Californios*, *Nuevomexicanos*, or *Tejanos* to identify themselves, and to denote the cultural gap between them and the Spanish authorities centered in Mexico City, hundreds of miles away and the seat of the vast Viceroyalty of New Spain. The brief Mexican republican period (1821–1846) did little to change things, though some locals would show loyalty to the republican institutions of the new nation by adopting the term *Mexicanos*.

The term *Spanish* (or *Spanish American*) became commonplace decades after the US takeover of northern Mexico, as the local Spanish-speaking people sought to reaffirm themselves culturally and politically vis-à-vis the new *Anglo* authorities.[3] Although the Treaty of Guadalupe Hidalgo that ended the war guaranteed US citizenship to the inhabitants of the newly conquered territories, Native Americans and other peoples of color remained excluded under US federal law. The term also served to reinforce long-standing Spanish racism against Indigenous persons, now supplemented by the racial policies of the United States toward Native Americans—which Hispanos were keenly aware of (S. Rodríguez 1992, 99). Hispanos were also cognizant of the fact that their legal citizenship did not necessarily confer on them social citizenship in the Anglo world, that is, being accepted as racial and cultural equals (Horsman 1981, chap. 12). According to Mai Ngai (2004, 2) Anglo presumption of their foreignness turned them into unassimilable "alien citizens" whose Americanness was always in doubt. Thus, in these racially mixed Hispanic societies, the term *Spanish* sought to publicly challenge demeaning Anglo stereotypes of the "Mexican" locals and instead force recognition of the latter as "whitelike," entitled to rights, and fully deserving of US citizenship (Gómez 2018, 90–91; Montgomery 2001, 60–62).[4] The term also became a symbol of ethnic pride and cultural resistance for the locals as they battled Anglo stereotypes and a postbellum status quo in which they were confined to play a subordinate role (Nieto-Phillips 2004, 8).[5] In particular, the lightskinned Hispano upper classes (i.e., *los ricos*—the wealthy) leveraged their Spanish ancestry as a way of retaining power and racial privilege in the face of an Anglo world where "Mexican" stood for brown and thus racially inferior (Gamio 1930, 54, 208–216). While in Texas, Arizona, and California the term *Spanish* (or *Spanish American*) never gained much traction because the locals were soon overrun by Anglo settlers, it was widely used in public by Hispanos in northern New Mexico and southern Colorado (and together with *Hispano*, it is still employed to this day). Ironically—or perhaps not—both the term *Spanish American* as well as *Mexican* meant different things to different groups in Colorado and New Mexico. For Hispanos, the former was a public demand for equality, while the latter was a private acknowledgment of a broadly shared culture. Anglos, on the other hand, tacitly accepted *Spanish American* when it was convenient for them (such as during New Mexico's bid for statehood[6]), while still generally viewing Hispanos as inferior through the prism of the racially loaded term *Mexican* (Nieto-Phillips 2004, chap. 2). These racial, ethnic, and cultural identifiers are not discrete, and Hispano groups and individuals used them as the situation dictated.

In the Upper Rio Grande, geographic isolation, spatial concentration, and demographic density allowed Hispano peoples and their culture to survive and thrive, even after the US takeover. Richard Nostrand (1992, chap. 1) argues that this territory represents a veritable Hispano homeland with distinct cultural characteristics among its population—characteristics that not only make New Mexico and Colorado Hispanos ethnically unique and different from Anglos but also different from other large Mexican American communities throughout the Southwest (where in many cases their ancestors migrated to the United States, mainly in the twentieth century) (Gallegos 2011, 88–90). Whether Nostrand's assertion is accurate or not (and this was widely debated by his academic peers), this Hispano "imagined community" (B. Anderson 2006) emerged in the nineteenth century, and it is still being historically constructed and shaped in a tripartite society that also includes Anglos and more recently arrived Latinxs (such as Mexicans and Guatemalans) in southern Colorado (MacAulay 2011), and Native Americans in northern New Mexico.

In 1851, New Mexican settlers founded the village of San Luis, the first of several agricultural communities that dotted the Valley—and Colorado's oldest continuously inhabited town.[7] These settlers were a mix of Hispano families and Anglo entrepreneurs (some of whom had married into local families and spoke Spanish). They took advantage of Mexican-government-issued *mercedes* (land grants), which had never been acted on because of the recurring Indian threat. For protection against Indian attacks, the US government built Fort Massachusetts in 1852; it was decommissioned shortly thereafter, when a new, more suitably located military outpost named Fort Garland was established in 1858. Hispanos streamed in from New Mexico, settling in parts of the San Luis Valley with enough water, wood, and grass for their animals; even digging by hand communal *acequias* (ditches) for irrigation.[8] These Hispanos tended to congregate in *plazas* (i.e., fortified compounds), small, tightly knit communities that allowed the settlers to help each other in these unforgiving frontier lands. These plazas were often named after the prominent families that founded them (e.g., Plaza de los Manzanares—nowadays the community of Garcia, Colorado). As other families joined them, *patrón*-client networks were established, just like in neighboring northern New Mexico. The *patrón* system was a semifeudal, socioeconomic arrangement in which a powerful *patrón* (i.e., local boss) provided paternalistic care to his people, in exchange for their allegiance. The *patrón* leased land and sheep to Hispano families, in exchange for produce and wool, but also served as a godfather, or *compadre*, who helped his protégés in times of need, thus cementing deeply rooted social networks with his people (W. Taylor and West 1973, 337–340). Agriculture and sheep and cattle ranching soon dominated the landscape of the Valley, and Hispano villages were largely self-sufficient. By keeping their numbers small and their impact on the ecosystem limited, Hispanic farmers eked out an existence from the lands of the San Luis Valley and fashioned resilient communal bonds solidified by a strong Roman Catholic folk faith.

In 1861, US Congress organized the territory of Colorado from portions of the Kansas, Nebraska, New Mexico, and Utah Territories, formally (and artificially) dividing the San Luis Valley between Colorado and New Mexico. Despite the large presence of Hispanos in the San Luis Valley and other parts of the new territory, Colorado was imagined as a white man's country—in sharp contrast with New Mexico, whose large Hispano and Indigenous population became a roadblock to statehood until the early twentieth century (Everett 2014, chap. 7). Hispanos in the new Colorado Territory opposed the partition of the San Luis Valley and even sought to remain a part New Mexico under a proposal for a nonlinear border that left the Valley out of Colorado, to no avail. Anglo interests dominated the congressional debate, and their insistence on a symmetrical, rectangular territory with straight lines prevailed. As it was becoming customary in the American West, Hispano pleas were ignored as issuing from a racially mixed, "foreign" people not fit to decide over the wishes and needs of white pioneers (Gonzales and Sánchez 2018).

The importance of the San Luis Valley suddenly increased when gold and silver deposits were struck in the San Juan mountains west of the Valley. With the Civil War over, and the forced removal of the Utes to reservations further west (Mitchell and Krall 2020, 321), the San Luis Valley became a supplier of foodstuffs to the mining boomtowns, as well as a transshipment point for goods flowing west into the mining camps and ore being transported east to Pueblo and Denver. Wagons roads were built across the valley as thousands flocked to the mining camps, sparking an economic boom in the region. The mineral wealth coming from Colorado and its dominant Anglo population strengthened the push for statehood, and on August 1, 1876, Colorado was admitted as the thirty-eighth state of the Union.[9] Soon thereafter, the Denver and Rio Grande Railroad (D&RG) company laid tracks over La Veta Pass and into the valley. Over the next decade, the railroad expanded throughout the San Luis Valley and into the adjacent mining towns in southwestern Colorado and northern New

Mexico, connecting them to the outside world. Alamosa became the center of rail operations for the company, making it into the most important town in the region (Publications Committee 1969a). The railroad also built new towns, something that it preferred to do rather than working rights-of-way with established towns. For example, the D&RG bypassed Conejos and created Antonito, as it expanded south of Alamosa (Loosbrock 2020, 364). As the railroad intruded and expanded into the San Luis Valley, new Anglo geographies that competed or overlapped with Hispano geographies were created, dictating the future patterns of trade and human habitation in the Valley (Wyckoff 1999, 196–198). As in other parts of the American West, the railroad was a catalyst of significant socioeconomic changes.

For Hispanos in the San Luis Valley, this was a period of rapid and unsettling changes. By the 1870s, most of the land in the Valley was still in the hands of Hispano subsistence farmers, but soon their communal, pastoral lifestyles clashed with the individualistic, entrepreneurial attitudes of Anglo settlers who saw land as a commodity to be exploited and speculated with. According to David Landis (1988, 26),

> The Mexican people of the Valley were desperately handicapped from the very start of their dealings with the Anglo-Americans. Despite their poverty, most of them were honest and devout, but they lacked an understanding of the aggressive American civilization. They were citizens of the United States but in name rather than in spirit. Even their Roman Catholic religion clashed with the dominantly Protestant creeds of their new Anglo-American neighbors.

Paradoxically, the US takeover provided new opportunities for Hispanos, as well as the new challenges. The expansion of the United States into the West concomitantly expanded the Hispano frontier into southern Colorado. US troops provided protection to fledgling settlements in the San Luis Valley, while Anglo entrepreneurs provided jobs (e.g., in railroads and mines) that helped Hispano settlers raise much-needed cash (Deutsch 1987, 17–19). Hispano sheepherders benefitted from the access that the railroad provided to markets in Denver, and the new rail lines "encouraged the development of sheep production into a major industry" (Simmons 1999, 254). On the other hand, Hispanos stood in the way of

Manifest Destiny, and "from the 1850s to the early 1900s, most Mexican-owned land in what is now the Southwest was lost to newly arrived Euro-American businessmen and families through litigation, force, coercion, sale, intermarriage, and squatters rights" (Aldama et al. 2011, 11). American jurisprudence insisted on accurate surveys, so US courts eventually dismissed many of the land claims that Hispanos had based on the long-term occupation of land grants issued by the Mexican government and that were verbally reaffirmed by US military governors after they occupied the territory. Many of these Hispano settlers had no title to their land, or their documents were not deemed valid in US courts, which rejected them on technical grounds (V. Sánchez 2020, chap. 1). The Conejos Grant, one of seven in what nowadays is Colorado, was eventually invalidated in 1900, after the case languished in US courts for decades. By then, many of the original Hispano settlers had lost their lands to Anglo newcomers attracted to the American West by the Homestead Act of 1862 (Sangre de Cristo National Heritage Area 2019a), including many army veterans who had served in Fort Garland (Simmons 1999, 132). Moreover, US land law did not recognize the "commons," lands where all the neighbors could gather wood or graze their animals (Brosnan 2002, 141).

In the 1870s, US Army officer George Wheeler spearheaded numerous surveying parties into the Western United States to accurately map and examine conditions in the region, including the San Luis Valley (Saenz 2020, 350). His detailed reports led the US federal government to claim ownership over millions of acres of common lands throughout the Southwest (deemed as "unsettled lands"), arguing that they had belonged to the Mexican government and not to the people who used them. These lands were ultimately placed under the control of new government agencies, like the US Forest Service, the Bureau of Land Management, the National Park Service, and other state and federal agencies, depriving the original users of access to the land and in many cases opening these lands to commercial exploitation by large timber, mining, and cattle-ranching industries (D. Peña 2005, 115). The new American authorities also taxed the land, not its produce. Cash for taxes, surveyors, and litigation quickly depleted the meager funds of most Hispano residents, who lived mostly in a barter economy, while a flock of bankers, land speculators, corrupt lawyers, loan sharks, and swindlers descended on the Valley to prey on its people.

Anglo cattle ranchers waged a range war with Hispano sheepherders in which property was destroyed, animals were killed, and violence flared often, while the Anglo authorities did little to stop it (R. Sandoval 1979). William Carrigan and Clive Webb (2013, 42) estimate that "between 1860 and 1884, mobs in Colorado lynched at least 23 Mexicans." In Trinidad, the largest Hispano town of the Colorado Territory, racial riots led by Anglos took place on Christmas Day, 1867. Martial law was declared, and federal troops had to be brought in to reestablish order (Brosnan 2002, 175). As a result of these events, the cultural divide between the Anglo and Hispano worlds paralleled a socioeconomic divide in which the former would come to control the region's (and the state's) economy and politics, while the latter increasingly became rural proletarians that provided the labor force that Anglo entrepreneurs needed (Brosnan 2002, 138–141). Manifest Destiny was realized as, in the words of the Pueblo Board of Trade (1883, 9), "the Indian and the Mexican speedily receded before this tide of emigration until ranches, mining camps, cities and towns sprung up to give solidity, strength and beauty to one of the most inviting sections of America." Outnumbered, orphaned from Mexico, and pushed aside by the Anglo world, Hispanos relied on each other to survive amid their powerlessness (Adams State College and San Luis Valley Historical Society 1980a, 1980b).

The arrival of the United States into what nowadays is Colorado accelerated what hitherto had been a slow but steady encroachment of Hispano settlements into Indigenous lands. Hispano villages quickly spread into southern Colorado thanks to the protection of US authorities and the new economic opportunities that Anglo businesses brought about. On the other hand, the village-centered way of life of Hispanos would be forever disrupted by the massive land grab that proceeded US annexation. Hispano villages in New Mexico and Colorado had been successful in an arid environment thanks to the careful use of resources in a balanced system of irrigated small holdings and common lands. When population pressures strained the ecological balance, young families would emigrate and re-create the village system in new lands. The arrival of the United States allowed for some expansion and reproduction of the village system but took away one of its key elements: the commons. Without these lands, the small plots of Hispano families were insufficient for them to survive—particularly in a capitalist, cash economy—forcing them to seek seasonal wage labor elsewhere. This situation dovetailed nicely with the demands of an expanding economy that relied on the cheap labor of immigrants and poor villagers (Deutsch 1987). As is the case elsewhere in the world, when peasants have enough land, they rarely sell their labor in the market. When they do not, they must become rural proletarians who move between farm labor at home and wage labor elsewhere, depending on the seasons, the availability of jobs, and their own needs. On top of the land grab, Anglo prejudices confined Hispanos to seasonal, back-breaking, low-paying jobs, while blaming the latter for their poverty. Hispanos resisted by falling back on their villages and traditions (W. Taylor and West 1973, 357), where tightly knit circles of extended family and friends provided solace and material support in times of need, and local traditions instilled in them a sense of continuity and cultural self-worth (MacAulay 2011).

Hispano Resistance and Survival

Hispano resistance took many forms, including violent attacks against Anglos and their properties in northern New Mexico (Arellano 2000, chap. 3). In Colorado, two noteworthy institutions are a prime example of the unique sociocultural traditions of Colorado's first Hispanics and their forms of resistance: Los Hermanos Penitentes and La Sociedad. Los Hermanos Penitentes, officially La Fraternidad Piadosa de Nuestro Padre Jesús Nazareno (Pious Fraternity of Our Father Jesus the Nazarene), or La Hermandad (the Brotherhood), as it also known, was a lay confraternity of Catholic men created in the absence of church officials in the former Mexican territory. The Penitentes had been a fixture of New Mexican rural society since colonial times—a fact of life that because of the lack of enough priests and resources for such a large territory, the Spanish Catholic Church had learned to live with. After its independence, Mexico removed Spanish clergy from its provinces, without fully replacing them with local priests, furthering the need of the locals for religious guidance. The loss of Mexico's northern territories to the United States further reduced the number of priests in these regions, while attempts to Americanize New Mexico's Catholic Church by bringing in French clergymen after the war, drove Hispanos to seek their own religious path.

Again, socioeconomic isolation in a racially segmented American society left Hispanos with no alternatives but their own cultural resilience. Los Hermanos Penitentes came to fill this void (R. Vigil 2006). La Hermandad reinforced Roman Catholic religious practices, helped the needy, and provided the social cohesion that an increasingly oppressed Hispano community desperately needed (Rivera 2016, 5–7). However, the popular, grassroots religiosity of the Penitentes put them at odds with the hierarchy of the US Catholic Church, which considered them a threat to its legitimacy and religious monopoly over its flock. The church tried in vain to bring the Penitentes in line with its official doctrine, only to drive them further underground, where they became an object of morbid curiosity for mainstream American society. Tales of Penitentes flagellating themselves in secret rituals filled stories back east that provided an air of exoticism and savagery to the isolated, unassimilated Hispano communities of northern New Mexico and Colorado. Moreover, the folk traditions of the Catholic Penitentes reinforced racial and religious prejudices held by mainstream Protestants regarding "Mexicans." More in line with reality, the Penitentes were expressing—and living—a practical Christianity, one that helped their communities survive the cultural and economic onslaught of the Anglo world while reinforcing deep-seated traditions of mutual help, charity, and pious lifestyles for others to emulate (López Pulido 2000). For example, in April 1881, Penitentes refused to work at the Engle Mine (south of Trinidad) for the religious celebrations around Holy Week, forcing the mine to shut down (Andrews 2008, 94).

La Sociedad, or Sociedad de Protección Mutua de Trabajadores Unidos (Society for the Mutual Protection of United Workers), was the most important *mutualista* among Hispanos in southern Colorado. *Mutualistas* were mutual aid societies and voluntary organizations that, like the Penitentes, provided help to those in need, helped strengthen social bonds, and reinforced the unique culture of Colorado's Hispanos. They fulfilled vital socioeconomic roles in the face of an aggressive American society that excluded Hispanos from its fold, forcing the latter to seek support and comfort among themselves. *Mutualistas*, for example, lent money for life's big events and emergencies (e.g., births, deaths, or marriages) to people with no access to banks, credit, or life insurance. They also sponsored social and cultural events (Rivera 2010, 9–11; M. Valdez 2001). La Sociedad, founded in Antonito, Colorado, in 1900, was a working-class organization that helped its members in case of illness, injury, or unemployment, as well as providing survivors' benefits in case of a member's death. It united unskilled workers, as well as farmers and sheep ranchers, in order "to protect each other against the injustices of tyrants and despots, the usurpers of law and justice, and those who steal our lives, honor, and property" (Rivera 2010, 21). The latter is an obvious reference to the changes taking place in the San Luis Valley as Anglo miners, homesteaders, and ranchers threatened the survival and ways of life of Hispano communities. As a survival strategy, Hispanos in the San Luis Valley sought jobs in the new capitalist, cash economy as employees in commercial farms, railroad laborers, and miners, becoming wage workers. La Sociedad quickly expanded as Hispanos sought jobs throughout the state and the region, eventually establishing lodges in Denver, Durango, Pagosa Springs, Montrose, Aguilar, Brighton, and Walsenburg in the 1910s–1920s, as well as in New Mexico and Utah (M. Valdez 2001, 13).

La Sociedad played a significant role in the 1914 *Francisco Maestas et al. v. George H. Shone et al.* court case, which challenged school segregation in Alamosa. The Alamosa School Board of Education had built a new "Mexican" school south of the train tracks that divided the Anglo and Hispano sectors of Alamosa, ostensibly to support Spanish-speaking children. Yet soon all Hispano children—regardless of their fluency in the English language—were forced to attend the new school. One of them, little Miguel Maestas, was forced to walk across the train tracks to the new Spanish-language school, despite the fact that he lived next to North Side School and spoke English. When efforts by Hispano parents to enroll their children at the Anglo school were rejected by school authorities (led by Superintendent George H. Shone), Francisco Maestas (Miguel's father) and other Hispano parents, with support from La Sociedad, took their case to court (Dokson 2022). The plaintiffs claimed that their children were being segregated on the basis of race (i.e., as "Mexicans"), which violated provisions regarding racial discrimination in schools found in the Constitution of Colorado. School authorities, on the other hand, argued that Hispano children were "white" (as citizens of the United States), but that they were being placed on the south side school because they only spoke Spanish and had to be taught English. When the affected children testified in court (in English, without the help of translators), the defendants' arguments collapsed, and the court ruled that all English-speaking children in Alamosa had to be enrolled at the school nearest them. *Francisco Maestas et al. v. George H. Shone et al.* was a clear example of Hispanos using the same system that oppressed them in order to seek legal redress. It was a significant victory for La Sociedad and Hispano parents, and it preceded other school desegregation cases in the nation by decades (Donato, Guzmán, and Hanson 2017).

It is worth noting that given the prevalence of anti-Mexican prejudice in the region (and the common use of the pejorative term *greaser* to refer to Latinxs[10]), the rise in jingoism as a result of American involvement in foreign wars (e.g., the Spanish-American War and World War I), and the arrival into the region of Spanish-speaking Mexican workers, La Sociedad sought to ameliorate Anglo hostility by portraying its members as assimilated Spanish Americans and not foreign "Mexicans." Thus, La Sociedad stressed the patriotism of its members by highlighting in its founding documents that they were Hispano-Americans (and not Mexicans) and making US citizenship a basic requirement for membership (Rivera 2010, 54).

The lack of ethnic solidarity with Mexican immigrant workers comes as no surprise given the fact that US-born Hispanos were US citizens (a very valuable asset, in their view) and that the presence of Mexican immigrants in their midst was often perceived as a setback on the road toward (hopefully) full acceptance into American society. These Hispanos also took advantage of their US citizenship and local majorities and pluralities to elect their peers to the territorial legislature and (later) the Colorado General Assembly (made up of a Senate and a House of Representatives). Thanks to the fact that the San Luis Valley had the only continuous communities of Latinxs,[11] for close to a century the southern Colorado counties of Conejos, Costilla, Huerfano, and Las Animas almost always had some Hispano representation. It led to what Fernando Padilla and Carlos Ramírez (1974, 191, 203) call "sub-state regional political potence"; that is, Hispanos from the San Luis Valley had token representation thanks to their numbers and spatial concentration, but because they made up just a small fraction of the Colorado General Assembly (which was dominated by Anglos), their political power at the state level was negligible. Smaller districts and a larger body meant that they were adequately represented in the House but "significantly underrepresented in the State Senate," where the districts are larger and the membership is smaller (Padilla and Ramírez 1974, 205). Thus, elite Hispanos participated in the Colorado General Assembly consistently and ran in the tickets of both the Democratic and the Republican Parties, but in the face of Anglo opposition and given the small number of seats they won Hispano legislators rarely had the votes to become an important voting block—at least until the advent of the Chicano Movement (see chapter 3).

These everyday forms of resistance (Scott 1985) helped Hispanos cushion the blow of Anglo institutions and prejudice and preserve their culture. From the relative safety and equality of their villages, Colorado's Hispanos would strategize how to survive in an Anglo world. This calculus included working their lands, wage labor in Anglo industries, or migrating out of the San Luis Valley altogether. It was neither total resistance nor succumbing to assimilation but what Eric Meeks (2020, 4) calls "resistant adaptation." Revolt was out of the question for Colorado's Hispanos, so they willingly adopted the latest gadgets supplied by US capitalism while preserving aspects of their culture that provided social cohesion and cultural comfort. Hispanos essentially sought to adapt to life in a new, Anglo-dominated world—a world "in which race and ethnicity shaped labor markets" (Meeks 2020, 4) and that largely excluded them as racial inferiors. Hispanos had no choice but to learn to navigate racialized American society the best they could. As documented by Virginia Sánchez (2020), elected Hispano elites in Colorado's territorial legislature were willfully ignored by their Anglo peers as they petitioned for things as simple as interpreters and translations of bills written in English so that they could do their jobs effectively. Moreover, just like the working-class people who elected them, Hispano political elites were subjected to widespread racial discrimination by Anglos in and out of the legislature. For Hispanos, there was no place to escape Anglo domination, only ways to adapt to resist it. By the end of the nineteenth century, the Anglo stranglehold on the Valley's Hispanos—and on their land—left the latter with no other choices.

In 1894, the nationwide economic crisis hit the San Luis Valley. Mining came to a standstill, and the Valley lost population as people abandoned their farms and mining towns. At the turn of the century, Hispanos began moving away from the San Luis Valley in search of jobs in Anglo industries in the homeland's periphery (e.g., the Front Range) and even farther away (e.g., Utah and Wyoming)—giving birth to a cultural "*manito* trail" of Hispano workers that extended across several states (L. Romero 2020).[12] This strategy allowed them to survive on what little land they had left by working seasonally elsewhere. In some cases, men would fan out in search of wage labor while women maintained the production of food in the household. In other cases, it became a permanent migration for the family to other parts of the state or the region, while still maintaining periodic contacts with their village of origin. Work in the railroads, mines, or sugar beet plantations allowed men to earn much-needed cash, while women found employment doing laundry, cooking, or working as house servants (Deutsch 1987, 33).

Large bituminous coal deposits were found in nearby Huerfano County and Las Animas County (just east of the San Luis Valley, on the east side of the Sangre de Cristo Range), providing employment to hundreds of Hispanos (V. Sánchez 2010). In fact, the towns of Trinidad and Walsenburg (originally La Plaza de los Leones) began as Hispano settlements that were quickly taken over by Anglos attracted by the natural resources of the region (Clyne 1999, 2–4).[13] The expansion of the D&RG into southern Colorado provided jobs for Hispanos and the transportation linkages that the coal industry required. In 1892, the merger of the two largest mining operations in the region led to the founding of the Colorado Fuel and Iron Company (CF&I), which owned coal mines and coking plants, as well as a steel mill in Pueblo. In 1903, it became part of the powerful Rockefeller financial empire and during the twentieth century a major economic force in southern Colorado (Scamehorn 1992). Life in the coal fields of southern Colorado was hard, and "Mexicans" were usually assigned the worst jobs in the mines (Gómez-Quiñones 1994, 74). Not only were mining jobs dangerous and backbreaking, but life in the isolated company towns was heavily regimented by the CF&I. The miners and their families often depended on the company for food, supplies, and housing. Losing your job meant that your family became homeless. European miners—initially from northern Europe but later from southern and eastern Europe—made up the bulk of the workers, but Hispanos were always a part of the labor force. The latter were not as ostracized as African American and Japanese workers but were never fully accepted as equals by the dominant European miners either. While some Hispanos resided in company towns, others lived in their traditional plazas, which provided them with some autonomy and cultural comfort—something the company was not necessarily fond of (Clyne 1999, 49–50). Hispanos featured prominently among the victims of the infamous Ludlow Massacre, when on April 20, 1914, soldiers from the Colorado National Guard and private guards from the CF&I fired on a tent colony of striking coal miners, killing twenty miners and their families, including women and children (Vallejo 1998). The strike, led by the United Mine Workers of America, was in response to appalling working conditions in the CF&I mines and part of the broader Colorado Coalfield War of 1913–1914 (Andrews 2008). While the coal mines provided year-round employment not far from the San Luis Valley, it was but one of several economic strategies that Hispano residents of the Valley utilized in their accommodation to the Anglo capitalist model. A more radical step was to leave the Valley altogether and work in the emerging sugar beet fields of Colorado's Eastern Plains (see chapter 2). While many Hispano families did end up relocating to the Eastern Plains, the San Luis Valley remained dear to them; it was a place of cultural pilgrimage that they would come back to in order to reconnect with the relatives and friends that they had left behind—and with the land, this Hispano homeland that stretched from southern Colorado to northern New Mexico and that embodied so much meaning for them (L. Romero 2020, 309).

The 1920s brought an increase in potato and lettuce production in the San Luis Valley, and with it, renewed demand for rural laborers. Potatoes became the most profitable cash crop in the Valley, and over half of the farmers (mostly Anglos) were soon growing them, which required large numbers of stoop laborers mainly to harvest them by hand. For Hispanos from the impoverished villages of southern Colorado and northern New Mexico, the opportunity to make $2–$3 a day became an important part of their survival strategy, and many young males spent days or weeks harvesting potatoes in the Valley. However, as the Valley's potato production increased, stoop labor needs went from occasional to regular, and entire Hispano families ended up working in the fields (Carlson 1973, 99–100).

Migratory farmworkers from California, Arizona, and Mexico—which included contingents of Asian Americans, Native Americans, and Mexican

Americans—became the latest arrivals into the San Luis Valley, reinforcing the subordinate condition of Hispanos and setting in motion regional and international migratory trends that continue into the present. The Valley's "Mexican" workforce made up of US-born Hispanos and Mexican immigrants now reflected the composition of the ethnic Mexican workforce thorough the American West more closely (with a mix of US-born and foreign-born "Mexicans") and was largely employed in traditional sectors such as railroads, mining, industry, construction, and agriculture (Gómez-Quiñones 1994, 73). The presence of new Mexican arrivals also exacerbated xenophobic feelings among those self-proclaimed "native" Anglos who opposed the importation of Mexican workers into the state, but farmers in the San Luis Valley needed all the cheap labor they could get as potato and vegetable production expanded. This first wave of migratory workers was short lived, though, as the Great Depression sharply reduced the demand for immigrant rural labor and the state authorities established patrols to keep them out (Publications Committee 1969b).

Governor Edwin "Big Ed" Johnson went as far as deporting Mexican workers (some of whom, it was found later, were US citizens) and declaring martial law to seal the state's borders. For two weeks in April 1936, the Colorado National Guard manned checkpoints on the state border with New Mexico, where soldiers intercepted and turned around "alien and indigent labor"—or anyone who fit the description in the eyes of the Anglo authorities.[14] The plan received strong condemnation from New Mexico's authorities (who threatened to boycott Colorado's products, forcing Johnson to back down), but it was popular among Johnson's white—and oftentimes blatantly racist—constituents, and he was easily elected to the US Senate a short time later (Meredith 2012). Perhaps not surprisingly, the governor also received letters from Hispanos supporting his plan and stressing that "as americans we like to be classify as americans not as Mexican as some politics callus [sic]" (Varsanyi 2020, 27). These Hispanos feared being the target of Anglo racial wrath by virtue of their looks, but they also resented the competition for scarce jobs that Mexican immigrant laborers represented during those tough economic times. Governor Johnson's antics, clearly designed for political theater (Leonard 1993, chap. 7), once again underscored the second-class nature of the state's Hispanic population, which the governor felt like he could push around and intimidate, without fear of significant short-term political repercussions or long-term impacts on his career.[15]

As shown in the introduction, by 1940 Hispanics still made less than 10% of Colorado's population. Considering that some Hispanics in the state were not US born, that they were mostly concentrated in southern Colorado, that they were generally poor, and that they had little political capital and agency due to their racialized "outsider" status, it is not hard to see why the state authorities in Denver ignored them. Unlike New Mexico, where Anglos had to contend with large numbers of Hispanics who outnumbered them (Gómez 2018, 7; Montgomery 2001, 60), in Colorado the reverse was true: Anglos vastly outnumbered Hispanics and could afford to overlook them—and would continue to do so well into the twentieth century.[16] Colorado's Hispanics had been effectively rendered invisible by the Anglo mainstream—save for the occasional "crisis" that called for the government's heavy-handed intervention, as was the case with Governor Johnson's made-up immigration charade during the Great Depression.

Post-World War II Changes

World War II brought renewed migration to the Valley, as part of the Bracero Program, an agreement signed with the Mexican government for the importation of migrant workers into the United States to alleviate the labor shortage caused by the war. These Mexican migrant workers began arriving in the San Luis Valley in 1943, where they worked in the sugar beet harvest initially, and eventually moved on to work in farms and for the railroad (Golden 2004, 42). Some of these Mexican workers came from the Texas Panhandle, where they had been previously employed in agriculture (Carlson 1973, 102–103). The war also mobilized hundreds of Hispano men, who volunteered to serve or were drafted—which temporarily reduced the Valley's agricultural labor pool. As in World War I, service in the military was a way for Hispanos to prove their patriotism to Anglo society, which in large part viewed them as suspicious "Mexicans," while also benefiting from programs like the G.I. Bill (Rivas-Rodriguez 2005, xvi–xviii). The war helped end the Valley's relative isolation, and in the postwar period the modernization and mechanization of agriculture, ongoing poverty for Hispanos, and the availability of jobs in urban centers set in place labor migration trends that continue to this day: As newcomers move into the San Luis Valley for work, business, or recreation, Hispanos—particularly the young—move to other parts of the state in search of better opportunities.

The postwar period also brought new challenges to the Valley's Hispanos in the form of renewed threats to traditional community lifestyles by logging, mining, and ranching interests. In 1960, Jack Taylor, a timber baron from North Carolina, purchased a large tract of land in what had been the Sangre de Cristo Land Grant. This originally 1-million-acre land grant had been awarded by the Mexican government to Narciso Beaubien and Stephen Luis Lee in 1843. Upon their untimely death in the Taos uprising of 1847, Charles Beaubien (Narciso's father) inherited the grant and used it to attract Hispano settlers from New Mexico into the San Luis Valley. The settlers were promised land for cultivation and grazing, as well as common access to the nearby mountains known as La Sierra,[17] for "pastures, water, firewood and timber" (Golten 2005, 462), which they had freely used since then. Taylor decided to fence off the land and deny access to *his* land to the locals, igniting a feud that pitted a wealthy Anglo outsider against poor Hispano farmers who had legally used La Sierra for generations ("The Public Domain" 1975). In November 1961, three young Hispanos caught trespassing into Taylor's ranch were badly beaten by his ranch hands. A local mob wanted to lynch Taylor and his men, who had to be taken into custody for their own protection. Locals retaliated by burning fences, cutting barbed wire, and ignoring Taylor's threats in a game of cat and mouse deeply set in a tradition of resistance to outside encroachment by the Valley's Hispanos (Sahagun 1993). For decades, Hispanos in the San Luis Valley (and northern New Mexico) had resisted takeovers by Anglo landowners and the federal government (e.g., the US Forest Service and the Bureau of Land Management). The ancient communal grazing, hunting, and logging practices of Hispanos bristled against US private property rights and federal land management policies, leading to numerous individual confrontations (Peña and Martínez 1998, 150). What set this latest case apart was the fact that Taylor had fenced off La Sierra, a valued economic and cultural resource of the people, and had employed bullying tactics to try to scare the locals away—a move that was universally condemned by Hispanos in the San Luis Valley and served as a catalyst for collective action (MacAulay 2011). Over the course of the next forty years, local Hispano residents (mostly from the town of San Luis[18]) organized around the Land Rights Council and took Taylor (and his successors) to court. Apolinar Rael, one of the region's elders, stubbornly refused to give up the fight, even after many of the locals were forced to leave the San Luis Valley in search of jobs elsewhere. After several legal setbacks, in 2002 the Colorado Supreme Court recognized the common law rights of Hispano landowners in the Culebra watershed to use La Sierra "to graze livestock, collect firewood, and harvest timber on land grant property that they and their predecessors have used for 150 years" (Golten 2005, 458).[19] The plaintiffs and other descendants of the original settlers were awarded keys to enter the ranch for the above-mentioned specific purposes only. Some 3,000 locals eventually ended up benefiting from this court decision.

However, during the time that Taylor owned the ranch, intense logging of La Sierra took place, threatening the Culebra watershed that provides much-needed irrigation to the agropastoralists of San Luis. The community resisted and, with the help of ecoactivists, tried blocking roads to stop trucks from going in and out (McBride 1997). Still, the logging went on. Another major environmental issue was the operation of a gold mine and mill just four miles from San Luis in the 1990s. Residents took Battle Mountain Gold to court to try to stop its mining operation because of concerns over the potential contamination of water sources, but the courts ruled in favor of the mine. Water is a commodity, and the company had the right to use water as it saw fit, according to the court's decision (D. Peña 1998a). Though the mining operation closed in 1997, lined pits full of cyanide and heavy metals remain behind, leaking into the Rito Seco Creek, which feeds the San Luis People's Ditch (Lutz 1999).

These environmental challenges go beyond the contamination of natural resources. For the Hispano agropastoralists of the San Luis Valley, the land is more than a commodity; it represents a way of life with deep roots into their past, a part of traditions that have been passed down from generation to generation (Valdez and Mondragón-Valdez 2000). For these Hispanos, the land is an integral part of an environmental ethic that finds it hard to reconcile Anglo attitudes of real estate as a commodity with Hispano cultural values of the land as a living entity that needs to be defended from depredation—an eleventh commandment of sorts (D.

Peña 1998a). The cultural ecology of the Hispano communities of the San Luis Valley rejects both the corporate industrial exploitation of nature by global capitalism, and the public land management policies of federal and state agencies that fault Hispanos for overgrazing a dwindling range while permitting extractive (e.g., logging and mining) and nonextractive (e.g., ski resorts) multiple uses of the land (Peña and Martínez 1998). In addition, Devon Peña (1998b) argues that Hispano communities have been good stewards of the land because their survival on an arid landscape has historically depended on learning from nature and working with its rhythms in order to utilize resources in a sustainable way. The building of *acequias* (i.e., ditches) owned by the community, the parceling of the land, the use of La Sierra in common, soil management practices such as the rotation of crops, and their intimate knowledge of local flora and fauna—among other practices—allowed Hispanos to thrive in northern New Mexico and southern Colorado without depleting the local ecosystem. If anything, it was the arrival of US corporate capitalism that began the large-scale destruction of the Valley's landscape and undermined Hispano sustainability practices, forcing the latter to extract a meager living—by any means necessary—from a diminishing land base.

Finally, the sociopolitical turmoil of the 1960s–1970s also impacted the San Luis Valley, though not to the same extent as other parts of the state (such as the Front Range). The Chicano Movement did not find many adherents in the rural, conservative Valley, where the politically charged Chicano identity and radical goals of the movement oftentimes clashed with traditional historical constructions of Hispano identity and more limited regional or local goals. Moreover, as in other parts of the state (and the American West), the movement was bisected by a generational cleavage, with most of its followers trending young. Anglo society reacted to the perceived threat of empowered Chicanxs with threats of its own. In Monte Vista, Colorado Mounted Rangers (a volunteer law enforcement auxiliary) were deputized by the local police department and accused of turning into vigilantes who went around harassing Chicanxs. Rangers Chief Henry Chafin infamously warned: "Any person who does not want to speak English should go back to Mexico. The name Chicano is anti-everything I've worked forty years for" ("Erroneous Enlistment or Induction" 1973). As such, the influence of the Chicano Movement in the San

Luis Valley was mostly limited to college students and community activists (e.g., the Land Rights Council[20]).

In Center, just northwest of Alamosa, Hispanos (who also referred to themselves as *mejicanos*) decided to challenge the political stranglehold that Anglos had on town politics. In 1970, Jennie Sanchez, a local activist who had challenged the segregation of *mejicanos* in the Center Consolidated School District and other local incidents of racism, organized a slate of Hispanic candidates who took over the town board. Five of the six seats went to *mejicanos* and their allies. From there, Sanchez organized lettuce workers to demand better wages and working conditions. The strike eventually ballooned into a regional movement, with the strikers marching to Denver and gaining national attention and the support of figures like Rodolfo "Corky" Gonzales and Cesar Chavez (Minor 2018). By pursuing legal actions and an electoral strategy that relied on their voting numbers and alliances with progressive Anglos, the *mejicanos* of Center turned the tables on the local Anglo establishment through nonviolent means (Wittevrongel and Sanchez 2017, chap. 4), an exceptional case in a region defined by the radical actions that were part of the militant ethos of the Chicano Movement (I. García 1997).

The Chicano student movement was centered in Adams State College (now Adams State University), the Valley's only college at the time and a significant avenue for social mobility for Hispanos in the region (Donato 2007, 117–119). In 1970, a chapter of United Mexican American Students (UMAS) was founded on campus. UMAS demanded more Chicano history courses, the promotion of Chicano culture, and tutoring for low-income students. Its members also staged a sit-in and fast in support of the striking lettuce pickers in Center. UMAS leaders were very active in the student newspaper, *The South Coloradan*, and periodically brought speakers to campus, including the controversial land rights activist Reies López Tijerina,[21] who was well known for his fiery oratory. Racial tensions on campus had increased significantly by 1973, particularly between white, Black, and Chicanx students—and within the groups themselves. Clannish behavior and disputes over turf, belonging, resources, and dates led to altercations. On May 14, 1974, physical confrontations between Black and Chicanx students sparked fights and a riot, leaving several students injured. The state police and national guardsmen were called in to keep the peace, and Black students—fearing for their safety—decided to leave campus before final exams (Holley 2006). The unfortunate clashes between African Americans and Chicanxs at Adams State College left a bitter aftertaste among those students fighting for equality and minority rights, and tainted the image of the local Chicanx students, now perceived as vindictive and power hungry. The end of the school year thus marked the heyday of the Chicano Movement and the eventual decline of student activism on campus, which never regained the intensity that it had between 1970 and 1974.

Multiple Hispano, Chicanx, and Latinx Identities

Although the San Luis Valley is often described as a segment of a larger "Hispano Homeland" that stretches north following the Rio Grande (the Rio Arriba region), Colorado's Hispanos have never lived in total isolation. The presence of Indigenous peoples and the US military, the arrival of Anglo homesteaders, and the eventual importation of workers from Mexico and elsewhere (e.g., Japanese Americans from California) have contributed to creating an increasingly diverse society in the Valley (Konishi and Crawford 2020; Simmons 1999, chap. 15). Hispano identity in Colorado is not—and has never been—frozen in time, as popular accounts of Hispanic cultural and linguistic isolation may proclaim (Maestas 2015, 8). It has been in flux for decades, and it "is continuously being constructed, deconstructed, and reconstructed" (S. Rodríguez 1992, 99).

The arrival of Mexican citizens into the San Luis Valley in the twentieth century helped replenish the Mexican American identity of Hispanos while complicating it too. On the one hand, Hispanos had remained culturally isolated for decades and the sudden influx of Spanish-speaking Mexican migrants added new yet familiar cultural imports. On the other, Hispanos did not see Mexican immigrants necessarily as equals. Decades of discrimination, pressure to conform, and a rising wave of patriotism during the two world wars transformed many Hispanos into liminal citizens that sometimes felt—or needed to feel—culturally closer to the Anglo mainstream than to the newly arrived Mexican workers. By then, many Hispanos were monolingual and fiercely proud of their US citizenship (witness the case of La Sociedad, mentioned earlier) and their contribution to the war effort; thus, relations with their Mexican "distant cousins" were not always amicable. Moreover, as has been the case elsewhere in the United States (D. Gutiérrez 1995; Jiménez 2010), some Hispanos felt that the arrival of Mexican immigrants set them back in terms of their hard-earned social gains and created confusion among those Anglos who could not (or would not) tell them apart; a fact that sparked feelings of resentment among Hispanos. Thus, Hispanos in the San Luis Valley wavered between welcoming the Mexican newcomers or rejecting them, sometimes on an individual basis, sometimes as a group. The position of Hispanos as Mexican American cultural hybrids that embraced a unique culture oftentimes made it difficult for them to identify with either Anglos or Mexicans and placed them in a cultural sphere of their own.

Mexican immigrants had their own identity issues, too. As monolingual Spanish speakers in an English-dominant (and Anglo-dominated) society, Mexican immigrants also had a hard time confronting—and conforming to—the San Luis Valley's socioracial pyramid. Rejected by Anglos—and sometimes by Hispanos too—Mexican immigrants found themselves relegated to the bottom of the barrel, peons working long hours for little pay and no recognition. Although Mexican immigrants saw some cultural commonalities with their Hispano "cousins," the latter's increasingly limited use of Spanish (particularly during the second half of the twentieth century) and their different backgrounds hampered a closer relationship. Paradoxically, Hispanos stereotyped Mexican immigrants as outsiders, unsophisticated peasants forced by poverty to migrate. Mexicans, on the other hand, stereotyped Hispanos as Americanized Hispanics who felt superior just because they had US citizenship but derided them because they lacked a strong Latin American identity, spoke halting Spanish, and were forced to live trapped between two worlds.

Oral history interviews in Alamosa, the unofficial capital of the San Luis Valley, corroborate these trends.[22] Some of my respondents witnessed these cultural conflicts growing up, and still see them to this day, particularly as the San Luis Valley has received more Latinx newcomers from other states, Mexico, and other countries in Latin America (e.g., Guatemala). These identity struggles overlap with an equally complicated relationship with Anglo culture, which is seen as dominant in the Valley and threatening to other cultures, but mastery of which is essential in order to make it in American society. Three main topics emerged from their narratives. First, the uniqueness of the Hispano experience in the US Southwest. Second, the challenges that immigrants face in adapting to a new society (including their US-born children). And third, uncertainty about their community's future. Oftentimes these topics overlapped, but for the most part they were treated separately.

Not surprisingly, the issue of Hispano identity (and other identities) came up in conversations time and time again. Hispanos make up the majority of Latinxs in the San Luis Valley, they are the Valley's oldest and largest ethnic "minority" (though in some counties, they are a demographic majority), and their standing vis-à-vis Anglos has shaped the nature of ethnic relations in the San Luis Valley for well over a century. Moreover, their deep historical roots in the region are a sort of historical anomaly in a nation where Latinxs are often seen as newcomers, even by immigrants themselves. Hispanos, in turn, reinforce their unique status by reproducing a narrative with strong ties to Spanish culture (MacAulay 2011).

Rosa,[23] a middle-aged Hispano female who works mainly with Latinx immigrants in the San Luis Valley, provided personal insights into the pan-Hispano worldview. "My dad would say: My ancestors came from Spain, not Mexico" according to her recollection. Some Hispanos in the San Luis Valley see themselves as part of a greater Spanish cultural sphere, relatively isolated for centuries and with distant influences from Mexico (which, after all, only ruled Nuevo México for twenty-five years). Though Hispanos would often use the terms *Mexicano* and *Mexicana* to refer to themselves and their culture (among other terms, including Spanish, Spanish American, *la gente*, and *la raza*), they stress the fact that they are different culturally from Mexican immigrants. Moreover, Hispanos of Rosa's generation still maintain their Spanish language, which has been passed down from one generation to the other, with its own New World linguistic characteristics (Bills and Vigil 2008; Vergara Wilson and Jenkins 2020). "Spanish was my first language; I learned English in school," she said with obvious pride. Rosa learned Spanish from her parents and grandparents, and to this day she speaks it at home with her husband—also a Hispano from the San Luis Valley. According to Rosa, not even the arrival of Mexican immigrants has altered the nature of the

Spanish language spoken by Hispanos. Hispanos feel that their culture is resilient and that Mexican immigration has added to it but not replaced it. Quite the opposite, Mexican immigrants—as new arrivals into the San Luis Valley—usually must learn the Hispanos' own vernacular, Rosa added with a chuckle.

If anything, for Rosa the biggest threat to Hispano identity is coming from the Anglo world. The homogenizing power of American culture—through public schools, media, and the workplace—is slowly undermining the linguistic traditions of Hispanos, particularly as the San Luis Valley becomes more integrated into the national mainstream. She put it succinctly: "My kids understand Spanish but won't speak it. The tradition has been lost." Carole Counihan (2009) observed a similar phenomenon in her study of Antonito, a small, mostly-Hispano town south of Alamosa. She found that "most of the town's youth born after about 1980 knew little or no Spanish" (26). Whereas local Hispanos and Anglos did not intermarry often in the past, interethnic marriages are becoming more commonplace nowadays as Hispanos have risen into the middle class. Hispanos have also moved on to other professions and out of the San Luis Valley, a cause of concern regarding the future of the Valley's Hispano community, as fewer Hispanos of the newer generations have ties to the land. To paraphrase Rosa's own words, the biggest threats to Hispanos are (Anglo) Texans and Easterners who are buying huge tracts of land in the San Luis Valley—not poor Mexican immigrants.

Dawn,[24] a young Hispano community advocate native to the San Luis Valley, also saw Hispano identity being defined in a similar way, as she recalled her parents' opinions on the subject. "We have been here longer," her parents used to say to highlight their deep historical roots in the San Luis Valley when referring to other Latinx immigrants. Dawn stressed the fact that "there is a separation"; that is, Mexicans are perceived as culturally different from Hispanos by the latter. Even when it comes to attending mass, Dawn remarked how Hispanos would go to English services while Mexican immigrants attend services in Spanish. Both communities also celebrate their own folk traditions separately. After the 2008 recession hit the region, some Hispanos in the San Luis Valley saw Mexican immigrants as competition for scarce jobs, or as moochers that abuse the system, according to Dawn. A handful of Hispanos were so resentful of

Mexican immigrants that "some Hispanos here would go out of their way to get Mexicans deported," a stunning revelation that clearly upset Dawn. As evidence, she mentioned that people would call the agency where she works by mistake in order to report undocumented Mexicans (her work number and that of Immigration and Customs Enforcement—ICE—are very similar). Even some of her relatives have done it, she confessed with a glint of shame in her eyes.

Dawn, however, personally feels a cultural connection with Mexican immigrants. She married a man from Mexico, and her family did not accept him initially ("it took a while," she recalled). Mexicans, on the other hand, stereotype Hispanos as lazy and too Americanized and oftentimes will call them Chicanos in a derogative manner. The cultural divide is even greater vis-à-vis Anglos, and Dawn spoke about her—and her own parents'—experiences growing up Hispano in the San Luis Valley. "My parents grew up at a time when discrimination was really, really high.[25] They were punished for speaking Spanish in school; they were belittled. He [her father] spent most of his kindergarten and first grade years in closets [as punishment] because he refused to speak English." As adults, when her parents had children, "they made a conscious decision to not teach us Spanish; so, we were really Americanized." Dawn did not feel discriminated against like her parents, who were very self-conscious about it and lived in a different time. Ironically, she learned Spanish from her former husband, a Mexican immigrant who was not fluent in English. But "when I had my son, my mother told me not to give him my last name, but his dad's [who is Anglo]. And I did. People treat him differently because of his last name. Even in 2012, Anglo kids get more recognition in school." Dawn's experience and that of her family is typical of other Hispanos in the San Luis Valley; widely discriminated against by Anglos for generations, they may discriminate against Mexican immigrants in turn as part of a perceived racial-ethnic pecking order based on skin color and national origin. Noel and Maryanne Dunne,[26] two Anglo pastoral associates, reiterated this trend, adding that "Hispanos are very wary of outsiders." Sometimes, "Anglo farmers are more sympathetic [toward Mexican immigrant workers]."

The Anglo cultural bias against Hispano culture and the Spanish language came up repeatedly during my interviews, with Hispanos feeling that their unique culture has been under siege for decades by an Anglo world that seeks to erase their identity—focusing on the elimination of the Spanish language in particular. These cultural and legal assaults on the Spanish language have been common throughout the history of the American West, and by the late twentieth century and early twenty-first century they had morphed into an English-Only movement that perceived languages other than English as divisive and un-American (Kuang 2018). Effective January 1, 1989, the Constitution of Colorado was amended to declare that "the English language is the official language of the State of Colorado" (State of Colorado 2022). The amendment was widely approved by voters, despite opposition by Governor Roy Romer and Denver Mayor Federico Peña, and it quickly led to misinterpretations and multiple instances of discriminatory behavior toward Spanish speakers (Coates 1989). On November 18–19, 1989, the National Conference to Combat the English-Only Movement was held in Denver. Ricardo Romero, one of the Chicanx activists in attendance, described the English-Only movement as "genocidal," while remarking, "We must destroy the English-Only movement because they want to destroy us (Mexicans) as a people" ("English-Only Means Genocide for Mexicans in U.S." 1989). To this day, linguistic policies—and their interpretation—remain a bone of contention between Anglo and Hispanic Coloradans.

Mexican immigrants, and other Latinx immigrants in the San Luis Valley (e.g., Guatemalans), face their own unique set of identity and everyday challenges. Approximately 10,000 immigrants live in the San Luis Valley (as per informal estimates by Rosa), where they work in agriculture, construction, and sometimes, the service sector. According to Rosa, it is jobs in agriculture that mainly attract Mexicans to the Valley, and the presence of Hispanos makes their accommodation relatively easier. Most Mexicans who come to work in the San Luis Valley are working-class immigrants hailing from rural locations in northern and central Mexico, and include some Indigenous peoples (e.g., Tarahumara), according to the Dunnes. Intermarriage between Hispanos and Mexicans has become more common, though some Hispanos are still reluctant to accept the latter ("they're not like us; they're womanizers" are common complaints, said Rosa). Moreover, most Mexican women come into the United States as part of family units, so it is usually single Mexican men who marry local Hispano women, a fact that creates competition and stirs resentment among Hispano men. On the other hand, marriages between Mexicans and Anglo women are extremely rare. According to Dawn, Anglos see Mexican immigrants as lower in the totem pole than Hispanos (because of their lack of US citizenship and the jobs they do), and oftentimes language is a big divide. Most immigrant workers in the Valley are young men and very mobile, moving from one place to the other, depending on which crop is in season (e.g., potatoes, lettuce, or spinach). Their lives—and those of their families—tend to revolve around their work schedules, with their children frequently attending two or three different schools in one academic year. After decades of Mexican migration to the San Luis Valley, however, over half of them have become homeowners by acquiring prefabricated, modular homes for their families, added the Dunnes. Unfortunately, police profiling of Mexican immigrants seems to remain a recurring problem for the latter, at the hands of Anglo as well as of Hispano police officers. On the other hand, Rosa commented that "some Anglos have taken them [Mexican immigrants] under their wings," a product of their common love for the land—although these cases are rare. And while outsiders often confuse Hispanos with Mexican immigrants—according to Dawn—most local Anglos are very aware of the Valley's ethnic pecking order.

Guatemalan immigrants, on the other hand, are seen as very different—even from Mexicans—because of their skin color, (Mayan) Indigenous looks, dress, language, and overall demeanor. A cohort of more than 400 Guatemalan immigrants and their US-born descendants make up a unique community in the San Luis Valley (Ludwig et al. 2012, 32). Q'anjob'al Maya from Santa Eulalia (in Guatemala's Huehuetenango Department) started arriving in the San Luis Valley in the late 1970s because of the country's protracted, low-intensity civil war, and the military government's periodic targeting of Mayan rural communities. The latter were seen by the right-wing military administrations as hotbeds of potential sympathizers of the left-wing insurgency, which in turn sought to recruit the Q'anjob'al into their ranks in order to bolster their numbers against government forces. Caught in the middle and fearing for their lives, young men started leaving their rural communities and making the perilous overland trip across Mexico and into the United States. Some began arriving in the San Luis Valley attracted by jobs in agriculture, while the area's relative isolation appealed to them as refugees who sought to leave behind a war-torn country.

Daniel,[27] a middle-class merchant in his hometown in Guatemala, was forced to leave because the war made his position untenable. The military demanded intelligence on the guerrilla's whereabouts from him, and he was then targeted in turn by the insurgents for cooperating with the government. After being warned that his life was in imminent danger, he left for the United States with other male relatives and crossed the US-Mexico border surreptitiously into Arizona. Unbeknownst to him, he spearheaded what eventually became a migratory wave of Q'anjob'al Mayans into the San Luis Valley. Because of the ongoing conflict in Guatemala, Daniel was able to secure political asylum and later became a legal resident of the United States, thanks to the Immigration Reform and Control Act of 1986, which provided unauthorized immigrants with a path to legalize their status. Like Daniel, most Guatemalans in the Valley worked for years at the Rakhra Mushroom Farm in Alamosa. Many of the first-generation Guatemalan male immigrants had just an elementary school education, while some of the women had none. In addition, not of all of them were fluent in Spanish, and even to this day many of the elders only speak Q'anjob'al. It is a closely knit community of war refugees who have been able to maintain their traditions (even across three generations[28]) and they represent a unique—and paradoxical—case of immigrants who despite being very different from the mainstream feel that they have received ample support from the Valley's local population. Daniel described how sometimes people (mainly outsiders) confused the Q'anjob'al with Mexicans, but after learning of their plight as political refugees, would become sympathetic. Whether this depiction is entirely accurate or just a perception, the status of the Q'anjob'al as war refugees certainly gives them a different outlook regarding their adoptive nation. Moreover, the tightly knit nature of their non-English- and non-Spanish-speaking community and their concentration in the mushroom industry perhaps helped insulate the Q'anjob'al from racial prejudices that Mexicans and Hispanos faced daily when engaging the outside world.

As seen, the generalized perception of the San Luis Valley as a Hispano homeland—while still accurate—can be somewhat misleading. The

Valley's Latinx population is a multilayered community of local Hispanos with deep historical roots in the region and waves of Mexican and other Latin American immigrants that have been arriving since the late nineteenth century. Except for the demographic preponderance of Hispanos in the mix, the San Luis Valley increasingly resembles other Latinx communities across the American West: mixed, diverse, and multigenerational.

Challenges for the San Luis Valley

Despite being the historical heart of Colorado's Hispano population, the San Luis Valley's Latinx community faces significant challenges. The Valley encompasses six counties in southern Colorado: Alamosa, Conejos, Costilla, Mineral, Rio Grande, and Saguache (see map 0.2). Except for Mineral County, the other five counties have large percentages (around 40%–50%) of Latinxs (see figure 1.2). Yet, the Valley's population is small: less than 50,000 inhabitants in 2020 (0.80% of the state population), of which 44.5% are Latinx, accounting for just 1.62% of all Latinxs in Colorado (US Census Bureau 2020). Alamosa is the commercial hub and largest city in the San Luis Valley, with roads radiating from it into neighboring communities—a result of the D&RG's nineteenth-century decision to found it as a rail center (Loosbrock 2020, 362)—but with less than 10,000 inhabitants as of 2020 (US Census Bureau 2020). If anything, the San Luis Valley is characterized by its tiny population and predominant rural character, with a handful of small towns spread around. The San Luis Valley also has a US national park, Great Sand Dunes National Park and Preserve, which is a major tourist draw and cash inflow in an otherwise poor region of the state. The Valley's poverty stands in sharp contrast with the image of Colorado as an affluent state, as represented by Denver's skyscrapers; the Front Range's sprawling suburbs; and multimillion-dollar compounds, glitzy ski resorts, and stately log cabins nested in its central mountains (Cronin and Loevy 2021b).

As of 2020, Costilla County was the poorest county in the state of Colorado (out of sixty-four counties), with 30.1% percent of its residents under the federal poverty level—whereas just 10.9% of Coloradans are listed as poor statewide. Alamosa County ranked fourth in the state in terms of poverty, while Conejos County ranked sixth, Saguache County ranked

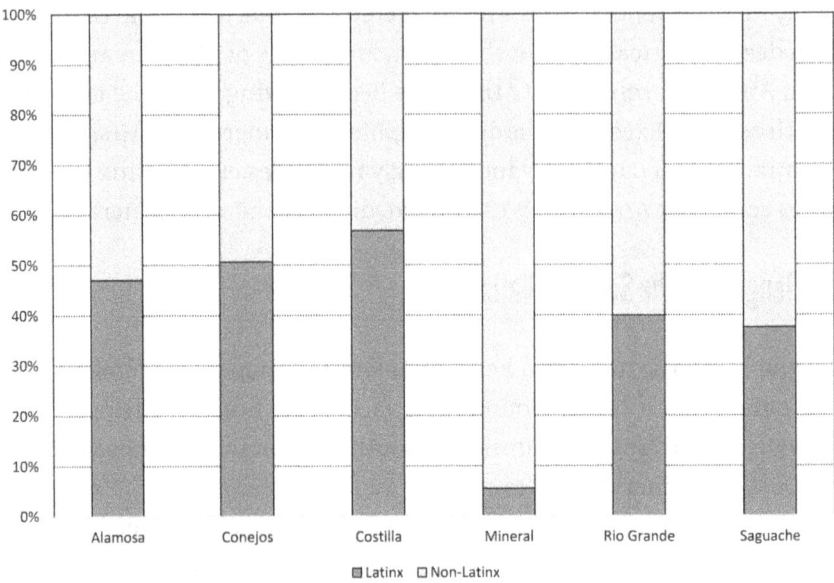

FIGURE 1.2. Latinx population of the San Luis Valley (percentage Latinx, by county), 1990–2020. Source: US Census Bureau.

eleventh, and Rio Grande County ranked thirteenth (Spaulding 2020). In most counties in the San Luis Valley, poverty is disproportionately concentrated in its Hispanic population, the result of decades of displacement and racial discrimination. For example, discriminatory practices in lending have prevented Hispanics in the Valley from becoming farmers and ranchers, while other locals have gone bankrupt and lost their land due to a lack of access to subsidized credit (Waddell and Martinez 2020). Without land, potential and former Hispanic farmers and ranchers have no choice but to move to urban areas (such as Alamosa) and seek meager employment, or to leave the Valley and move to the Front Range urban areas. Young Hispanics see few opportunities for themselves in the San Luis Valley and move out, leaving behind a graying population (San Luis Valley Community Action Agency 2020, 9–10). Generalized poverty compounds the provision of health care to an older population spread out over large, underpopulated counties. Not surprisingly, in a study of fifty-eight Colorado counties, the healthiest counties were all in the Front Range or included resort towns such as Telluride and Vail. In contrast, counties in the San Luis Valley ranked toward the end of the list when it came to health indicators: Rio Grande County at 47, Conejos County at 50, Alamosa County at 51, Saguache County at 56, and Costilla County dead last at 58 ("Valley Low in County Health Rankings" 2018). San Luis Valley counties outpace the state in poor health indicators, such as smoking, obesity, and physical inactivity; as well as negative socioeconomic indicators, such as higher rates of unemployment and children living in poverty.

Even the agricultural bounty of the San Luis Valley is facing challenges, in the form of drought induced by climate change. The San Luis Valley lies in an arid region, so years of below-average snowpack, excessive well pumping by farmers, and a plan to divert Valley water to Front Range cities threaten the viability of ranching and agriculture in the San Luis Valley, where "one of every three dollars of basic income . . . comes from agriculture" (Obmascik 2021). Valley crops like potatoes and alfalfa require enormous amounts of water, which is increasingly difficult to get, as the state has halted the drilling of new wells for several decades now. On top of that water deficit, state courts ruled that Valley irrigators have a 2031 deadline to replenish 400,000 acre-feet of water to the underground aquifers. Failure to meet the deadline will likely force the state government to shut down local wells, a worst-case scenario that Valley farmers dread, as it would bring about economic ruin (Coleman 2020). Ranching and agriculture, the rural industries that once attracted New Mexican settlers to the San Luis Valley, led to the development of a regional Hispano culture that was deeply rooted in the land and the rhythms of the seasons in the Valley. As elsewhere in the West, climate change is imperiling rural America, its agricultural bounty, and the welfare of its people. In the San Luis Valley, these environmental challenges dovetail with generalized poverty, decades of discrimination against Hispanics, and lack of economic opportunities, to paint a bleak picture of the Valley's future—particularly for Hispanics. The ancient way of life of Hispanos, their traditions, and their love for the land are at a tipping point. As more young Hispanics leave the San Luis Valley in search of better economic opportunities elsewhere, the Hispano homeland that once housed Colorado's first permanent settlements and became the heart of the state's Hispanic community is in danger of losing its resilience and cultural distinctiveness—not to mention its traditional economic livelihood (Rivera 2016, 13–14).

Conclusion: The Birthplace of Hispano Colorado

The US-Mexican War enabled the settlement of Colorado by its first Latinx/Hispanic people: the Hispanos of the San Luis Valley (originally *Nuevomexicanos* settling the northern territory of New Mexico). A byproduct of US imperial expansion and settler colonialism, Hispanos (and Native Americans) were overtaken and socially displaced as the United States sought to expand its territory—a process that continued unabated well into the late nineteenth century (J. Hernández 1997). In a classic case of internal colonialism, the lands that nowadays make up the American West were captured, occupied, and exploited by Anglo settlers and corporations that turned the local Hispanos into a cheap labor force that they could rely on (Acuña 2000). The ideology of Manifest Destiny fueled this westward expansion and buttressed the racial pecking order that led Anglos to claim the Western lands as theirs while racializing Hispanos into foreign Others (Horsman 1981, chaps. 11–12). Anglo America would come to imagine Hispanos (i.e., "Mexicans") as a brown people, a non-white inferior race, except when it was convenient for political reasons (e.g., pleading for New Mexico's statehood). Hispanos unfortunately entered the US racial landscape as racialized Others, a position of inferiority reinforced by subsequent waves of immigration from Mexico, and as bearers of a stigma that would persist well into the present.

Yet, these imperial schemes also played a role in allowing the expansion of Hispano communities into the territory that would eventually become the US state of Colorado. As had been the case elsewhere, US internal colonialism displaced the Indigenous peoples of the region, disrupted traditional ways of life, and introduced an aggressive capitalist economy where corporate interests reigned. The imperial onslaught hit Hispanos hard, yet it also sparked new forms of resistance among them that bolstered their cultural resilience and led to new strategies for survival in a hostile Anglo world. Neither helpless victims nor passive onlookers, Colorado's Hispanos challenged, contested, and accommodated to their new reality, eventually expanding their geographical reach and establishing new communities throughout the state (Deutsch 1987, 9). For as much as Manifest Destiny was seen as "evidence of the innate superiority of the American Anglo-Saxon branch of the Caucasian race" (Horsman 1981, 1),

US imperialism in the American West faced the same dilemma as colonial powers elsewhere: The newcomers ultimately depended on the cheap labor of the locals. As such, one of its unintended consequences was the survival, consolidation, and expansion of the Hispano Homeland—to include southern Colorado and other parts of the state.

However, it must be kept in mind that Colorado's Hispano community is the product of not just one empire but three: Spain, Mexico, and the United States. It was Spain's conquest of the Rio Grande region and its subjugation of Indian Pueblos that allowed Hispanos to settle in what eventually became New Mexico and claim it as their own, while Mexico's land grants fueled their expansion further north—a process finalized by the US armed presence in the San Luis Valley (S. Rodríguez 1987). Thus, all three countries played an imperial role in establishing Hispano communities at the expense of the region's Indigenous peoples. Even the Hispano claim to a homeland vis-à-vis Anglo newcomers is predicated on the erasure of Indigenous claims to the same land by both parties. And while Hispanos could technically make a claim to the land by virtue of their mestizo and Indigenous ancestry, the Hispano Homeland is usually imagined as more Hispanic than Indigenous. It will not be until the dawn of the Chicano Movement that the children of these Hispanos (and other Mexican Americans) will seek to reclaim their Indigenous ancestry while rejecting their Hispanic cultural roots as part of an anticolonial discourse (see chapter 3). Such is the nature of borderlands in the American West, where the claims of advancing and retreating empires overlapped in myriad ways with competing claims from local Hispanos and Native Americans. Even as Colorado became a "bordered" territory when it was separated from New Mexico (Adelman and Aron 1999), the Hispanos of Colorado's San Luis Valley remained an important part of a cultural borderland, one that became more complex and transnational with the passing of time and the arrival of Mexican immigrants from south of the new US-Mexico international border (R. Gutiérrez and Young 2010).

While Hispano identity helped shield and unite those peoples acquired by the United States via the Treaty of Guadalupe Hidalgo, and to this day remains a significant cultural and ethnic identifier throughout southern Colorado (e.g., *manito* identity), being part of an imagined Hispano community is just one of the many ways in which Colorado's Latinxs identify themselves. Even though the state of Colorado in general and the San Luis Valley in particular are historically connected to Spanish and Mexican culture, and Latinxs have been the area's largest demographic minority for decades; historical, generational, national-origin, linguistic, and even ethnic differences among the Valley's Latinxs present a complex picture in terms of identity formation. Whereas the original Hispano population lived in relative cultural isolation for decades, the arrival of Mexican immigrants and other Latinxs since the early twentieth century has added layers of complexity to the old Anglo-Hispano divide. The San Luis Valley resembles a multilayered cake with a Hispano foundation onto which Latinx immigrants have added cultural layers as they have arrived. While these layers oftentimes touch (and sometimes overlap), they have not blended with each other entirely, leaving distinguishable communities of Hispanos, Mexicans, and other Latinxs (mainly Guatemalans) that interact with each other and with the Anglo community in different ways. As such, Hispano cultural strands radiate outward from the San Luis Valley and help shed light on identity formation processes in the birthplace of Colorado and throughout the Centennial State.

2

THE EASTERN PLAINS

Sugar Beets and Braceros

Carmel "Chuck" Solano's back hurt—a lot. As a young boy, he started working in the sugar beet fields of eastern Colorado and did not stop until he was a grown man. His family, originally from New Mexico, were itinerant field workers who moved from farm to farm, and state to state, in search of work. Chuck's days started very early; he would get breakfast, head for the fields, and work thinning the sugar beets with his family. Thinning beets required him to be constantly bent over, using a short hoe to remove the weeds that grew in between the sugar beet plants (Solano 2013, 41). Chuck would work a long row of beets, and upon reaching the end, he would get up, crack his back, and start with the next row.[1] This repetitive work took a toll on his body, and he was not alone. Thousands of fellow Mexican Americans and Mexican immigrants toiled in Colorado's sugar beet fields for most of the twentieth century, becoming an essential component of the industry's labor force. Hundreds of these laborers would eventually call the plains of eastern Colorado home, raise families, and establish flourishing communities that would leave a distinct Latinx imprint on the region.

This chapter examines the use of "Mexican" (i.e., Hispano, Mexican, and Mexican American) labor in the sugar beet fields of eastern Colorado and its impact on the development of Latinx communities in the state's Eastern Plains region (see map 0.1). It describes how Mexican and Mexican American labor was incorporated into the state's thriving sugar beet business, the numbers and migratory circuits of laborers, the role of the Bracero Program in funneling large numbers of Mexican laborers to this region, and, finally, the creation of multilayered Latinx communities in Colorado's Eastern Plains—a place hitherto devoid of them. Moreover, it argues that whereas these imported workers were perceived as temporary sojourners by their employers, permanent Latinx communities were eventually established, and they grew deep roots, altering the demographic and cultural landscape of Colorado's least populated region, and (in the process) expanding the Mexican American cultural borderlands further north.

Beet Sugar in Colorado

White Gold. The Silver Wedge. These nicknames for beet sugar reflect how valuable this cash crop once was for Colorado's Eastern Plains—to the extent that sugar production had become Colorado's chief resource by 1930, easily besting the profits from the state's much-touted gold and silver mines (May 1989, 429–430, 439). Since the early nineteenth century, Europeans had been extracting sugar from beets in order to supply a growing demand from consumers hungry for sweet calories in their diets. It would take a few decades for sugar beet seeds and the technology to extract sugar from them to make it to the United States, and it was not until 1899 that the first sugar manufacturing plant in Colorado opened in Grand Junction (Abbott, Leonard, and Noel 2005, 173). Several developments contributed to the state playing a major role in the US sugar beet sector. First, Colorado's soils and climate were ideal for growing sugar beets. Some regions of the state—like the Eastern Plains—lacked the necessary rainfall, but this challenge was met by the construction of irrigation canals, thus opening parts of the "Great American Desert"[2] to intensive cultivation. Second, the region targeted by the sugar beet industry—mainly the Eastern Plains—was sparsely populated by the late nineteenth century,[3] and land was cheap and plentiful. Third, the Industrial Revolution produced the technology and supplied the machinery needed for the large-scale processing of sugar beets at substantial profit margins. Fourth, the Dingley Tariff Act (1897) and the Spanish-American War (1898) had stimulated the production of US domestic sugar by making overseas sugar imports more expensive (Irwin 2017, chap. 6). And fifth, railroads now crisscrossed the American West, facilitating the transportation of processed sugar to eastern markets, where it had big demand. As a result, Colorado's sugar beet production would center mostly on the state's Eastern Plains (with smaller operations in the Grand Valley, on the state's Western Slope region), transforming its featureless countryside and ushering in major economic and social changes for the region and the state—changes in which Latinx workers played a major role.

The first sugar manufacturing plants in Colorado were built in Grand Junction (1899) and Rocky Ford (1900). The first plant on the Front Range opened in Loveland in 1901, and it was soon followed by several more throughout the region (in Greeley, Eaton, Fort Collins, and Longmont), making Colorado the leading producer of sugar beets in the nation by 1909. Great Western Sugar Company—a pioneering sugar producer with operations across several states—consolidated several of these plants in 1905 and began expanding operations throughout the Eastern Plains, acquiring a plant in Sterling, and building new ones in Brush and Fort Morgan. By the 1920s, Great Western Sugar Company and other minor producers had over a dozen sugar plants in operation in northeastern Colorado (around the South Platte River Valley), with vast expanses of sugar beet fields dominating the landscape of the state's Eastern Plains. Further south, the American Beet Sugar Company, Holly Sugar Company, and other minor producers transformed the Arkansas River Valley into the state's other major sugar-producing region (Twitty 2003, 50–51). The sugar business operated mainly as a trust, and thus large companies such as Great Western also controlled railroads and had interests in coal mines and lime quarries. Finally, irrigation projects became the lifeblood of Colorado's sugar beet industry. The Newlands Reclamation Act of 1902 helped transform the Great American Desert into fertile farmland with the building of dams, ditches, and canals, and the sugar beet industry thrived as a result (2003, 34–47). When World War I wreaked havoc on

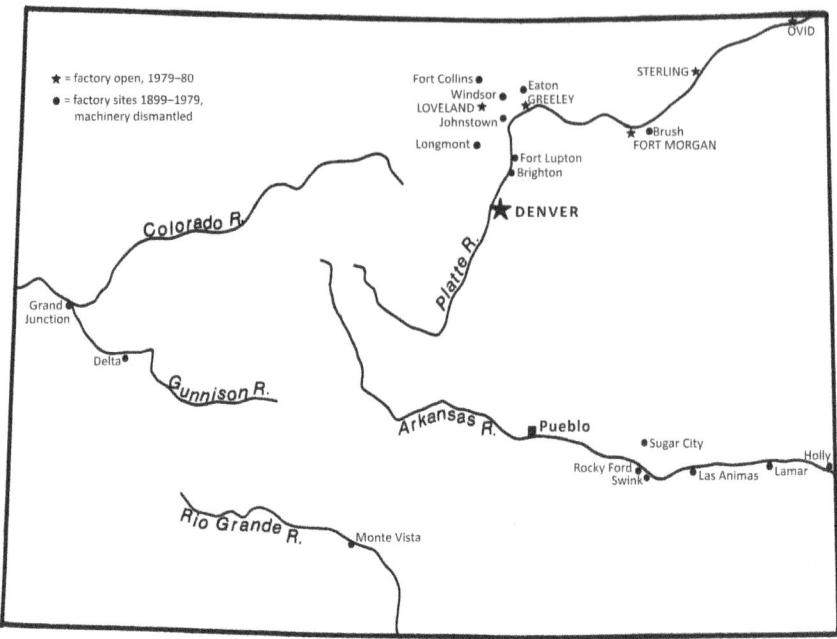

MAP 2.1. Beet sugar factory locations in Colorado, 1899–present. Source: Sabin 1986, 294.

Europe's agriculture and disrupted shipping, US beet sugar production stepped in to fill the void. Accordingly, new sugar factories were built in Brighton, Delta, and Fort Lupton during the Great War. In 1926, after a slump in prices and new protective tariffs, Great Western built two new factories in Ovid and Johnstown (see map 2.1). By 1927, Colorado was the largest sugar-beet-growing state in the nation, with 30.2% of beet acreage and 35.6% of beet sugar production (P. Taylor 1930, 99).

Large-scale, extensive sugar beet cultivation required experienced laborers who worked intensively on the beets throughout the season. Initially, the industry relied on German Russians who had experience with beets and could be persuaded to migrate to the United States. Japanese workers were also employed to some extent, but the practice declined after the Gentlemen's Agreement of 1907 blocked Japanese immigration to the United States. In the case of German Russians, World War I and the Russian Revolution eventually brought an end to their further immigration. Ironically, the German Russian migrants were initially stigmatized as racialized stoop laborers who relied on child labor to succeed. Within a generation or two, most of these families had acquired land and, with it, social standing in a system where land ownership defined whiteness. In turn, farmers of German Russian ancestry came to employ (and exploit) the next large source of racialized cheap labor in the beet industry: "Mexicans"[4] (Legg 2005).

Mexican Labor Migration

A major component of sugar beet production in Colorado was the widespread use of so-called Mexican labor. These workers were far from being the first Hispanics in the region. Mexican trappers had explored and exploited the resources of the land along with French Canadian and American partners in the early nineteenth century. In 1835, Franco-Spanish trapper Louis Vasquez established a fort and trading post near present-day Platteville,[5] while Mexican mountain man Mariano Medina settled with his family and others near present-day Loveland (Duncan 1988, 6; Jessen 2019). In 1842, Anglo mountain men founded a plaza and trading fort named El Pueblo. These were Hispanicized Anglos; they had Mexican wives, spoke Spanish, and followed local customs, and some had even converted to Catholicism and become Mexican citizens. Moreover, the inhabitants of El Pueblo were mostly Mexicans, connected by trading networks to Taos. Eventually, Fort Pueblo was abandoned after it was destroyed by a war party of Utes and Jicarilla Apaches in 1854 (Haverluk 2002, 47–49). The history of these Hispanic individuals and their contributions would be lost with the arrival of thousands of Anglo settlers, but more important, their historic connections to Mexico, New Mexico, and the "Mexican" workers coming from the South remained unacknowledged. For all intents and purposes, these migrant workers were aliens in a "white" American West.

The beet sugar industry was labor intensive, particularly when it came to the planting, thinning, and harvesting of the sugar beets, and Mexican laborers were to play a major role in the development of the state's sugar beet industry through their hard work in the beet fields. Local Spanish-speaking Mexican (i.e., Spanish American) workers started joining the sugar beet industry of southern Colorado in 1900, and by 1903 they were being employed in the northern part of the state. In 1912, for the first time, Mexican workers began to be imported from out of state (May 1989, 287). Unlike previous waves of German Russian and Japanese workers who usually came with their families, these Mexicans were mostly young men hired just for the season. They came from two sources: Mexican nationals (primarily recruited in Texas, New Mexico, and Arizona) who migrated north into the United States looking for seasonal jobs; and Hispanos (i.e., Spanish/Mexican Americans) from northern New Mexico and southern Colorado who often supplemented their annual income by working in the beet fields (Varsanyi 2020, 13). This short-term hiring strategy worked well for a while, but soon, labor needs and competition from other sectors (like the mines and railroads) made the sugar companies realize that they needed a more stable pool of cheap labor, as desertions among the migratory labor force were numerous (Hamilton 2009, 281).

By the 1920s, the companies began encouraging the migration of Hispanic family units, starting with Great Western in 1922. The companies also built—or helped build—housing units to accommodate these Mexican and Mexican American workers and their families. The settlements (known as *colonias*) provided workers with a place to live, but no land of their own that they could farm (Valdés 1990, 113–114). *Colonias* consisted of basic homes (made of clapboard or adobe) arranged in small neighborhoods, built by the sugar companies for their Hispanic workers and their families, and oftentimes lacking water, sewer, and electricity. Sometimes, the sugar companies provided the materials, and the workers built their own homes. In all cases, the sugar companies intended their workers to remain in place yearlong and encouraged other economic sectors (e.g., the railroads) to provide jobs for their Mexican workers during the offseason. The much-publicized rationale was that if the sugar companies could save money on labor, those savings would translate into better prices for beet farmers at harvest time (May 1989, 410–411). In other words, what was good for the sugar companies was good for society in general. For the inhabitants of the *colonias*, these permanent homes were a step up from the boxcars, cabooses, and wooden shacks often used by beet farmers to house itinerant workers and their families. They were a shot at a decent life for their families and perhaps an education for their children.

The first *colonia* of the Great Western Sugar Company was built in Fort Morgan in 1922. It was quickly followed by several others, including one in 1924 located northwest of Greeley known as "the Spanish colony" (officially Española Subdivision), because it originally harbored Hispano families recruited by the company in New Mexico (Lopez and Lopez 2007, 13–14, 34). Initially, the homes (which the workers built by themselves using adobe bricks) were rented to the workers, but at the end of their five-year lease, the Great Western Sugar Company encouraged the families to purchase their homes and provided them with payment plans in an attempt to secure an experienced, stable labor force. The *colonias* were the perfect example of the spatial segregation that reinforced the second-class racialized status of Mexican workers. For example, Great Western built four *colonias* in Fort Collins; three of which (Alta Vista, Andersonville, and Buckingham) were built on company land located on the other side of the railroad tracks (and of the Poudre River), close to the company's sugar plant but away from the city's downtown (nowadays known as Old Town). The other Mexican *colonia* (Holy Family, named after its Roman Catholic church) lies west of downtown in an area first settled by African American families that eventually became a Hispanic neighborhood (Hamilton 2009, 285-I; Thomas 2003, 4–10).[6] Its church provided services in Spanish in a town in which race and religion usually went hand in hand; part of a region in which the Mexicans' Roman Catholic faith was another strike against them (Sabin 1986, 134). *Colonias* were spatially segregated from the main part of towns because of objections by Anglo residents, who "won't let the Mexicans come any closer" (P. Taylor 1930, 209). In Greeley, Anglos were concerned about the location of the Spanish Colony—nine miles away (Donato 2007, 37–38). Unlike other parts of the country where white families could not escape mingling with people of color, in eastern Colorado the "absence"[7] of Asians, African Americans, and Native Americans, coupled with the relatively small numbers of Mexican laborers, allowed for the spatial segregation of the latter and the creation of the fantasy of a "white American West" (Pierce 2016).

In its ongoing search for a reliable labor force, the Great Western Sugar Company went as far as producing slick films in Spanish designed to attract potential Hispanic laborers. These short films portrayed living conditions in the *colonias* and work in the fields in the best possible light (Great Western Sugar Company 1924). But unlike the German Russians and Japanese workers that preceded them, Mexican *betabeleros* (i.e., stoop labor in the beet fields) were never given the opportunity to become landowners. The low wages that they earned were not sufficient to provide decent lives for their families, much less to accumulate the necessary capital to buy farmland (May 1989, 417). They were rural proletarians solely employed to work in the fields, particularly for the backbreaking stoop labor of blocking, thinning, and harvesting the beets (Hamilton 2009, 279). By the late 1920s, about 10,000 families lived in the *colonias*, which functioned as company towns. Because the company did not pay workers until the end of the season, these families relied on store credit from the local storekeeper, who provided them with food and cash advances to make it through, thus further tying the beet workers to the sugar company by way of their indebtedness (Valdés 1990, 115–116). In essence, the sugar beet companies instituted a plantation-style system of debt peonage that guaranteed them reliable cheap labor whenever they needed it (Vargas 2005, 29).

Many workers in the sugar beet fields came from northern and central Mexico, a country that underwent major structural changes in the late nineteenth century. The administration of strongman Porfirio Díaz (in power from 1876–1911), bent on transforming rural Mexico, promoted "modernization" schemes that included the continued dismantling of the *ejido* system,[8] the construction of vast railroad networks, and the opening of the country to foreign investment. As in the case of the American West, railroads, mining, and agribusinesses began to dominate Mexico's rural economy, opening the country's northern region to capitalist development (Moreno-Brid and Ros 2009, chap. 3). Landlessness increased, and thousands of former peasants and rural workers sought better conditions in the United States, where there was a big demand for Mexican laborers and wages were significantly better. For example, average wages for rural workers in Mexico's haciendas were about 12¢ a day in the early 1900s. In contrast, average wages in the United States during the same period ranged from 50¢ to $3.00 a day depending on the industry, with mining offering the best-paying jobs (Cardoso 1980, 22–23). It also helped that northern Mexico's dominant industries were the same as in the American West, thus providing US companies with experienced laborers willing to work for lower wages than US citizens would accept. Demand simply met supply.

In 1910, the Mexican Revolution ushered in a period of economic uncertainty and political upheaval, displacing thousands of Mexican peasants from their lands, and forcing some into the United States, where jobs were available for them (Aguayo 1998). Between 1909 and 1927, Mexicans went from being 9% of the labor force in the Great Western Sugar Company to becoming (by far) the largest ethnic group employed by the company, at 59% of its labor force (Hamilton 2009, 278). Colorado's Mexican-born population increased drastically between 1917 and 1920—almost fivefold (Sheflin 2019, 181). This labor surge was thanks to the efforts of the Great Western Sugar Company sending Hispanic agents throughout the Southwestern and Midwestern states to recruit workers. These bilingual, bicultural recruiters could establish a rapport and earn the trust of field workers, who would return year after year to the beet fields of Colorado. Great Western agents were particularly successful in Fort Worth and San Antonio, Texas, as well as in the Lower Rio Grande Valley, where most of the workers held seasonal jobs in winter and could be convinced to come to Colorado in the offseason (Hamilton 2009, 278; May 1989, 408). Workers coming from northern Mexico followed the Mountain States' labor stream, crossing at El Paso, Texas, and moving north to Colorado (Vargas 2005, 17). Company agents signed six-month contracts on behalf of individual beet farmers, who agreed to provide housing and water to the workers while the company provided one-way transportation (Reisler 1976, 88–89). Thus, sugar beets played a significant role in the migratory circuits of Mexican workers who followed the seasons, moving from one region of the country to another as the harvest progressed. Thousands of Mexican immigrants arrived in the beet fields of Colorado in the 1920s, supplementing a labor force of Hispanos already in place.

The arrival of thousands of Mexicans to Colorado created racial tensions with the white community and with Hispanos. For the former, Mexican immigrants represented a brown horde of undesirable, inferior aliens. Mexicans were tolerated because they served as cheap labor—a "necessary evil" (Sabin 1986, 128)—but were denied any equality with white Americans and were segregated through a system of informal discriminatory practices that took decades to be dismantled. By the early

1920s, the Ku Klux Klan (KKK) was very active in Colorado, controlling the state legislature, state offices, city councils, and even judgeships. Denver Mayor Ben Stapleton (1923–1931, 1935–1947) and Colorado Governor Clarence Morley (1925–1927) were prominent members of the KKK (Goldberg 1981). Mexicans (who were non-white Catholics) became an easy target for the Klan's vitriol, and the KKK was very active in beet towns, burning crosses and participating in parades in order to intimidate people of color (Donato 2007, 50–53). For example, in Boulder County the Klan organized parades in which hundreds of members (in full KKK regalia) and dozens of cars participated, burned crosses in front of homes belonging to Catholic families and on Flagstaff Mountain, endorsed political candidates, called for the firing of non-Protestant staff at the University of Colorado (and helped defund the university in 1925 when its president refused to comply), supported friendly merchants, and by the mid-1920s controlled Longmont's city government (McIntosh 2016, 116–123). However, perhaps because of the subordinated position of Mexicans and their spatial segregation, they were not seen as an urgent, threatening issue by the Klan in Colorado as elsewhere, and most of the Klan's activities consisted of harassment and public displays designed for intimidation (unlike the lynchings and murderous racial violence of the US plantation South). *Colonias* and other Mexican neighborhoods were usually located on the other side of the tracks—or in a segregated area—so as to physically exclude Mexicans from the main part of town. Living on the other side of the tracks made Hispanics keenly aware of their inferior status in American society—even as children they were upset about it (Salazar 2004, 6). Also, "sundown towns" were commonplace throughout rural Colorado.[9] Signs like "No Mexicans After Night" or "White Trade Only" further reinforced the spatial and cultural segregation of Mexicans (Delgado and Stefancic 1999, 756). For example, Loveland, Colorado, nowadays known as the Sweetheart City for its world-famous Valentine's Day remailing program, stood out as a very white sundown town among the sugar beet towns of the Front Range. Loveland's few Hispanic residents were segregated to its east side, and "No Mexicans Allowed" signs hung in downtown restaurant windows and water fountains (Rayes 2021). As a real estate agent put it bluntly, "We try to keep the Mexicans in their own part of town and don't rent to them in certain parts" (P. Taylor 1930, 209).

Elsewhere, oral histories collected from longtime Hispanic residents of the Front Range painfully tell how Anglo bars and pool halls in towns like Longmont and Louisville were off-limits to people of color. Even decorated Hispanic veterans returning home from World War II had to endure the humiliation of being denied service for not having the right complexion. Schools were equally segregated—even though it was against the law—by arguing that Mexican children did not speak the language or needed remedial education. In larger districts, Anglo children and Mexican children attended separate schools; in smaller districts, they were segregated into separate classrooms or Mexican children had to sit in the back of the room (Donato 2007, chap. 4; Salazar 2004, 6). The real reason was crudely stated by a Weld County superintendent of schools: "The respectable white people of Weld county do not want their children to sit along side of dirty, filthy, diseased, infested Mexicans in school" (P. Taylor 1930, 216). The unofficial segregation of Mexicans also extended into (Italian American) Catholic churches and movie theaters, where Mexicans were instructed to sit apart from Anglos (Duncan 1988, 31–34). For Mexicans and Mexican Americans, life in Colorado revolved around work in the fields and their Hispanic communities, with occasional forays into the white part of town for shopping in those establishments that would cater to them. Anglos were thus reassured that Mexicans would not displace Anglo farmers or threaten the racial status quo (May 1989, 409).

Spatially segregated and culturally isolated, Mexicans and Mexican Americans had no hopes or desire to integrate, yet they were often blamed for failing to assimilate. Mexicans formed their own religious clubs, baseball teams, and fraternal organizations (Donato 2007, 42). Two parallel societies coexisted, with Anglos rarely crossing the racial line to join Mexican organizations (baseball teams proved to be the exception) and Mexicans largely being prevented from joining Anglo groups. Still, Anglos pointed out the Mexicans' inability to assimilate, and oftentimes contrasted them to the more successful (and white) German Russians. According to Frank Van Nuys (describing the failure of assimilation programs in the American West), "Lessons in English, American history, and civics, along with tutoring in the domestic arts or whatever else fit one's definition of Americanism, did not alter the calculus of racial privilege and power in the New West" (2002, 191). If anything was preventing or retarding the assimilation of Mexicans, it was the hysteric reticence of Anglos fearful of racial contamination, a fact sometimes noted in passing by scholars studying the social conditions on Mexicans in Colorado's beet fields. William Wilson Bundy, writing about the "Mexican problem" in Otero County while completing a graduate degree at the University of Colorado in 1940, laid the blame on Mexicans and their culture for their own wretched conditions but could not overlook the fact that they were widely segregated everywhere they went: shops, restaurants, dance halls, and movie theaters (qtd. in Donato 2007, 43–44). An informal but socially enforced segregation system was firmly set in place in the beet fields of eastern Colorado and surrounding communities in which—not unlike South Africa's infamous apartheid—Mexicans were forced to reside outside of Anglo towns, were allowed occasional forays into the Anglo world to work and shop, and were deemed useful only to the extent that they could be exploited as cheap labor for the benefit of sugar companies. Moreover, Mexican culture was deemed inferior and pernicious to that of Anglos, and racial discrimination underpinned the whole socioeconomic structure (Nash 1985, 10). During the first decades of the twentieth century, Jim Crow segregation and its racialized labor structure transcended the geographical confines of the US plantation South and was informally reproduced in the sugar beet plantations of Colorado's Eastern Plains—this time against a wholly different racialized group.[10]

For Hispanos, Mexicans presented a problem too, as Anglos often confused and treated both as one—accidently or deliberately. Hispanos considered that their hard-won gains in American society were being undermined by Mexican immigrants, and too often felt themselves the racial sting of being confused with foreigners they viewed as inferior (Van Nuys 2002, 190). Hispanos shared a *manito* culture that overlapped with that of the Mexican *surumatos* (i.e., those coming from south of the border), but geographical, linguistic, and legal status cleavages were significant cultural factors that sometimes separated them into two camps. Hispanos perceived Mexicans as unrefined peons forced by poverty to emigrate to a foreign country. (Paradoxically, poverty also drove Hispanos to leave their homeland of southern Colorado and northern New Mexico for the beet fields of the Eastern Plains.) For their part, Mexican immigrants viewed Hispanos as Anglicized Mexicans with a superiority complex yet lacking a strong culture and a fatherland (P. Taylor 1930, 212–216). These cultural divisions were sometimes exacerbated by employers who preferred Mexican immigrants over local Hispanos. The former—by virtue of being immigrants with few rights—were seen as more docile and hardworking, while the latter—who were US citizens—were seen as more problematic. "The Mexican is all right in his place," according to a Great Western sugar grower, echoing the nonthreatening position of the Mexican rural worker in the racial pecking order of the American West at the time (May 1989, 401). Overall, both groups of Hispanics were largely viewed and treated the same way by Anglos—with racial contempt—and widely labeled as "Mexicans," a racially loaded term when used by Anglos, and "greasers" (Acuña 2000, 205; Reisler 1976, 135). Both groups ended up living side by side in the *colonias*, where intermarriage between the two groups was commonplace (Valdés 1990, 117–118). Despite some tensions between Hispanos and Mexicans, the two groups worked in the fields together and lived under the same conditions, as wave after wave of Mexican immigrants would eventually blend with Hispanos with deep historical roots in Colorado.

Life for Hispanic beet workers and their families in the fields of Colorado was harsh. Stoop labor was backbreaking and poorly paid, with Mexican workers earning less than German Russians or the Japanese (May 1989, 415). In a system reminiscent of feudalism, Anglo growers allocated plots of land for a migrant family to work. Initially, field workers were paid per day of labor or by acre harvested, but starting in 1924 pay was by tonnage, which meant that workers' wages varied depending on the exact weight of the beets that they could harvest. Thus, during low yield years, growers effectively shifted financial risk to their workers and saved money on wages (Hamilton 2009, 307). Whereas in the 1920s a Mexican family would earn a paltry $600–$800 annually working in the sugar beet fields, by 1932 this amount went down to about $100 per year—starvation wages. The workers went on strike, but amid the Great Depression and a hugely decreased demand for labor, they failed (Leonard 1993, 72–74). Local law enforcement arrested and intimidated strike leaders, accusing them of being communists, threatened beet workers with eviction, and even deported some organizers who were Mexican nationals (Vargas 2005, 72–73). Moreover, work in the sugar beet fields was seasonal, usually spanning a period of about six months, from late May to late November (P. Taylor 1930, 121–122), which contributed to the workers' financial dependence on the beet farmers and the companies and made labor organizing extremely difficult.

The rhythm of work in the beet fields was brutal. Field workers spent long hours in the fields constantly bending over while planting, blocking, thinning, and harvesting beets. In between operations, workers were idle, forced to seek part-time employment elsewhere. The work regime was particularly intense during the harvest season, and every available hour of sunlight was devoted to harvesting beets. Harvesting beets by hand was a particularly risky process. Workers used sharp knives with a hook at the end to pluck the beets out of the ground and then top them (i.e., remove the leafy top). The quick pace of work during harvest time and the long days were major contributing factors to accidents when wielding a sharp beet knife. Cuts, gashes, loss of fingers, and constant back pain were common occupational hazards. During the beet harvest, women and children contributed to the family's income by joining men in the fields—including pregnant women and children as young as six. Their workdays began before sunrise and went for as long as enough sunlight was available to be out in the fields, which made for very long days during the summer. The work in the beet fields extended into the winter season because the longer the beets were in the ground, the more sugar they held. Therefore, it was not unusual for Mexican families to be working in freezing weather, topping beets that had been covered by the first snowfalls (Duncan 1988, 14). According to Zaragoza Vargas (2005, 30), blocking and thinning an acre of beets required that children crawled on their hands and knees about five miles. Whereas the use of child labor was a source of public concern when German Russians worked the beet fields, Colorado authorities looked the other way once Mexican labor became commonplace (Legg 2005). The children of Mexican laborers "were not considered part of the community" (Sabin 1986, 140); they routinely missed school during the harvest, and they would start working in the fields as soon as they were big enough to use a short-handled hoe (which was banned eventually because of the back problems its use caused). The extreme weather conditions of the plains (which can be cold and windy in fall, winter, and spring, and searing hot in summer), the harsh work regime, poor nutrition, and accidents all took a toll on their developing bodies, aging them prematurely (Vargas 2005, 30). The authorities either downplayed the work conditions or justified the use of Mexican labor by stereotyping the latter as belonging to a different caste, naturally suited for that kind of labor (Donato 2007, 25–26).

Moreover, Colorado sugar companies never attempted to negotiate wages with their Mexican workers, who toiled without the benefit of unions and collective bargaining (Nash 1985, 52–55). Their status as foreigners (at least in the case of Mexican nationals), their racialization and exclusion by mainstream Anglo society, and their utter lack of labor options in the American West left them with no choice but to accept their fate. Some of them complained to the Mexican consul in Denver, who reported to his superiors on the low wages for sugar beet workers, their appalling living and working conditions, and the prevailing racism and segregation that Mexican citizens had to endure (Donato 2007, 41). But there was little that Mexican consuls could do, except voice their displeasure to the local authorities (who routinely ignored them). Hispanos, being US citizens, had no consul to advocate for them. Both groups of "Mexican" workers had few friends to defend them.

The field workers' seemingly docile demeanor was interpreted as a byproduct of cultural pessimism (i.e., a stereotypical *mañana* attitude) by Anglos bent on justifying the exploitation of Mexicans (May 1989, 403). Paternalistic attitudes—liberally imbued by racial prejudices—led Anglo farmers to draw their own conclusions about the Mexicans' presumed inferiority:

> "The Mexicans are like the plantation Negroes in improvidence, lack of foresight, or desire to do other tasks." "The Mexicans understand servitude next to the Negro, who is a born servant. When a Mexican doesn't take his hat off to you it's time to let him go." "A Mexican is the best damn dog any white man ever had." (qtd. in P. Taylor 1930, 154–155)

Local intellectuals contributed to the reproduction of racial stereotypes regarding Mexicans, passing off their opinions as scientific fact. For example, Rubén Donato (2007) quotes F. A. Olden (writing for the *Greeley Tribune* in 1925), who boldly asserted that Mexicans "had minds no more developed than that of sixteen-year-old children, had primitive eyes for bright colors, were unthrifty, and did not know how to live within their means" (38). As a result of the nexus that the world of sugar beets developed between race and labor, stoop labor became racialized as "Mexican labor"; shunned by whites and lowly regarded, as well as poorly paid. An ethnic division of labor spread through the fields of Colorado and the American West, in which Mexican rural proletarians were relegated to backbreaking stoop labor in the fields, while Anglos owned the land or performed other (better-regarded and better-paid) jobs. It also led to Anglo farmers and sugar beet companies becoming dependent on cheap Mexican labor in order to grow crops profitably in the arid West (Valdés 1990, 120). According to an editorial in the *Eaton Herald*,

> To our mind the whole question resolves itself into the question of beets or no beets. If we are going to raise beets, and it looks as if they are the only thing that will put the country on its feet, we must have labor to care for them. The Mexicans appear to be the only ones available. (qtd. in P. Taylor 1930, 233)

Farmers wanted cheap Mexican workers while the general populace rejected and segregated them as racial inferiors (Twitty 2003, 53). The economic conundrum was ineluctable: Mexican labor was needed, but Mexicans were unwanted. "Ideally growers wished for the appearance of multitudes of Mexicans at the proper time and their complete disappearance at the termination of the harvest," according to Mark Reisler (1976, 90). The uneasy compromise was to keep them at bay, working in the fields, living apart, and denied opportunities for social mobility—"all separate, but not equal, to those [spaces] of people with European ancestry" (Hamilton 2009, 279, 281). But if they were to become too numerous or problematic, then the solution was to get rid of them, as the residents of Rocky Ford did in 1900 by expelling two camps of Mexican beet workers (Sabin 1986, 128). In the words of Berkeley zoologist and eugenicist Samuel Holmes (1926, 27): "Are you going to sacrifice our children for the sake of assimilating the Mexican?" This conflicted, paradoxical, and unequal relationship between Colorado farmers and ranchers and Mexican labor continues to this day.

Despite some vocal Anglo resistance, these incipient Mexican / Mexican American communities began growing deeper roots during the first decades of the twentieth century, and by 1930, well-established communities of Hispanic *betabeleros* dotted Colorado's Eastern Plains. The arrival of entire family units changed the formerly transient nature of Hispanic field workers, and the sugar companies went to extremes to keep their cheap labor force, oftentimes trapping the workers in debt to keep them from leaving (Sheflin 2019, 184185). Pauperized and lacking options, the lives of Mexican beet workers and their families revolved around periods of intense labor at low wages in the beet fields, followed by periods of dependence on welfare handouts during the offseason (May 1989, 417–419). This vicious economic cycle was commonplace throughout Colorado's sugar beet industry, and it is typical of plantation societies, where "the company" keeps its cheap labor pool in check through financial mechanisms that tie workers to the plantation (Beckford 1999, appendix 2; Merleaux 2015, 217).

The Great Depression and Mass Deportations

The Great Depression provided the first major test for this economic compromise. With the economy stalling and prices falling, the sugar beet industry found itself in dire straits. The federal government came to its aid, with the passing of the 1934 Jones-Costigan Amendment of the Agricultural Adjustment Act (Edward P. Costigan was a US senator from Colorado). The act (aka the Sugar Act of 1934) stabilized the sugar industry by setting quotas and guaranteeing a basic price for producers (Twitty 2003, 55). Ordinary Americans were not so lucky. Millions of US workers lost their jobs during the economic crisis, and the Dust Bowl of the 1930s left thousands homeless throughout the Great Plains—including Colorado (Sheflin 2019). From 1930 to 1935, severe drought reduced Colorado's sugar beet harvest in half, leaving over 7,000 *betabeleros* without work (Vargas 2005, 41). Banks foreclosed on farms, and rural dwellers left in a desperate search for jobs all over the region. Mexican rural laborers, unable to find employment, also moved, often to urban centers, where they swelled the ranks of the poor who depended on government welfare for survival. Soon, calls to deport Mexicans by the public became commonplace. The rationale put forward by those demanding the deportation of Mexican aliens was that during tough economic times, the few available jobs should be set aside for US citizens and not for foreigners. Some voices further argued that white men ought to be the nation's priority when it came to jobs, and that Mexicans and "colored" Others were taking away the jobs that whites could use. Colorado Governor Edwin Johnson happily obliged and declared "the possibilities of employment ... for only native sons [i.e., Anglos]" while threatening to use the state's National Guard to round up and expel foreigners (Balderrama and Rodríguez 2006, 71, 89). As covered in chapter 1, Governor Johnson followed up on his threats by mobilizing the National Guard and closing the state border with New Mexico in 1936, ostensibly to keep foreigners (i.e., Mexicans) away from Colorado (Meredith 2012). Overnight, Mexicans went from being the essential cheap labor that Western agriculture relied on, to being stereotyped as unfair competition for white laborers. In addition, Mexicans (including US-born Mexican Americans) were portrayed as burdens for a state in which scarce welfare funds should be destined to feeding white, American families. There was even a concern that Mexican workers would get used to government handouts and refuse to work, according to local Anglo officials (Vargas 2005, 44–45). The Federal Emergency Relief Administration (FERA) provided some help for indigent Mexican families, going against the wishes of Governor Johnson, who proposed to round them up in a concentration camp near Golden before eventually deporting them (Leonard 1993, 74). But New Deal policies designed to create jobs and relieve Americans' suffering excluded farm laborers and disproportionally favored Anglos, meaning that most Mexicans and Mexican Americans (as well as other communities of color) were on their own (Krainz 2005).

The xenophobic hysteria snowballed, and the authorities, eager to please white voters during these uncertain times, began "repatriating" Mexicans—a misnomer intended to whitewash the removal of undesirable non-white "aliens." The repatriation push forced nearly 20,000 Mexicans (including US-born children) out of Colorado and into Mexico (Sheflin 2019, 190). In 1932, the Boulder County Commissioners appropriated money "for the transportation of said families to the Mexican border," a move that coincided with a strike by sugar beet workers and unrest among miners as wages were being cut (McIntosh 2016, 127–131). In 1935, Governor Johnson expelled thirty-two Mexicans from the state, twenty of whom were US citizens, leading to a diplomatic spate with Mexico

(Leonard 1993, 74). Many Mexican families left voluntarily, fearing arrest and the loss of their possessions, but others were forcibly deported by state and federal authorities—even though the former have no jurisdiction over immigration matters. Those who repatriated themselves lost their properties or had to sell them at a loss, forced by circumstances and Anglo buyers that took advantage of their plight. In 1936, the Colorado State Vigilantes, a surreptitious anti-immigrant organization, distributed threatening handbills in Greeley and Rocky Ford urging Mexicans to leave "at once" (Donato 2007, 56). Race riots, that is, the violent expulsion of racialized Others by Anglo mobs from towns around the American West, has a long and troubling history in the region—including Colorado (Leonard 2002; Pierce 2016, chap. 8). The Great Depression simply took it to a new level, as the generalized economic crisis exacerbated nativist passions, while the active participation of state and federal authorities increased the scope of the roundups and deportations. Moreover, the mass repatriation of Mexicans (along with the collusion of local authorities) would foretell the mass displacement and incarceration of Japanese Americans in internment camps only a few years later. In both cases, xenophobic hysteria led federal authorities to violate the most basic human rights of communities of color (including many US citizens), reduce them to an inferior category by virtue of their race, and justify their forced removal from "native" Anglo spaces. Mexicans and Mexican Americans were easily deported across the US southern border in the 1930s to a country that received them (Balderrama and Rodríguez 2006), but in the case of Japanese Americans on the West Coast, an even worse fate awaited them in US internment camps during World War II (Marrin 2016).

The Bracero Program Era

The opening salvos of World War II brought renewed demand for cheap Mexican labor in the American West, particularly after the attack on Pearl Harbor forced the sudden entry of the United States into the war at the end of 1941 (Nash 1985, 50–51). As millions of men joined the military, and women replaced them in workplaces, the US economy was abruptly reoriented towards the war effort. Some Hispanos / Mexican Americans were able to find jobs in the defense industries and programs that sprouted in

Colorado, but anti-Mexican discrimination followed them there. Available jobs sometimes would go to Anglos from neighboring states, while local Hispanos would be hired solely for menial, dirty jobs, segregated from Anglo employees, and paid "Mexican" wages (Vargas 2005, 218–219). The federal government received multiple discrimination complaints, but little was done save for cosmetic changes.

As the United States entered the war, demand for agricultural goods rose sharply, and Western farmers suddenly and once again needed cheap labor—lots of it. The US federal government's solution to the urgent need for imported labor was the signing of the first bilateral agreement with Mexico for the large-scale, legal importation of Mexican field hands (i.e., *braceros*). The Bracero Program (as the Mexican Farm Labor Agreement became popularly known) was implemented in 1942 and proved so popular that it would outlast the war for decades to come. Mexican workers had been the mainstay of farms, ranches, mines, railroads, factories, construction sites, and pretty much every Western economic sector that relied on cheap labor (Nash 1985, 11). About 2 million braceros came to the United States during the lengthy life of the program (1942–1964), ushering in a new era of dependency on imported Mexican labor for US agribusinesses (Mize and Swords 2011, 3). In Colorado, farmers were used to—and craved—Mexican labor, and by 1944, 10,000 Mexican braceros were working in the state (Sheflin 2019, 211–213). Despite their racial misgivings, Anglo farmers recognized that Mexicans were hard workers who were willing to endure tough labor and housing conditions—conditions that prevented their replacement as white laborers historically had refused to take on these arduous jobs. The signing of a binational agreement for the importation of Mexican braceros did not necessarily translate into better working and living conditions in the beet sugar fields. For example, braceros were initially bused from Mexico by the Great Western Sugar Company, either using chartered buses or eventually acquiring their own. However, by the 1950s, in an effort to cut costs, the company began using private contractors who brought in immigrant labor to Colorado using overcrowded trucks. Eventually, the federal government had to step in and regulate the interstate transportation of migrant workers to prevent overcrowding (May 1989, 424–425). Housing conditions also varied in quality (depending on location), and finding employment during the offseason remained a major challenge for these workers. Whereas the company paid for the laborers' transportation from Mexico to Colorado, once the harvest season was over, the workers and their families were usually on their own. Unable to pay their way back to Mexico, many gravitated to urban areas such as Denver to seek employment or go on welfare (Nash 1985, 109). The massive inflow of Mexican workers during the Bracero Program era, the inconsistent application of federal and local regulations, and Anglo apprehensions about Brown people in their midst, would eventually lead to the implementation of the ill-named Operation Wetback, a massive roundup of undocumented "Mexicans" ordered by the Dwight D. Eisenhower administration in 1954 (Lytle Hernández 2006). The operation, coordinated by Army General Joseph May Swing (as new head of the Immigration and Naturalization Service), deported over a million undocumented workers to Mexico, paradoxically, at the same time as tens of thousands of Mexican workers were still being imported legally into the United States under the terms of the Bracero Program. Such are the contradictions inherent in Mexican labor migration to the American West.

The Bracero Program ended in 1964, but by then beet sugar production was on its way down, and by the 1970s it was a shadow of its former self. Low sugar prices, driven by ample production overseas (mainly of cane sugar), meant that Colorado producers were simply surviving thanks to government controls that protected US sugar. In 1974, the Sugar Act was not renewed by Congress, effectively eliminating the tariffs that kept US sugar producers in business (Markoff 1979, 176). Global sugar prices rose in the 1970s, but the introduction of high-fructose corn sweetener was a major blow to the industry. Sugar consumption declined as corn sweetener overtook the food industry, and Colorado's beet sugar producers never recovered. By 1979, sugar factories across the Arkansas River Valley and the Western Slope had shut down, leaving only a handful of Great Western Sugar Company factories operating in northeastern Colorado (Markoff 1979, 177–178). Eventually, even an industrial giant like Great Western succumbed to sugar's new era, getting sold to foreign interests in 1985. In 2002, it became Western Sugar Cooperative, pooling together over 1,000 sugar beet growers in four Western states. In Colorado, only the sugar-processing facility in Fort Morgan remains in operation (Western Sugar Cooperative 2022).

Nowadays, sugar beet planting and harvesting is a highly mechanized operation, no longer reliant on the cheap labor of hundreds of Mexican field hands, and it is usually carried out by the farmers themselves. Yet, the legacy of sugar beets looms large over Colorado's Eastern Plains. According to William May, the labor policies of the Great Western Sugar Company "transform[ed] agriculture in the North and South Platte River valleys from the relatively small-scale family farm structure into large-scale, industrialized farming" (1989, 426). Although the industry has now come full circle (i.e., back to family farming), the ripple effects of decades of Mexican labor imports into eastern Colorado are clearly visible in the formation in the state's Eastern Plains of permanent Latinx communities—the heirs to the Hispanos and Mexican braceros who planted their own roots in the region.

The Sugar Beets-Coal and Steel Nexus

Although the sugar beet industry dominated the agroindustrial landscape of Colorado's Eastern Plains for decades, it was not the only corporate giant of the region. As mentioned in chapter 1, the discovery of significant coal deposits in southern Colorado led to the construction of the largest steel mill west of the Mississippi River in Pueblo, Colorado, a town strategically located on the banks of the Arkansas River (Haverluk 2002, 49–51), with easy access to rail lines coming from the Great Plains (and points east) and the Front Range (and points north and south).[11] The Minnequa Steelworks' steel mill, owned by the Rockefeller family, was the linchpin of the Colorado Fuel and Iron Company's (CF&I) vast empire of coal, calcite, and iron ore mines; lime quarries; and railroad networks that stretched across three states (including New Mexico and Wyoming). As of 1910, the CF&I employed about 15,000 workers, and it became the state's largest industrial corporation by the 1920s (Rees 2010, xi). The CF&I put Pueblo on the map; the town became a major industrial center in a region previously known only for its ranching and farming, and a "company town" and classic example of an economic enclave that had few horizontal linkages, instead dominated by a vertically integrated corporation. As in the case of the beet sugar industry, another large corporation from the East with deep pockets and politically well-connected, had a free reign to exploit the American West, its resources, and its peoples in a quasi-colonial fashion.

From its inception, the CF&I employed a multinational workforce, consisting of immigrants from northern, eastern, and southern Europe, as well as local Hispanos and Mexican immigrants. However, the CF&I's management thought of Hispanos as "foreign" as the European immigrant miners that worked alongside them. Though the CF&I managers were cognizant of the centuries-long presence of Hispanos in the New Mexico territory,[12] one predating the Treaty of Guadalupe Hidalgo, and though management knew that the Hispanos were native-born US citizens, the latter's culture and language set them so apart from the Anglo mainstream that they were treated by the company as foreign "Mexicans" in need of assimilation (F. Montoya 2006 30–31). In this case of Eastern colonialism of the American West, the CF&I corporate managers acted as agents who not only ruled over their employees but also put in place a racial pecking order that turned local Hispanos into "foreigners" while treating Anglo outsiders as "native" whites and real Americans. This socioracial order, the product of settler colonialism, would have an impact on the fate of Mexican workers at the CF&I, regardless of their citizenship status. Even though Mexican immigrants and Mexican Americans (i.e., Hispanos) made up an increasingly large proportion of the CF&I's labor force, they rarely rose beyond the most menial positions or were selected as representatives for the workers. The number of Mexican workers at the CF&I increased as a result of World War I and new US immigration laws in the 1920s that restricted European migration. For example, by 1924 Mexican miners made up 34% of the employees at the Trinidad District, up from 23% in 1916 (Rees 2010, 90), as the United States was entering the war. But Mexicans were mostly confined to the dirtiest, lowest-paid positions. They rarely became bosses in the mines or held the specialized, salaried positions from which most of the workers' representatives came. In addition, Mexican workers at the CF&I lacked job security. They were frequently let go and rehired on multiple occasions—which made it almost impossible for them to earn seniority status (Rees 2010, 92–100). Even by the mid-1970s, a report by the Equal Employment Opportunity Commission revealed systematic discrimination toward Chicanxs by the CF&I. The report indicated that the CF&I

placed whites in clean jobs and Spanish-surnamed individuals in the coke ovens or ore preparation—the dirtiest jobs in the mill. Moreover, in one of its subsidiaries (Fountain Sand and Gravel Company), no Spanish-surnamed individuals held a white-collar job, and no Spanish-surnamed females were employed ("CF&I, Unions Charged with Race/Sex Discrimination" 1976).

In between hirings and firings at the mines and the steel mill, Mexican workers gravitated to the beet fields. As a matter of fact, Great Western and CF&I worked closely to hold a monopoly over cheap labor in Colorado's Eastern Plains. Great Western, which had imported many of the immigrant Mexican laborers, wanted to keep them around after the beet harvest concluded (rather than lose them to other states), and encouraged CF&I to hire Mexican workers during the offseason. CF&I happily obliged, as Great Western was a buyer of its coal, and the agreement guaranteed a steady supply of cheap labor whenever the companies needed it the most (Rees 2010, 99–100). A similar informal arrangement existed in Boulder County, an area dotted with sugar beet fields and coal mines. Field laborers worked the beets most of the year, moving to jobs in the coal mines during the winter months, which helped Latinx families stay in the area year-round. Wages in the coal industry were better and the work was steady (though dangerous), which most men preferred to the stoop labor of the beet fields (McIntosh 2016, 72–83). Still, these were just survival strategies that helped Latinx families make ends meet. The great beneficiaries were the sugar beet and coal companies that always had their share of cheap labor within easy reach.

Job insecurity was more than a fact of life for Mexican workers in Colorado's Eastern Plains; it was a deliberate strategy by big corporations to keep them underemployed and thus maintain a cheap labor pool—a perfect example of industrial giants colluding against their workers' best interests. Sugar beets, coal, or steel offered little financial security to Hispanos and Mexican immigrants in Colorado. At best, they were desperate means for survival in an Anglo-dominated world. At their worst, they were industrial meat grinders who destroyed their bodies through hard, dangerous work, with little for workers to show in return. According to Gerald Nash (1985, 110): "A majority, especially the older generation, endured their lot in silence. They had been culturally attuned to deprivation in and outside the United States for centuries, had limited aspirations, and reflected a conservatism often associated with people from peasant backgrounds." The stereotype of the pliant Mexican worker—a widespread trope in the American West—was about to become undone by the rise of the Chicano Movement, a direct response to decades of oppression at the hands of the Anglo establishment.

The 1960s and Pueblo's Chicano Movement

Although the Chicano Movement was centered in the Denver metro area (see chapter 3), Pueblo's blue-collar roots and the small college campus of Southern Colorado Junior College (later renamed Colorado State University Pueblo in 2003) provided militants for El Movimiento and fueled protests and boycotts. Pueblo's Chicano Movement was instigated by Alberto "Al" Gurule, an empowered social worker who, appalled by the socioeconomic conditions of Latinxs in Pueblo and their treatment at the hands of Anglo authorities, decided to organize the Chicanx community. In 1969, he joined the national grape boycott organized by Cesar Chavez and, together with local Chicanx students from the Movimiento Estudiantil Chicano de Aztlán (Chicano Student Movement of Aztlán, or MEChA—Spanish for "fuse"), picketed Safeway supermarkets in town. The grape boycott was quickly followed by a boycott against Coors beer, due to the Colorado-based company's racist hiring policies.[13] Gurule then accepted a position with Pueblo United, where he organized and provided services to Chicanx youth. One of his most controversial actions was the development of the Black Berets, a militant Chicanx organization based on California's Brown Berets. The Black Beret Creed contained allusions to violent action and getting rid of *gringo* businesses and led to Gurule becoming a notorious target for Pueblo's Anglo community. Ultimately, the pressure coming from the Anglo establishment (and some Latinxs) was too much to bear, and Gurule was forced to resign his position (Marquez 1983).

MEChA took up the mantle and led by Martín Serna (Gurule's right-hand man), students targeted educational disparities in Pueblo's District 60—a largely "Mexican" school district. The students presented a list of demands that included courses in Chicano history and the hiring of

Chicanx teachers and counselors. When the school authorities dismissed the demands, a massive walkout ensued at Centennial High School in May 1970 (followed by a "walk in" when the school authorities threatened to expel those students involved in the walkout), combined with a civil rights lawsuit. Tensions ran high for months, and the Chicanx organizers received threats and hate mail for their efforts. For example, Louis "Lugs" Garcia, a Brown Beret and community activist from Pueblo's predominantly Chicanx/Mexican Salt Creek neighborhood, received an anonymous letter suggesting to him that "if you all feel so put out in our country—why don't you zip down to Mexico and see how many handouts you get there!" ("A Letter from a Very Unhappy 'White'" 1972). The ("white") author of the anonymous document asserts, in no uncertain terms, that this is "our country" and that Chicanx activists belong in Mexico—a common trope employed by nativist Anglos to portray Chicanxs as "foreign" and "Mexican," and the United States as an Anglo nation (i.e., "our country"). In 1973, the lawsuit against the Pueblo School District was settled, and the students' demands were met (Marquez 1983). It was a major victory for Pueblo's Chicano Movement and its Chicanx student militants, who had defied the odds and finally gained a degree of respect from the Anglo authorities.

An interesting, parallel development to the Chicano Movement in Pueblo was the creation in 1966 of the New Hispano Party, a movement that grew out of the dissatisfaction of Mexican American political activists with the prevailing two-party system (Gómez-Quiñones 1990, 74–75). Its constituents argued that their pleas were ignored by mainstream Anglo politicians, who routinely paid lip service to Hispanic voters but consistently failed to nominate Mexican American candidates to elective positions. Levi Martinez, a prominent Mexican American attorney from Pueblo, was its nominee for governor, but the party did poorly at the polls. It faced the opposition of the Democratic Party—which commanded most of the Latinx vote—and popular leaders of the Chicano Movement such as Rodolfo "Corky" Gonzales. The party was riddled by divisions and dissent, and it seemed like some of its leaders were in it just for personal gain, to use it as leverage so that they would be considered for future nominations by the Democratic Party. Moreover, despite its progressive political goals, its emphasis on Hispano and Spanish American identity was quickly becoming outdated and smacked of elitism during this period of militancy and political upheaval centered on demands for a more egalitarian society (D. Sandoval 2011, 249–251).

Finally, Pueblo was the headquarters of *La Cucaracha*,[14] one of the most prominent newspapers produced by Colorado's Chicano Movement. Founded in 1976 by Juan and Deborah Espinosa, David Martinez, and Pablo Mora, *La Cucaracha* was a constant thorn on the side of the Anglo establishment and a rallying voice for Chicanx militants. It ceased publication in 1983 but has been revived as of 2023 as a quarterly publication (Lewis 2023). Apart from Pueblo, the Chicano Movement bypassed the Eastern Plains. Unlike the lightly populated, rural plains to its east, Pueblo is an urban enclave with a history of discrimination against communities of color (mostly its large Hispanic minority cohort) but also with a record of labor activism. Both factors combined to make Pueblo a small, if symbolic bastion of the Chicano Movement outside of Colorado's Front Range proper.

Meatpacking Plants and New Immigrants

The end of the sugar beet era and the decline of production in Pueblo's Minnequa Steelworks brought about major demographic and economic changes to Colorado's Eastern Plains. Except for major cities such as Greeley, most towns and counties on the Eastern Plains lost population as their economic fortunes declined. Starting in the 1970s and into the present, predominantly rural counties in eastern Colorado witnessed a steady outmigration of young (twenty–twenty-nine-year-old) people leaving the region for urban areas, while the share of older folks remained steady or increased slightly (Lawson 2017). The graying of the Eastern Plains translated into a declining availability of young workers and the lack of a younger generation to take over family farms. Farmers switched to more profitable, less labor-intensive crops such as alfalfa, corn, millet, and wheat—which began replacing sugar beets (Fort Morgan Museum 2015).

The economic downfall of the Eastern Plains set up the stage for agribusinesses looking for cheap land and labor, and meatpacking became the new dominant industry of the region. Cattle ranching had always been a fixture of the Eastern plains, but beef carcasses were usually processed elsewhere. As described in Upton Sinclair's classic novel *The Jungle* (1906), the meatpacking industry was still concentrated in large urban areas like Chicago in the early twentieth century, connected by railroads to rural areas throughout the Midwest and the West, which supplied them with meat. Once carcasses were delivered to meatpacking plants, hundreds of immigrants toiled in appalling conditions processing the carcasses, with the finished products then being shipped out to consumers mainly in eastern markets. In the second half of the twentieth century, the meatpacking industry suffered three radical transformations.

The first major transformation of the meatpacking industry was its relocation to rural areas, closer to the source of the product. Cattle from ranches in the region were gathered in huge feeding lots to fatten them weeks before they were slaughtered nearby, then sent to large industrial plants where the carcasses were disassembled into small cuts and boxed. From there, the meat products were shipped to markets across the country by train or truck (thanks to the new interstate highways) using refrigerated containers (Schlosser 2001, chap. 7). By spatially concentrating all aspects of production, meatpacking companies saved money, and they no longer had to rely on plants located on expensive urban real estate, which were highly regulated by city authorities.

The second major transformation was increased competition that led to attrition, leaving the meatpacking industry concentrated in the hands of a handful of large, powerful agribusinesses (e.g., Cargill, JBS Foods, National Beef Packing, and Tyson Foods). Small ranching and farming operations are now beholden to these industry giants, which control over 80% of all beef slaughtered in the United States, as well as significant portions of the pork, poultry, corn, and soybeans industries (Ogburn 2011). These agribusinesses also have an international footprint, with operations across the globe—led by JBS Foods, whose parent company (based in Brazil) is the world's largest beef packer.

The third and final transformation of the meatpacking industry was the mechanization, industrialization, and streamlining of the disassembly process (aka "de-skilling"). Whereas as in the remote past an experienced butcher would cut up a carcass into different cuts of beef, by the twentieth century the process was being carried out in a factory-like setting, where dozens of unskilled workers work shoulder-to-shoulder in a disassembly line, performing the same repetitive task hundreds of times a day. As new technology helped speed up and simplify the disassembly process, employees were required to work faster, putting a greater strain on their bodies, leading to more workplace accidents; repetitive-use injuries of arms, hands, and fingers; and higher turnover rates—up to 400% annually (Schlosser 2001, 160).

One feature of the meatpacking business has not changed in over a hundred years, though: its reliance on cheap, immigrant labor. From Upton Sinclair's eastern European laborers to today's Mexican, Central American, Asian, and East African immigrants, the industry is a meatgrinder of immigrant bodies. Hired at low wages, receiving few benefits, and disposed of when no longer needed, immigrant labor is relied on by the meatpacking industry in a steady supply in order to deal with the high turnover rates at the plants. This constant turnover translates into very few employees staying long enough to qualify for full benefits and makes unionization harder. The regional debt crisis known as the "lost decade" hit Latin America's economies hard in the 1980s, providing the impetus for people to flee economically depressed areas for the United States. That massive migrant flow, coupled with the restructuring and industrialization of US rural industries, funneled Latin American migrants into rural areas in the United States, where they became cheap labor (including Colorado's Eastern Plains) (Gouveia 2005, 11–14).

From 1980 to 2000, the meatpacking industry began relying more and more on Mexican (and other Hispanic) labor. Whereas in 1980 only 8.5% of all meat-processing employees across the United States were Hispanic, by 2000 that figure had increased to 28.5%, and the percentage of those Hispanics who were foreign born went from 49.7% in 1980 to 82% in 2000 (Kandel and Parrado 2005, 459). As native-born workers were turned off by the industry's low wages and dangerous labor practices, Latinx immigrants filled in the niche. For migrants coming from Mexico and Central America, the US meatpacking industry's wages were more attractive compared to what they could earn back home, and the industry's deplorable labor conditions were somewhat tempered by their new First World living standards (e.g., increased purchasing power, better housing, schools for their children, etc.). The tradeoff is part and parcel of the immigrant experience: hard sacrifices and a life of toil in the hopes that your children will have a shot at the American Dream. Thus, Latinx immigrants flocked to meatpacking jobs in rural counties as non-Hispanic whites and others left the industry, a process well described by Michael Piore (1979) when he examined the US economy's bifurcation into "primary" and "secondary" sectors. In his dual labor market theory, meatpacking jobs fall squarely within the new "secondary" sector of the economy: dangerous, unstable, poorly paid, lacking benefits, and with high turnover ratios. Moreover, as more and more Mexicans and other Latinx immigrants occupied this labor niche, entry-level meatpacking jobs became racialized; that is, they became "Mexican" jobs that no self-respecting Anglo would do—not only for the low wages but also on cultural and racial grounds.

In Colorado's Eastern Plains, meatpacking agribusinesses loom large. Some of the Mexican *braceros* that came to work the sugar beets ended up getting hired year-round. As beet production declined during the last decades of the twentieth century, they began working in the ranches and feedlots that became the economic mainstay of the region. In Greeley, the Monfort meatpacking operation became an industrial colossus located just north of the city. The family's success turned Greeley into a company town where the Monforts held a stranglehold over the city's economic base and its politics (eventually branching out into state politics). The Monfort companies employed hundreds of workers, mainly from Mexico and Central America—many of whom were undocumented (Andreas 1994, chap. 2). These vulnerable workers became an essential part of a revolving door industry that went through dozens of employees every month but knew there were always more to replace those who left or were fired. Fort Morgan is another classic example of a Colorado company town; the Cargill meatpacking operation also employed Latinx immigrants there but eventually began hiring East African refugees (mainly Somalis) who had been resettled in the area, held work permits, and were desperate for entry-level jobs in the United States (J. Anderson 2016).

In the specific case of Mexico, the implementation of NAFTA in 1994 helped funnel cheap immigrant labor into the United States. A trilateral agreement between the United States, Canada, and Mexico, NAFTA was intended to lower trade barriers and foster trade between the three countries of North America. While NAFTA did in fact increase trade significantly between the United States and Mexico, it also had deleterious impacts on Mexican agriculture, as cheap US agricultural imports flooded Mexico and put small farmers out of business (Mize and Swords 2011, chap. 10). As family farms throughout central Mexico failed, the new economic challenges sparked a major migratory wave of working-class Mexicans. They started migrating internally, to Mexico City, to other secondary cities (e.g., Monterrey), and to industrial towns on the US-Mexico border; but they also increasingly headed for El Norte (i.e., the United States), as generations of Mexican laborers had done before them (Massey, Durand, and Malone 2002). The thousands of NAFTA-driven migrants that came to the United States in the 1990s–2000s supplied the cheap labor that US agriculture needed, including Colorado's rural counties in the Eastern Plains.

In what now has been a recurring trend in the American West, the NAFTA wave of Mexican immigrants joined previously established, multigenerational communities of Hispanos, Mexicans, and their descendants. The new arrivals also represented fresh cultural imports from different parts of Mexico, thus reinforcing the "replenished ethnicity" of Mexican American communities throughout the United States (Jiménez 2010). In Colorado, they joined previous generations that had established deeply rooted communities along the Front Range (e.g., Fort Collins, Loveland, and Longmont) and the Eastern Plains (e.g., Greeley, Fort Morgan, and the Arkansas River Valley). To no one's surprise, NAFTA benefitted the meatpacking industry handsomely: First, it got meatpackers the cheap immigrant labor they needed to become profitable and expand their operations; and second, NAFTA opened up new markets for meatpackers' exports in Mexico, which now was being flooded with US agricultural products. More than the sugar beet industry ever did, the meatpacking industry globalized labor and export products in Colorado's Eastern Plains.

The arrival of the NAFTA wave of immigrants stirred controversy in receiving communities and brought back old ugly tropes regarding Mexican labor in the United States. This immigrant wave also arrived during a time of increased enforcement of migratory controls, both at the US-Mexico border, which was becoming increasingly militarized in the 1990s–2000s, and further inland, where the Immigration and Naturalization Service (INS) carried out raids designed to placate the demands from elected officials and the American public for action regarding the immigration "crisis" (Nevins 2010). Meatpacking plans became an obvious target, given the common knowledge that large numbers of unauthorized migrants worked there. In the summer of 1991, INS agents targeted the Monfort plant in Greeley, where it was estimated that at least half of the foreign workers were using fake documents. Yet, despite the arrest of employees and some deportations, the Monfort company was not fined for employing undocumented workers (Andreas 1994, 21–23). Things changed drastically after the September 11, 2001, terrorist attacks, with xenophobia on the rise across the nation amid fears of a porous southern border. The attacks led to the largest reorganization of the US federal government since World War II, and the creation of the Department of Homeland Security, which now housed the US Border Patrol and the newly created successor to the INS: Immigration and Customs Enforcement (ICE). On December 6, 2006, a massive ICE raid targeted the Swift plant in Greeley (owned by JBS Foods)—as well as those in four other states—and arrested a total of 1,297 undocumented workers (273 Swift employees were arrested in Greeley on that day). The ripple effects of that raid were widespread and very disturbing. Federal agents did not bother to inform local authorities about the raid. As a result, when many parents did not pick up their children after school because they had been detained or were too scared to show up, school authorities were left scrambling for solutions, desperately calling parents and relatives who were hesitant to pick up the phone, while having to look for places to shelter the children in the meantime. Immigrant families were split, and children were traumatized when they lost one or both parents to the raid. Their lives were further upended when—because of a parent being deported—the family had to make the heart-wrenching decision of returning to Mexico and taking their children who were born or raised in the United States with them, or leaving them in the care of relatives in the hope that those deported by ICE would be able to sneak back into the United States. In the long term, hundreds of undocumented migrants and their families hid in fear for weeks, took their children out of school, or left town altogether (Lofholm 2013). In 2011, a smaller ICE raid hit Fort Morgan's Wildcat Dairy—this time with the cooperation of the local sheriff's office. Twenty workers were arrested and accused of using forged documents to gain employment in the United

States. Again, undocumented workers were arrested and deported, but no legal action was taken against the company that employed them (Roberts 2011). To counter the harmful impacts of ICE raids on Colorado's immigrant communities, several immigrant-rights organizations joined forces in 2016 to form the Colorado Rapid Response Network. The network reports ICE raids in local communities and dispatches volunteers to help families affected by the arrest of loved ones, but usually there is little that they can do in the aftermath of such traumatizing events.

In the early twenty-first century, more than a century after the sugar beet industry radically altered the landscape of the Eastern Plains, Mexican and other Latinx laborers are still needed but unwanted. Though the local economy relies on them, Anglo society largely rejects their presence. Unlike any other crop in Colorado before or after it, sugar beets required copious amounts of labor during its cultivating and harvesting phases—a demand that could only be met by importing Mexican and Mexican American labor (May 1989, 437). Similarly, the modern meatpacking industry relies on the cheap labor of immigrants to remain competitive in a cutthroat global business environment. In both cases, Latinx immigrants are/were the weakest link in the production chain. They work(ed) in backbreaking, dangerous jobs, performing repetitive, mind-numbing tasks for low wages and little recognition. Their immigrant, sometimes undocumented status, made them easy prey for human traffickers, employers, and an Anglo society that despised them because of their race and non-US origins. Colorado's Eastern Plains have not been a welcoming place for Latinx workers, domestic and immigrant alike. Yet, Latinxs came to the region and stayed, forming communities that have survived—and thrived—to this day, a testament to the fortitude and resilience of generations of migrant workers who dug roots in a new, Anglo-dominated land against all odds. Nowadays, those Latinx communities are an integral part of Colorado's Eastern Plains.

Latinx Communities in the Eastern Plains

One of the striking features of the Eastern Plains region is its vastness. One can drive for hours and see nothing but ranches and farmland, with small towns dotting the seemingly endless landscape. Thus, another major characteristic of the Eastern Plains region is its rural nature, which remains to this day. This semiarid region accounts for almost 40% of Colorado's territory, and it is the state's agricultural heartland. Yet, it is sparsely populated—quite a departure from the highly urbanized Front Range lying just a few miles to its west. Only 8% of Colorado's population lives in the Eastern Plains—less than half a million people—and some of its counties have been steadily losing population since the late twentieth century (US Census Bureau 2020). Extreme temperatures, strong winds, tornadoes, and water scarcity have historically made human settlement difficult in the region. Add to that a graying Baby Boomer population of farmers and ranchers, and the flight of their grown children to urban areas, and the region's demographic decline stands in sharp contrast with the state's rapidly growing (urban) population (Rice 2021).

In this region of declining fortunes, Latinxs are one of its bright spots. Latinxs make up almost 30% of the Eastern Plains population (a larger percentage than on the Front Range), and in some Eastern Plains cities—like Greeley, Fort Morgan, Las Animas, La Junta, and Lamar (see map 0.1)—Latinxs are between 38% and 51% of the population. The city of Greeley, with over 109,000 inhabitants, is by far the largest city in the Eastern Plains,[15] and part of a county-wide metro area of over 328,000 inhabitants—the fastest growing metro area in Colorado in large measure thanks to its rapidly growing Hispanic population (McCoy 2021). Greeley also anchors Colorado's new (as of 2023) Eighth Congressional District, which extends south from Greeley towards Denver's northern suburbs.[16] The Eighth boasts the largest percentage of Hispanics of any congressional district in the state (at 39%), and it was the result of the work of the new Colorado Independent Redistricting Commission in 2021, which sought to maintain the partisan balance in Colorado's other seven congressional districts while adding a new competitive district (Paul 2021).[17] Democrat Yadira D. Caraveo, a pediatrician whose parents came to the United States as undocumented immigrants from Mexico, became its first representative in 2023. Caraveo won the 2022 election by a slim margin in this evenly split district, due to the Latinx vote, 75% of which favored her (Aguilar 2022). In 2024, Caraveo lost her reelection bid to Gabe Evans, a Latino Republican who defeated her by less than 2,500 votes (Paul 2024).

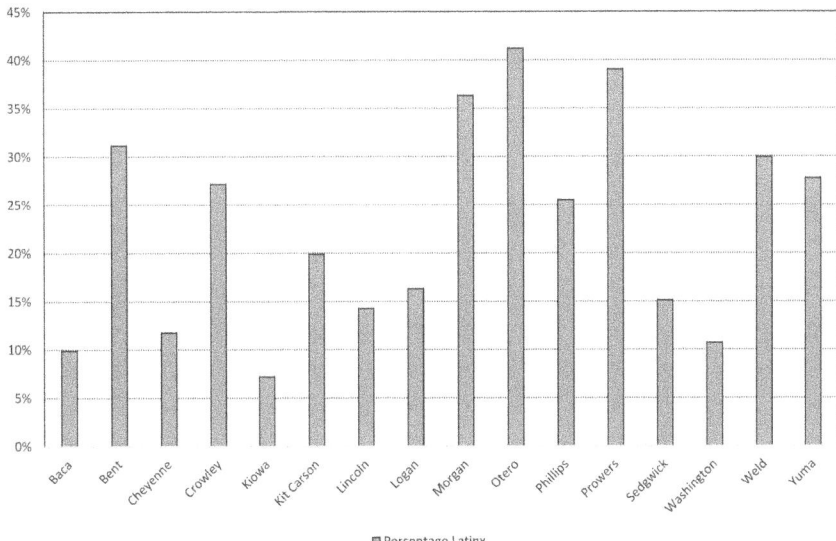

FIGURE 2.1. Latinx population of the Eastern Plains (percentage Latinx, by county), 2020. Source: US Census Bureau.

In Bent, Crowley, Morgan, Otero, Phillips, Prowers, Weld, and Yuma Counties, Latinxs make up more than a quarter of the county's population (see figure 2.1 and map 0.2). Except for Morgan and Weld, these Eastern Plains counties have very small populations (less than 20,000 inhabitants each), so the presence of Latinxs in these rural communities helps keep these counties' economies afloat (Simpson 2017). These rural Latinx communities are the result of the long-term presence of Latinxs in the region (dating back to the sugar beets era), as well as new arrivals from other US states, Mexico, and Central America attracted by jobs in agriculture, ranching, and the oil and gas industry. In addition, meatpacking plants, construction labor, and service jobs are attracting Latinxs to Weld County's greater Greeley metro area—paralleling as well as fueling the county's rapid growth. As in other parts of the state, the presence of Latinxs has ripple effects into the future, as their children make up a large percentage of public-school enrollments. For example, 63% of students in the Greeley 6 School District, 65% of students in the Fort Morgan RE-3 School District, 69% of students in the East Otero R-1 School District (i.e., La Junta), and 74% of students in the Rocky Ford R-2 School District are Hispanic (as of

2021)—just to name a few (Annie E. Casey Foundation 2024). In essence, Latinxs have become a fundamental part of Colorado's Eastern Plains region and a permanent fixture too, their presence there now as ubiquitous as that of Hispanos in the San Luis Valley.

Conclusion: A Rich Latinx Legacy

When the first beet sugar factories opened in Colorado at the turn of the twentieth century, very few people could foresee how this agricultural commodity would come to transform not only the Eastern Plains but the state itself. And Latinxs were a part of that transformation. Their hard labor, often under unforgiving conditions, made the Eastern Plains bloom and enriched the state coffers. Sugar beets—and the fortunes that the crop created—would not have been possible without "Mexican" labor. But Latinxs were much more than transient laborers. They were family units, many of them extended, that populated an area of the state often imagined as "empty" by those living in large cities. The deep-seated culture and sense of community of Latinxs challenged Anglo assumptions of Mexican workers as inferior beings, as birds of passage that could contribute little to the state besides their cheap labor. A point well made by Lourdes Gouveia (2005, 6): "Although Latinos are found at the core of this country's rural life, they remain marginal to the nostalgic imagery and historical narratives of rural America." Their working-class status also reinforced prevailing racial prejudices regarding "Mexican" workers, who were seen as inferior racialized Others not only vis-à-vis Anglos but even when compared to recent European immigrants such as the German Russians. In the sociocultural pecking order of Colorado's Eastern Plains, Latinxs occupy the bottom rung in Anglo narratives of white farmers making the land bloom, adding to the former's invisibility as worthy members of Colorado's social landscape.

It is time to acknowledge that Colorado's Eastern Plains became as Mexican as they were Anglo, and nowadays it is impossible to think of the region's history without considering its Mexican heritage. The romanticized but inaccurate image of entrepreneurial Anglo farmers "taming" the Plains needs to be balanced out with that of hardworking Mexican

FIGURE 2.2. "The Hand that Feeds" sculpture, Fort Collins, Colorado. Source: The author.

braceros growing and harvesting the crops we eat—both key elements in the success of Colorado's rural industries.[18] And as the meatpacking industry has come to replace sugar beets, new immigrant cohorts add their own cultures to this rich social mix. Mexicans, Central Americans, and other immigrants are replenishing local ethnic identities as well as effecting changes in host communities, a "back-and-forth set of adjustments and readjustments in which both newcomers and established individuals work out, through interactions with each other, what it means to belong," according to Tomás R. Jiménez (2017, xiv). Just like the Hispanos of the San Luis Valley had done before, the Latinxs of Colorado's Eastern Plains created a cultural borderland in the region by the mid-twentieth century. Hispanos, Mexicans, and Mexican Americans interacted with Anglos (and each other), under trying conditions, to form transregional and transnational communities that diversified a "white" region and laid a foundation for multiracial, multiethnic communities that enriched

Colorado. The history of Colorado's Eastern Plains is far from over. It is being (re)written daily through the hard work of countless Latinxs who are (re)defining what it means to be a Coloradan.

Finally, there is one more important, often overlooked legacy left by the thousands of Hispano and Mexican laborers that came to toil in Colorado's Eastern Plains: They paved the way for the state's Chicano Movement. Their children and grandchildren, born, raised, and educated in the United States, had a shot at the American Dream—or at least they thought they did. When the promises of equality did not materialize, Chicanos poured into the streets of US cities to protest their second-class status in Anglo society (see chapter 3). Colorado's early- and mid-twenty-century "Mexican" workers raised a generation of urban(ized) Mexican Americans that came of age in the 1960s–1970s, mainly in the cities of the Front Range. Educated in US public schools, conscious of the plight of their forebearers, and exposed to Anglo racism and discrimination in school, the workplace, and everyday encounters with the Anglo world, these Mexican American activists that styled themselves *Chicanos* would not back down and take it. They organized, they marched, and they demanded a radical restructuring of racial relations in the state and the nation—and in doing so, they changed the rules of the game for Latino Colorado.

3
THE FRONT RANGE
El Movimiento

The Chicano Movement in Colorado has two histories. One is the "official" story covered in newspapers and government documents. That story is the history of a radicalized group of young Chicanas and Chicanos during the Cold War. In the best of cases in this story, Chicanx activists are suspected of being communist sympathizers[1]—naive college students who are a headache for local and federal authorities as the latter seek to control unrest during the turbulent decades of the 1960s and 1970s. In the worst of cases, Chicanx activists are seen as dangerous destabilizing agents who under the influence of foreign powers are bent on undermining the US government and the American way of life through violent means ("These Our Their Leaders" 1976). Either way, Chicanas and Chicanos are portrayed in this "official" story as problematic, un-American racialized "Others"—a threat to American values and society.

The other history is the story of young men and women who decided to assert their rights to end decades of oppression and exclusion at the hands of Anglos in the American West (Acuña 2000). Chicanxs in

Colorado witnessed how their parents and grandparents had—for the most part—been relegated to a life of hard labor in the fields, the mines, the steel mill, or the local service industries. Chicanx workers were Colorado's cheap labor pool, and a system of official and unofficial practices had been implemented over decades to keep them "in their place" (see previous chapters). Very few young Chicanxs had access to higher education, and Anglo society—by and large—thought or expected little of them. Public schools were to provide young Chicanxs with basic literacy skills or vocational training, but not necessarily send them to college. And once they were in the workplace, ethnic labor segregation prevented Chicanxs from rising through the ranks. In essence, Colorado was a land owned by Anglos but worked by Chicanxs. As described by Chicano activist Francisco "Kiko" Martínez: "We knew [that] there had been a war against Mexico, but we didn't understand that that war involved us" (Freedom Archives 2017). For Chicanxs, this story was about achieving equality in American society, and having a shot at the American Dream. As they were tired of waiting for decades for things to change, militancy and confrontation would become necessary tactics in order to effect change and gain respect as a political force to be reckoned with. These two diverging narratives competed for the public's attention during the 1970s, with the "official" story enjoying broad access to mass media outlets and cloaked in a mantle of governmental respectability, while the subaltern discourse of the Chicano Movement in Colorado struggled to reach even those within the Latinx community. In this classic David-versus-Goliath struggle, competing versions of "the truth" presented radically different versions of events, actors, and victims. In the end, "the truth" is not necessarily what really happened during those years but what each side believed it to be.

This chapter looks at Colorado's Chicano Movement from the point of view of its actors. Through archival research and oral histories, I have cobbled together a narrative of El Movimiento that utilizes a research justice approach to place Colorado's Chicano Movement in its proper historical context. Research justice "is a strategic framework that seeks to transform structural inequities in research and recognize marginalized communities as experts and key stakeholders in the management of the data and knowledge produced" (Colin Powell School for Civic and Global Leadership 2021). Rather than rely exclusively on official sources,

I examined publications written by Chicanx activists for the Chicanx community. In addition, I employed an extensive collection of oral histories by Chicanx militants to fill in the gaps and provide a more nuanced understanding of what the Chicano Movement meant for those who lived through those tumultuous—yet exciting—times. Finally, the chapter also places the Chicano Movement in the context of Colorado's Front Range, a highly urbanized corridor that contains most of the state's population. The presence of large numbers of Hispanics in the Front Range (mainly of Hispano, Mexican, and Mexican American origin) provided the critical mass that El Movimiento required to thrive in Colorado—a state where Hispanics had been publicly unacknowledged and rendered invisible for close to a century. By the late 1960s, the Chicano Movement was about to radically disrupt Colorado's Anglo-imposed status quo, with the force and suddenness of the tornadoes that periodically wrecked life in the Eastern Plains.

Chicanxs in the Front Range: What's in a Name? What's in a Place?

In its most simple definition, Chicanxs are Mexican Americans who not only straddle both cultures but who have also created a new, hybrid culture resulting from their interaction with the local environment. Chicanxs are a distinct sociocultural phenomenon of the American West, the product of an Anglo takeover of Indigenous and Mexican lands and people after 1848, and the latter's resistance (J. D. Vigil 2012). But this basic definition has been challenged as not an entirely accurate one, because even though Chicanxs are US citizens, Anglos see them as mere "Mexicans," as well as an incomplete one, because it glosses over (or completely ignores) the deep Indigenous roots of Chicanxs. As defined by David Byron Young,[2] Chicanxs are racially Indigenous but culturally a mixture of Indigenous, Spanish, Mexican, and American influences (particularly in Colorado and New Mexico). Their hybridity makes of Chicanxs a unique demographic cohort, culturally different from their Mexican ancestors (who see them as too Americanized to be "authentic" Mexicans and derisively call them *pochos*), from Anglos (who see them as Brown people that are not their racial equals), and even from federally recognized Native Americans (who may see Chicanxs as "wannabe Indians") (Young 2011, 126). Moreover, Chicanxs strongly reject the assimilationist strategy of generations of Mexican Americans ("Mexican American or Chicano" 1969), who hoped that by keeping their heads low and not ruffling any feathers the Anglo establishment would eventually accept them. For Chicanxs, full assimilation into Anglo America is not only implausible but unappealing (Meier and Ribera 1993, 218–219). For Chicanxs, assimilation into the US mainstream implies the acceptance of white tropes regarding the inferiority of Brown people and Anglo (mis)interpretations of Mexican American history and culture (Almaguer 1971, 1974). Needless to say, Chicanxs also reject the strategy of Hispanos to highlight their Spanish roots vis-à-vis Anglo culture (Muñoz 1989, 7–8). In the Chicanx worldview, the Spanish empire was but the first in a line of colonial oppressors and enslavers that eventually came to include Mexico and the United States in the early and mid-nineteenth century, respectively (Reséndez 2016).

More than any other term used to describe the Mexican-origin population of the United States, the gendered term *Chicana/Chicano* is laden with political meaning (M. García 2021, 3–4). First, the term seeks to empower those who have been powerless for decades by providing them with a term of their own, one that inspires pride in those that use it, rather than an assimilationist term imposed by mainstream America (e.g., Mexican American) (Baca 2021). Second, the term (ostensibly derived from *Mexicano*) corrects historical wrongs by establishing a connection with the land and the Indigenous roots of the Chicanx people, whereas other terms ignore or gloss over such heritage (Rosales 1997, 261). And third, the term reflects a political commitment to the community and a rejection of a mainstream Anglo America that in turn has historically rejected Chicanxs as racialized "Others." According to Ignacio García (1997), the confrontational political stance of the Chicano Movement was the result of a militant ethos encapsulated by the ideology known as *Chicanismo*.

The foregoing definition of Chicanxs dovetails nicely with Benedict Anderson's (2006) depiction of an "imagined community." Bound together by a common heritage and similar experiences of exploitation and rejection at the hands of Anglo society, Chicanxs constitute a nation within a sovereign state, with some Chicanx activists even calling for full nationhood in the form of their own nation-state ("Professor Predicts

'Hispanic Homeland'" 2000).[3] In their militancy, Chicanxs rejected Anglo oppression and saw the solution to their woes by circling the proverbial wagons and focusing on their communities and seeking their own solutions, much like their Hispano ancestors did generations ago. Following on Young's (2011) arguments for the recognition of the Indigenous roots of the Chicanx people, it can even be argued that Chicanxs represent an extended ethnic group in the American West, just like Navajos and Utes (and other Native Americans).[4] The use of the term *La Raza* by Chicanx activists to refer to themselves and their historical connection to *Aztlán* (the ancestral homeland of the Aztecs) add two major cultural elements that bolster the ethnic claim.[5] Moreover, Chicanxs were/are racialized and otherized by Anglos, just like the case of dozens of Indigenous tribes of the United States. A byproduct of the conquest of the American West, Chicanxs are an ethnic component of the Western landscape that Anglos took by force. Not only did Chicanxs see and imagine themselves as a separate people, but the establishment treated them as such too—decades before Chicanx intellectuals laid the basic tenets of Chicanismo (Rosales 1997, 20). Ethnicity—like race—is a social construct, and it is defined and imagined by insiders as well as outsiders (Hutchinson and Smith 1996). As such, Chicanxs represent an ethnic group within the United States, and their Indigenous roots anchor them into the geographical context of the American West. Their rise also complicated the formation (and definition) of Latinx cultural borderlands throughout Colorado and the American West. While claiming to be a separate—and novel—cultural entity, Chicanxs also partook of Hispano, Mexican, and Mexican American communities, making them part of a cultural borderland with ties across the US-Mexico border. More often than not, Chicanxs looked across the border for cultural referents in Mexico, while their ranks were augmented by Mexican immigrants and their children who lived transnational lives.

One caveat, though: Imagined communities (such as ethnic groups) may challenge origin stories. Thus, in the case of Chicanxs throughout the American West, the demographic composition and lived experiences of Chicanxs can be quite diverse (Muñoz 1989, 9–11). While many Chicanxs in Colorado and New Mexico have deep Indigenous roots, others in places like Texas and California may lack those and instead emphasize regional allegiances and shared experiences as the defining elements of their Chicanx identity (Richardson 1999; G. Sánchez 1993). In California, student protests and labor struggles (the latter under Cesar Chavez and Dolores Huerta) characterized the objectives of the Chicano Movement (Bardacke 2011; García and Castro 2011). In New Mexico (under Reies López Tijerina[6]) El Movimiento was a messianic struggle over Hispano lands in the face of Anglo encroachment and the land use policies of the US federal government (R. Gutiérrez 2022). In Texas, the creation of a Chicanx political party (La Raza Unida Party) under the leadership of José Angel Gutiérrez gave the movement an electoral twist (Navarro 2000). And in Colorado, student protests and the mobilization of Chicanos on the urban Front Range wrote a new chapter on the history of the Chicano Movement.[7] From Texas to California, the goals, tactics, and leadership styles of the Chicano Movement differed. But under the tenets of Chicanismo, all Chicanxs were on the same boat, united by a common experience of discrimination and racialization at the hands of Anglos (I. García 1997, 43–44). In theory, a light-skinned Chicana student from Texas's Lower Rio Grande Valley had an equal claim to the Chicanx "imagined community" as a Chicano from New Mexico who identified as Indigenous, as did a recent Mexican immigrant versus the members of a Hispano family that settled in the American West (then El Norte) before there was a United States of America. According to Richard White (1991, 593), the positive aspect of the term was that "*Chicano* submerged all the complicated sectional, class, and social divisions of the Mexican and Mexican American community under a single term." Chicanos also shared the American West with non-Mexican-origin Latinxs, recent immigrants, and other people of color (e.g., African Americans, Asian Americans, and Native Americans), some of whom supported the Chicano Movement, as they too suffered discrimination at the hands of Anglos (Treviño 2017).[8] Although there were racial, class, regional, and cultural differences among them, Chicanxs shared common struggles with discrimination, displacement, and social invisibility, and they—in large numbers—turned to militancy to confront the Anglo-imposed status quo in the 1960s–1970s. Chicanxs were demographically and culturally diverse but could come together in the struggle against a common political oppressor (i.e., Anglo America).

The geographical setting also influenced the local nature of the Chicano Movement in Colorado. Unlike the case of New Mexico, where

Hispanos—turned into militant Chicanxs—fought for their land, in Colorado El Movimiento was mainly an urban affair that took place along the Front Range. Though there were rumblings in rural areas such as the San Luis Valley and the Western Slope (see those respective chapters in this book), and Chicanx militants hailed from all over the state, it was in the cities of the urban corridor known as the Front Range where the large protests, marches, and clashes that defined Colorado's Chicano Movement took place. But what made the Front Range urban corridor the ideal—and perhaps the only viable—incubator for the development of a large-scale Chicano Movement in Colorado?

Colorado's Front Range is a mountain range that lies on the east side of the Rocky Mountains, facing the Eastern Plains (see map 0.1). Its piedmont offers a comparatively good climate in contrast to the weather extremes found in the mountains to its west or the plains to the east. Not surprisingly, this region is where one finds Colorado's largest human settlements—by far. The Front Range urban corridor began as a base for prospectors looking for riches in the intermontane valleys east of the Continental Divide in the mid-nineteenth century. Denver, founded by the South Platte River in 1858, would quickly become the territory's de facto—and later, official—capital (Abbott, Leonard, and Noel 2005, chap. 4). Its location turned it into a critical transportation hub that linked the central Rocky Mountains (and its mineral riches) to markets in the Midwest and the East via the railroad. As gold rushes brought more people to the territory (and after 1876, the state of Colorado) other towns sprouted north and south of Denver, such as Fort Collins, Longmont, Boulder, Aurora, and Colorado Springs. Prospectors, farmers, merchants, and professionals came to Colorado lured by the promise of a new start and a good quality of life (Leonard and Noel 2016, 28). Yet, development along the Front Range urban corridor came in fits and spurts, tied to the vagaries of the mining industry and agriculture. The fortunes of boom-and-bust mining towns in the mountains had a ripple effect on the population of the urban corridor in the late nineteenth century, and by the early twentieth century, the ebbs and flows of sugar beet production likewise affected livelihoods in the Front Range (Wyckoff 1999, chaps. 3–5).

It was not until World War II that the Front Range urban corridor took off (after some very tough years during the Great Depression). The war brought an influx of federal money, wartime industrial production, and the mobilization of thousands of Coloradans (Abbott, Leonard, and Noel 2005, chap. 17). Since then, Denver and the surrounding Front Range urban areas have been the destination of thousands of new arrivals, particularly as the industries of the Old West (e.g., mining, oil and gas, and farming and ranching) began coexisting with the industries of the New West (e.g., services and technology, tourism, and real estate) during the second half of the twentieth century (Abbott, Leonard, and Noel 2005, chaps. 18, 22). The breakneck pace of population growth continues unabated, making Colorado in general and the Front Range urban corridor in particular, one of the fastest growing states and regions in the nation. This region—roughly from Fort Collins to Pueblo—now constitutes an almost-continuous urban corridor that houses the majority of the state's population (Lang and Muro 2008). And Latinxs are a big part of this story.

As Denver and other Front Range cities grew in size, so did their Latinx populations, which were mostly of Mexican origin (either Hispanos from southern Colorado and New Mexico or Mexican migrants from south of the border). Just like the Anglos who came from the Midwest and the East, Latinxs were attracted to the Front Range cities by job opportunities, urban amenities, and services (e.g., running water, electricity, hospitals, and public schools for their children) that added quality to their lives (Leonard and Noel 1990, 388–389). But unlike the Anglos that were received with open arms, Latinxs in the Front Range had to endure the same discriminatory treatment that they had experienced in other parts of the state. Housing and labor segregation forced them to live in the poorest neighborhoods and work in the most physically taxing jobs (Dorsett 1977, 226, 242). They were excluded from meaningful participation in the sociopolitical lives of these cities and were perpetually perceived as "outsiders," in contrast to Anglo newcomers, who quickly claimed to be "locals."[9] Several generations of Mexican-origin Latinxs created Mexican American enclaves in Denver's west (e.g., Westwood) and north sides and other cities of the Front Range (oftentimes on the other side of the tracks, as was the case in the American West), and their labor contributed to the development of these thriving locations (Deutsch 1987, 132). By 1920, an estimated 1,390 "Mexicans" lived in Denver—some moving there temporarily during the winter months when there were no jobs in the sugar beet industry. In 1930, at the start of the Great Depression, close to 7,000 Mexicans resided in the city, driven there by the safety net that the city provided (such as welfare and public health services), and by the beginning of World War II the number had grown to over 12,000 (Dorsett 1977, 226).

Needed but unwanted, Mexican Americans toiled at their workplaces so their children could have a better future and a shot at the American Dream—to no avail. Just like their Mexican American parents, Mexican-origin children were perceived as cheap labor in Anglo-dominated economic sectors (Meier and Ribera 1993, 219). Despite their US citizenship and command of the English language, they experienced limited vertical social mobility as a result of being denied educational opportunities, promotions in the workplace, and access to political structures (Dorsett 1977, 283–284). Mexican Americans had fared better in the cities, but racial discrimination and structural prejudices still hounded them (White 1991, 592). Middle-class Mexican American organizations had achieved some success in desegregating public spaces in the 1930s–1950s, but they never represented a serious threat to the well-entrenched Anglo establishment that basically controlled all levers of power (M. García 1989). In the early twentieth century, organizations such as the Order of Sons of America (made up of World War I Mexican American veterans) emphasized the naturalization of Mexican immigrants, assimilation, and US political participation. This strategy implied a clean break with notions of an eventual return to Mexico or at least the maintenance of strong cultural bonds with a Mexican fatherland. Other Mexican American organizations, such as the League of United Latin American Citizens (LULAC)[10] and the American GI Forum straddled a middle path, with calls to assimilate and integrate into US society but from a position of ethnic pride (M. Rodriguez 2015, 8–9). Something that all these organizations had in common were their ultimate goals: to fight discrimination against Mexican Americans through legal strategies and show Anglo America that the former were valuable, loyal members of US society. These organizations also promoted social mobility through education and made school desegregation one of the top priorities. By the late 1950s and early 1960s, though, their rhetoric began mirroring that of the civil rights movement and they blamed racism as the main culprit for the plight of Mexican Americans

(Rosales 1997, chap. 6), laying the ground for the future demands of the Chicano Movement. Likewise, the 1960 presidential election sparked the involvement of a generation of young Mexican Americans in national politics through the Viva Kennedy clubs (I. García 2000). Mexican Americans identified with Senator John F. Kennedy's religion (Roman Catholicism), ethnic background (exploited Irish Americans), and outsider status (running against Richard Nixon, the establishment's candidate). Most important, Kennedy's running mate was Texas Senator Lyndon B. Johnson, a sympathetic ally of the Mexican American community.[11] The Viva Kennedy clubs elevated the political stature of the Mexican American community in key battleground states such as Texas and provided Mexican American leaders with valuable political experience and Washington connections. Still, it is likely that this socioeconomic status quo that exploited and relegated most Mexican Americans to second-class status would have remained largely unchanged throughout the American West had it not been for the social, political, and cultural upheavals of the 1960s (O. Martinez 1980).

The generation that had endured the Great Depression and survived World War II gave birth to the Baby Boomers—America's largest generational cohort until the twenty-first century. Anglo Baby Boomers grew up in a world of relative peace and affluence, benefiting from suburban amenities, the proliferation of television, and the best public education system in the world. But change was around the corner. The United States was divided by deep inequalities along class, racial, and gender lines, exacerbated by the traumatic overseas conflict in Southeast Asia commonly known as the Vietnam War.[12] Boomers, empowered by their education and white privilege, protested the war, the status quo, and pretty much everything that their parents stood for. The anti–Vietnam War protests; the hippie movement; the women's liberation movement; and the drugs, sex, and rock and roll culture embraced by the Boomers were more than social movements in a shifting America; they were profoundly destabilizing sociocultural phenomena that widened existing cracks in the status quo (Cogan and Gencarelli 2015), cracks that provided people of color with opportunities to make their own demands for change. The civil rights movement, led by courageous African Americans in the Jim Crow South was—without a doubt—the most disrupting social movement of the times as it challenged institutionalized white supremacy in one of the most conservative regions of the nation (Eagles 1986). It would spark parallel militant movements led by Chicanxs, Native Americans, gay people, and working-class people—all demanding their rightful place in American society (Suarez 2013).

Geography and militant politics combined to fuel the Chicano Movement along Colorado's Front Range, for a variety of reasons. First, the Front Range had the numbers of Chicanx activists needed to create a critical mass that could sustain the movement long term. By 1970, 85% of the Mexican American (i.e., Spanish-surnamed) population of the US Southwest lived in urban areas (White 1991, 592). Although Latinxs in Colorado were proportionally significant in areas of the state such as the San Luis Valley (the historical heartland of Latino Colorado), numerically the largest concentrations of Latinxs were in Denver and other cities of the Front Range urban corridor. By 1950, the Denver Area Welfare Council estimated the "Spanish American" population of the city at 30,000–45,000 individuals. In 1960, the US federal census listed 43,147 Spanish Americans in Denver; by 1970, 86,345; and by 1980, 91,937—a significant increase (Leonard and Noel 1990, 389–390). In 1956, Bert A. Gallegos was elected to Colorado's House of Representatives; he was the first Mexican American to represent a Denver district. His election signaled a Latinx demographic shift, decades in the making, from the heavily Hispano counties of the San Luis Valley to the urban areas of the Front Range around metro Denver (Padilla and Ramírez 1974, 206).[13] Despite their minority status in cities like Denver, Chicanx activists along the Front Range consisted of hundreds of individuals, rather than a few dozen. These numbers translated into a massive outpouring of Chicanx militants on the streets of cities like Denver, augmented by Chicanxs coming from other parts of the state (Conan 2011). Smaller cities like Alamosa or Grand Junction, for example, witnessed protests by Chicanxs, but they consisted of a handful of individuals, even when joined by others coming from afar (see chapters 1 and 4, respectively).[14]

Second, Denver and Front Range cities are at the center of the action. Denver, as the state capital, holds the offices of the state government and the city and county of Denver, as well as federal, state, county, and local courts. It also happens to be Colorado's largest city, with the most population, the largest workforce in the state, the most college and high school students, the largest police force, and so on. Denver is also crisscrossed by highways that connect it (and the Front Range) to the rest of the state and the region. As a major trade and transportation hub, literally everything goes through Denver. Television and radio stations that cover the state are also based in the Denver metro area, ensuring that events happening there (e.g., a march or protest by Chicanxs) are covered right away and in depth. Given it disproportionate demographic, political, and economic weight vis-à-vis the rest of the state, events that took place in Denver in the 1960–1970s had an impact across the state (and the region),[15] and if something newsworthy was happening in Colorado, it was more likely than not happening in Denver. In the state of Colorado, Denver is the hub of the wheel, and the nearby Front Range cities are its spokes. Thus, it comes as no surprise that Colorado's Chicano Movement reached its zenith in Denver. It was there—in the heart of the Front Range—that the Chicano Movement would have the most impact.

Third, there were spatial and cultural advantages to growing up and living in a major metro area like Denver. Urban Chicanxs had greater access to education and services than their rural counterparts did (White 1991, 592). Young Chicanxs in Denver lived in close proximity to each other and attended large public schools with dozens of other Chicanxs. This spatial concentration facilitated their organization and mobilization, the spread of information, and their tactics—something that was harder to achieve in rural areas of the state (Deutsch 1987, 154). Chicanxs in the Front Range were able to develop their own urban culture that provided them with a social bond, influenced by their access to national and local media, to each other, and to other communities of color in the metro area (e.g., African Americans). Hundreds of young Chicanxs watched on television how white policemen beat up Black activists their own age in southern cities, how Black demonstrators resisted, and how they eventually triumphed over those that wanted to keep them down. And they began asking themselves: If African Americans prevailed under extenuating circumstances, why could Chicanos not do the same against Anglos in Colorado? The end of Jim Crow dovetailed nicely with the rise of the Chicano Movement, altering the political landscape in Colorado (Olden 2017, 49). From the Deep South to the West Coast, examples of historically marginalized groups marching for their rights abounded, and they inspired Chicanxs in Colorado into action. These young Chicanx urbanites had unprecedented access to education and information that their Mexican American parents lacked a generation before, witnessed the valiant examples of other communities of color across the nation demanding equality, and grew up in an era when protesting the establishment was practically a rite of passage for progressive youth (Muñoz 1989, 47–52). Once they reached high school and college, young Chicanxs knew what they had to do. The multiple generations of Mexican Americans who toiled in the fields and mines of Colorado, who endured privations that threatened their wellbeing, and who resisted Anglo exploitation and discrimination (sometimes actively, as in the case of labor unions), to eventually give their children a better life in the cities of the Front Range, planted and watered the seeds of the Chicano Movement (R. Hernández 2020).

Fourth, it was in the cities of the Front Range where the social disparities that Latinxs had to endure were the most apparent and the pushback stronger. In the face of widespread Anglo discrimination, Hispanos in the San Luis Valley sought refuge in their villages and communal life (see chapter 1), while Mexicans and Mexican Americans in the beet fields of the Eastern Plains endured years of hard labor hoping to eventually give their children a better life in the cities of the Front Range (see chapter 2). But the young urban Chicanxs of the 1960s–1970s thought differently. They had been raised to believe in the American Dream. They had an education. They had been promised a brighter future, only to realize that Anglo America wanted them to end up like their parents—poor manual laborers without a future (Dorsett 1977, 284). Stephen Leonard and Thomas Noel (1990, 392) paint a damning picture of the living conditions of Mexicans and Mexican Americans in Denver:

> A 1950 study, "The Spanish-American Population of Denver," conducted by the Denver Area Welfare Council, revealed that the average Spanish-American family made only $1,840 a year. Black families earned $1,930 and Whites made over $3,000. The council estimated that 60 percent of Hispanics lived in substandard housing, 90 percent did not complete high school, 50 percent sought help from social welfare agencies; that

they occupied 30 percent of all public housing and constituted over a third of the city's jail inmates; that their infant mortality rate was six times greater than that for residents of more affluent areas.

Whereas Mexican American rural workers had to endure hard work and oppressing poverty, and still shrug off racial microaggressions by Anglos, Chicanxs bristled at the status quo. Whereas Mexican Americans feared the Anglo police force, Chicanxs demanded accountability from law enforcement. Whereas their parents had learned to keep their heads down in order to survive in an Anglo world, Chicanx children would not back down. Unapologetic and unafraid, Chicanxs pushed back against the Anglo status quo. Feeling they deserved a better fate than their parents in a diversifying America, their "relative deprivation" (Gurr 1970) at the hands of an Anglo establishment that routinely crushed their dreams left them angry and upset—and willing to mobilize. Practically all Latinx communities in Colorado experienced racial discrimination, but none were as prepared, as positioned, and as willing to fight back as the Chicanx youth coming of age in Colorado's Front Range in the 1960s–1970s.

And fifth, Denver and most of the cities of the Front Range urban corridor had a liberal bent that the rest of the state lacked. The Eastern Plains, the San Luis Valley, and the Western Slope were profoundly conservative regions. That conservatism included the older members of the Mexican and Mexican American communities, who still thought that assimilation—rather than confrontation—was the key to gain an equal footing in American society and had a hard time accepting the tactics of the radicalized youth of the Chicano Movement.[16] Metro Denver and other liberal enclaves (like Boulder and Fort Collins[17]—both college towns) provided a fertile soil for the demands that characterized the era, such as the student protests against the Vietnam War ("Boulder Anti-War Protest May 1972" 2015; McNeill 2017a, 2017b; Stewart 2009). Anglo liberals in Colorado were willing to support some of the demands of the Chicano Movement—lest it turn into something worse—and offered concessions when it came to labor discrimination issues, educational reforms, and the validation and dissemination of Chicanx culture. But despite the somewhat liberal bent of Front Range cities,[18] the Chicano Movement was largely seen as a major threat to the Anglo establishment in Colorado, and it was harshly repressed by local, state, and federal authorities (Barrera 2004, 117–119; O. Martinez 1980).

Chicanas Led the Way

The Chicano Movement, just like many other social movements throughout history, is commonly seen as having been led by men while minimizing the role of women. In this traditional narrative, reproduced by some Chicanx militants, the press, academics, and mainstream American society, the Great Man Theory lives on (Carlyle 1841, 1–2). More specifically, the Chicano Movement is imagined as the product of the actions of four great men: Cesar Chavez, the union leader who organized Mexican American field workers in California; Rodolfo "Corky" Gonzales, the community organizer behind the Crusade for Justice in Colorado; José Angel Gutiérrez, the founder of La Raza Unida Party in Texas; and Reies López Tijerina, the activist who led the fight for the land rights of Hispanos in northern New Mexico (Conan 2011; López 1992, 79).[19] According to this narrative, these men rose to the occasion and made a difference in the lives of thousands of Chicanxs and other people of color in the American West during the 1960s–1970s. They displayed unique leadership abilities; put their life on the line by facing arrest, beatings, and threats on their lives; and eventually developed a loyal following that made the Chicano Movement possible. Some, like Chavez, even partook in the mortification of the flesh by fasting for prolonged periods, creating a devout, cult-like following (Bardacke 2011, 298–303). As a result, the *HIS*tories of these four men give the Chicano Movement quasi-religious, hagiographical overtones.[20]

While it is undeniable that the leadership abilities of these men inspired countless Chicanxs to believe in something greater than themselves (perhaps for the first time in their lives) and gave those who had been rendered powerless by the Anglo establishment the agency that they had been lacking, this narrative is both incomplete and factually inaccurate (Facio 2011). While leaders like Chavez, Gonzales, Gutiérrez, and Tijerina played a defining role in El Movimiento, the Chicano Movement cannot simply be reduced to their stories (M. Montoya 2016). It was a social movement of thousands of unnamed, courageous activists—men, women, and children who challenged the Anglo establishment and shocked US society with their defiance. Many of them were leaders of the Chicano Movement that because of their gender, age, or role did not get the attention and press coverage of Chavez, Gonzales, Gutiérrez, and Tijerina. Such was the case of the indefatigable Dolores Huerta, a Chicana leader and union organizer with her own merits and great accomplishments (Sowards 2019) but oftentimes reduced to playing second fiddle in traditional narratives of the Chicanx labor rights struggle in California (as in the usual practice of mentioning her name after that of Chavez—as in "Cesar Chavez *and* Dolores Huerta"). Chicanas constructed a "distinctly female ethnic identity" apart from Chicanos and Anglo women that "interpenetrated their interpretation of themselves as women workers" (Deutsch 1994, 7). Unfortunately, the empowerment of Chicanas also sparked a backlash among some Chicanos, who felt that their leadership—and their manhood—were threatened by militant women. According to Elisa Facio, "A number of women . . . were threatened, physically and verbally abused, and coerced into sexual relations (known today as date rape) because of their Chicana feminist or woman-ist standpoint" (2011, 356). A worst fate befell Chicana feminist lesbians, who were often silenced by the cultural and nationalist politics of El Movimiento, which supported a heteropatriarchal status quo. Even though it is historically called the *Chicano* Movement, Chicanas were the unacknowledged and underappreciated backbone of El Movimiento at the same time as they challenged the system at large, Anglo feminism, and the inherent machismo of Latinx culture in what became known as "Chicana Power" (Blackwell 2011).

In Colorado, the local Chicano Movement received a major boost thanks to Guadalupe Briseño, a Chicana organizer whose struggle and defiance grabbed the headlines as Chicano activist Rodolfo "Corky" Gonzales was also becoming a household name. In mid-1968, Briseño organized workers at the Kitayama Corporation, where she worked. The floral plant mainly employed Mexican American women, who endured long working hours in appalling conditions: low wages with no overtime pay, high humidity, muddy and slippery floors, no protective clothing, a lack of sanitary facilities, and verbal abuse and harassment from managers (Falcón 2003, 142). Under Briseño's leadership, the plant laborers organized the National Floral Workers Organization (NFWO), and on July 1, 1968, they went on strike. The workers received ample support from the Chicanx community, but they still had to endure months of a protracted strike. At one point, in a symbolic act of defiance, the floral workers chained themselves to the plant's gates. At the urging of Kitayama, the police responded in force, tear-gassing the strikers, cutting off their chains, and hauling them away from the plant's entrance. After months of striking, conditions at the plant improved, but the NFWO was never recognized by Kitayama, and the plant closed shortly thereafter (Allyn 2019b).

Although Briseño and the plant workers failed in having all their demands met, this seemingly little strike at a floral plant in Brighton had a ripple effect on the Chicano Movement throughout Colorado. The brutality displayed by the police, the intransigence of Kitayama, the resilience of the strikers, and the extraordinary courage displayed by ordinary women who—in addition to their jobs at the plant—were also mothers and wives, inspired Chicanxs all over the state (Falcón 2015). Whereas Corky Gonzales was a former boxer and activist who sought confrontation as a way of attracting attention for his cause, Briseño and the striking plant workers found themselves thrust into the headlines as unexpected victims of state-led violence against women. For many, the strike was an eye-opener that showed how little regard the Anglo establishment had for Chicanas and women of color—as well as their capacity to confront injustice with dignity and aplomb. The scenes of defenseless women being tear-gassed and manhandled by the police sparked anger and moved Chicanxs in Colorado into pursuing more confrontational tactics vis-à-vis the authorities. The tears of Guadalupe Briseño and the striking floral workers of the NFWO symbolically watered the seeds of Chicanx resistance in Colorado.

Chicanas challenged not only the Anglo establishment but also the widespread machismo and heteropatriarchy within El Movimiento, in line with parallel changes taking place in American society. Forced to fight on two fronts (both Anglo society and the domestic front), Chicana activism sparked a long-overdue conversation in Latinx communities regarding the equality of women. Chicanas were thrice oppressed by the intersectionality of race, class, and gender, as working-class women of color. Traditional gender roles derived from Anglo and Latin American cultural norms relegated them to supporting their parents, husbands, and children and left them with little agency to speak for themselves.

The "Chicana Power" movement radically disrupted that trend. Whereas Chicanos pressed for changes in their political, socioeconomic, and cultural relationship vis-à-vis Anglo America, Chicanas saw that struggle as incomplete if it kept them subordinated to men in Chicanx households (Facio 2011). Equality, if it was to be achieved by militant means, meant equality for all—including women. So they marched.

The Denver High School Walkouts

The lack of concern over the working conditions of Chicanx workers displayed by the Anglo establishment reflected a much greater problem: In Colorado (as in other parts of the American West), Chicanxs were neither seen nor heard. They had been rendered invisible by a discriminatory system that treated them as second-class citizens suitable just for toiling in low-wage occupations (Leonard and Noel 1990, 388, 391–392). Indeed, many Mexican Americans could aspire to nothing more than long hours of backbreaking labor, but they also believed in America's promise and endured miserable working conditions in the conviction that their children could achieve the American Dream. Getting a decent education has always been the ticket to vertical mobility in American society, and both parents and children from communities of color understood the importance of making sacrifices so that the children could have a better future. Yet the educational system failed to see them too. Denver's public schools largely ignored Chicanx students, their needs, and their demands. Its educational system did not believe in the need to provide Chicanx children with much of an education, the reasoning went, as they were destined to become blue-collar laborers anyway. Although the city of Denver and the state of Colorado never had any formal segregationist policies put in place in public schools (as was the case in the Jim Crow South), the selective implementation of policies regarding the selection of sites for school buildings, the gerrymandering of school boundaries, and the deliberate busing of students created "Anglo," "Black," and "Mexican" schools in the city and throughout the state.[21] As a result, Mexican American students in Denver had "the highest drop-out rate of any group of students and the lowest educational attainment levels in the city" (Olden 2017, 44–45). Even within schools, academic tracking and placement in special education created informally segregated classrooms of "Mexicans." There was not to be an American Dream for the Chicanx youth of the 1960s. It was either working in the same jobs that their parents had for generations or fighting in the Vietnam War. But Chicanxs were determined not to be invisible anymore.

By 1969, tensions in West High School, a "Mexican" school in Denver, had reached a boiling point. Years of demands by Chicanx students that the school's administrators failed to address had left the former frustrated and angry. The tipping point was reached over the racist comments of an Anglo social studies teacher, who belittled Chicanx students by reportedly telling them things like "If you eat Mexican food, you'll look like a Mexican" and "Spanish students are stupid because their parents are stupid" (H. Sanchez 2019). On March 20, 1969, dozens of West High School students staged a massive walkout after trying to present a list of nine demands to end "racist attitudes" at the school, including "courses in Chicano history, culture and language: bi-lingual education from elementary school through college: Chicano literature in the West High library, and a school board for the West High Neighborhood Complex with no at large members" (Sorensen 1969). They left their school and marched to Sunken Gardens Park, where they met with other Chicanx activists. From there, they marched to Baker Junior High, where more students joined the protest, and then marched with them back to West High School. The large-scale protest immediately drew the attention of the authorities, and Denver police officers were sent in force to contain the demonstrators. The Chicanx activists were ordered to leave the grounds, and as the police started pushing on them a violent confrontation ensued. Denver police beat up and used pepper spray on the protestors, who fought back ("Summer in March" 1969). The violent arrests and overreaction by the police only added fuel to the fire, and the protestors decided to march to City Hall and other downtown buildings (Anthony 1969). The next day (March 21), more Chicanx activists and their allies joined students from at least four Denver schools to stage an even larger protest. Like the day before, confrontations between the police and demonstrators took place, with activists responding to police brutality by throwing rocks and bottles at the authorities. The Chicanx students and activists paid a heavy price, with dozens injured, but the Anglo authorities finally listened to their demands. Denver Public Schools Superintendent Robert D. Gilberts agreed to hire new teachers, the offending social studies teacher at West High was transferred to a different school, and the curriculum was changed to make it more representative of the student body (H. Sanchez 2019). For Chicanxs, it seemed as if the authorities only paid attention to them whenever things turned ugly. That lesson was not lost on the activists, and the militant nature of El Movimiento was further reinforced by the reticence of the Anglo authorities to take their demands into consideration, the brutality displayed by local law enforcement, and the antagonizing—if not outright hostile—coverage by the Anglo mainstream media. If Chicanxs wanted equality in American society, they would have to fight for it.

The Crusade for Justice

On March 17, 1973, Denver police officers confronted members of the Crusade for Justice in front of its offices (housed in an apartment building owned by Corky Gonzales). An explosion ensued, and shortly thereafter a member of the Crusade for Justice was killed by the police. This violent incident highlights the serious challenges that El Movimiento faced at the time, and it—unfortunately—helped color the perception that many Coloradans have of the Crusade for Justice and the Chicano Movement in general: as a time of extreme radicalism and bloody confrontations. Yet, the Crusade for Justice was a lot more than violent clashes with the police. It was an organization that improved life for Denverites and specifically the lives of those Chicanxs that it served for the better. Its gains benefited then current and future generations of Chicanxs, Latinxs, people of color, and the city in general. The Crusade for Justice was also an empowering movement that transformed the lives of countless Chicanxs in profound, nontangible ways. For many Chicanxs, the Crusade for Justice made them feel valued, seen, and heard—perhaps for the first time in their lives. The newly acquired pride and self-worth of these young Chicanxs inspired them to do greater things, like getting an education, having a career, and giving back to the community. Finally, the Crusade for Justice put Colorado on the map of the Chicano Movement. According to David Byron Young (2013, 10), "Denver was the navel of the

Chicano movement." Next to what was going on in California, Texas, and New Mexico in the 1960s–1970s (states with much larger Mexican American and Chicanx populations), Chicanxs in Colorado seemed like minor players within the greater Chicano Movement. The Crusade for Justice changed that perception, making Colorado an equal player on the mental landscape of El Movimiento. The actions and thoughts of Corky Gonzales and others in the Crusade for Justice transformed the nature of the Chicano Movement, gave it intellectual coherence, and blazed a new path forward. Unlike Chavez, Huerta, or Tijerina, Corky Gonzales imagined El Movimiento in theoretical terms as something greater than the local battles that were being fought throughout the American West. For Corky Gonzales, El Movimiento was more than an abstraction; it was literally a massive, regional undertaking toward a collective goal of Chicanx self-preservation, community empowerment, and cultural pride—a long-overdue coming together of sorts. It is in Colorado where El Movimiento truly evolved into a regional political movement, and for Chicanxs across the nation nothing would be the same ever again.

Rodolfo "Corky" Gonzales was your typical Mexican American kid from Denver. Raised by his immigrant father after his mother died, Corky Gonzales was keenly aware of his Mexican heritage and how his family struggled to make it in America. He tried to get a college education but had to drop out because he could not afford it. He then boxed for a few years (and was very good at it), retired from professional boxing, ran for office a few times (and lost), and owned a couple of local businesses (including a bail bonds agency) before settling into a government job for the city of Denver by the mid-1960s. These experiences exposed Gonzales to the inequities and abuses that Chicanxs faced in Denver: poverty, unemployment, a subpar educational experience, incarceration, and—particularly—police brutality. His restless nature did not sit well with a desk job, and after becoming increasingly frustrated with the establishment and getting involved in some personal tiffs, he was fired by Denver Mayor Tom Currigan in 1966 and became a full-time community activist. True to his nature, Gonzales had cautioned others about his intentions when he was hired by the city of Denver: "I'm an agitator and a troublemaker. That's my reputation and that's what I'm going to be. They didn't buy me when they put me into this job" (Denver Public Library 2009).

Gonzales finally discovered his calling when he founded the Crusade for Justice in 1966, a community organization devoted to helping Denver's Chicanx population. The Crusade for Justice had evolved from Los Voluntarios, a mainstream volunteer organization for the Spanish-speaking people of Colorado, of which Gonzales was a member. Los Voluntarios had been involved in highly visible cases of police brutality against members of Denver's Mexican American community—to no avail (no police officers were fired or convicted for their crimes) (E. Vigil 1998, 159, 193). By then, Gonzales had also become highly critical of Mayor Currigan, other city authorities, and the federal War on Poverty programs (which had led to his firing). He founded the Crusade for Justice as an outlet for his many struggles against the Anglo establishment, which eventually outgrew local issues in Denver and went on to include national and international issues. For example, Gonzales and the Crusade for Justice became allies of Reies López Tijerina in the struggle to recover the lands that Hispano farmers had lost at the hands of the US federal government. This alliance became even more controversial after the arrest of Tijerina and his followers after their armed takeover of the Tierra Amarilla (New Mexico) courthouse on June 5, 1967 (López Tijerina 2000, 92–93). Gonzales briefly visited northern New Mexico, where he took over the affairs of Tijerina's organization until the latter was freed on bond. Gonzales was also an outspoken critic of the Vietnam War. He criticized the unnecessary deaths of Chicanxs in a foreign conflict run by Wall Street while their needs back home remained unaddressed. Gonzales also traveled widely and met with national leadership figures such as Cesar Chavez (who visited Denver and was hosted by the Crusade) and Dr. Martin Luther King Jr. (eventually joining Dr. King's Poor People's March on Washington in 1968) and rubbed elbows with many of the most well-known 1960s human rights and radical political activists from around the nation (Gómez-Quiñones and Vásquez 2014, 117–118). Denver's Anglo press struggled to reconcile the image of the local boxing legend with that of the militant antiestablishment figure. Once idolized by sports columnists who saw in the young fighter the embodiment of American ideals, Gonzales was eventually demonized as an agitator when his ideals challenged the Anglo status quo (T. Romero 2004b).

Gonzales quickly became more than a local nuisance who spoke embarrassing truths to power. His growing political stature and radical antiestablishment views raised serious concerns by the Federal Bureau of Investigation (FBI), which began surveilling him and documenting the activities of the Crusade for Justice (Federal Bureau of Investigation 1968). His racial militancy even caught the attention of FBI Director J. Edgar Hoover himself, who had the Crusade and other "leftist" movements in his sights, with plans to undermine them as early as 1968 (Vargas 2017, 317). For the FBI, Gonzales and the other leaders of the Chicano Movement were dangerous radicals who posed a threat to the status quo, particularly in the context of the Cold War and the Cuban Revolution.[22] The FBI and other government agencies saw the hand of communist infiltrators and agitators behind these ethnic mobilizations, whose intent—the government deducted—was to sow disunity in American society and destabilize it from within (E. Vigil 1999).[23]

The Crusade for Justice took the fight against police brutality in Denver to a new level. Corky Gonzales—unlike Cesar Chavez—relished his role as a disruptor of the Anglo status quo and criticized both political parties (Democrats and Republicans) alike. His confrontational style led him to organize street protests that would turn into political rallies, and sometimes clashes with the police, as Gonzales called on his followers and Chicanxs in general to fight back against the establishment. The deaths and beatings of Chicanxs at the hands of what Gonzales described as a racist police force protected by a corrupt establishment sparked numerous protests, and calls for investigations and the firing of police officers and their supervisors. Denver's Anglo establishment had never dealt in the past with an empowered community of color that demanded accountability from its police force. Corky Gonzales changed that dynamic. His reluctance to back down from a fight and his proclivity to attack the sacred cows of the Anglo establishment (like the mayor) in personal terms certainly irked Denver authorities, who were not used to such attacks and considered Corky Gonzales and his Chicanxs militants as troublemakers who were beneath them. But it was Gonzales's incendiary rhetoric that scared authorities the most, as when he unambiguously stated at a public forum with the police (in support of the angry words of a Crusade member): "If it takes retaliation and violence to gain justice and equality, that's what is going to be" (E. Vigil 1999, 49). Denver's Chicanxs were done talking. They demanded action—or else—a scary prospect for the authorities.

By the mid-1960s, Gonzales's thoughts regarding the place of Chicanxs in American society had fully developed into a comprehensive worldview, and he turned to poetry to convey his innermost feelings on Chicanx identity to a community that he saw as lacking direction. His epic poem *Yo soy Joaquín* (*I am Joaquín*) describes the existential paradox of the Mexican American / Chicanx trapped between two cultures (and belonging to neither one), while being mercilessly exploited by Anglo society. Gonzales wastes no time in getting to the heart of the matter in the first few lines of the poem, when he proclaims (1967):

> Yo soy Joaquín,
> perdido en un mundo de confusión:
> I am Joaquín, lost in a world of confusion,
> caught up in the whirl of a gringo society,
> confused by the rules, scorned by attitudes,
> suppressed by manipulation, and destroyed by modern society.

Despite the unbearable oppression, Gonzales makes the case throughout his poem that Chicanxs should be proud of who they are, their heritage, and their potential. He details how Chicanxs are the descendants of Indigenous rebels who resisted Spanish colonialism, heroic nineteenth-century Mexicans who crafted a new nation, and modern revolutionary leaders who fought for social equality. Contrary to the condescending messages emanating from Anglo society regarding the presumed inferiority of Mexicans (and Mexico), Chicanxs have nothing to be ashamed of. Theirs is a beautiful and proud history too, and one to match the likes of George Washington and the Anglo Founding Fathers. Finally, *Yo soy Joaquín* is a clarion call for action. Armed with this historical knowledge and secure in their identity, Chicanxs must empower themselves, confront their oppressors (the Anglo establishment), and claim their rightful place in American society (Gonzales 1967):

> I am Joaquín.
> The odds are great
> But my spirit is strong,
> My faith unbreakable,
> My blood is pure.

I am Aztec prince and Christian Christ.
I SHALL ENDURE!
I WILL ENDURE!

Yo soy Joaquín became an instant classic of El Movimiento and inspired countless Chicanxs across the nation to come to terms with their hybrid identity, and to demand change from a complacent, indolent Anglo establishment that not only exploited them, but belittled them too. The poem was widely reproduced, read publicly, cited in rousing speeches, and even turned into a play. And the fact that it was penned not by a scholar but by an ordinary Chicanx from Denver, a former boxer turned community organizer, made it more relatable to thousands of Chicanx youth who faced the same lack of options to make it in Anglo society as a young "Mexican" by the name of Rodolfo Gonzales once did. For these Chicanx youth, Corky nailed it. Corky spoke to them, they related to him, and he inspired them into action. If Cesar Chavez (a mild-mannered, Christ-like figure) was the soul of the Chicano Movement, and Reies López Tijerina (aka "El Tigre"—"The Tiger") was its hardened fists fighting back against the Anglo establishment, Corky Gonzales became its fiery, beating heart, pumping fresh, oxygenated blood (in the form of Chicanx youth) into radical action. Corky's vision of Chicanxs was unifying and, above all, inspirational.

In 1969, the first Chicano Youth Liberation Conference was held in Denver, hosted by the Crusade for Justice, which had been promoting itself as the vanguard organization of the Chicano Movement (Muñoz 1989, 75). It was well attended by Chicanx youth from all over the United States, as well as representatives from other communities of color, with more than 1,500 youth from over 100 organizations in attendance (Navarro 2000, 87). The conference's highlight was the proclamation of "El Plan Espiritual de Aztlán" (Spiritual Plan of Aztlán), a nationalist call to action penned by Gonzales, with a preamble by California Chicano poet Alberto "Alurista" Urista ("Alurista" 2019). The plan emphasized the racially mixed, mestizo character of Chicanxs and Latin Americans in general, with references to a "Mestizo Nation" and a "Bronze Continent" who were the rightful owners of the land—in stark contrast to the "brutal Gringo" and "foreign Europeans" (E. Vigil 1999, 97–98). That language reflected the foundational myths and racial policies of several Latin American countries (but mainly Mexico), who sought to forge national unity in their heterogenous societies by rallying their citizens around the idea of a mestizo melting pot. The "Bronze People" imagery specifically evoked Mexico's former Secretary of Education José Vasconcelos's writings about Latin Americans becoming a "fifth race"—which Vasconcelos labeled *la raza cósmica* (i.e., "the cosmic race") (Telles 2014, chap. 2). Moreover, the plan portrayed Chicanxs and Latinxs (and their culture) as humanists vis-à-vis the greedy capitalist Anglos (Muñoz 1989, 77), echoing the arguments of Uruguayan writer José Enrique Rodó and a whole generation of Latin American intellectuals who read his masterpiece *Ariel* (Rodó 1988) and used it to launch a moral salvo against the profit-driven societies of western Europe and North America. Even the plan's concluding sentence—"Por la raza todo, fuera de la raza nada" (For the people, everything, beyond the people, nothing)—echoed Fidel Castro's oft-quoted dictum "Dentro de la Revolución todo, contra la Revolución nada" (Within the Revolution everything, against the Revolution nothing), a well-known slogan among the radical militants of the 1960s–1970s (Castro 2016, 87).

Besides its flowery preamble, the plan concluded that "social, economic, cultural, and political independence is the only path towards total liberation from oppression, exploitation, and racism" ("El Plan Espiritual de Aztlán" 1969). Yet, besides a general call for unity; for Chicanxs to assert control over the economy, education, and institutions; and for the promotion of Chicanx self-defense and cultural values, the plan was short on details. Its main goals revolved around nationalism, calling for "a free and autonomous nation, culturally, socially, economically, and politically," and at the very end, a battle cry: "Liberation!" ("El Plan Espiritual de Aztlán" 1969). Nationalism was promoted as the great unifier of the Chicanx people—a feeling so powerful that it could transcend the major cleavages (such as class) that divided them (E. Vigil 1999, 100). Unrealistic goals and generalities aside, the plan sought to define Chicanxs as a nation; that is, a people with defined cultural traits, a shared history, and a future in common—much like Benedict Anderson's "imaged community" (2006, 6). The only element missing for Chicanxs to truly become a nation was sovereignty, thus Gonzales's call for Chicanxs to assert control over all aspects of their lives. It was obvious to all that achieving the goals of the plan—particularly those concerning economic and political autonomy—was not practical. Chicanxs were divided regarding how far to take the movement, the Mexican American community (and particularly older folks) were not onboard with the plan, and it faced the opposition (and hostility) of Anglo society.[24] If anything, the Plan was aspirational and—most important—inspirational, and it represented a clean break with the Mexican American assimilationist tactics of the past (Gómez-Quiñones and Vásquez 2014, 191). Despite the paranoid scenarios that the FBI had developed around the threat presented by Gonzales and the Crusade for Justice, Chicanxs were in no position to imperil US national security. There would not be a campaign of terror followed by a war of national liberation, the United States would not be dismembered into separate ethnic nations, and there would not be a communist takeover.[25] Corky Gonzales simply wanted Chicanxs to believe in something greater than themselves, to dream of alternative futures, and to muster those nationalist feelings as fuel for political action (Navarro 2000, 83). His merit lay in the fact that he dared to go big. Unlike other leaders of the Chicano Movement, Corky Gonzales thought in national—and nationalist—terms. Although his political activism was limited in its goals to local issues, his political thinking extended well beyond Colorado to imagine a sovereign Chicanx nation, free of Anglo exploitation and interference. Corky Gonzales was—more than any other major leader—the ideological pillar of the Chicano Movement.

The formation of La Raza Unida Party (LRUP) in 1970 was an attempt to turn some of these lofty ideals into reality—albeit the goals were more modest and short term in light of the significant, real-life political challenges that Chicanx activists faced. La Raza Unida Party could be best described as "a state-centered party that made the disparities between Mexican-Americans and Anglos the focal point of its platform" (Márquez and Espino 2010, 292), although some of its members were quick to point out that LRUP was not a political party—at least not in the traditional sense (Keller Montez and Aleman 1973, 6). Described as a "feeling...a way of life," LRUP sought to restore a traditional Chicanx lifestyle disrupted by Anglo society (Alire 1972). Unlike most Anglo voters, Mexican Americans still represented a distinct ethnic group over a hundred years after the war with Mexico, a result of almost-constant migration and cultural replenishment from Mexico (Jiménez 2010), coupled with widespread segregationist practices toward people of color throughout the American West. Thus, the activists of the Chicano Movement found fertile ground for the creation of an alternative political party that appealed to this particular ethnic constituency. Although the credit for the creation of LRUP goes to José Angel Gutiérrez and other Chicanx political activists from Texas, Corky Gonzales was one of its founding leaders too.[26]

From the start, significant schisms developed over regional, strategic, and personality differences among LRUP leaders. Although LRUP eventually aimed to become a movement with national influence, its organization resided mainly at a grassroots level, particularly in states outside of Texas. For Chicanx activists in Colorado, this strategy was part of a deliberate choice to keep the party close to the people and not to emulate the model of mainstream Anglo parties. Chicanx militants in Colorado argued that LRUP was heading in the wrong direction by following a conventional organizational and campaigning model, and they even accused Gutiérrez of being a sellout and trying to impose his will over party members outside of Texas (*El Gallo* 1974). But these regional, ideological, and strategic differences also paralleled (and sometimes masked) the main cleavage in the party: the strong personalities and diverging worldviews of Corky Gonzales and José Angel Gutiérrez over the direction of the Chicano Movement in general and LRUP in particular. Whereas both were key leaders of the Chicano Movement, Gonzales and his followers saw themselves as the pure embodiment of the highest ideals of Chicanismo (i.e., Chicanx nationalism) and promoted a "no-compromise" position, while Gutiérrez and his followers embraced a more pragmatic approach to politics (I. García 1989, 107–109). According to Amando Navarro (2000, 84), "A doctrinaire purity permeated Gonzales's thinking as well as that of CJ's [Crusade for Justice's] secondary leadership and membership." Moreover, Colorado's Chicanxs accused those in Texas of betraying the principles of El Movimiento and of belittling them and treating them as colonial subjects of the Texas LRUP (*El Gallo* 1974). These accusations (and counteraccusations) would lead to splits within LRUP, with each regional (i.e., state) chapter acting on its own. But most important, Gonzales and Gutiérrez were highly charismatic leaders with their own regional constituencies who rarely gave ground or compromised. Simply put, there was no room for both men in a national Chicanx political party. The personality clashes came to a head during the 1972 convention of La Raza Unida Party in El Paso, Texas. There, Gutiérrez easily outmaneuvered a confident Gonzales to become LRUP's national chairman. Whereas by then Gonzales was El Movimiento's most charismatic leader, Gutiérrez and his cadres were effective lobbyists who had won local elections (I. García 1989, 115). Gonzales returned to Colorado defeated, although he still claimed to be the moral leader of the Chicano Movement.

The debates over personality differences, nonaligned strategic choices, and the particular cultural ethos of regional LRUP chapters spilled out into the community by way of public meetings, rallies, and newspapers articles, thus giving the voting public the impression of a party in disarray and its leaders fighting for personal power, rather than for the people. For example, Al Gurule, the party's candidate for governor of Colorado in 1970, declared that the Democratic Party was LRUP's "chief enemy" and called Hispanics who ran on the Democratic ticket "coconuts—brown on the outside but white on the inside" (i.e., Brown people defending white interests) (B. Martinez 1970). Such incendiary rhetoric—popular with LRUP's young base—did not sit well with the moderate and conservative sectors of Colorado's Mexican American and Hispano community. As a result, LRUP achieved some minor victories in south Texas but fared poorly elsewhere, particularly in Colorado where not a single statewide LRUP candidate gathered more than 5% of the vote—far less than the required 10% to gain official recognition (Navarro 2000, 94). The LRUP faithful tried to spin its poor showing by taking the high moral ground and arguing that the party was winning the hearts of the Chicanx people by defending their real interests, but those appeals only convinced the hardcore militants (Gabriel Jose 1972). Most Mexican Americans and Chicanxs eventually rallied back to the Democratic Party.

It is incredibly difficult to break up the partisan stranglehold of the US two-party system, plus there are major limitations to what ethnicity-based political movements can achieve. The main problem with LRUP was that it depended on a critical mass of Chicanxs voting for its candidates, something that it could only achieve in local races in places with a large Chicanx community that could overwhelm the Anglo vote. Moreover, alliances were out of the question in states like Colorado. According to Corky Gonzales himself: "No party controlled by Gringos will ride on our back" (*El Gallo* 1974, 6). Outside of those ethnic enclaves, and without alliances with other political parties, LRUP had a hard time convincing non-Chicanx constituencies (including other communities of color, such as African Americans) to vote for its candidates. In places like Colorado, where Latinxs were in the minority in most urban areas, and felt historically disempowered and disenfranchised as a community, and where the LRUP decided to pursue its own independent path rather than seek alliances with the Democrats, the results were dismal. Finally, the destiny of LRUP in Colorado was tied to that of the Crusade for Justice—the former being an extension of the latter. As the Crusade for Justice and its leader Corky Gonzales became embroiled in bitter struggles with the authorities, LRUP suffered as a result. The party was built around Corky's charisma, and when Corky's popularity declined, so did LRUP's star (Navarro 2000, 106). Colorado's LRUP thus remained in the realm of unfulfilled aspirational goals, rather than a concrete reality. Its main goal was "arousing anger among Chicanxs, not winning elections or even influencing legislation" (I. García 1989, 96). Although it was described by Chicanx militants as a powerful, inspiring organization, it never got off the ground.[27]

On the one hand, the Chicano Youth Liberation Conference and the founding of La Raza Unida Party were major successes for Corky Gonzales and the Crusade for Justice. Both extended their regional reach and made of Gonzales a national leader, while achieving his stated goal of raising the consciousness of Chicanxs across the nation and getting groups of young Chicanx to organize and coordinate actions with each other (Muñoz 1989, 78). On the other hand, the themes of the conference, its radical attendees from all over the United States, their incendiary speeches, and the resulting Plan Espiritual de Aztlán attracted the attention of local and federal authorities. Brimming with confidence after the success of the Chicano Youth Liberation Conference, Corky Gonzales committed himself to more radical causes at the national level, including support for the American Indian Movement (AIM) and the armed occupation of Wounded Knee (South Dakota) carried out by Oglala Lakota people and AIM militants that began on February 27, 1973. The cooperation and seeming coordination between Chicanx and AIM activists alarmed FBI agents, who reported on a march in Denver in support of the takeover on March 6, 1973. According to an FBI report, 400–500 protestors gathered as speakers called for the "unity of Chicanos and Indians against the common oppressor" (E. Vigil 1999, 205). If Corky Gonzales had been a local problem beforehand, he now represented a potential threat at the national level. Surveillance and concerns by the FBI would only increase as Gonzales became a sought-after speaker and ally of radical minority leaders and their causes.

March 17, 1973, marked the beginning of the end. Shortly after midnight, a confrontation between Denver police officers and young Chicanx militants ensued in front of the Crusade for Justice headquarters (which by then included a small apartment building with tenants). The confusing incident led to several arrests, shots being fired, police officers and Chicanxs getting injured, the death of Crusade activist Luis "Junior" Martinez at the hands of the police, and a suspicious explosion that destroyed one of the apartments (Girón 2011, 284). The police report blamed Chicanx militants, who were accused of shooting at the police and storing explosives in one of the apartments, leading to the explosion ("Felony Assault Charges Filed" 1973). The Crusade leadership countered these accusations by arguing that police officers had started the violence that led to the melee and that it was the authorities who had fired an explosive device at the Crusade apartments (Leonard and Noel 1990, 386–387). As usual, the local press reproduced the official police story practically verbatim, while the Chicanx community trusted the word of their own members (E. Vigil 1999, chap. 11).

This violent incident and its legal repercussions (arrests, trials, jail time) represented major blows for the Crusade for Justice. For Chicanx activists, it seemed as if the authorities had switched from harassing militants and Chicanxs in general, to pursuing a strategy of carrying out a frontal attack on the Crusade for Justice and what it stood for. Not surprisingly, some members and the Chicanx public left the Crusade for Justice and stayed away from its events. Even its marquee program, Escuela Tlatelolco, a school for Chicanx children with a culturally appropriate curriculum, saw its enrollment diminish (E. Vigil 1999, 231).[28] The periodic arrests and indictments of Chicanx activists on various charges deflated the zeal of Crusade members and slowed down the Chicano Movement's momentum. For example, the charges against Alberto Mares (accused of bank robbery) and John Haro (accused of possessing explosives), both well-known members of the Crusade for Justice, cast an unflattering light on the Crusade (E. Vigil 1999, chaps. 14, 16). The 1973 shooting of Richard Castro, a moderate Mexican American politician, by a member of the Crusade, followed by a crude warning by *El Gallo* newspaper (published by the Crusade for Justice), reinforced the view in the public's mind of the Crusade as a radical and dangerous organization (Leonard and Noel 1990, 397). Years of unrelenting harassment, negative press coverage, legal prosecution, tactical errors, constant confrontation with the Anglo establishment, over-the-top pronouncements, and violent deaths took their toll on Corky Gonzales and the Crusade for Justice. By the late 1970s, the organization was in steep decline, a shadow of its former self.

By the 1980s, as President Ronald Reagan led a national conservative backlash (Dallek 1999), the Chicano Movement was losing steam. The formerly young militants of the 1970s had turned into adults, formed families, and moved on with their lives. Personal and tactical divisions had hampered Chicanx unity, and Corky Gonzales's fiery personality and his zealousness in exerting control over every aspect of the Crusade for Justice (which was, after all, *his* personal pet project) did not help, either. Moderate Latinxs bristled at the Crusade's tactics and rejected its anti-Vietnam War rhetoric, which they saw as unpatriotic and casting a suspicious light on people long considered "outsiders" by Anglo society (Leonard and Noel 1990, 396). For Mexican Americans bent on assimilation, Corky's nationalism, his criticism of the US political establishment, and his call to oppose the war effort did not help their cause (Navarro 2000, chap. 4). Issues of machismo also permeated the Crusade for Justice in particular and the Chicano Movement in general, including on college campuses (Facio 2011; "La Chicana: Recognize Her for What She Is" 1975). Women complained about being relegated to secondary roles as supporters of the movement, rather than being given equal standing as leaders too (Vargas 2017, 318). Moreover, the Crusade's successful model "could not be emulated outside of Denver," relegating it to the city despite the national appeal of its message (Gómez-Quiñones and Vásquez 2014, 116). Corky was the Crusade, and the Crusade was Corky's, who was its *jefe* (Navarro 2000, 83); and one could seemingly not exist without the other.

Most important, the national mood had changed. Radical change was not a priority anymore for the aging Baby Boomers and for the generation that followed them (Generation X), and as a result, the nation's politics became more conservative. Americans were exhausted by the social convulsion and political polarization of the 1960s, the national trauma of the Vietnam War, the assassinations of major political figures like Martin Luther King Jr. and Robert F. Kennedy, and the economic woes of the late 1970s, and they simply desired a return to normalcy—epitomized by Ronald Reagan's 1984 presidential campaign ad "It's Morning Again in America" (New-York Historical Society 2020). Still, Corky Gonzales turned the Chicano Movement into a regional force to be reckoned with by reshaping it into a nationalist cause. Moreover, his militancy redefined Anglo-Chicanx relations in Denver and throughout the state. Without a doubt, the political ascent of Corky Gonzales and the Crusade for Justice represented a watershed moment for Colorado's Chicano Movement.

While it is apt to highlight Corky Gonzales's significant contributions to Colorado's Chicano Movement, he was but one of many leaders and participants of El Movimiento in Colorado. There were other Chicanx leaders who were less publicly visible than Gonzales but nonetheless quite influential on the direction of the movement in the state. Likewise, the participation of hundreds of mostly anonymous activists created a critical mass of militants that gave Colorado's Chicano Movement a powerful momentum, enabling it to challenge the Anglo establishment. Some of those cases are examined in the sections that follow.

The Murder of Ricardo Falcón

On August 30, 1972, Ricardo Falcón, a Chicano activist from Colorado, was on his way to El Paso, Texas, where he was due to attend the first national convention of La Raza Unida Party. When the car he was traveling in overheated, Falcón and his companions stopped at a gas station in Orogrande, a small town in southern New Mexico, less than an hour away from their destination. While Falcón and his friends sprayed water on the car's hot radiator, a discussion ensued with the gas station owner, Perry Brunson, who accused them of wasting water and demanded payment for it. The heated discussion turned physical, and Brunson shot Falcón, who died on the spot. Brunson, a white supremacist who belonged to a racist right-wing party, argued that he shot Falcón in self-defense, and he was eventually acquitted of manslaughter charges by an all-white jury in nearby Alamogordo (a conservative military outpost).

Falcón was a well-known Chicano activist in Colorado, where he helped found UMAS at the University of Colorado Boulder (CU Boulder) campus. He participated in marches with the Crusade for Justice, the United Farm Workers (UFW) union, and the American GI Forum ("Falcon Gave His Life For La Gente" 1977). Falcón was also former director of the United Mexican American Students Equal Opportunity Program (UMAS-EOP) at CU Boulder, an advocate for the rights and education of incarcerated Chicanxs, and—at the time of his death—a candidate for Weld County sheriff ("Ricardo Falcon Presented by Priscilla Falcon" 2022). He was such a charismatic leader that CU Boulder President Frederick P. Thieme once remarked about him (in a concerned tone) that "Falcón is looked up to by the Chicanos as a 'Jesus.'" Pres. Thieme—in an interview with the FBI—further told federal law enforcement agents that he was worried that "certain persons have gained control of UMAS and have utilized it as a political organization attempting to gain control of the university and operations of the federal government" (Juan Espinosa 2019a, 4). Thieme's unfounded and wildly exaggerated concerns led him to fire Falcón from the program and try to undermine UMAS, describing the organization as a "junior mafia."

The fact that the murder of Ricardo Falcón went unpunished underscored the belief that Chicanxs were still second-class citizens in the American West—Brown bodies with no rights that an Anglo had to respect. Brunson's acquittal was evidence that little had changed since the days when Anglo vigilantes or Texas Rangers could kill "Mexicans" (oftentimes US citizens of Mexican ancestry) with impunity: They would simply not be charged after a hurried investigation by the authorities or a sympathetic, racially prejudiced Anglo jury would quickly acquit them of all charges (Muñoz Martinez 2018). Seemingly, all that it took for a Chicanx life to be in peril was a wrong turn, a traffic stop, or a disagreement with an armed Anglo. That is how precarious Chicanx lives felt (and still feel[29]). Chicanx youth, and their parents, lived in constant fear—ironically, on the land that their ancestors had occupied for generations. An op-ed, written by CU Boulder students shortly after Falcón's murder, put it succinctly (John Espinosa and Moore 1972):

Until the state of mind which drives men like Brunson is changed, all Chicanos have reason to live in fear.

Brunson has reminded us who we are—just Mexicans. Sometimes we forget and find ourselves believing we are Americans with all of the rights of citizens. In the eyes of the racists we are nothing, our struggle has only begun.

Que viva la Raza y que viva Ricardo Falcon!

The Kiko Martínez Case

Francisco E. Martínez, widely known by his nickname "Kiko," was one of the pillars of Colorado's Chicano Movement. Born in Alamosa, in the San Luis Valley, Kiko became a lawyer and a thorn on the side of the establishment because of his defense of Chicanx activists and prisoners of color, going as far as suing the state's penitentiary system for gross violations of the inmates' civil and human rights. He also took on cases of police brutality against Chicanxs and was part of the legal team sent by the Mexican American Legal Defense and Education Fund (MALDEF) to investigate the murder of Colorado Chicanx activist Ricardo Falcón in southern New Mexico in 1972 (Nieto 2011, 367). Kiko was also a militant in the Chicano Movement who participated in local and national meetings, marches, and protests in support of El Movimiento and other causes. After a police raid on the building owned by the Crusade for Justice, Denver Police alleged that it had found and deactivated explosives throughout the city, and in October 1973 Kiko was indicted on charges of mailing explosive packages. Kiko evaded the authorities and fled to Mexico, where he spent the next seven years—though the Denver mainstream media concocted the story that he had fled to Cuba, which was typical of individuals with communist sympathies at the time (Barrera 2004, 126–128). In 1980, Kiko was arrested in Nogales, Arizona, while attempting to reenter the United States under an assumed name. His arrest led to a lengthy legal process that ended in mistrials, charges being dropped for lack of evidence, and just one guilty verdict: for lying to a customs officer when he crossed the border into the United States. By then, Kiko Martínez had spent a decade of his life on the run or fighting trumped-up charges in court. The government had raided his home, interrogated his family and friends, and put him through hell as part of a personal vendetta designed to crush him and intimidate others in the Chicano Movement. Even the courts concurred that the federal government had acted with vindictiveness in his case (E. Martínez 1982).

Unfortunately, Martinez's legal saga did not end with his exoneration. Kiko Martinez continued to be harassed by the authorities for years after winning his freedom, and after the 9/11 terrorist attacks he was placed on a watch list known as the Violent Gang and Terrorist Organization File due to his previous indictments on explosives charges. Afterward, even minor traffic stops prompted lengthy interrogations from law enforcement officers until—hours after being detained—Martinez would be set free. Kiko Martinez was also placed on a "no fly" list, which prevented him from boarding planes (Lydersen 2007). Tired of the periodic harassment, Martinez decided to sue the federal authorities over these clear violations of his civil rights, and he won settlements in all cases ("Alamosa Activist Settles U.S. Suit over Traffic Stops" 2007; "Colo. Man Wins Watch List Suit" 2007).

As is often the case with incidents related to the Chicano Movement, two stories emerge from Kiko's saga. The first one is that of a terrorist sought by the FBI; the other one is that of a Chicanx community activist the government wanted to put away for good. Character assassination tactics were routinely employed by local newspapers that echoed the government's position, and *The Denver Post* even went as far as offering an additional $2,500 reward for Martinez's capture when the latter was on the run from the authorities (E. Martínez 1982, 93). Despite the lack of evidence, Anglo public opinion had no qualms in passing judgment on Kiko Martínez a priori. But for the Chicanx community, Kiko Martinez was one of them: persecuted, hunted down, and stripped of his humanity, like so many Chicanxs before him. Martinez had to run away to avoid capture by the authorities or—even worse—murder for being considered "armed and dangerous" and "resisting arrest"—a familiar ending for many fugitives in the Chicanx community. Kiko Martinez paid a steep price for his activism, but in the end he prevailed. He escaped with his life, won in federal court, and to this day he remains a powerful symbol of the El Movimiento in Colorado.

The Chicano Student Movement in Colorado

Although Corky Gonzales is considered the public face of the Chicano Movement in Colorado, dozens of Chicanx college students and their allies grabbed the headlines, too. They—like scores of young people around the nation—opposed the Vietnam War, supported women's rights, and joined the Chicano Movement to demand their share of the American Dream. Their struggle, sometimes in obscurity, but often mischaracterized by society at large, infused the Chicano Movement with fresh blood and ideas, and nurtured a new generation of up-and-coming leaders who were to lead their communities for decades to come. Just like the history of the Vietnam War cannot be written without mentioning the massive antiwar protests on college campuses across the nation, the history of the Chicano Movement is also incomplete without mentioning the mobilization of thousands of high school and college students who defied the authorities (and sometimes their parents) to claim what was rightfully theirs: equality and recognition in American society.

As more Chicanxs moved to urban areas around the World War II period, and as more of them joined the ranks of the urban working and middle classes, the Baby Boomer generation that came of age in the 1960s–1970s represented the first large-scale cohort of Chicanxs to go to college in the United States (including in Colorado) (Arce 1976). As was the case elsewhere around the American West, these Chicanx students soon found out that being accepted into college did not translate into feeling welcomed on campus. Quite the opposite, Chicanx college students at institutions like CU Boulder felt isolated, outnumbered, and unwanted (McIntosh 2016, 225–230). Moreover, they faced a traditional "canon" of courses that did not reflect their historical experience and the culture they came from. There were no Chicano studies courses and few Chicanxs who taught classes or worked in the administration. Unlike their Anglo classmates, Chicanxs felt utterly unrepresented at CU Boulder. In line with developments on other college campuses nationwide, Chicanx students began mobilizing. In 1969, the United Mexican American Students organization was founded at the CU Boulder campus to organize Chicanx students, demand the creation of a Chicano studies program, and increase

FIGURE 3.1. UMAS logo. Source: United Mexican American Students Papers (CSUP-UMAS), Colorado Chicano Movement Archives, Colorado State University Pueblo.

the recruitment of Chicanx students and faculty (Juan Espinosa 2019a, 4) (see figure 3.1). UMAS also published its own student newspaper: *El Diario de la Gente* (The People's Daily). The efforts of UMAS initially paid off with the establishment of the Chicano Studies Program in 1969 and the Equal Opportunity Program (UMAS-EOP) in 1972, but they soon stalled. By the spring of 1974, after waiting for months for their financial aid and dissatisfied with the UMAS-EOP administrators, Chicanx students took direct action ("Occupation at TB-1" 1974). From May 13 to May 31, 1974, a group of Chicanx students occupied Temporary Building #1 (TB-1) on the CU Boulder campus to demand their financial aid and the resignation of UMAS-EOP Director Joe Franco and Assistant Director Paul Acosta. Eventually, university administrators negotiated with the occupiers, leading to the resignation of Franco and Acosta, and an amnesty for those involved in the takeover (J. Vigil 1974).

But UMAS's victory was marred by the death of six Chicanx activists off campus. On May 27, 1974, an explosion destroyed a car in Chautauqua Park, Boulder, killing two activists (Reyes Martínez and Una Jaakola) and a CU Boulder UMAS student (Neva Romero). On May 29, 1974, another car explosion killed three Chicanx activists (Florencio "Freddy" Granado, Heriberto Terán, and Francisco Dougherty) and injured a fourth (Antonio Alcantar), who lost a leg and suffered serious burns and was maimed for life. The police argued that the victims were assembling bombs in their cars when the devices detonated. The FBI and a grand jury investigated the incidents, but no one was ever charged in their deaths. In a forty-eight-hour timespan, six Chicanx activists and their allies (known thereafter as "Los Seis de Boulder") had died near campus under mysterious circumstances ("Car Bombings Claim 6 Lives" 1974)—a development that shook the Chicano Movement in Colorado to its core. Had their deaths been accidental, as the authorities claimed? Had they been set up by a traitor working for the police? Or had they been murdered with explosive devices planted in their cars by establishment forces, acting under orders or on their own, who sought to crush the Chicano Movement at a time of rising activism? Half a century after these tragic events, it is unlikely that the truth will ever be known, but different versions of it still fall neatly within ethnic lines. For conservative Anglo Coloradans, the official version of clumsy, amateurish bomb makers who killed themselves while trying to put together explosive devices while sitting in a car appealed to long-held stereotypes of Chicanxs as prone to violence but not very intelligent.[30] Front Range newspapers, TV stations, and other mainstream media reproduced the official version of events, propagating it widely, and it was accepted by the Anglo public without much questioning (Woodcock and Bowie 2019). Any suggestions of foul play by the authorities were dismissed as paranoid conspiracy theories without any grounds.

For the Chicanx community, the truth lay elsewhere. For six Chicanx activists to die in a similar fashion in two separate incidents in less than forty-eight hours was more than an unfortunate coincidence (Crusade for Justice 1974). The activists had no prior history of being involved in violent acts and had no training in explosives; no one could determine how they acquired the explosives that ultimately killed them. Quite the opposite, Los Seis were either model students or community activists who had distinguished themselves for their struggle in favor of the Chicanx community. They had been sometimes confrontational—as was common at the time—but never violent, neither in word nor in deed. Thus, the official version provided by the authorities made no sense to the Chicanx community, particularly in light of a troubling history of decades of racial profiling; police brutality against Chicanxs; arrests under false or trumped-up charges; and sloppy, careless investigations when Chicanxs were the victims of a crime ("DA Said Lax on Police Beatings"). The two car bombings were eerily similar, raising suspicions of a murder conspiracy among the Chicanx community. According to this alternative theory, a third party bent on dismantling the student movement could have planted the bombs in the cars, targeting then current and former students known for their activism ("Car Bombings Claim 6 Lives" 1974). Historical distrust of the police only begets more distrust, and the death of Los Seis marked a low point in relations between Colorado's Chicanx community and the Anglo establishment. The eventual involvement of federal law enforcement in the criminal investigation did not make things better, particularly at a time when revelations of the "dirty tricks" used by US federal authorities against war dissenters, civil rights leaders, and other protestors became public (Church Committee 1976).

For most Chicanxs, the details of the story just did not add up. Rather, it seemed like Los Seis had been set up by the authorities or murdered as a warning to others (Chicano Law Students, University of Colorado 1974). But by whom specifically? At that point, and given the lack of evidence, it was impossible to tell. However, that really did not matter as much as the fact that six young Chicanx activists were dead, and for the Chicanx community their deaths were both a widely felt tragedy and a stark reminder of the power of the Anglo establishment. The death of Los Seis de Boulder was seen as an act of war by the Chicano community; it was viewed as the most brutal reprisal on the part of the establishment in decades and one that had a chilling effect on Chicanx activists. Many Chicanxs—whether they were involved in the Chicano Movement or not—left CU Boulder or were brought home by parents who feared for their children's lives (Young 2015). The lack of a definitive explanation for the death of Los Seis de Boulder created uncertainty and stoked widespread fears among the Chicanx community that anyone could be at risk—but particularly young people.[31]

While CU Boulder was at the forefront of Chicanx activism among Front Range educational institutions, students at other college campuses mobilized as well. For example, at Colorado State University (CSU), Chicanx students founded the Mexican-American Committee for Equality (MACE) in the spring of 1969. Within a few months, MACE renamed and became an affiliated chapter of UMAS. On September 16, 1969,[32] CSU students affiliated with UMAS joined thousands of young Chicanxs across the nation in a massive walkout of junior high, high school, and college students (Ramos 1969). In Denver, more than 2,500 students marched. The activism of Chicanx college students (and their allies) in Colorado increased public awareness about their neglect by university administrators and would bring about concrete changes, including the admission of more students of color; the creation of programs to attract and retain minority students; the hiring of Chicanx faculty and staff; and the development of programs in Mexican American, Chicano, and race, ethnic, and women and gender studies. Colorado was becoming an increasingly diverse state, and soon college campuses across the state started reflecting that new reality—all thanks to the radical actions of the Chicano Movement.

Conclusion: No Longer Invisible

Latinxs in Colorado have been historically characterized by their invisibility. They were rendered invisible by a white majority that saw Latinxs as either relics of the past or foreign newcomers and treated them as racialized Others that did not belong here, in Anglo America. Colorado's Chicano Movement challenged this narrative in new and unprecedented ways, forcing a reckoning by the Anglo establishment, opening new spaces for Latinxs in Anglo society, and, most important, sparking conversations among Latinx communities regarding their place in the Centennial state. Colorado's Chicano Movement (symbolically tied to Rodolfo "Corky" Gonzales) had—besides its militant ethos—a strong ideological component that provided a powerful sense of autochthony to Chicanxs, imbuing them with ethnic pride and countering the alienating discourses stemming from Anglo society. In essence, Chicanxs turned the Anglo process of racialization on its head by proclaiming that yes, they were Brown people—and proud of it. The Chicano Movement by no means ended Anglo racial and ethnic prejudice regarding "Mexicans" or the stereotypes surrounding people of color, but instead confronted these deep-seated social ills in unprecedented ways. And as argued by Marc Rodriguez, it ultimately "created a framework for the expansion of rights and the expression of personhood in an increasingly multiracial, mixed-race North America" (2015, 165).

In Colorado, the Chicano Movement fought for most of the national goals of El Movimiento: civil rights, educational opportunities, equal treatment before the law, labor rights, historical land claims, political empowerment, and so forth. In addition, Colorado's Chicano Movement fought for something even more basic and primordial: recognition by the Anglo establishment. In a white state where its largest community of color was (alternatively) seen as "outsiders" or not seen at all, recognition was a significant first step toward the achievement of all the other goals of El Movimiento. According to David Gutiérrez (1993, 524), "ethnic Mexicans' awareness that they had been rendered insignificant as human beings in this manner has provided one of the major forces driving both their efforts to achieve full political rights in American society and their attempts to recapture and rewrite their own history." The Chicano Movement in Colorado shook the foundations of the Anglo establishment to such an extent that mainstream society had to recognize Chicanos on their own terms (D. Gutiérrez 1993, 531–534). Anglos were forced to publicly acknowledge the presence of Chicanxs in the state as Coloradans—no longer as "Mexicans," or euphemistically as "Spanish Americans" or "Mexican Americans," but as *Chicanos*, with all the political connotations and ideological ramifications of the term. Chicanxs were confrontational, militant, and unwavering in their demands, and Anglo society had to learn to live with that. Whether out of fear or respect, Chicanxs gained social and political standing in Colorado.

Colorado's Chicano Movement also forced open doors for those who came afterward (Allyn 2019a; Esquibel 2015, 21). Gains in labor rights, educational opportunities, and political recognition enabled late Baby Boomer and Generation X Chicanxs to climb up the social ladder. More Latinxs attended colleges and universities, started small businesses, and moved into the middle classes in the 1970s–1980s than ever before. Although large sectors of Colorado's Latinx community remained mired in poverty and lagged in socioeconomic achievements behind Anglos, progress was noticeable. The fear of a radical, militant, nationalist Chicano Movement bent on undermining the status quo also convinced Anglo politicians to work with moderate elements within the Latinx community. Not all Chicanxs, Mexican Americans, and other Latinxs embraced El Movimiento's radical politics, but they benefited from the backlash that it sparked among the Anglo establishment in states throughout the American West (Márquez and Espino 2010). Political elites in Denver and other cities along the Front Range realized the need to placate Latinx demands, lest they embrace the disruptive politics of Chicanx extremists. As a result, Front Range cities and counties devoted a larger share of their economic pie to their Latinx communities in the form of programs, schools, and jobs. Nowadays, Latinxs in Colorado are present at the table as recognized members of the political establishment—perhaps not to the extent that their numbers would warrant but well above and beyond their scant representation in the 1950s–1960s. Even current Latinx immigrants benefit from the spaces in American society that the Chicano Movement forced open half a century ago (M. Rodriguez 2015, 168–169).

However, I argue in hindsight that such achievements were to be expected. They were—after all—at the heart of the Chicano Movement's demands and had been part of the long-term goals of the Mexican American community for decades. If anything, the changes were long overdue but not surprising once they took place. Colorado's Chicanxs had the numbers, the confidence, and a national changing mood on their side. Were this examination to end here, Colorado's Chicano Movement would not be more or less remarkable than those social movements taking place elsewhere in the American West, where young Chicanx militants also forced the Anglo establishment to acknowledge their demands and effected major social changes in places like California and Texas. But in Colorado, El Movimiento went much further than that. The merit of Colorado's Chicano Movement lies in its boldness to dream big, to inspire Chicanxs nationally, and to dabble in the imagined community of Aztlán.

Corky Gonzales's poems, the 1969 Denver Youth Conference, and its "Plan Espiritual de Aztlán" transformed the nature of Colorado's Chicano Movement from a local endeavor to a national struggle. His emphasis on Chicano cultural nationalism provided Chicanxs with an ideal that they could rally around and a source of deep pride, while El Movimiento's militant ethos (I. García 1997, 92–99) caught the attention—for different reasons—of Chicanx youth, the older Mexican American generations, and the Anglo establishment. By going against prevailing ideas of assimilation in American society, Chicanxs in Colorado distinguished themselves from others in the Chicano Movement and placed El Movimiento alongside Third World national liberation struggles (albeit briefly). As unrealistic as Gonzales's goals of Chicanx self-determination were, the mere imagining of a Chicanx nation, free from Anglo encroachment, reflected a community coming of age, maturing enough to the point where it could see itself standing on its own and confident enough of its strength that it could—and would—reject the Anglo world. In Colorado, the Chicano Movement became the imagined nation of Aztlán—even if just for a short while—and Anglo America was put on notice.

In conclusion, Colorado's Chicano Movement was a multifaceted endeavor with clear local goals but broad national repercussions. Its symbolic leader, Rodolfo "Corky" Gonzales, was a shooting star that confronted the local Anglo establishment in unprecedented ways, achieved some victories, and ultimately faded out due to repression and the changing times. But he also inspired Chicanx youth to dream big, imagine a united Chicanx community, and consider the (very remote) possibility of making the nation of Aztlán into a reality. This national perspective added a unique element to Colorado's Chicano Movement that—despite its small numbers and geographical isolation in the interior Mountain West—positioned it ideologically at the forefront of El Movimiento. Colorado's Latinxs practically went from invisible followers to symbolic leaders and in doing so changed the tenor of the conversation regarding El Movimiento, its goals, and its possibilities. To be clear, Chicanxs in Colorado and elsewhere built on the achievements of preceding generations of Mexican American activists, and largely their immediate goals (e.g., school desegregation, civil rights, and socioeconomic opportunities) overlapped those of their elders, but the unexpected, strident militancy of the Chicano Movement was a rude awakening for the Anglo establishment. Anglo America (both locally and nationally) had no choice but to confront this new reality of empowered Chicanxs, acknowledge it, and pursue new strategies to deal with it. Those strategies ranged from repression to accommodation, but for the first time since the end of the United States war against Mexico in 1848, the Mexican-origin communities of the American West were the ones making (their own) history, while the Anglo establishment just reacted. No longer seen as a passive, dormant community by the late 1960s, Colorado's Chicanxs led the charge as they called on Chicanxs across the nation to unite under a common ethnic banner, regardless of class, regional, or ancestral differences. The unprecedented nature of this bold challenge to the Anglo establishment placed Colorado under the national spotlight and finally gave political visibility and sociocultural prominence to a formerly excluded people that had been "unseen" for well over a century. As pointed out by Chicana activist Priscilla Falcón: "The state underestimates the power of history, and history rarely stays put in a forgotten, disconnected past—and that is the door that we have opened today" (Freedom Archives 2017).[33]

4

THE WESTERN SLOPE

NAFTA's Legacy

One of the intrinsic qualities of racial prejudice in the twenty-first century is that as much as you know that it still exists and it is out there, it never fails to shock you when you see it manifested.* And that is exactly what happened to me one morning at a busy rest stop in Colorado's Western Slope. There it was, for all visitors to see: "Go Home Beaners!" written in black marker on a bathroom wall (see figure 4.1). Perhaps what shocked me the most was not the message, for I had heard it many times before, but the setting. Glenwood Springs, Colorado, is an idyllic small town located at the mouth of one of the most visually stunning canyons in the state and known for its hot springs that draw thousands of tourists every year. It is your typical, jaw-dropping, postcard-perfect Colorado setting. Yet, as I was driving on I-70 marveling at the natural beauty of Glenwood Canyon, I could not stop pondering about the anti-Mexican graffiti that I

---

* Adapted from *The North American West in the Twenty-First Century*, edited by Brenden W. Rensink, by permission of the University of Nebraska Press. Copyright 2022 by the Board of Regents of the University of Nebraska.

FIGURE 4.1. Anti-Mexican graffiti, Glenwood Springs, Colorado. Source: The author.

had seen just minutes before. It was the summer of 2007, and for over a year the United States had been rocked by massive pro-immigrant rights' rallies as the US Congress debated punitive measures against undocumented immigrants. The fate of an estimated 12 million human beings was on the line, and an acrimonious debate on the role of immigrants (and their labor) in American society had been going on for months across the nation (Román 2013). Colorado was no exception. The state's natural beauty belied the rapid socioeconomic changes that had been taking place in the American West for decades, and its newfound reliance on Latinx immigrant labor. In response, local right-wing reactionaries such as Representative Tom Tancredo (from Denver) spewed hateful messages that blamed undocumented immigrants for the economic dislocations that blue-collar Americans had experienced and promised a quick fix by deporting all "illegal" immigrants (Mulkern 2005; Tancredo 2006).

A part of Tancredo's rant was true. The state of Colorado experienced major socioeconomic changes in the last two decades of the twentieth century, just as the militancy of the Chicano Movement was declining. Around the nation, the radical social activism of the 1960s–1970s over civil rights and the Vietnam War gave way to the conservative "Reagan Revolution" of the 1980s (Dallek 1999) and the end of the Cold War. In Colorado, the economic boom years of the 1990s, the aging of the Baby Boomers, and the attractive amenity lifestyle of Front Range metro areas fueled rapid demographic shifts, with thousands of transplants from other states moving in during the 1990s and 2000s. New companies set up shop in Colorado, while other existing businesses decided to relocate from the East Coast and the Midwest, creating hundreds of jobs and attracting new talent to the state. The Old West economy of agricultural production and cattle ranching diversified into a New West economy of high-tech industries (including defense), tourism, and real estate, which coexisted with traditional agribusinesses (farming and ranching), mining, and oil and gas extraction (Wyckoff 2014). As thousands of newcomers from around the nation moved into the state of Colorado, international migrants followed suit, also attracted by the new job opportunities.

Starting in the 1990s, a new population layer bolstered the long-standing presence of Latinxs in Colorado: the arrival of thousands of Mexican immigrants after the implementation of NAFTA. The stated goal of NAFTA was to lower—and in some cases, eliminate—trade barriers between the United States, Canada, and Mexico, thus boosting international commerce and creating a large trading bloc that would rival the European Union. The economic shock waves of this agreement penetrated deeply into Mexico's rural areas, where agricultural imports from the United States forced traditional small-scale farmers to seek opportunity elsewhere (Boskin 2014). Thousands of Mexicans would eventually migrate to Mexico City and other large urban centers, to the maquiladora towns of the northern border,[2] and to the United States (Massey, Durand, and Malone 2002, chap. 5). In Colorado, many of these new immigrants ended up in the state's large metro areas, such as Denver, Aurora, and Colorado Springs—traditional destinations for previous waves of immigrants from Mexico. However, the NAFTA migrants also found jobs and settled in parts of the state hitherto devoid of a sizable Mexican population,[3] such as the Western Slope—a trend that quickly reshaped the region's demographics.

Colorado's Western Slope occupies the western third of the rectangular-shaped state, and it encompasses most counties west of the continental divide, which runs along the spine of the Rocky Mountains (see maps 0.1

and 0.2). The area is sparsely populated. Decades ago, its economy relied upon oil and gas extraction, ranching, and agriculture, but the economic boom of the 1990s fueled the expansion of the resort industry in ski towns along the I-70 highway corridor and other parts of the region (Childers 2012). Moreover, an aging Baby Boomer generation and the rapid population increase of the state led to the growth of regional trade and service hubs such as Grand Junction and Durango.[4] This rapid economic expansion and diversification created thousands of jobs in ranching and agriculture, but mostly in the construction and service sectors, where Mexican immigrant workers met the demand for cheap, low-skill labor (Shumway 2015, 415). The NAFTA immigrant cohort initially came for the jobs, but a generation later it represents an integral part of the region's population. Thousands of Mexican immigrants (and their descendants) now live and work throughout the Western Slope, where they make up a large segment of the population. Equally important, this new labor force occupies a vital space in an affluent economy that relies on cheap labor.

This chapter examines the twentieth-century history of the Western Slope and the rapid demographic changes that have taken place in the region since the mid-1990s, focusing on the role that (mostly) Mexican immigrants have played in its booming economy. On the one hand, it argues that recent Mexican migration to Colorado's Western Slope is not a "new" historical development but rather the latest iteration of a long-term trend with local, regional, and global repercussions. On the other hand, this new Mexican migratory cohort has such unique characteristics (e.g., different places of origin, new settlement patterns, and modes of insertion into a New West economy) that it can be argued that its recent migration represents a "new" development in Colorado and the New West. There is little published on the history of Latinxs in the Western Slope, so this chapter reconstructs this history by relying on interviews with Latinx immigrants, community leaders, and staff from local community agencies, as well as research carried out in libraries throughout the state.[5]

A History of Latinxs in the Western Slope

As examined in the introduction, Colorado's Latinx history is often seen by non-Latinx Coloradans as consisting of two distinct periods: old

Hispano families who had settled in the Southwest before the war with Mexico and recently arrived Latinx immigrants—with little historical context in between. According to this popular trope, a handful of Mexican citizens of mixed Indigenous and Spanish ancestry originally inhabited the territory occupied by the US military during the 1846–1848 war with Mexico (and eventually purchased and annexed by the United States after the signing of the Treaty of Guadalupe Hidalgo in 1848). These locals eventually gave way to the thousands of Anglo miners, ranchers, and pioneer families that arrived after the war. Fast-forward a century and a half, and these Hispanos are supplemented by thousands of (mostly) Mexican immigrants who have come to the state in the last few decades. Two distinct eras, two demographic cohorts, two simplified views of Latinxs in Colorado—all exist with little regard given to the continuous presence of Latinxs in the state by the Anglo mainstream. Latinxs are imagined as both ancient relics of a distant past (like Native Americans) and as "new" (in the form of Mexican immigrants), but they are rarely seen as part of Colorado's (or the American West's) mainstream (Limerick 1987, 255). The mainstream narrative is still one of audacious Anglo trappers, miners, and pioneer families who settled an "emptied" territory.[6] In this historical omission, Colorado's Latinxs disappear in the popular imagination, and they do not come back into the picture until well into the twentieth century—and then mostly as immigrants. This stereotypical view is particularly the case when looking at the history of Latinxs in Colorado's Western Slope, a region of the state that does not have the large "old" Hispano and Latinx communities of places like the San Luis Valley but that more recently has been receiving many of the "new" waves of Latinx immigrants (Lopez Tushar 2007, 48–49).

Ironically, it was not until the end of the US-Mexican War and the arrival of Anglo settlers that Latinxs became a permanent fixture in Colorado's Western Slope region (Nostrand 1992, 99). Native resistance had thwarted previous Spanish and Mexican attempts to establish permanent settlements in what is now Colorado (e.g., in the San Luis Valley). The founding of US army outposts throughout the territory, significant defeats of Native Americans at the hands of the US military, and the eventual confinement of Indigenous peoples into reservations (particularly the Utes and Navajos that inhabited western Colorado) opened up the

Western Slope to American settlements (Abbott, Leonard, and Noel 2005, 116–117). Most of the settlers were Anglos, though some Hispanos from the San Luis Valley and northern New Mexico also came to southwestern Colorado. Like Anglos, Hispanos came attracted by the opportunity to work in the expanding industries of the region (mining, railroads, and cattle and sheep ranching) and settled in the new towns of Durango, Mancos, and Cortez. Such was the case of the Archibeque family (originally sheepherders of Navajo, Ute, Pueblo, and French Basque ancestry), which in the 1870s migrated north from Bloomfield, New Mexico, to southwestern Colorado, eventually settling in Mancos and Cortez, and becoming one of the oldest Hispano families in the area.[7]

In Durango, a prosperous transportation hub founded in 1880 to service nearby mining towns (and that housed a smelter), the worlds of the Anglo majority and the "Mexican" (i.e., Hispano and Mexican) minority were well defined early on: Sixth Street divided them, with "Mexicans" being forced to reside south of it (aka "south of the border") and on the west side of the Animas River. Many of the "Mexicans" worked at the smelter or had the lowest-paying jobs in town and were subjected to harassment by the Ku Klux Klan, which was very active in Durango during the 1920s and oftentimes burned crosses on Smelter Mountain, a prominent point visible from all over the town (D. Smith 1992, 91, 120–122).

Other parts of the Western Slope, such as the Grand Valley (home to Grand Junction), were settled later. The construction of irrigation canals in the late nineteenth century boosted commercial agriculture in the area, which specialized mostly in the production of fruit crops (such as grapes, peaches, and apricots) and, later, of sugar beets. In fact, the first sugar beet factory in the state opened in Grand Junction in 1899, attracting dozens of Hispano families from northern New Mexico and southern Colorado to the area (Carr and Kempa 2015, 24). Hispanos had been leaving the San Luis Valley in search of work since Anglo settlement and US courts deprived them of their lands (see chapter 1), as the expansion of American capitalism in the late nineteenth century sparked a demand for cheap labor throughout the state. Although most of these Hispano workers sought work and eventually settled along the Front Range (see chapters 2–3), others opted to work in the Grand Valley's fruit orchards, in its railroad industry, and as stoop laborers in the growing sugar beet industry (Abbott, Leonard, and Noel 2005, 354–355). World War I brought about record high prices for sugar, as sugar beet fields across Europe were laid to waste. Moreover, the construction of the Grand Valley Diversion Dam in 1916 and the Government Highline Canal in 1917 made available thousands of additional acres for sugar beet cultivation, further increasing the demand for cheap labor provided by Latinx workers (Carr and Kempa 2015, 27). For example, the Lucero family (originally from the San Luis Valley) came to the Grand Valley to do stoop labor after their family farm in Hoehne, Colorado, failed in 1925. As recalled in an interview with Mr. Santiago Jorge Bernal,[8] in 1927 Plácida Lucero married José Celso Bernal, whose family had come to the Grand Valley from Ocate, New Mexico. In time, the Luceros and the Bernals rented a farm in Loma, Colorado (just west of Grand Junction), where they grew sugar beets and sold them to the Holly Sugar Company. One of their children, Santiago Bernal, would eventually come to own a farm in Loma (which the family purchased from Jesús Maldonado, a Hispano from the San Luis Valley). The Bernals and the Luceros were part of about twenty Hispano land-owning families in the area; all of which are now gone—save for the Bernals.

Despite significant intra- and interstate migration, the existing Hispano families from southern Colorado and northern New Mexico were not sufficient in number to satisfy the labor demands of a thriving sugar beet industry (L. Herrera 1991, 4), and Mexican immigrants soon filled the void. In the 1910s, Mexico was rocked by its revolution, which destroyed vast swaths of productive land in the interior, forcing hundreds of thousands to flee (Henderson 2011, chap. 1). Many of these refugees crossed the border and sought work in the Western United States, including the Grand Valley, where they worked as *betabeleros* for the Holly Sugar Company. These seasonal workers often returned home to Mexico at the end of their contracts. In an effort to secure a steady pool of laborers, Holly built quarters near its factory in Grand Junction to house workers and their families. The housing comprised "a row of connected adobe homes" with outhouses and an outside communal faucet but lacking electricity or heat, "except for a wood stove" (L. Herrera 1991, 8). This area became a Latinx neighborhood known as Las Colonias, shared by Hispano and Mexican immigrant families (Carr and Kempa 2015, 38–39).[9] As elsewhere throughout the state (and the American West) Latinxs in Las Colonias lived segregated lives, always mindful of potential Anglo discrimination, enduring harassment by the Ku Klux Klan (which was "active in Grand Junction during the 1920s"), and unwelcomed in some local businesses that displayed "No Mexicans Allowed" signs (L. Herrera 1991, 14). Although the Great Depression crippled the region's economy, more Mexican workers came to the Grand Valley with the World War II–era economic revival and the implementation of the Bracero Program, an international agreement between the governments of Mexico and the United States that legally imported hundreds of thousands of rural Mexican workers into the American West (Mize and Swords 2011, chap. 1). These *braceros* and their descendants intermarried with the Hispano families already living in the Grand Valley, giving rise to a multigenerational, diverse Latinx community that exists to this day. Moreover, their second- and third-generation children moved out of the fields and into urban, middle-class occupations thanks to public education and their command of the English language. As a result, Grand Junction, the commercial hub of the Western Slope, has a Latinx core, and for decades cities and small towns throughout the Western Slope have had significant Latinx populations.

The end of the Bracero Program in 1964 did not stop the arrival of Mexican immigrants into the United States. Instead, unauthorized workers filled the need for cheap agricultural labor in the country. Most important, the Bracero Program left a major legacy in the United States: the children of the *braceros* that arrived in the 1940s–1960s grew up to become the activists of the Chicano Movement as they came of age in the 1960s–1970s (see chapter 3). Although El Movimiento (as the Chicano Movement was known by its members) had deep roots in Colorado, it mostly bypassed the Western Slope (E. Vigil 1999). Some of the second- and third-generation Mexican Americans in the region started identifying as Chicanxs in the 1960s–1970s, but several factors conspired against the growth of the movement in Colorado's Western Slope. First, the area did not have the sheer demographic numbers—and geographical concentration—of Mexican Americans that parts of the Front Range (such as Denver, Colorado Springs, and Pueblo) had. With the exception of Las Colonias in Grand Junction, most Latinxs were dispersed throughout the Western Slope and their numbers were small in comparison to Front Range metro areas. Unlike places like the San Luis Valley (where Hispanos oftentimes made up the majority of the population), Latinxs in the Western Slope were disenfranchised racial minorities who had learned to survive in an Anglo world by keeping their heads low, trying to assimilate, and not challenging the system.[10]

Second, at home, Hispano and Mexican parents encouraged their children to assimilate into the Anglo world, fearing that their children would be discriminated against by mainstream society. Thus, comparatively few Latinxs from the Western Slope joined the Chicano Movement. Third, the Western Slope was—and to a certain extent still is—a geographically and socially isolated region, conservative in its cultural and political outlook, and worlds apart from the hustle and bustle of the Front Range. Thus, Latinxs residing in the Western Slope did not have the same exposure to the Chicano Movement as their counterparts on the Front Range did, and their conservative milieu and perennial minority status meant that few of them were inclined to join El Movimiento. Most still identified as Mexican Americans or Hispanos. And fourth, the Western Slope, a rural, isolated area in a big Western state, did not have the institutions of higher education that became incubators of the Chicano Movement elsewhere in the state (such as at CU Boulder). Grand Junction had Mesa College, but very few Latinxs attended the local college. According to Mr. José Chavez, a Chicano activist from Grand Junction who attended Mesa College in the mid-1970s, there were only about twenty Latinx students on campus at the time. They founded a chapter of UMAS, over which he presided from 1975–1976, but because of their small numbers, they usually ended up going to the San Luis Valley or the Front Range to meet and march with fellow Chicanx activists there. His political activism with UMAS felt threatening and unpatriotic to conservative Anglos, and as a result Chavez received death threats in the mail.[11]

The Coming of NAFTA

Even after the decline of the sugar beet industry in the 1970s, the Western Slope remained a destination for Mexican immigrants who sought work in the region's orchards, farms, and ranches, as well as in a budding service industry in Grand Junction and other towns (Curry 1977). The region's economy, also based upon extractive industries such as uranium, coal, and oil, went through boom-and-bust cycles in the 1980s–1990s, placing the region's inhabitants on an economic rollercoaster ride of unemployment and underemployment, and causing much distress in small towns that found themselves without consistent tax revenues to provide basic services. For example, for decades seasonal immigrant laborers have been coming to Palisade, a major fruit-producing town in the Grand Valley (just east of Grand Junction), to work in the orchards. According to Ms. Karalyn Dorn,[12] executive director of Child and Migrant Services (a local nonprofit that helps migrant workers), every year dozens of mostly male migrant laborers arrive in Palisade from Mexico. They hail mainly from the states of Michoacán and Aguascalientes, and from northern Mexico. Since the late 1980s, most come with H-2A visas,[13] which allow them to work temporarily in the United States. Their work in the fields begins in the spring (when they plant and thin the fruit trees), picks up during the summer (with apricot and cherry picking in June, and the peach harvest from July to September), and winds down by the fall (when they prune the fruit trees). Packing fruit (mostly done by women) takes place during the harvest season, and there are countless odd jobs to be done before winter sets in. By late fall, most of the migrant workers are gone, though some eventually stay year-round and try to regularize their immigration status. María (last name withheld),[14] a Mexican migrant from Sonora, related to me how she and her husband left Arizona for Colorado, where they have worked in Palisade's vineyards for several years (with occasional stints by her husband into the oil industry), harvesting grapes during the warm months and spending winters in Sonora, Mexico.

This economic picture, however, is incomplete. As was the case in other parts of the state (and in the American West generally), new economic sectors were also replacing or supplementing traditional extractive industries. The Old West of uranium mining and oil production now coexisted with an expanding New West of real estate sales and recreational activities. Western Slope cities and towns like Aspen, Durango, Glenwood Springs, Grand Junction, Montrose, Pagosa Springs, Telluride, and Vail began growing in size. Moreover, an increasing number of people moved there, attracted by the weather, the lifestyle, and jobs in the new technology and service industries. The economic and demographic changes were more drastic along Colorado's Front Range but equally noticeable in the small cities and towns of the Western Slope. The other newcomers to the region were retirees, most of them Baby Boomers who sought an amenity lifestyle, sparking a real estate and construction boom in the aforementioned towns—and conjuring up renewed fears about the "Californication" of Colorado (Fulcher 2018). Finally, these newcomers were joined by hundreds of thousands of tourists, as the recreation industry took off and became one of the pillars of Colorado's economy. The economic and demographic growth created thousands of new jobs; some of these in industries that needed cheap labor, such as the retail and hospitality industries. As ski resorts, hotels, and restaurants thrived in the new economy, thousands of servers, dishwashers, maids, clerks, and other entry-level positions needed to be staffed (Power and Barrett 2001). Palisade is a good example of how the Old West and the New West converge in a small Western Slope town. Besides its fame as a producer of apples, apricots, berries, cherries, peaches, plums, and grapes, Palisade's vineyards have become a major tourist destination in the Grand Valley. Agritourism in the form of wine-tasting tours, festivals, and vacation packages that include a stay in local wineries have created new economic opportunities in the region (Widener 2022). Moreover, Colorado's economic prosperity in the late twentieth century and early twenty-first also sparked a construction boom in the Western Slope. All these transplants, retirees, and tourists needed homes; apartments; condos; hotels; and places to work, shop, and have fun. Construction required cheap labor too, and the demand for workers remained high (Travis 2007). Mexican immigrants filled that void—as they have done so many times before in our nation's history.

The 1980s–1990s were particularly challenging for Mexico's poor. The country had borrowed heavily in order to fund ambitious infrastructural development projects and import substitution industrialization programs in the 1960s–1970s. When oil prices plummeted in the early 1980s, Mexico found itself unable to pay its external debt (Bulmer-Thomas 2003, chap. 1). In 1982, Mexico's finance minister announced that the country could no longer service its debt, triggering a regional financial crisis known as "the lost decade" in Latin America (Massey, Durand, and Malone 2002, 75–77). The crisis forced Mexico to cut back on social spending, restructure its economy, and accept conditions imposed by the International Monetary Fund (IMF) in order to secure bailout loans. A new slate of technocratic presidents in Mexico embraced globalization, opening up the country's economy, and culminating in the signing of NAFTA with Canada and the United States in 1992. The agreement (implemented on January 1, 1994) significantly increased trade between the United States and Mexico, and more American companies began investing in Mexico. Dozens of assembly plants known as *maquiladoras* opened up in Mexico's interior and along the border, taking advantage of Mexico's low taxes and cheap wages, and creating thousands of entry-level jobs for Mexico's poor (Orme 1996). But NAFTA also had significant deleterious effects on Mexico's countryside. US agricultural imports soon flooded Mexico's consumer market, making it impossible for family farms to turn a profit. Mexican farmers began abandoning the countryside by the thousands, seeking jobs in Mexico's industrial cities (e.g., Mexico City and Monterrey), the rapidly growing *maquiladora* border towns (e.g., Tijuana and Ciudad Juárez), and El Norte (i.e., the United States) (Rivera, Whiteford, and Chávez 2009).

The ripple effects of NAFTA not only sparked a new wave of Mexican immigration to the United States but also altered the nature of the flow (Jiménez 2010, chap. 2). Whereas in the past the majority of Mexican immigrants to the United States came from Mexico's northern states (such as Sonora and Chihuahua), by the 1990s central and southern Mexican states (such as Jalisco, Guanajuato, Guerrero, and Michoacán) produced the bulk of emigrants. Most were young men who sought seasonal or temporary employment in the United States, sent remittances back home to their families, and eventually returned to Mexico, completing a migratory circuit that they would likely repeat in the future (Henderson 2011, chap. 5). Increased law enforcement and the building of new barriers along the US-Mexico border by the US government at the turn of the century (particularly after the September 11, 2001, terrorist attacks) disrupted this circular migration pattern—which ebbed and flowed according to the demand for cheap immigrant labor in the United States. Violence on the borderlands also increased as Mexican cartels fought over control of the drug trade, extortion rackets, and the smuggling of immigrants into the United States. All these factors combined to make the journey to the United States a more difficult and expensive proposition for most ordinary Mexicans (Slack, Martínez, and Whiteford 2018). Still, the potential to earn significantly higher wages in the United States drove thousands of

Mexicans to risk it all and head north. Hundreds died in the desert or at the hands of smugglers (known as coyotes) and the Mexican drug cartels, who frequently rob, beat, and rape those attempting to cross.[15] As a result, what used to be a (kind of) routine circular trip has become a one-way road, with entire families (including children) trying to make it into the United States. These powerful "push" factors, combined with the myriad of "pull" factors that Colorado's rapidly expanding new economic sectors provided, assured a steady flow of cheap immigrant labor for Colorado's thriving industries at the turn of the century.

New Mexican Migrants in the Western Slope

The 1990s witnessed a surge of Mexican immigration to Colorado's Western Slope—unlike anything that the region had witnessed since the days of sugar beets and the Bracero Program. Most of the immigrants came from Mexico's central states, though traditional migrant flows from northern states (e.g., Chihuahua) continued. Some Central Americans, mainly from El Salvador and Guatemala, came too. They were young men (at least initially) from rural backgrounds and with little education beyond elementary school. Besides the traditional agricultural occupations (farm labor, cattle ranching, and sheepherding) these Latinx immigrants also found better-paying jobs in the booming construction sector, restaurants, hotels, and other businesses related to the growing tourism and recreation industries of the Western Slope. While men tended to concentrate in construction, landscaping, and agriculture, women found jobs in hotels, restaurants, and domestic service. According to Ms. Karla Gonzales García,[16] who at the time led a community service agency in Telluride, although the male-dominated industries paid better wages, Latinas had the most stable jobs among immigrants, particularly as construction work dried up after the 2008 recession.

In 1990, Latinxs represented just 8.06% of the population of the Western Slope, but by the turn of the century (2000 decennial census) they comprised 11.49% of its population (US Census Bureau). Numerically, the Western Slope's Latinx population went from 26,433 individuals in 1990, to 52,781 in 2000—a 100% increase![17] And the numbers would just keep on rising during the first two decades of the twenty-first century, to

TABLE 4.1. Latinx population of Colorado's Western Slope, 1990–2020

	1990	2000	2010	2020
Number	26,433	52,781	88,050	102,250
Percentage of the region's population	8.06%	11.49%	15.93%	17.46%

Sources: Colorado Department of Local Affairs, State Demography Office, "Race and Hispanic Origin" (2022a); US Census Bureau.

88,050 Latinxs in 2010 and 102,250 in 2020. Unfortunately, it is impossible to determine specifically how many Mexican immigrants arrived in Colorado during this period (or any given period). The US Census Bureau does not ask questions about immigration status, and immigrants are less likely to answer census questions. For example, for the 2020 Census, 891,760 individuals in Colorado indicated Mexican ancestry, which is about 70% of all Latinxs in the state. Assuming a similar percentage of Mexican ancestry for Latinxs in the Western Slope, that is about 71,575 individuals of Mexican ancestry living in the region—though it is impossible to tell which ones are (or identify as) Hispanos, Mexican immigrants, Mexican Americans, Chicanxs, and so on. Thus, this work relies upon data for Latinxs as a whole, and it broadly assumes that trends for the Western Slope's Latinx population are mainly reflective of the region's Mexican immigrant population.

Table 4.1 sums up the growth of the Western Slope's Latinx population. The fastest growth took place in the 1990s (as the state's economy started to boom and NAFTA was being implemented), with the Latinx population doubling in size. By 2010, Latinxs had become 15.93% of the Western Slope's population—a 66.82% increase in a decade—and by 2020, the US Census Bureau showed that the region's Latinx population had increased to 17.46% (Colorado Department of Local Affairs 2022a). These figures still pale in comparison to the hundreds of thousands of Latinxs who live in Colorado's Front Range, but the demographic trends reflect a rapidly growing population in a region of the state with historically below-average numbers for Latinxs. Moreover, the trend points to the Western Slope's Latinx population eventually matching the state's average of 22% Latinxs, and it could even surpass it in the near future given the region's relatively small population.

Equally important is where these Latinxs choose to live and work. The Western Slope is not only a sparsely inhabited region of the state of

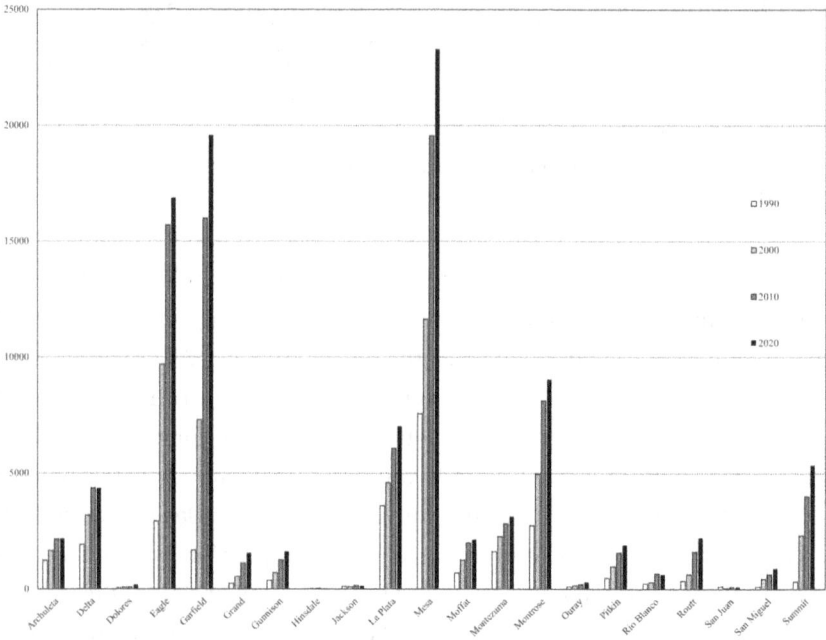

FIGURE 4.2. Latinx population of the Western Slope (by county), 1990–2020. Sources: State of Colorado, Department of Local Affairs, State Demography Office; US Census Bureau.

Colorado, but also an unevenly inhabited one. The rugged topography of the region (broken up by mountains, mesas, and canyons) means that most of the population in concentrated in valleys, lowlands, and highway corridors. Some counties—like Hinsdale or San Juan—have fewer than a thousand inhabitants overall, whereas Mesa County (where Grand Junction is located) has over 150,000 residents (Colorado Department of Local Affairs 2022b). Moreover, ski resort towns (like Aspen, Telluride, and Vail) are well known for having a small year-round population but hundreds of part-time "residents" who own a second home and usually visit during the winter season. These ski resort towns are also pricey, which means that some of the "locals" cannot afford to live there and are forced to commute from places where rents are cheaper. Figure 4.2 shows how the Western Slope's Latinx population reflects these regional trends. As expected, the larger counties (in terms of population) received the largest influx of Latinxs, particularly during the 1990s–2000s. For example, Mesa and La Plata Counties, home to Grand Junction and Durango (respectively the largest towns on the Western Slope), saw a large influx of Latinxs as a result of their construction booms. Both towns went through a growth spurt in the 1990s–2000s that spilled over into neighboring areas. In both cases, traditional jobs in ranching and agriculture attracted Mexican immigrants, but the cities also provided jobs in retail, hospitality, and tourism. Moreover, entrepreneurial members of the Mexican immigrant community started small businesses that nowadays cater to the Latinx community, such as Mexican restaurants, *taquerías* (i.e., small taco restaurants or trucks), grocery shops, clothing stores, butcher shops, bakeries, and service centers to send remittances back home. Some of these stores are veritable multipurpose businesses where people can shop, eat, and send money home to Mexico.

The growth of Grand Junction and Durango (and their Latinx populations) during the 1990s–2000s was somewhat expected, as these are the only significant metro areas in the Western Slope. The most surprising development in the last few decades, however, has been the growth of Latinx communities within driving distance of ski resort towns such as Aspen, Telluride, and Vail. It is particularly noticeable in figure 4.2 when one looks at the large influx of Latinxs to Eagle, Garfield, and Summit Counties. These three counties are on the I-70 corridor, a major highway that connects several ski resort towns just west of the continental divide. Eagle County is home to Vail, an affluent world-class ski resort destination, and other ski areas lie near I-70, including Breckenridge in Summit County. The region is also dotted with small gateway towns, like Frisco and Silverthorne, with dozens of places to shop, eat, and stay. This recreation-based economy generates millions of dollars in revenue annually and relies on the hard work of Latinxs (mainly Mexican immigrants) who clean, cook, and cater to the thousands of tourists that flock to the ski slopes every winter. Latinx immigrant workers are usually found behind the scenes, though, laboring in restaurants, hotels, and other service industries, doing the countless low-paying jobs that keep the show running.[18]

But most Latinx workers cannot afford to live in those well-to-do places. Their wages are too low to afford the high rents (driven up by astronomical real estate prices in a market that caters to luxury homes and condos), so instead they live further down I-70, away from the resort towns, in mobile home parks or substandard housing (the only places they can afford) trying to make ends meet (Griego 2019). For example, Ms. Rocío Guzmán (pseudonym),[19] a middle-aged immigrant from central Mexico, worked back-to-back eight-hour shifts in two fast-food establishments in Vail in order to make her long commute from Gypsum (a small mining community about forty miles away) worth her while. Luckily for her, there is a bus service to Vail from Gypsum, and her two jobs are in the same strip mall, so at the end of her first shift Ms. Guzmán just changes clothes and walks next door to her second job.

Other immigrant workers are not so lucky, and they endure long, treacherous commutes in winter to and from work. Moreover, besides working double or extended shifts, immigrants in the area employ other survival strategies, such as living with extended family members and pooling their resources, in order to afford the high cost of living in Colorado's ski country. A similar story occurs near Aspen (another world-class ski resort) and Glenwood Springs (a tourist destination with hot springs right on I-70). Tiny Pitkin County (mostly Aspen and unincorporated areas) has the priciest real estate market in Colorado, with a median home value of $662,964 and a third of its homes valued at over a million dollars, as of 2019—just before the COVID-19 pandemic hit (Stebbins 2019). By 2021, as the economy roared back and the uber-rich sought homes in the area (but real estate inventory remained low), median prices for single-family homes in Aspen surged to $8.9 million and for condos to $2.15 million. Those prices quickly doubled within months (by late 2022), when single-family home median prices in Aspen skyrocketed to $17.8 million and condo median prices to $4.9 million (Mohammadi 2022). These jaw-dropping prices make of Aspen the most expensive real estate market in the nation (on a price-per-square-foot basis). Middle-income workers such as teachers, police officers, and city workers cannot afford to live in a place that has become the winter playground of business moguls and celebrities who fly in their private jets into the local airport for a quick ski vacation. Needless to say, this recreation mecca is largely unaffordable to the Mexican immigrants who work there, so they reside further down the I-70 corridor in mining towns like Silt, Rifle, and Parachute, and commute to work from there. Aspen's spectacular growth was made possible—and it is still sustained—by the labor of Mexican immigrants who drive long distances to work lengthy shifts in Colorado's most expensive town. The luxury living and environmental privilege of Aspen's residents and tourists stand in sharp contrast to the old, dilapidated housing that Mexican immigrants workers rent in run-down boom-and-bust mining towns miles—and a world—away from there (Park and Pellow 2011).[20]

Telluride is another good example of a New West economy that depends on immigrant labor. The old mining town set in a stunning Rocky Mountain valley has become a major luxury ski resort destination (second only to Aspen), and its growth has spilled over into a new development next door (Mountain Village), connected to Telluride by a gondola. In spite of efforts by the city of Telluride to provide affordable housing to middle-income workers, most of them cannot afford to live there—as is the case with other resort towns throughout the American West. According to Ms. Jenna Hagen,[21] a teacher at the local high school, some young teachers resort to sharing apartments with roommates, others try to get a rent-subsided apartment in Mountain Village (where there is a long waiting list), or just live farther away, in small rural communities such as Norwood or Naturita, and commute to Telluride. Unfortunately, most new teachers leave after a few years because they cannot afford to live and raise a family in Telluride. The lack of affordable housing in a tiny resort town (population of 2,607 according to the 2020 Census) was a vexing problem when Telluride went through its construction boom in the 1990s and early 2000s. It needed hundreds of construction and service workers, but there was no affordable housing for them. Immigrants filled this void. Over a thousand Latinx immigrant workers commuted on a daily basis from Montrose and Olathe to Telluride (a trip of more than an hour). Those immigrants came to the area mostly from northern and central Mexico (though there were also some Central Americans). Initially they were attracted to the agricultural jobs in the Montrose area (because of their rural backgrounds), but they soon moved into construction and service jobs in Telluride that paid better—such as landscapers, maids, and kitchen staff—according to Mr. Ricardo Pérez,[22] head of Hispanic Affairs Project, a grassroots organization that serves immigrants in western Colorado (Hispanic Affairs Project 2022). Entrepreneurial immigrants acquired vans and earned a living by making several rounds trips a day from the Montrose/Olathe area to Telluride, ferrying hundreds of immigrant workers to Telluride's booming economy. A few lucky immigrants were able to get rent-subsidized apartments in Telluride after the city built Shandoka Apartments, including Ms. María Perla,[23] a Salvadoran immigrant who earned a living working in the hospitality and food preparation industries. Currently, there is a waiting list of over 130 families to get into one of these coveted apartments. A look at figure 4.2 shows a steep increase in Montrose County's Latinx population in the 1990s and 2000s; but no such increase is evident in San Miguel County (home to Telluride), where most immigrant workers (and other middle-income employees) simply cannot afford to live.

A similar phenomenon—albeit on a much smaller scale—can be seen in Gunnison, where male Mexican immigrants came attracted by ranching and sheepherding jobs in the 1980s. By the 1990s, they had brought their families with them and created a community that now works primarily in the service and hospitality industry. From Gunnison it is a short, thirty-minute drive to Crested Butte, where the former Club Med was one of the first ski resorts to hire Mexican immigrants in the 1990s. Nowadays, dozens of them commute to work in Crested Butte's ski resorts, mansions, and ritzy vacation condos, while residing in Gunnison, where the cost of living is substantially cheaper. An interesting feature of Gunnison's Mexican immigrant community is that over half of them are Cora people, an Indigenous group from the mountainous region of the state of Nayarit (in central Mexico), whereas the rest tend to hail from Tabasco or Chihuahua. Some Coras originally migrated to the Montrose area before moving to Gunnison in search of better job opportunities. That was the case of Ms. Paula (last name withheld)[24] and her husband, who came from Tepic (Nayarit) in 2000 and worked in ranches and farms in Olathe (near Montrose). Their former jobs involved hard, physical labor, so they moved to Gunnison in 2010, where she now works in a hotel. The Coras are a very tightly knit community, and some of them are not fluent (or very fluent) in Spanish, which means that there are ethnic divisions between them and other Spanish-speaking Mexican immigrants who often view the Cora as backward Indians, according to Ms. Marketa Zubkova,[25] who leads the Hispanic Affairs Project's outreach efforts in the Gunnison / Crested Butte area. Gunnison's Coras are twice discriminated: first by their Mexican compatriots (who have brought with them prejudices against Indigenous people prevalent in Mexican society) and then by Anglo society at large, which views people of color in general and Indigenous people in particular as inferior. In addition, the Coras' lack of fluency in Spanish (and/or English) and their status as immigrants (including some who are undocumented) put them in a particularly precarious situation. In 2023, Marisela Ballesteros, a second-generation Cora born in Montrose but raised in Gunnison, was elected to the Gunnison City Council, a significant political development that promises to give the Cora community a greater say in local government (Lofholm 2023).

Finally, a small number of Latinx immigrants have been coming to Colorado's Western Slope to work as sheepherders since the 1990s. Most of them hail from South American countries with deep-seated pastoralist traditions, such as Bolivia, Chile, and Peru, where they are recruited by agents with connections to ranches in the American West. These recruiters help them get contracts and the necessary paperwork to apply for H-2A visas at the nearest US consulate. With visas in hand, these immigrant workers (usually young males) fly to the United States, where they are picked up at the airport by a ranch hand and taken straight to work. That was the case with Mr. Ignacio Alvarado,[26] a seasonal worker originally from Puerto Montt (in southern Chile) who came to Colorado in 1990 and worked as a sheepherder in the Craig area for several years. At the time, just Anglos and Mexicans worked in the sheep ranches, so he was one of the first South American sheepherders in the Western Slope. Mr. Alvarado was put in charge of 12,000 sheep and 5,000 head of cattle in a territory that spanned 100–200 square miles. He spent most of the summer months by himself, with a shepherd dog and his horse for company, and a high-powered rifle to protect the animals from the occasional predatory bear and the coyotes. His spartan quarters consisted of a small, old camper trailer with no running water, where he prepared his meals from canned food. He rarely took baths and he wore the same clothes for days on end. Every couple of weeks, a ranch hand came by to check on him and supply him with water and food. The job was lonely and boring—not to mention potentially dangerous. Mr. Alvarado's greatest concern was suffering an accident and becoming incapacitated and unable to call for help. His worst fears almost came true when he became very sick with a tick-borne illness and could not get out of bed for days. Luckily, a ranch hand stopped by just in the nick of time and rushed him to the hospital.

For hours and hours of field work seven days a week, Mr. Alvarado was paid just $650 per month ($900 once he got his US permanent residency card—aka "green card"). After doing the math, he figured out that after three years on the job, his wages amounted to about 99¢ an hour.

In 2018, after years of intense opposition from powerful Western ranchers, wages for sheepherders were raised by the US federal government to $1,200 per month, which according to Mr. Alvarado averages out to $2–$3 per hour when one factors in the 24/7 nature of sheepherding. In addition, ranchers exercise an inordinate degree of control over the lives of their immigrant sheepherders, determining whom they see, when they get paid, what they eat, and when they get medical care. Sometimes ranchers even keep their workers' documents and threaten them with deportation if they do not comply with the labor conditions (K. Jones 2016). Anglo ranching families are a powerful special interest in the Western Slope, and their political connections and conservative leanings remain a significant obstacle to immigrant rights. Many of these ranchers see Latinxs as second-class citizens and have no incentive to change the status quo that protects their interests and benefits them—particularly at the urging of "outsiders" who work for US federal government agencies. In the words of Mr. Larry Archibeque,[27] these ranchers are "entitled, entrenched, and embittered."

Thus, for these immigrant workers, who have family back home who depend on their remittances, there are few good options. Erácleo and Reynaldo (last names withheld),[28] two immigrant workers from the rural outskirts of La Paz, Bolivia, shared similar stories. They arrived in Colorado in the late 1990s and have spent years working in cattle and sheep ranches in southwestern Colorado (near Durango), an experience they summed up in three words: *soledad, clima, y terreno* (loneliness, climate, and terrain). Loosely translated, their main complaints revolved around the loneliness that their jobs entailed (such as having to spend weeks in the backcountry all by themselves), the harsh mountain weather (with both cold and hot spells, as well as dangerous hail and thunderstorms), and the rough terrain (over which they have to move around thousands of head of cattle and sheep, trying to keep their losses to a minimum). These sheepherders are some of the most exploited immigrant workers in the state, yet their plight is largely unknown outside of some immigrant rights' agencies because of their isolation, vulnerability, and small numbers. According to estimates by the Hispanic Affairs Project, about 300 H-2A immigrant workers toil in Colorado's backcountry (K. Jones 2016). As in the case of NAFTA and Mexican migration to the Western Slope, these H-2A immigrant workers from South America are being funneled to Colorado by a globalized migratory system that relies on cheap labor. Nowadays, the relative ease of communications and air transportation allows ranchers in remote parts of Colorado's Western Slope to recruit shepherds from the Global South—an unthinkable prospect just decades ago. For these immigrant workers from South America, a few seasons of hard work in Colorado's backcountry represent an opportunity to feed their families, save some money, and perhaps may even open the door to permanent residency in the United States (at least for the lucky few who are eventually sponsored by their employers, as was the case with Mr. Alvarado). The work is hard, the risks are great, and the rewards are meager, but desperate immigrant workers from South America still flock to Western Slope sheep and cattle ranches (Jordan 2022).[29]

A Changing Ethnic Landscape

Compared to the huge post-NAFTA migration of Mexicans to Colorado's Front Range, the small numbers of Mexican immigrants in the Western Slope may seem relatively irrelevant. However, raw numbers do not tell the whole story, particularly in a region characterized by few cities, small towns, and vast rural areas that only holds about 10% of Colorado's population. A look at how quickly these population changes took place, and the current standing of the Latinx immigrant population in the Western Slope, help us make better sense of the powerful impact of recent Mexican immigration into this sparsely populated region of Colorado. Mexican migrants have profoundly transformed the Western Slope's ethnic landscape—as they (and other Latinxs) are transforming the American West as well (Wyckoff 2014, 178).

Figure 4.3 shows the rate of change of the Latinx population in Colorado's Western Slope counties between 1990 and 2020. Almost all counties in the Western Slope witnessed the growth of its Latinx population in the 1990s, but it comes as no surprise that the greatest changes (by

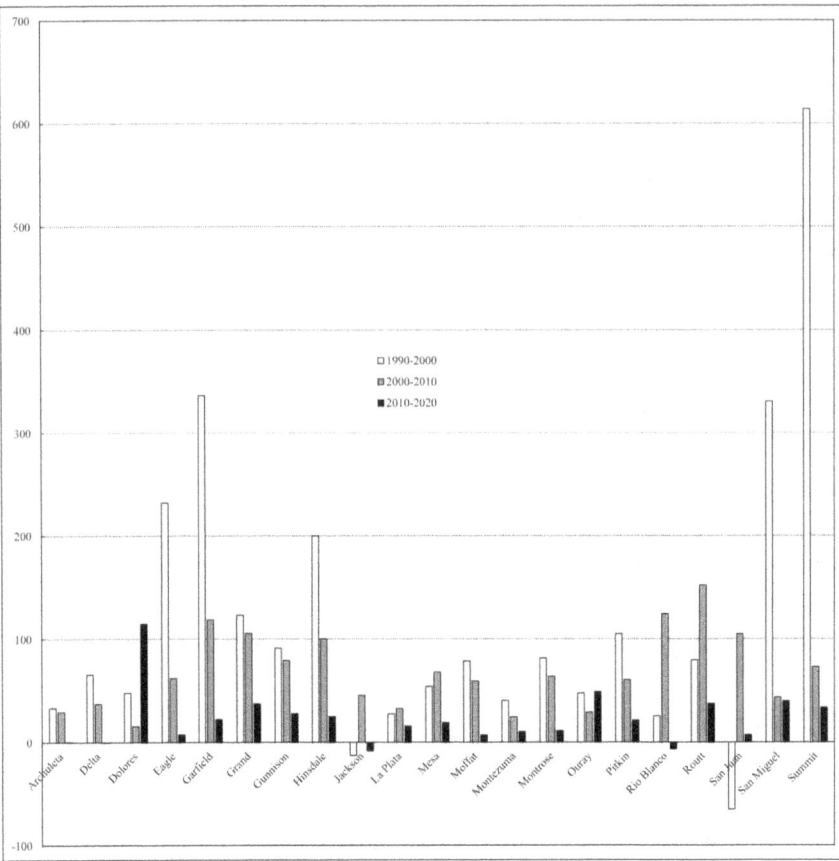

FIGURE 4.3. Rate of change of the Latinx population of the Western Slope (by county), 1990–2020. Source: US Census Bureau.

far) took place in rural areas hitherto devoid of Latinx communities that saw a sudden influx of Mexican immigrants in the 1990s (as NAFTA was being implemented). Eagle, Garfield, and Summit Counties experienced triple-digit growth rates from 1990 to 2000 as Mexican immigrants flocked to construction, service, and hospitality jobs in the I-70 ski resort towns of Aspen and Vail. These were counties in which few, if any, Latinxs resided before 1990, unlike places like Grand Junction, which had a long-standing Mexican American / Chicanx community. In the 2000s, Garfield County's Latinx population recorded triple-digit growth too, as Mexican immigrant workers kept moving there looking for cheap housing. Also noticeable is the greater rate of change in 2000–2010 (compared

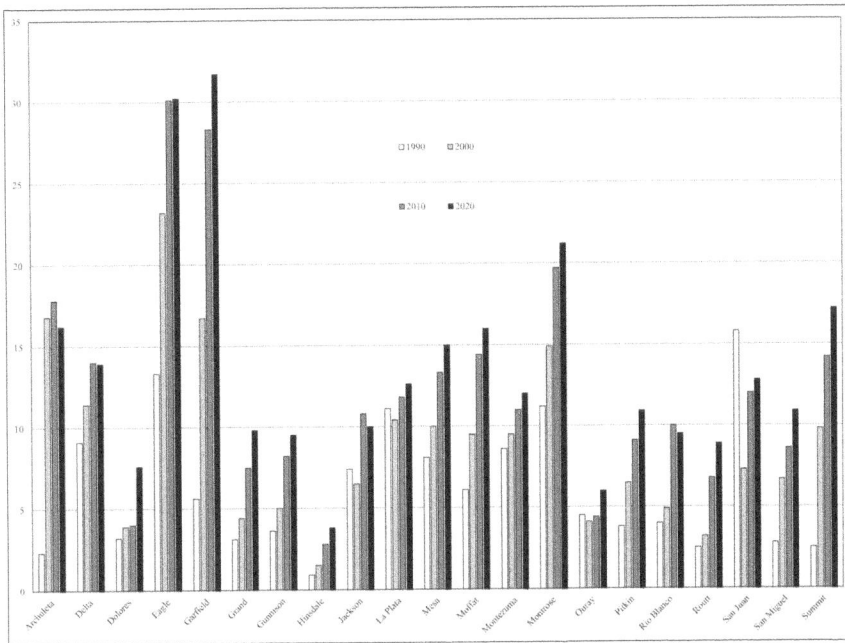

FIGURE 4.4. Latinx population of the Western Slope (percentage Latinx, by county), 1990–2020. Source: US Census Bureau.

to 1990–2000) for Rio Blanco and Routt Counties (in northwestern Colorado), as immigrants began "discovering" these places and moving there for jobs in ranching, agriculture, and mining but also in the service industry of Steamboat Springs (a ski resort town). San Miguel and Hinsdale Counties are statistical outliers: the former because few Latinxs could afford to live in Telluride until some affordable housing was built in the 1990s, the latter because only four Latinxs lived in lightly populated Hinsdale County in 1990. The same can be said about Jackson and San Juan Counties, which showed little—if any—growth in their Latinx population. Both are rural counties with tiny populations, so even a minor change in the number of Latinxs can skew the graph one way or the other.

Figure 4.4 tells the rest of the story by examining the percentage of the population of Colorado's Western Slope counties made up by Latinxs. Again, the biggest Latinx populations (percentagewise) can be found in the rapidly growing immigrant bedroom communities of Eagle and Garfield Counties, where small mining towns became affordable destinations for Mexican immigrants working in Aspen and Vail. Garfield County (home to low-cost rural communities like Parachute, Rifle, and Silt) saw its Latinx population grow from 5% of the population in 1990 to 31% in 2020, while in neighboring Eagle County, close to a third of the population is now Latinx. Similarly, 21% of Montrose County's population and 14% of neighboring Delta County's population is now made up of Latinxs—a direct result of Telluride's economic boom. Even Archuleta County, home to vacation resorts in Pagosa Springs (the gateway community to Wolf Creek ski area), is now 16% Latinx, compared to just 2% back in 1990. Across the board, all counties in the Western Slope saw increases in their Latinx population (with the exception of tiny San Juan County). These increases—both numerically and percentagewise—are the direct result of Mexican immigration flows in the 1990s and 2000s, fueled by NAFTA's woes in Mexico and Colorado's booming economy.

These impressive numbers only reflect the tip of the iceberg. Public school enrollment by race/ethnicity for selected Western Slope school districts shows an up-and-coming second generation of young Latinxs who are on the verge of becoming adults, entering the workforce, and voting. For example, the Summit RE-1 School District is 39% Hispanic, the Eagle County RE-50J School District is 52% Hispanic, the Garfield RE-2 School District is 54% Hispanic, and the Roaring Fork RE-1 School District (which covers Glenwood Springs and Carbondale, near Aspen) is 57% Hispanic (as of 2021). Further out, the Montrose County RE-1J School District (within commuting distance of Telluride) is 39% Hispanic, and the Lake County R-1 School District (which covers the remote mountain town of Leadville) is 64% Hispanic (Annie E. Casey Foundation 2024). Within a generation, these Latinx children will be entering American society as young adults, under vastly different conditions from their parents, and they will keep on altering the demographic dynamics of the region.

This sustained labor migration came to a screeching halt when the US economy entered into a recession in 2008. The recession not only slowed down Mexican migration across the nation but seems to have provoked a net reverse flow as more immigrants left for Mexico than came into the United States (Gonzalez-Barrera 2015). The 2008 recession hit the immigrant community hard. Mexican immigrants found themselves without jobs as construction projects stopped. Moreover, with fewer people traveling and taking vacations, retail and hospitality jobs dwindled across Colorado's Western Slope. Even in a wealthy, paradisical Western Slope location like Telluride, many immigrant men found themselves without jobs after the halt in construction. According to Ms. Karla Gonzales García,[30] co-executive director of San Miguel Resource Center, immigrant women then became the main breadwinners at home, leading to increased levels of alcohol abuse, marital conflicts, and domestic violence among immigrant families as traditional family structures broke down. Faced with few decent job prospects and having to support extended families in two countries, some immigrants returned home. Entire families were (again) uprooted by the economic crisis, which tore apart the social fabric of the immigrant community, displacing people that were in the process of establishing stable lives in the United States—a systemic challenge for community agencies like the Hispanic Affairs Project, according to Mr. Ricardo Pérez.[31]

Moreover, anti-immigrant feelings grew among Anglos as they too felt the impact of the economic crisis. A public opinion survey carried out in the Intermountain West listed feeling the impacts of immigration as the second-ranked item on a list of issues mentioned by respondents. Across the board, most respondents wanted to see a greater involvement of the federal government in dealing with immigration, although opinions regarding immigrants differed sharply by class. College-educated whites were more likely than working-class whites to believe that immigrants "enrich our culture and strengthen our economy" (62% versus 42%, respectively) and that immigrants should be allowed to stay in the United States and eventually become US citizens if they have lived here for years, have not committed any crimes, and pay a fine (65% versus 50%, respectively) (Teixeira and Bowman 2010, 10–12, 27). As it has happened many times in our nation's past, immigrants were being scapegoated and accused of stealing jobs, depressing wages, and draining off social services (Román 2013). A letter to the editor of *The Cortez Journal* from a clearly upset reader asked for the elimination of "free handout programs" for immigrants and questioned "to what extent does someone who knowingly . . . illegally immigrates into the United States have rights[?]" (Black 2011). The huge linguistic and cultural gap between Anglos and Mexican immigrants did not help bridge their differences. In a town like Grand Junction, home to retirees and affluent Anglos, these two worlds rarely overlap. In the words of Professor Tom Acker (Colorado Mesa University),[32] who has a multiracial and multicultural family, "Anglos see Latinos as a mystery."

In Durango, an outdoorsy town made famous by hard-playing yuppies, Anglo transplants from California and the East Coast that came in the 1990s are being displaced (i.e., priced out of the real estate market) by affluent white Texans. This conservative influx has turned a former liberal college town into an increasingly reactionary bastion less welcoming to Latinx immigrants, according to Mr. Danny Quinlan,[33] who directs Compañeros: Four Corners Immigrant Resource Center, an agency that helps mostly Latinx immigrants in the Durango/Southwest Colorado region. A letter to the editor of *The Durango Herald* boldly asserted: "There are people living in Durango right now who have moved here to get away from the crimes and systemic stresses caused by heavy illegal-immigrant populations" (Sigman 2012). Previously, the same individual had penned a letter to the editor describing Mexico as "a corrupt, near-lawless country that has taken advantage of U.S. largesse for a long time" (Sigman 2010a) and had complained about a series of articles on immigration (published by *The Durango Herald*) for its apparent sympathy toward undocumented Mexican immigrants, without mentioning the detrimental effects that undocumented Mexican migrants had on US citizens and American society at large (Sigman 2010b). In nearby Cortez, a conservative enclave, a candidate for county commissioner promoted an "unusual ethnocentric religious doctrine [that] maintains that people from England and northern Europe will be favored by Jesus in his kingdom, a comforting belief for most white people in Montezuma County" (Jobin 2014).

This sometimes-uneasy mix of Latinx immigrants and Anglo "natives" reflects the increasing diversity of the region and of Colorado's Third Congressional District, which covers most of the Western Slope, the San Luis Valley, and Pueblo. The Third Congressional District tends to lean slightly conservative (Cook Political Report 2022), and it has been traditionally dominated by agricultural, mineral, and ranching interests. Although the district is heavily rural, it can be surprisingly diverse, with wealthy, progressive enclaves such as Aspen and Telluride surrounded by more modest, conservative areas (Burness 2020). Its two biggest urban centers are Grand Junction, a blue-collar, conservative city that sits on the district's western edge, and Pueblo, a heavily Latinx, unionized, and more liberal city located on the district's eastern corner. As a result, the district has historically switched hands between Democrats and Republicans. For example, from 1993 to 2005, Scott McInnis, a moderate Republican from Mesa County, served as the district's representative. Upon McInnis's retirement, John Salazar, a moderate Democrat from the San Luis Valley, won the seat (Farer 2004) and held it until he was defeated in 2010 by Scott Tipton, a mainstream Republican from Cortez (Lawrence 2010). But in 2020, in a shocking upset, Tipton was defeated in the Republic primary by Lauren Boebert, an unabashedly pro–Donald Trump conspiracy theorist who went on to win the general election (Luning 2020). Her reactionary views on immigration, religion, and cultural issues turned Representative Boebert into a political lighting rod in her Western Slope district, and she is considered one of the most controversial members of Congress (D. Valdez 2021), barely winning reelection in 2022 by a handful of votes. With Boebert's surprising move to the Fourth Congressional District in 2024 (Biller 2024; Isenberg and Garrison 2023),[34] it remains to be seen if Colorado's Third Congressional District will return to its moderate political roots.

More recently, the COVID-19 pandemic wreaked havoc among Latinxs in the state. With the nation's economy coming to a standstill in the spring of 2020, many Latinxs in the Western Slope lost their jobs or had their work hours cut. Others—such as supermarket employees and farmworkers—still had jobs to do because they were designated as essential workers (Sullivan 2020) but endured months of fear and uncertainty at the workplace before vaccines became available, while their employers tried to ride out the economic downturn (often without success). Overall, the state's Latinx workers, who are overrepresented in blue-collar occupational sectors where they are in close contact with their coworkers and the public, did not have the option of doing remote work (as was the case with mainly Anglo white-collar workers) and were hit the hardest by the pandemic-induced economic slowdown—particularly in Colorado's Western Slope, where a majority experienced food insecurity or had trouble paying their rent or mortgage (Bunch 2021). On top of that, those Latinxs without a legal presence in the United States did not qualify for the enhanced unemployment benefits or the economic stimulus checks offered by the federal government (Borowsky 2020). But in spite of these hardships, Mexican and Latinx immigrants to the Western Slope have managed to create stable communities, with deep roots, that are now extending into a second (and a third) generation.

Creating Immigrant Communities

In American popular discourses, Mexican immigrants are often portrayed as sojourners who come to the United States just to work and send money home, without developing meaningful attachments to the places where they reside—or the country that has welcomed them. This stereotype is fueled by the huge cultural gap between Anglos and Mexicans, and by the extended family connections in Mexico that most first-generation immigrants keep. Harvard Professor Samuel Huntington even turned this trope into the topic of his controversial book *Who Are We? The Challenges to America's National Identity* (2004), in which he argued that Mexican immigrants and their unassimilated children were eroding American culture and US democratic values. But this particular stereotype, like most, is overblown. Mexican immigrants to the Western Slope (and their children) reside in thriving ethnic communities and their second-generation children are now moving into the US middle class—just like every immigrant wave to America that preceded them. They are also investing in their new homeland. Mexican shops and restaurants have sprung up across the Western Slope, as well as community organizations that cater to immigrants (e.g., Hispanic Affairs Project, Compañeros, and Child & Migrant Services), the Western Colorado Latino Chamber of Commerce (based in Grand Junction), and even monthly Spanish-language newspapers: *La Voz del Pueblo* (The People's Voice) and *Entérate Latino* (Find Out, Latino). These immigrant-owned businesses and community organizations cement the presence of immigrants in American society, contribute to revitalizing local communities in the Western Slope, and provide newcomers with a stake in the host country. Over time, the newcomers from Mexico and other parts of Latin America are slowly becoming a part of America. But just as Mexican and Latinx immigrants are being transformed by their presence in Colorado's Western Slope, they are at the same time transforming social spaces in the region. Their demographic numbers, cultural practices, economic impact, and emerging political power are changing the face of the Western Slope and forcing a reexamination of a region in Colorado previously imagined as "white." These can be dramatic, unanticipated changes that may spark an Anglo backlash because of the fear of a "Mexican" takeover (D. Gutiérrez 1998; Román 2013), particularly in small communities where the changes are more noticeable (e.g., Eagle, Garfield, and Summit Counties).[35]

These Mexican/Latinx communities in Colorado's Western Slope are also highly transnational. They maintain cultural, economic, and even political ties with their country of origin; a vibrant regional identification; and a very close, personal connection to their hometowns. Transnationalism is broadly defined as "the processes by which immigrants forge and sustain multi-stranded social relations that link together their societies of origin and settlement" as these migrants "take actions, make decisions, and develop subjectivities and identities embedded in networks of relationships that connect them simultaneously to two or more nation-states" (Basch, Glick Schiller, and Szanton Blanc 1994, 7). These transnational social relations and related activities between immigrants in the host society and their home countries have been facilitated by major advances in communications and transportation technology since World War II (e.g., telephones, email, electronic remittances, and commercial aviation, among others).[36] Mexican migrant transnationalism has been widely documented in various contexts (Gill 2018; Jiménez 2010; Odem and Lacy 2009; Rouse 1992; R. Smith 2006), and the multinational, multigenerational Mexican/Latinx communities of the Western Slope are no exception. For example, first-generation Mexican immigrants in the Western Slope tend to be deeply religious and observant of Catholic festivities ("very ritualistic," in the words of Mr. Ricardo Pérez[37]). As such, these Western Slope immigrants required of religious services that were mostly unavailable when they arrived. The Catholic Church quickly responded by sending the Misioneras Guadalupanas del Espíritu Santo (Guadalupian Missionaries of the Holy Spirit) from California to help meet the spiritual needs of the immigrant community. But their local religious needs are only part of the picture. Members of these immigrant communities stay in touch with their friends and relatives back home and keep abreast of their hometowns' religious festivities. Some contribute money for the festivities, while others actually travel back home to participate in them. According to Ms. Marketa Zubkova,[38] who works with the immigrant community of Gunnison, for the Indigenous Cora people who make up a large portion of Mexican immigrants there, Holy Week is extremely important, as a time of the year when major festivities of the Cora cosmic worldview take place. Coras who can do so (because they have documents) will travel from Colorado to Nayarit to participate in Holy Week festivities such as "La Judea," a syncretic festival that combines pre-Hispanic traditions of fertility and Catholic rituals (CDI Mx 2016). Other Mexican migrants will travel home for the celebration of their hometown's patron saint festivity, a time when they reconnect with old friends and their extended family, bring them gifts from the United States, and engage in acts of charity.

Economic transnationalism takes the form of remittances and investments in businesses and real estate. Most Mexican migrants in the Western Slope that I interviewed indicated that they had family in Mexico that depended on remittances that they usually wired on a monthly or biweekly basis. In 2021, remittances to Mexico reached an all-time high of US$51.6 billion—94.9% of which originated in the United States (Aguilar Rangel 2022). The Mexican states of Guanajuato, Jalisco, and Michoacán received the most in remittances—states that are well represented among Mexican immigrants in Colorado's Western Slope. These remittances buy food, clothes, appliances, and pretty much whatever dependent families in Mexico need, but they are also utilized for investments such as setting up a small business (oftentimes a tiny grocery store built on the front porch of the family home), acquiring farmland, or buying a retirement home for homesick migrants in the United States. Mexican migrants living overseas also organize in hometown associations to raise funds for much-needed public projects back home, such as sport venues, clean-water systems, and streetlights (FitzGerald 2008; Lahiri 2004). Political forms of transnationalism are less common among Mexican migrants but can take the form of campaign donations to politicians, voting in Mexican national elections by mail from the United States, and even travelling back home to run for office in local elections (Zorrilla-Velazquez, Alfaro Ponce, and García-Hernández 2021). Overall, Mexican migrants in the Western Slope live highly transnational lives, are constantly in touch with family and friends back home, and remain engaged—sometimes remotely but occasionally in person—in the seasonal rituals and daily life of their hometowns.

Transnationalism usually wanes with the second generation. The children of immigrants (or those that immigrated to the United States at a very young age) lack the hometown connections that the adult immigrants cherish. Their world is the society of the host country, mixed in with the culture of their parents. As such, second-generation children face a different set of challenges from that of their parents but also enjoy opportunities that their parents lacked (Portes and Rumbaut 2001). They must face prevailing racist attitudes and discriminatory practices toward "Mexicans" that are well ingrained in the history of the American West. These attitudes and practices have become formidable obstacles in the educational trajectory of second-generation Mexican Americans and are a source of concern regarding their integration and potential for success in American society. Second-generation Mexican American students have to endure forms of discrimination unknown to their non-English-speaking parents and are—by most standards—an "at risk" demographic cohort (López and Stanton-Salazar 2001). While their immigrant parents expect—and endure—a life of hard work and privation in the United States because of their immigrant status, second-generation Mexican American children are led to believe in the American Dream and the promise of equality in American society, only to encounter other forms of racial discrimination in school and the workplace. In the words of Tom Acker,[39] this "racist overlay" makes life hard for second-generation Mexican/Latinx students. They speak English and strive to get a decent education, only to be treated like "Mexicans" by an Anglo mainstream that cannot see beyond their skin color and Spanish surnames. Most second-generation children are curious about their roots and try to balance the weight of family expectations (e.g., to get an education and a good job) with the challenges and demands of US society. But they lack good role models, so boys tend to focus on work and paying the bills, while girls seek the long-term strategy of pursuing an education, according to Telluride high school teacher Ms. Jenna Hagen.[40] Many feel angry about not fitting in and live in homes with extended families separated by immigration and/or deportation.

These contradictions inherent to the Mexican American experience—and their powerful impact on outcomes—are succinctly described by David López and Ricardo Stanton-Salazar (2001, 61):

> In some ways, the Mexican example reflects the *normal* run of things in American immigration history: The children of immigrants get the minimal education offered by their new homeland and find jobs somewhere between the dirty work their parents did and the carers of more privileged groups. In other important ways, however, the history of incorporation of *Mexicanos* is categorically different from the cycle of assimilation experienced by white ethnics. When the burdens of historical segregation, economic exploitation, and enduring racial stereotypes are added to their socioeconomic disadvantages, then low Mexican-American achievement levels become more comprehensible.

Despite these challenges, the second-generation, US-born children of Mexican immigrants, because of their US education and fluency in the English language, have found employment in pink-collar occupations (mainly the females), while males are keen to join the US military—a ticket to see the world beyond the Western Slope that also provides gainful employment. Intermarriages with the Anglo population and with Hispanos and Chicanxs are slowly taking place too, according to Martín Valdez,[41] publisher of *La Voz del Pueblo*. In that sense, the second-generation children of Mexican immigrants are behaving just as scores of previous immigrants before them did: They are being assimilated and acculturated by schools and other socializing agents while still retaining traces of their parents' culture (such as bilingualism). This process takes place simultaneously with the arrival of new immigrants to the region, thus giving the appearance (to casual Anglo observers) that the community remains wholly "Mexican" and does not intend to become Americanized, a phenomenon known as "replenished ethnicity" (Jiménez 2010, chap. 4). But the trope of the "unassimilable Mexican" runs deep throughout the American West, and it seeks to delegitimize Latinxs by alleging that they—because of their cultural ancestry—cannot become full-fledged Americans. The struggle for legitimacy in American society is one that Hispanos faced in the past and that Mexicans and other Latinxs still face to this day (Huntington 2004, 230–247).

While racial prejudice and daily microaggressions against "Mexicans" are still commonplace, the second-generation Mexican Americans of the Western Slope are deeply immersed in American society and worlds away from their parents' lived experiences as immigrants. Meanwhile, the progress of the old Hispano and Chicanx families in the region goes on. Most form part of a solid middle class, made up of businesspersons and professionals, such as Mr. Levi Lucero,[42] a realtor and Grand Junction icon who played a key role in renaming Mesa State College to Colorado Mesa University in 2011. In 2000, another one of these middle-class Latinxs, Cindy Enos-Martinez,[43] became the mayor of Grand Junction—the largest city in the Western Slope. Some Hispanos have successfully assimilated into American society and trend conservative politically, but others retain their Latinx identity and see in the plight of recent Mexican immigrants the story of their own families, thus supporting efforts for comprehensive migratory reform, to provide the undocumented with driver's licenses, and for Congress to pass the DREAM Act, as expressed to me by Mrs. Nicole Bernal Ruiz,[44] who used to work for the Hispanic Affairs Project in Grand Junction.

Finally, Mexican immigrants are major contributors to their communities and to a robust economy in Colorado. They still build homes, clean rooms, and pick fruit, but increasingly they also operate as small business owners and have moved up into pink-collar and white-collar professions. Moreover, throughout the American West, Latinx immigrants have infused rural counties with new blood at a time when the Anglo population is getting older, and their children are leaving for jobs and education in the big cities (Pohl 2017a, 2017b). In rural Colorado, most ranchers and farmers are older white men, but their workforce is Latinx. In 2012, the average farmer in Colorado was fifty-nine years old (Quinton 2019). As the children of Anglo farmers and ranchers increasingly move to urban areas, Latinx immigrants from rural backgrounds have picked up the mantle—Anglos and Mexicans united by their love for the land. John Harold, the king of Olathe's Sweet Corn, employed thousands of Mexican immigrant workers over the course of more than two decades, some of whom now return with their grown children to harvest corn in his fields. When the Harolds were criticized for hiring immigrant labor from Mexico, John came to their defense. Currently, one of Mr. Harold's children (who married a Mexican immigrant) grows sweet corn in Mexico, thanks to the connections that the family developed over the years with their Mexican workers (McKelvey 2016). In a surprising turn of events, Mexican corn, once devastated by NAFTA's subsided imports, is making a comeback thanks to the migration of Mexican workers to US farms.

Colorado's Western Slope is being transformed by the forces of global capitalism. NAFTA, enacted three decades ago, set in motion forces within Mexico's rural areas that had widespread ripple effects in Mexico, the United States, and the Western Slope itself. The latter region's economic growth required hundreds of cheap laborers for its emerging sectors (e.g., construction and services), demand that transnational migrants from Mexico (and other parts of Latin America) would meet. In doing so, Mexican migrants fueled the region's economic growth but also effected its sociocultural transformation. The Western Slope nowadays boasts vibrant Hispano, Chicanx, and Mexican/Latinx communities which have become an integral part of the social fabric of the region. Historically disconnected and isolated from the hustle and bustle of the Front Range, the Western Slope increasingly mirrors the demographic patterns of the state at large, with a fast growing, multilayered, multigenerational Latinx population: a new, up-and-coming batch of Latino Coloradans.

Conclusion: Transforming Colorado's Western Slope

Contrary to xenophobic tropes describing Mexican immigrants as moochers and criminals who take advantage of Americans and the US government (Black 2011; Sigman 2012), or as unassimilable newcomers, the reality is far less extreme. Just like thousands of immigrants before them (including the European ancestors of the current US Anglo majority), the immigrants from Mexico and other Latin American countries who have moved to the Western Slope in the last two to three decades simply want a shot at the American Dream. They are willing to cross dangerous international borders, live in the shadows of American society, and endure economic exploitation and racial prejudice for their families to have a better future. Many—like the European immigrants who preceded them over a century ago—seek to escape nations that deny them these opportunities, oppress their citizens and exploit them, or cannot guarantee public safety. These Latinx immigrants have flocked to Colorado's Western Slope because of the job opportunities that are available to them and a safe environment in which to raise their children. And most have been able to achieve their own particular version of the American Dream. The immigrants I interviewed in Colorado's Western Slope were generally optimistic about their future—though cognizant of the challenges that they and their families faced in the United States. Despite obstacles like anti-Mexican discrimination and structural racism, their second-generation children, like the children of previous immigrants, are attending school, learning English, and slowly making it in American society. The US assimilation process is still quite vibrant and effective—as it was a century and a half ago. US schools, media, social networks, and their own peers provide the Latinx second generation with a vastly different social milieu than the one their parents experienced in their sending societies (Portes and Rumbaut 2001; Rumbaut and Portes 2001).

Moreover, the transnational migration of Mexicans and Latinxs to the Western Slope is not taking place in a vacuum. The combined forces of global capitalism and international labor migration are funneling them to the Global North in general (Sassen 1988) and the Western Slope in particular, where the development of new economic sectors has sparked a demand for cheap labor which these immigrants meet. Supply simply meets demand, though in complex ways. Transnational migratory networks provide would-be migrants with information about when and where to migrate, where the jobs are, how much they pay, where to live, where to shop, the pros and cons of different locations, and local quality-of-life standards for their families. Furthermore, the historical presence of Hispanos, Chicanxs, and other Latinxs in the Western Slope region has helped channel their migration and facilitate their incorporation through previously existing transnational social networks. The NAFTA cohort of Mexican migrants to the Western Slope is neither the first migratory wave to the region—nor will it be its last. Like in a multitiered cake, today's cohort of transnational migrants (mainly) from Mexico simply adds another demographic layer to the Western Slope's growing Latinx communities, replenishing their cultural capital, fueling economic development, revitalizing small towns and rural areas, increasing the region's diversity, and in the process enriching Colorado's society at large. It is but the latest Latinx cultural borderland in our state. Finally, the movement and/or arrival of transnational migrants to the Western Slope mirror regional trends in the Mountain West: "The Hispanic population is moving out of or new Hispanic immigrants are not moving to, the historically Hispanic core" (Shumway 2015, 412). The San Luis Valley, the historic heart of the state's Latinx population, has been losing relevance to metro areas like Denver and the rapidly growing communities of the Western Slope. Latinxs, whether they are immigrants or US citizens, gravitate to where the jobs are, as pretty much the rest of the US population does. The Western Slope, with its rich mix of Old West and New West industries, is Colorado's latest economic frontier.

Unfortunately, this latest Latinx cohort is not immune to the racialization processes that previous waves had to endure. As if history insists on repeating itself (or at least, rhyming) the NAFTA cohort of Mexican labor is stereotyped, racialized, dehumanized, and exploited, in ways similar to the displacement of the Hispanos of the San Luis Valley in the nineteenth century, the exploitation of the braceros of the Eastern Plains in the first half of the twentieth century, and the exclusion of the Chicanos of the 1960s–1970s. Even as overt racial prejudice is nowadays politically incorrect, the same racially based mechanisms of exploitation are at work in extracting profits from cheap immigrant labor, while racialization processes help keep Latinx immigrants "in their place" regarding mainstream Anglo society. At a time when Colorado (re)defines itself as a "progressive" state in twenty-first century America, some things never seem to change.

In the immediate post-NAFTA period, transnational migrants from Mexico have become the latest cohort in Colorado's lengthy Latinx history. These migrants are major contributors to the state's economy and have built resilient communities in the face of adversity; their second-generation children are moving into the ranks of the American middle class. When NAFTA was signed in 1992, few thought that Colorado's Western Slope would be so radically transformed in a time span of just three decades by the influx of thousands of migrants from Latin America. In hindsight, their arrival is not a new story but a new chapter in the history of Latinxs in Colorado.

CONCLUSION

Colorado's Latinxs and the New American West

Race has always played a role in the American West—and Colorado is no exception to that fact. Popularly imagined as a white territory and state, the presence of Latinxs in Colorado is characterized by their invisibility in the mainstream's cultural landscape, historical neglect by state and local authorities, and a lack of acknowledgment of their role(s) in the region's economy. Even though Latinxs have long been Colorado's largest ethnic minority (after Indigenous peoples were massacred and pushed out of the territory and state or into small reservations in the late nineteenth century—as was the case with the Utes) and the main source of cheap labor for most of the state's industries, a popular perception has remained that Colorado was an "empty" landscape suitable for white settlement. Unlike California, New Mexico, and Texas, where Anglos had to contend with much larger populations of "Mexicans," in Colorado the numbers of Latinxs remained small (when compared to the Anglo population) for decades after the end of the US-Mexican War in 1848. Overall demographic size may have rendered Colorado's Latinxs invisible in the popular imagination but not for the state's economic sectors that depended on their labor. As examined in the previous chapters, generations of Hispanos, Mexican Americans, and Chicanxs toiled in the fields, mines, factories, and service sector industries of the Centennial State.

By the twenty-first century, the invisibility of Colorado's Latinxs unfortunately remains in place to a large extent, but it is not as striking as in decades prior. Substantial domestic demographic growth, new patterns of international labor migration, the social gains of the Chicano Movement, and evolving cultural mores have brought Colorado's Latinxs out of obscurity and into the public eye. The sheer reality of Latinx demographic growth and socioeconomic mobility mean that Colorado's Latinxs are occupying more social spaces than ever before. For example, the Denver metro area has a thriving Latinx middle and professional class that owns hundreds of small businesses and is well represented in both the public and the private sectors (Colorado Hispanic Chamber of Commerce 2018). Watershed political events like the Chicano Movement of the 1960s–1970s and the tenure of Federico Peña as mayor of Denver in the 1980s–1990s forced Anglo Coloradans to reckon with the fact that Latinxs were an integral part of the state's social landscape, not just as racialized outsiders who did backbreaking labor but as legitimate political actors on their own, vying for and occupying spaces that were formerly reserved for whites (de la Garza 1979). Those political changes sparked a shift in cultural perceptions too. It may seem minor nowadays, but when Federico Peña became mayor of Denver, he was properly addressed as *Peña* (with the use of the Spanish letter *eñe*) and not by its common Anglicized form as *Pena*. Finally, the historical contributions of Latinxs to Colorado began to be acknowledged by the authorities for the first time, even if sometimes stereotyped as quaint relics of the past by the emphasis on nineteenth-century Hispano history—as in the case of some state and federal tourism campaigns (Colorado Tourism Office 2023; Sangre de Cristo National Heritage Area 2019b).

This chapter reexamines Colorado's racial landscape and reassesses the role(s) played by Latinxs at the local, state, and regional levels. The first section analyzes the gains made by Latinxs at the local and state levels while delving into the challenges remaining for the achievement of equality between Latinxs and Anglos in Colorado. The second section takes the case study of Latinxs in Colorado and frames it within a regional perspective, in order to point out how their experiences dovetail with those of Latinxs throughout the American West and reinforce narratives of otherness and belonging in this historically contested—and iconic—region of the United States. Finally, the third section summarizes some of the book's main points while introducing questions and potential themes for future research.

City and State: Latinxs Entering the Mainstream

As examined in chapter 3, the Chicano Movement burst the doors open for the participation of Latinxs in Colorado politics. The Anglo establishment, fearful of the radical, oftentimes violent politics of El Movimiento, sought to co-opt Latinxs into its ranks. In particular, the Democratic Party, which had broadly supported the civil rights movement, decided to pursue a new national electoral strategy that involved building a multiracial coalition of voters, which included African Americans in the South and urban centers of the Northeast and the Midwest, and Latinxs in the West, as a way to offset Republican gains in the South and the Mountain West (DeSipio 1996; Francis-Fallon 2019; Kazin 2022). That electoral realignment allowed some Latinxs in Colorado to make it onto the Democratic ticket and gain elective office in the last decades of the twentieth century, a trend that carries on into the twenty-first century as the Front Range's Latinx and non-white populations have increased. For example, by 2010 Denver was only slightly more than half non-Hispanic white, and Aurora had already become a majority-minority major urban center in the Denver metro area. Despite being imagined as an Anglo enclave for decades, the reality is that Denver has never been a culturally homogeneous city (Goetz and Boschmann 2018, 76). It has always been a city of immigrants (mainly white ethnics but also including Latinxs, African Americans, Asian Americans, and Native Americans) that by the twenty-first century has become a diverse melting pot of races (T. Romero 2004a).

Denver's diversity, which had been building up over decades, was historically hemmed in by segregation and redlining. Hispanic neighborhoods lined up along the South Platte River Valley, just outside of the downtown district, in areas characterized by industrial and commercial uses, and railroad lines. Other Hispanic neighborhoods, such as Auraria, no longer exist (see chapter 3), while neighborhoods formerly occupied by white ethnics (e.g., Italians and western Europeans), such as Highland (in northwest Denver), became increasingly settled by Hispanics as the former moved out (Goetz and Boschmann 2018, 79). Ironically, "postwar white flight to the suburbs made it possible for Hispanic families to buy houses in neighborhoods once occupied by the white immigrant working class," leading to high rates of Hispanic homeownership (Tracey 2020, 172–173). This phenomenon created a class of Hispanic homeowners who were more invested in local affairs and metro politics than the itinerant sugar beet workers of the 1920s–1940s who gravitated in and out of Denver during the offseason (see chapter 2). A stable, growing postwar Hispanic population in the Denver metro area (and other parts of the Front Range), coupled with the visibility of the Chicano Movement of the 1960s–1970s, allowed emerging Hispanic/Latinx (though mainly Mexican American) political leaders to enter the political mainstream during the 1970s–1990s. Colorado's Latinx politics was no longer limited to San Luis Valley counties. It was now centered in Denver, Colorado's capital and the heart of the state in more ways than one.[1]

Pauline "Polly" Baca is, without a doubt, the state's preeminent Latinx electoral trailblazer, achieving a number of "firsts" for Latinxs, people of color, and women in Colorado. Baca, from Greeley, Colorado, got involved in politics while attending Colorado State University in the 1960s. After short stints working in Washington, DC, California, and Arizona, she moved back to Colorado. Baca was elected to the Colorado House of Representatives in 1974, as the first Latina representing Adams County, and in 1978 she became the first Hispanic state senator in the state. She chaired both the House Democratic Caucus and the Senate Democratic Caucus during her tenure, which ended in 1986. In addition, Senator Baca worked with several Democratic presidents, going all the way back to the Lyndon B. Johnson administration, and she became a fixture in national Democratic Party politics (Democratic Party of Denver 2023). Baca struggled against racial and gender prejudices in a world still dominated by Anglo men, but her perseverance motivated generations of Latinxs to enter local and state politics.

Federico Peña, a lawyer and out-of-state transplant who originally hailed from south Texas, followed in Baca's footsteps. Peña moved to Denver in 1972, where he worked as a legal advisor for Mexican American / Chicanx nonprofit organizations. Running as a Democrat, Peña was elected state representative in 1978 and quickly rose to become minority leader at the Colorado House of Representatives. In 1983, he defeated several establishment candidates (including incumbent Mayor William "Bill" McNichols) in both the primary election as well as the runoff, to become the first Hispanic mayor of Denver—a surprising political development in a city where Latinxs did not constitute a significant voting block at the time. But Peña defied expectations (and tropes) about Latinxs by being a nonthreatening, picture-perfect candidate, moderate in his policies, who appealed to centrists (Leonard and Noel 1990, 404). Moreover, Peña's unexpected electoral success hinged on inspiring Denverites to dream big, enabling him to transcend his ethnicity, despite efforts by his opponents to portray him as a radical Chicanx lawyer (M. Vigil 1987, 98–100). Death threats prevented Peña from attending his own postelection party, and his autobiography details numerous indignities and instances of racial prejudice directed at him because of his Hispanic ethnicity (F. Peña 2021). Yet, Peña rose to the occasion and indeed challenged Denverites to dream big: He was responsible for the construction of the new Denver International Airport, a massive undertaking on the outskirts of the city that almost did not happen; a new convention center in downtown Denver, known as the Colorado Convention Center; and he also brought to Denver the Colorado Rockies, the city's first Major League Baseball team. All were huge political and financial risks at the time that would eventually pay off handsomely.[2] Over a quarter century after the end of his tenure as mayor, Peña is considered one of the best mayors Denver has ever had (Silverman 2021) and a source of inspiration for aspiring Latinx politicians in Colorado and across the nation. His postmayoral service as US secretary of transportation and US secretary of energy under the Bill Clinton administration only added to his local and national stature. Most important, Mayor Peña normalized Latinxs in the eyes of the Anglo public as people capable of performing at the highest levels of government—and being quite successful at it.

The first three decades of the twenty-first century have witnessed the election and appointment of more Latinxs to higher office in Colorado—including representing the state's constituents at the federal level. Examples are brothers Ken and John Salazar, from Colorado's San Luis Valley. Kenneth "Ken" Salazar, a lawyer and descendant of Hispano settlers who came to the area from northern New Mexico, was elected state attorney general in 1998. In 2004, he launched a bid to become US senator, running as a moderate Democrat. After securing his party's nomination, Salazar went on to successfully run against beer magnate Pete Coors (the Republican candidate) and become Colorado's first Latinx senator and the first Latinx to be elected to statewide office in the state. Ken Salazar served briefly in the US Senate—just four years—before accepting the position of secretary of the interior for the Barack Obama administration in 2009 (United States Congress). From 2021 to 2025, Senator Salazar was US ambassador to Mexico. His older brother John Salazar, a farmer and rancher in the San Luis Valley, was elected to the Colorado House of Representatives as a Democrat in 2002, before becoming a US representative for Colorado's Third Congressional District in 2005 (Farer 2004). John Salazar represented the Third Congressional District (which encompasses the Western Slope, the San Luis Valley, and Pueblo) for six years, before losing reelection in 2010. Nowadays, the Third leans Republican and has not elected a Democrat since Representative Salazar's defeat in 2010. Despite the fact that the Salazar family has deep roots in the region that date back to the founding of Santa Fe, New Mexico, in 1610, their Hispanic ancestry made them the target of prejudice and racial discrimination as they sought—and reached—higher office: "I've been taunted, called names—from dirty Mexican to lots of other names—as I was growing up, and even now as a United States senator," according to then Senator Ken Salazar (Johnson 2006). It is a sober reflection on prevailing racial mores in American society, when even the most prominent Latinx officeholder in Colorado is not immune from ad hominem attacks and readily becomes a "Mexican" in the eyes of some bigoted Anglos. Unfortunately, what these three case studies of Latinx elected officials from Colorado (Baca, Peña, and the Salazars) have in common is not just a story of personal achievement and political success but also the fact that all of them had to overcome deep seated anti-Mexican, anti-Latinx racial prejudices in order to make it in US politics. Despite the enormous social obstacles in their path and the discrimination that they had to endure, these Latinx leaders forged ahead and blazed a path for future generations of Latinxs (and other people of color) in the state.

Several Latinxs have traveled down this path, and nowadays Latinxs are regularly elected to the Colorado General Assembly, where some have reached leadership positions in both chambers. In 2015, Crisanta Duran, a Democrat representing northwest Denver, became majority leader of the Colorado House of Representatives, and in 2019 she was elected speaker of the house—the first Latina to become speaker in state history (Frank 2019). In 2015, Senator Lucía Guzmán (a Democrat representing Denver) became minority leader of the Colorado Senate, followed by Senator Leroy Garcia, a Democrat from Pueblo, who became minority leader in 2018. When his party retook control of the body in 2019, Garcia became president of the state's upper chamber (Goodland 2018). Still, despite the political success of some Latinxs at the state level, political representation for the state's largest ethnic cohort lags behind their numbers. Lack of US citizenship status has a lot to do with it, particularly for a community with a significant number of migrants. Youth is another strike against Colorado's Latinxs. Being a young demographic cohort (at least when compared to non-Hispanic whites) means that many Latinxs in Colorado are minors—and still not eligible to vote. As a result, just about half of Colorado's Latinxs are eligible to vote, a stark contrast to the 80% of the state's white population that can do so. And while Latinxs represent over 22% of the state's population, they only make up 15% of eligible voters in Colorado. Other hurdles stand in their path to political empowerment, namely, low educational attainment and higher-than-average poverty rates, two social factors that conspire to tamper formal political engagement. About a fifth of eligible Latinx voters in Colorado have less than a high school education and an annual household income that is less than $30,000. On the other hand, over 40% of white voters in Colorado have a bachelor's degree, and over a third of them have annual household incomes of over $100,000 (Pew Research Center 2016). This socioeconomic chasm between Anglos and Latinxs parallels historical patterns of inequality and racial discrimination against the latter to make of Colorado a state still dominated by Anglo interests—despite the substantial gains made by Latinxs in the last few decades.

The road to success in America usually begins with education, and at the start of the twenty-first century that path is still riddled with potholes and bumps on the road for Latinxs. Latinxs in Colorado have made significant strides when it comes to education (e.g., a 20% increase in high school graduation rates), but there is still plenty of catching up to do, particularly when Latinx educational levels are compared to those for Anglos. A recent analysis of US Census data for 2010–2020 carried out by the Colorado News Collaborative highlights entrenched educational gaps between non-Hispanic whites and Colorado's communities of color—particularly Latinxs. Despite gains at the high school level, where 75.4% of Latinx students graduated as of 2020 (Robles 2022), college graduation rates for Latinxs in Colorado are 31 percentage points lower than for whites and 10 percentage points lower than for African Americans—the largest such gap in the nation (Hubbard and Griego 2022). This unsettling gap ironically coexists with the fact that Latinxs account for three out of every four new high school students in the state. Whereas Colorado is a tony college destination for out-of-state students attracted by the state's outdoorsy lifestyle, painfully little investment took place to help in-state students during the last decade. The double whammy of the 2008 recession and the COVID-19 pandemic slammed the brakes on economic growth, affecting Latinxs and other communities of color in Colorado (e.g., African Americans) disproportionally. The slow recovery from these economic crises slowed investment in education and social services that get underserved students and first-generation students into college. The stakes could not be higher: as is the case around the nation, Colorado's white Baby Boomers are retiring in large numbers, but Millennial and Gen Z Latinxs in general do not have the same levels of education to replace them. Colorado's workforce desperately needs significant investments in education so that aging white Baby Boomers can be replaced by an up-and-coming younger demographic cohort that is mostly Latinx.

Finally, despite the persisting socioeconomic gap between Latinxs and Anglos in Colorado, recent polls have shown that Latinxs are heavily invested in the political system, share similar concerns with the state's population at large, and support policies that are in line with Colorado's recent politically progressive turn (Daum et al. 2011; Osgood and Frank 2020).³ For example, a 2022 poll listed the three main concerns of Latinx Coloradans: the rising cost of living (i.e., inflation), the economy, and improving wages and income—all of them priority issues for the population at large as salaries could not keep up with inflation and gas prices soared during the summer of 2022. The other priorities for Latinx respondents also dovetailed nicely with the state's progressive agenda: addressing gun violence, creating affordable housing, lowering health-care costs, protecting women's reproductive health/abortion rights, education, and discrimination/racial justice (Colorado Organization for Latina Opportunity and Reproductive Rights et al. 2022, 1, 6). The emphasis of Latinxs on these issues and their preference for government-based solutions (e.g., environmental regulations, restrictions on gun ownership, rent controls, abortion rights, universal health care, and protecting same-sex marriage) clearly favor the Democrats (2–3). Not surprisingly, 47% of Latinx respondents identified as Democrats, 28% as independents, and just 17% as Republicans. On the ideological spectrum, Latinx respondents classified themselves mostly as somewhat or very liberal (44%) and moderate (40%), with just 17% of them identifying as conservative (16). These numbers do not bode well for Colorado Republicans, who have struggled to recruit Latinxs, particularly after the likes of Tom Tancredo, Lauren Boebert, and Donald Trump—and their fiery rhetoric—keep pushing the Republican Party into the ideological fringe, turning it into a white nationalist, xenophobic, anti-immigrant movement in the eyes of potential Latinx voters. Republicans do have an electoral angle, though, as Colorado's Latinxs express a deep concern for their economic well-being—an issue where Republicans could exploit voters' feelings of anxiety over the economy. But instead, Colorado's Republicans have painted themselves into a corner by embracing nativism, conspiracy theories, and a general disregard for the well-being of Colorado's Latinx population (Korecki 2022; Woods 2022). As the size of Colorado's Latinx population continues to increase and as they become a larger share of the state's electorate, it looks like they will help swell the ranks of Colorado's Democrats and moderate and liberal independents and make the state even bluer than it currently is. In turn, as the Democrats depend more on the Latinx vote in Colorado as a reliable constituency, it is likely that the former will field more Latinx candidates (as was the case with the successful candidacy of Dr. Yadira Caraveo in Colorado's Eighth Congressional District in 2022) and pursue policies that are amenable to the issues that Latinxs have identified as their top priorities. The intimate political nexus of Colorado's Latinxs with the Democratic Party actually reflects nationwide trends seen among Latinx voters—with the major exception of Cuban Americans in south Florida (Krogstad 2020) and, more recently, Mexican Americans in south Texas (Svitek and Choi 2022)—but further facilitated by the state's very progressive political landscape.

The Region: Latinxs in the New American West

Although this work has limited itself to examining the experience of Latinxs in Colorado, it also sheds light on certain themes germane to the (re)definition of the role and standing of Latinxs in the twenty-first century American West. Latinxs (including recent waves of Mexican migrants) are such an intrinsic part of the American West that their presence practically touches on most Western historical themes, as well as on some that are unique to Latinx communities in the West. Following are some connecting themes and questions intended to contribute to this ongoing conversation (Rensink 2022).

LATINXS/HISPANICS ARE NOT FOREIGN; THEY ARE PART OF THE AMERICAN WEST. Despite nativist political discourses that sought—and still seek—to portray Latinxs as perpetually "foreign" (Gómez 2022), the latter have always been part of the American West. From the Hispano populations that settled parts of the West long before it became part of the United States, to the waves of Mexican, Central American, and other Latinx immigrants that have arrived in the last few decades, the presence of Latinxs in the West has been a long-standing defining feature of the region. Hispanos from New Mexico were the first Americans to settle the territory that eventually became the state of Colorado (see chapter 1). As their descendants throughout southern Colorado are keen to say: "I didn't cross the border; the border crossed me"—a reference to the signing of the Treaty of Guadalupe Hidalgo in 1848 that created a new international border between the United States and Mexico (DiPrince 2023).

Ironically, much of the "othering" of Latinxs (and other communities of color) has been carried out by Anglo groups claiming nativity after only a generation or two in the American West. In the second half of the nineteenth century, Native Americans and Hispanos were quickly racialized as "foreign" Others by Anglos predating on their lands—part of a political project designed to undergird a large-scale land grab and the establishment of a pliant cheap labor pool. Presently, Colorado's Latinxs are oftentimes seen as "foreign" by Anglo transplants surprised by the presence of "Mexicans" in *their* state, regardless of whether these Latinxs are old-stock Hispanos or more recently arrived immigrants from Latin America. In contrast, the leaders of the Chicano Movement (see chapter 3) argued that Chicanxs were native to the American West because of their Indigenous ancestry (and therefore, whites were the actual "foreigners"). The Western Slope, with a growing population of Anglo transplants and retirees, and small but growing Latinx communities made up of large numbers of immigrants, is a good case study of this pernicious trend of othering Latinxs (see chapter 4). Throughout the American West, whiteness still amounts to unquestionable nativity, whereas communities of color have never been able to totally shed the stigma of foreignness (Pierce 2016).

The perception of Latinxs as "foreign" in the American West also has to do with sustained migration (mainly) from Mexico. Unlike Anglo Westerners whose ancestors migrated to the Eastern United States but eventually moved west in the nineteenth and twentieth centuries, or new, twenty-first-century Anglo transplants from other US regions, ongoing international migration defines the Mexican Western experience, "buttress[ing] the association between Mexicanness and foreignness" (Jiménez 2010, 258). For most Anglos in the American West (and thorough the United States), migration is a chapter in their families' history that is buried deeply in the past. Their ancestors came from Europe, they endured hardships (and some discrimination too) but eventually assimilated and became "Americans." It is now settled history, and time and space provide a safe distance from which contemporary Anglos can view and evaluate their own migratory background. There is even a certain nostalgia about the plight of their ethnic ancestors among Western Anglos, exemplified by the availability of Colorado "Pioneer" and "Italian American" license plates (Division of Motor Vehicles 2023). Despite this ongoing romanticizing and imagining of their own migrant ancestors, contemporary Anglos would not find many actual differences between their foreign ancestors and current Latinx migrants. Both cohorts would probably share similar histories of poverty and persecution in their home countries, a desire to "make it" in America, a lack of familiarity with the language and the culture of the host nation (i.e., culture shock), and looks that were not typically "American." Tom Tancredo's Italian grandparents were probably as out of place in Denver as the recent Mexican immigrants that he loves to demonize.

Jiménez (2010, chap. 8) argues that the Mexican-origin population of the American West is unable to engage in such nostalgic thoughts—and it pays a price for it. The fact that Mexican migration has been fairly consistent since the late nineteenth century (and it is still ongoing) means that Mexicans are racialized in the American West not only because of their looks but also because of this permanent connection to immigration. Unlike Anglo migration, there is no closing chapter in Mexican migratory history. There are no ethnic grandparents who are by now but a hazy memory sparked by a blurry black-and-white portrait in the hands of their American descendants. There is no Statue of Liberty and Ellis Island. Mexican-origin individuals, regardless of the time of arrival of their ancestors (including those who did not arrive but were annexed after the 1846–1848 war with Mexico), are still being defined by Anglo society through the lens of the ongoing migration of their peers. Ethnicity remains salient in the Mexican-origin community to an extent that is unknown—and misconstrued—in Anglo circles. Mexican-origin people are neither an unassimilated community of immigrants (and the children of immigrants), as Samuel Huntington (2004) argued; nor a separate ethnic nation, as Chicanx activists struggled for; nor assimilated, hyphenated Americans, as Mexican Americans hoped for. They are all of those things—and more. The Mexican-origin communities of the American West resemble a multilayer cake made up of multigenerational, citizen and immigrant, documented and undocumented, assimilated and unassimilated cohorts—all bound together by a common narrative: the Mexican migratory experience. In Anglo eyes, the ongoing Mexican migratory experience racializes *all* "Mexicans," turning them into a permanent immigrant group in the United States (Jiménez 2010, 259).

Moreover, for Anglo nativists, the US-Mexico border is no Ellis Island but rather a problem that begs a solution; and the Mexican presence in the United States is not a welcome development that enriches the social fabric of America but rather a direct result of failed law enforcement and migration policies. Thus, in dominant Anglo narratives, there is no room for Mexican-origin "real" Americans.

Regardless of whether the Mexican and other Latinx presence in the American West is perceived as beneficial or not by the Anglo mainstream, the fact remains that there has always been a Mexican presence in the region. It is one that will not go away; rather, the Mexican-origin and other Latinx populations of the American West have been increasing in their size, visibility, and impact. As much as Anglo nativists may try to portray "Mexicans" as foreign, they are an intrinsic part of the American West, helping define it historically and contemporarily as the multicultural region that we know nowadays.

WESTERN LABOR IS "MEXICAN" LABOR. Mexicans may not had been a good fit for Anglo standards of whiteness, but they always had a place in Western industries as cheap laborers (Kim 2012). The West is a "Third World" region of the US First World, which has many elements in common with other frontier territories: dependent on big government, extractive industries, and tourism; geographically distant from the centers of power, decision making, and capital; conquered and exploited from elsewhere; and vast, rural, and underpopulated. In the American West, the "Mexican" label became a placeholder for Hispanos, Chicanxs, Mexican Americans, and other Latinxs who toil in economic sectors where labor is racialized, low wages and harsh working conditions are the norm, and Anglos rarely work alongside Mexicans. Since 1848, "Mexicans" have been the preferred cheap labor force in Western farms, ranches, mines, and other industries (e.g., the railroad industry). As the Old West transitions to—and coexists with—the New West, "Mexicans" continue to be the main cheap labor force of the twenty-first century American West. In a sense, Mexican migrants travel from the Global South to a peripheral region of the Global North. For example, construction sites, retail businesses, and the hospitality and amenity industries of Colorado's Western Slope rely on "Mexican" labor to turn a profit while maintaining labor costs down—as is the case throughout the West (see chapter 4). The background of the workers has changed in the last two centuries, with more immigrants from central and southern Mexico, Central America, and some South American countries (e.g., Bolivia, Chile, and Peru), but their racialization in Western industries continues unabated. Throughout the Western Slope, Peruvian sheepherders, Cora housekeepers, and Guatemalan mushroom farmworkers perform "Mexican" labor: racialized, low-paying, menial jobs that Anglos would not do. In American society, arduous labor often goes beyond a low wage and a job description—it involves race, too. Hired in large numbers during boom years, but compelled to leave during bust periods, "Mexican" labor maintains a long-standing, continuous presence in the American West, unlike other regions of the United States. There would not be an American West without "Mexican" labor. It is simply unimaginable but remains largely unacknowledged.

The racialization of "Mexican" labor represents an obstacle to the full acceptance and achievement of equality among Latinxs in the American West. As long as Latinxs are perceived as "Mexicans" fit only for "Mexican" labor, Anglos will have a hard time accepting them as their equals—or in positions of social leadership and political power. Major investments in the education of the Latinx community are needed, not only for its own improvement but also for the benefit of society at large.

WHAT IS THE AMERICAN WEST—AND DO LATINXS GET TO (RE)DEFINE IT? Our (American) West is a geographical figment of the nation's imagination, based on the westward expansion of the United States. We have a West just because American society looked at it from the East. For Asian migrants, it was their East, while for Indigenous peoples, it is home. For Latinxs, the American West has been their North (El Norte), a designation that overlaps with distinctions between the Global North (which includes the American West) and the Global South (which includes Latin America). Therefore, for Latinxs, El Norte is more than a geographical label; it is a socioeconomic realm with sharp economic distinctions but blurred cultural ones. El Norte can be an extension of home but also a foreign land. The borderlands—a cultural zone that extends far away from the international border into the Western United States and northern Mexico—blend the Global South into the Global North as much as they blend Mexico into the United States. Here, history moves in a northerly fashion, north from Mexico (and before that, New Spain). Yet, the borderlands are also a region on their own, distinct from points further north and south but connected by transnational networks (Gutiérrez and Young 2010): a Hispano and Chicano homeland that also partakes in the American West's ethnic diversity and links to lands abroad. When Mexicans migrate to Colorado's Eastern Plains and Western Slope, they encounter an unfamiliar land with familiar faces—a region foreign in a domestic sense. Therefore, for Latinx peoples, the American West revolves on a north-south axis, as visualized from the Global South. From this perspective, Anglos are not native to the area but newcomers, and Latinxs have always been part of the history of El Norte.

The American West is—and has been for a long time—home to Latinxs (Iber and De León 2006). Despite efforts by the Anglo establishment to portray Latinxs as racialized, foreign Others (Pierce 2016), the American West is home to Latinxs whose presence, labor, and culture helped build and fashion it into the iconic region that it is nowadays (Wyckoff 2014, 164–165). Without its mainly Mexican-origin Latinx influences, the *American* West would not exist, for the American West's largest demographic minority called this region home for a good century before the arrival of *los americanos*, and to this day millions of Mexican-ancestry Hispanos, Mexican Americans, Chicanxs, and Mexican immigrants reside in this region, define it, and make it prosper. Moreover, in the American West, Latinx demographic minorities have become over time demographic pluralities and, in some cases, majorities at the state and county level (e.g., in California, New Mexico, and Texas). If anything, the American West is more Latinx than ever.

Colorado also happens to be a good case study of how Latinxs (re)define the American West. Despite Anglo tropes about enterprising white prospectors and hardy pioneer families settling the territory and the state, Hispanos led the way and were present at every step of the territory's creation and its transition into statehood—even if under unequal terms with Anglo society (V. Sánchez 2020). Eventually settling into every region of the state, where their labor has proven key to the success of local economies, Latinxs are part and parcel of Colorado's history and its culture (Wyckoff 1999). From the vast Eastern Plains to its rugged Western Slope, no region of Colorado has been left untouched by the presence of Latinxs (Simpson 2017). And just like in other regions of the American West, their socioeconomic and cultural impact has amplified as their numbers have increased. With over a fifth of all Coloradans claiming a Latinx identity (which will become a fourth soon), the time has come to proclaim Colorado a Latinx state in the same vein as Arizona, California, New Mexico, and Texas. For Latinxs in Colorado, the state is not only a borderland where Anglos and transnational Latinx cultures overlap but also a homeland that the latter get to define. The "orphaned" Hispanos of the northern San Luis Valley who were cut off from New Mexico when the Colorado Territory was created in 1861 probably never imagined that one day their presence would come to define the political entity that had just annexed them. In hindsight, the adoption of the Spanish-language term *Colorado* for the territory and the state was a harbinger of things to come. And as we look into the future of our state, the increasing numbers of Latinx Coloradans point to a greater influence in the state's economy, politics, and culture. I look forward to a point in time when Colorado's Latinx culture will be a part of the mainstream and not something that has to be constantly pointed out as a reminder, as an addition to an incomplete history, missing—either by omission or by design—a key, foundational component of its own identity.

IN THE MULTICULTURAL AMERICAN WEST, ASSIMILATION IS A TWO-WAY STREET. The dual, competing narratives about Mexicans and other Latinxs who are either assimilating (kind of) just like other waves of immigrants, or are not assimilating because of their own or society's fault, hide an important component of Western society: the Hispanicization of the American West. Just as the Spanish conquistadors adopted—and adapted—Indigenous ways in order to survive in the New World, and Anglo pioneers adopted Mexican ways as they settled Tejas/Texas, today's American West (and increasingly, US society) is being influenced by Mexican and Hispanic/Latinx culture. According to Terrence Haverluk (2003, 166): "In many respects Hispanic culture now defines what is Western." I would take his argument even further and tacitly extend it to the rest of American society, as the Hispanic presence increasingly reaches into all US geographical regions and corners of American life. From cowboy (i.e., *vaquero*) apparel to today's *quinceañera* coming-of-age parties, Anglo culture in the American West is infused with Hispanic influences. For example, Denver's Cinco de Mayo Festival attracts over

400,000 visitors—many of whom are not Latinxs—and has become one of the largest in the nation ("Cinco de Mayo celebration in Denver" 2023). Mexican restaurants are ubiquitous throughout the American West and are nowadays found in even the smallest Western towns. And while the increased interaction between Latinxs and Anglos (and other demographic groups) in the American West has led to cultural borrowing, the appropriation of Mexican cultural artifacts by the dominant Anglo society, and—lest we forget—the commercialization and trivialization of Latinx cultures (Dávila 2001; D. Gutiérrez 1993, 523–524), it also true that it has led to the Hispanicization of Anglo culture. Mexican and Latinx culture is now becoming mainstream in the American West—and it looks like Anglos cannot have enough of it.[4] While political pundits argue over the pros and cons of Latinx immigration, complain about the porous US-Mexico border, or declare that the United States is on the verge of being "invaded" from the south, Anglos in the American West go about their lives interacting with Hispanics on a daily basis, eating Mexican food, listening to popular Latinx music (whether it is Mexican musical genres or Hispanic Caribbean reggaeton), and learning a word of Spanish here and there. And in the case of their children, they are likely attending a school where many—if not most—of their classmates are Latinxs, leading to an even greater degree of multiracial and multicultural interactions. Of course, let us not forget that this newly found Anglo fascination with Hispanic culture takes place as Latinxs "still suffer from economic and political marginalization" (Haverluk 2003, 181).

The Hispanicization (or Latinization) of the American West is plainly visible even in Colorado, a state where Latinxs have been historically rendered invisible by the Anglo mainstream. Whereas Anglo businesspeople in states like California, New Mexico, and Texas realized decades ago that they could make money by selling to local and out-of-state tourists the illusion of time travel to a placid past where Hispanic culture dominated a pastoral landscape, Colorado has been a latecomer to this marketing strategy. But starting in the 1980s, as the Chicano Movement lost its radical edge, "Mexican" culture became safer and more palatable to Anglo Coloradans. Casa Bonita, an iconic, kitschy Mexican restaurant in Lakewood (a Denver suburb), epitomizes the conspicuous Anglo consumption of Mexican culture. For generations of Anglo Denverites, a trip to Casa Bonita, with its all-you-can-eat Mexican buffet, mariachi music, and famous cliff divers, was a rite of passage—an immersion into a cartoonish Hispanic world, but from a safe distance.[5] More recently, Pueblo, Colorado—a city known for the labor and housing segregation of its Mexican American and Chicanx population; significant socioeconomic challenges related to poverty, crime, and drug use; and a patently clear Anglo-Mexican racial and ethnic divide—is burnishing its rough, steel town image thanks to the revival of Hispanic culture. Pueblo chile (aka chili) peppers have become famous around the region (even rivaling New Mexico's Hatch chiles), and the city now boasts a Pueblo Chile & Frijoles Festival, a new motto ("Experience the Flavor"), and a major source of revenue for local businesses (The Greater Pueblo Chamber of Commerce 2023).[6] Chiles and *frijoles* (i.e., beans), once considered by Anglos as part of the lowly diet of impoverished Mexicans (Haverluk 2002, 50), have been transformed nowadays into moneymaking cultural icons that anchor Colorado's local identity. A typical example of *neolocalism*, the Pueblo Chile & Frijoles Festival is but one of many similar events found throughout Colorado and the American West that highlight a romanticized, sanitized version of Hispanic culture where Mexican and New Mexican items, such as *ristras* (i.e., strings) of chiles, are available for sale to tourists wishing to take home a local "ethnic" souvenir (see figure 5.1). As Haverluk (2003, 179) poignantly put it: "Ironically, after one hundred years of trying to hide their Spanish legacy, Western chambers of commerce are now cashing in on their failure to fully assimilate Hispanics and stamp out Hispanic material culture." Things have certainly come full circle, as the descendants of the Anglo invaders of the nineteenth century are nowadays "discovering" Hispanic culture and embracing it in an attempt to "feel" a local connection to the region—all part of the contested nature of racial and ethnic relations in the American West (Limerick 1987).

In conclusion, Latinxs (i.e., Hispanos, Chicanxs, Mexicans, and others) represent an element of continuity in the American West. They were here before the arrival of the United States to its "West," and they remain an intrinsic part of the American West (their *Norte*) to this day. Moreover, Latinxs have shaped the West into a homeland, an element that they hold in common with Indigenous peoples, Mormons, and other communities

FIGURE 5.1. Chile ristras at the Pueblo Chile & Frijoles Festival, 2019. Source: Pueblo County, Colorado.

(re)created in the American West. Yet, in spite of historical continuities, twenty-first-century Latinx migration brings an element of diversity, disruption, and discontinuity to the West. Latinxs are as much a part of the New West as they were of the Old West. As this study points out, Latinx immigrants are not only adding a new layer to the long-standing presence of Latinxs in Colorado, but they are also establishing a new presence—and creating new communities—in places from which they had been absent. For some Latinxs, the American West is still a frontier, a new frontier that may involve vast distances, economic uncertainty, and personal peril. But as in the distant frontier past, global forces still set people in motion. And they, in turn, (re)shape the character of the American West into the early twenty-first century. Latinxs are major agents of continuity and change in this ongoing Western (hi)story, and in Latino Colorado, they are no longer invisible.

A Colorado Latinx Research Agenda

More than a comprehensive examination of Latinxs in Colorado, this work is but a point of departure, a call to action. Given the historical invisibility of Latinxs in Colorado, much more scholarly work is required in order to place Latinxs in their rightful place in the state's mainstream narratives. Topics such as the Hispanos of the San Luis Valley and Denver's Chicano Movement have been well covered, but a new Latinx research agenda should encompass themes that reflect the socioeconomic changes taking place in Colorado's Latinx community and its growing diversity. For example, what about the Latinx middle class that has become a major economic force in Denver and other parts of the state? Latinx businesses in the state generate millions of dollars in tax revenue, and Latinx consumers are the fastest-growing market demographic in Colorado and the nation. Unlike historical tropes that uniformly see Latinxs as poor laborers, there is a vibrant Latinx middle class in the state whose contributions—and potential—remain unacknowledged. A good socioeconomic study of Colorado's Latinx middle class is long overdue.

The Western Slope is also fertile terrain for anthropological research on the social interactions between Anglos and Latinx immigrants. Here is a part of the state that has been hitherto isolated from major migratory waves but for the last three to four decades has been experiencing significant Latinx labor migration—not only from Mexico but also from other parts of Latin America. Excellent ethnographic work about the sociocultural and economic impacts of Latinx immigration into the New South and the Pacific Northwest is now available (Jimenez Sifuentez 2016; J. Jones 2019; Murphy, Blanchard, and Hill 2001; Odem and Lacy 2009; Sarathy 2012; H. Smith and Furuseth 2006; Stuesse 2016), and there is no reason why Colorado's Western Slope should remain understudied. Based on my limited research work in the region, the Western Slope could provide an ideal case study for the examination of the ripple effects of Latinx settlement in a mostly white, rural, conservative region of the American West, one that also attracts Latinx migrants because of the availability of entry-level jobs in ritzy resort towns and the region's service sector. These socioeconomic and cultural dualities that are so prevalent in Colorado's

Western Slope—a region shared by oil and gas industry roughnecks as well as ski bums and hordes of tourists—probably make of the area a unique setting for such a study.

In the state's Eastern Plains, Latinx and other immigrant workers keep the region alive. Decades of economic decline and depopulation have altered the demographic makeup of eastern Colorado, brought in new economic players, and reshaped the fate of small-town America. While the industrialization of rural America thanks to meatpacking plants, animal feedlots, and other agricultural agribusinesses has been studied, the socioeconomic role of Latinx (and other immigrant) workers in towns like Greeley, Fort Morgan, Sterling, Lamar, and La Junta, their assimilation (or lack thereof) into American society, and the fate of their second-generation children call for an in-depth examination.

Finally, although most of Colorado's Latinx population is of Mexican origin, the Front Range (particularly the Denver and Colorado Springs metro areas) have witnessed an increasing national-origin diversity among its Latinx population. Thousands of Puerto Ricans, Cubans, Venezuelans, and other South and Central American Latinxs are diversifying and complicating the historical portrait of Latinxs in Colorado, particularly around the Denver metro area. Denver metro is no longer just a Mexican, Mexican American, or Chicano enclave but increasingly a Latinx one too, where younger generations of Latinxs and new immigrants are redefining *latinidad* as a pan-ethnic phenomenon—a trend seen in other urban areas throughout the nation (Aparicio 2019; De Genova and Zayas 2003; Portes and Rumbaut 2001). Moreover, the post-NAFTA arrival of thousands of new Mexican immigrants (many of them from nontraditional immigrant-sending regions of the country) also complicates the oftentimes homogenous portrayal of Mexican-origin Latinxs in Colorado. Immigrants from central and southern states in Mexico, ethnic Indigenous Mexican immigrants, and urbanites from the Mexico City metro area have been adding new layers of complexity to the Mexican-origin Latinx experience in Colorado. These recent arrivals also differ in terms of their class, race, education, and legal status in the United States, thus providing a rich resource for a wide-ranging research project on Colorado's increasingly diverse Latinx population.

Colorado is more than just a state; it is also a state of mind. Though visualized by millions of tourists and recent transplants as this picture-perfect outdoors paradise where people spend their days seeking fresh powder, drink craft beers, and are universally happy (aka "Colorado nice"), the state—like most territories in the American West—has a complex history hidden behind its stunning natural beauty. Its progressive politics, which goes hand in hand with a high quality of life for its residents, seems far removed from its early origins as a territory deemed suitable for white settlers, where Indigenous peoples were dispossessed of their lands and "Mexicans" became the indispensable, cheap labor force for the state's booming industries (e.g., mining, railroads, and agribusinesses). For well over a century since the American takeover in 1848, Colorado (the territory and the state) was no paradise for the thousands of Latinx workers who toiled in invisibility, needed but unwanted, separate and not equal. And as Colorado was transformed in the late twentieth century by the irruption of New West industries (e.g., services, amenities, and real estate development), Latinxs once again were called to undergird the state's progress. If Anglo capital and technology helped build Colorado, Latinx labor made it possible. Yet, here we are, in the early twenty-first century, seeking to place Latinxs in their proper context in a state that seems to have a hard time remembering their contributions and seeing them as equals.

Initiatives such as those by History Colorado to highlight the Spanish and Mexican origins of the Colorado Territory, its early inhabitants, and the Chicano Movement are important first steps in the right direction (Allyn 2019a, 2019b; DiPrince 2023; Flores 2019; "Press Release" 2015). But events by History Colorado, as important as they may be, still conjure up images of Colorado's Latinxs among the general public as "historic" and not contemporary—despite the best efforts of History Colorado to place these exhibits in their proper context and highlight their connections to the present. Even this book, I am afraid, might be considered as a "history" text by some, still unaware of the fact that Latinxs have always been—and remain—an intrinsic part of Colorado. Heritage tourism may be another good way to educate the general public about Latinxs in Colorado, but as it is usually the case around the American West these initiatives, festivals, and experiences usually portray a sanitized version of history. Coloradans and out-of-state tourists deserve an honest appraisal of Colorado's history—warts and all—and not a "Colorado nice" version of it (which, I do realize, may not be good for business).

Definitely, more needs to be done. For being close to a fourth of the state's population, Colorado's Latinxs barely register in the state's—and the nation's—popular imaginary. Few visitors and recent transplants think of Colorado as a Hispanic state, in the same vein as California, New Mexico, or Texas. Quite the opposite, Colorado is still imagined by most Americans as a white place and its Latinxs as recent newcomers. Here is where the government should play a role in giving credit where credit is due. Not only should more state funds be allocated for the education of Latinxs (as a key emerging component of the state's labor force), but more funding should also be allocated to educate all of our students about Latinxs. The only way the Anglo establishment will finally come around to acknowledge the presence of Latinxs in Colorado's society—past, present, and future—is by educating the new generations about Latinxs and other communities of color in the state. My hope is that at some point in the near future, more Latinxs will be elected to higher office (e.g., governor, and more US senators and representatives), thus increasing the visibility and political power of Latinxs. But ultimately, equality between Anglos and Latinxs will only be achieved when it is no longer newsworthy that a Latinx has been elected to higher office; when there are no more "firsts" (or "seconds") to report, when having Latinxs wield political power will not raise any eyebrows, and their opponents will point out to their policy record and not to their ethnicity.

In the meantime, Latinxs are slowly shedding their invisibility in the state by way of demographics: one child, one worker, and one voter at a time. If current trends persist (despite slowdowns caused by the 2008 recession and the COVID-19 pandemic), Colorado's Latinx population will increase steadily, and—soon—one out of every four Coloradans will be Latinx. In the face of timid gestures by the establishment to acknowledge the state's Latinx community, population numbers will have to tell the story, particularly along the Front Range, where Latinxs are becoming a political force to be reckoned with. A new *movimiento* is needed in Colorado, this time not to seek an independent path away from Anglo society but to fully integrate Latinxs—as equal partners—into the American mainstream. Not to assimilate Latinxs necessarily, but to render them equal with Anglos. A Colorado "Latino Movement" of sorts. If history serves as a guide, such a movement may not be ultimately and completely successful, but it will force the Anglo establishment (again) to make institutional changes; changes that will open doors, create opportunities, and—perhaps most important—increase the visibility of Latino Colorado in the New American West.

NOTES

Introduction: Latino Colorado

1. The terms *Hispanic* and *Latina/o/x* are used interchangeably in this work. While the original (male) term Latino, its female counterpart, Latina, and its nongendered version, Latinx, have gained ascendancy due to their use by the US Census Bureau and dozens of community organizations and academic units, the older term *Hispanic* is still commonly used, particularly in Colorado and New Mexico. Many activists prefer the term *Latinx* (and versions of it) over *Hispanic* because they feel that the latter places too much of an emphasis on Spanish cultural roots and ancestry, to the detriment of Indigenous, African, and other legacies, whereas the former points to the multicultural and multiracial Latin American ancestry of its people. However, as we shall see, Spanish ancestry remains a matter of cultural pride for many Hispanics in southern Colorado and northern New Mexico to this day (who call themselves Hispanos), and it plays a defining role in the community. Similarly, the terms *Chicana/o/x* will be used to refer to those that identified with the Chicano Movement of the 1960s–1970s.
2. Some recent academic works include Aldama et al. (2011); De Baca (1998); Donato (2007); Rivera (2010); and E. Vigil (1999).

3. Colorado is nicknamed the "Centennial State" because it achieved statehood in 1876, as the United States of America celebrated the 100th anniversary of the signing of its Declaration of Independence (Colorado State Archives 2023).
4. *Manifest Destiny* is defined as the belief in the inherent superiority of the Anglo-Saxon race and the American nation, which was destined by Providence to control large parts of the continent. The phrase was coined by newspaper editor John O'Sullivan in 1845 (Horsman 1981).
5. The Treaty of Guadalupe Hidalgo granted US citizenship to the inhabitants of the territories annexed by the United States in 1848. However, because US citizenship was exclusive to whites, those individuals classified as Native Americans were not eligible. In other words, Mexicans could become "legally white" but Indigenous traits could make one ineligible for US citizenship (Gómez 2018, 145).
6. Other racialized "Others" did not fare much better. See Milner (1996) for essays on the experiences of African Americans, Asian Americans, and Native Americans in the American West. Latinxs—in some situations—would gain certain legal and social advantages by virtue of claims to whiteness while occupying an ambiguous liminal state between Anglos and unassimilable Others (Dowling 2014; Gómez 2018; Lukens 2012; Nieto-Phillips 2004).
7. The term *Chicano* had been used pejoratively in the past to refer to Mexican Americans, but in the 1960s it became a powerful symbol for activists committed to rewriting their own history from a standpoint of cultural pride.
8. For example, Federico Peña served as the first Hispanic mayor of Denver for two terms (1983–1991) and Joseph "Joe" García (former president of Colorado State University Pueblo) became the state's first Hispanic lieutenant governor (2011–2016).
9. The concept of the "borderlands" has been an interesting development among historians of the American West, who have vigorously debated its merits since the 1980s–1990s (Adelman and Aron 1999). Originally developed in the early twentieth century to counter hegemonic narratives of an expanding (and eventually closed) American frontier (Turner 1894), the concept has evolved from a mainly geographical location on the edges of empires, such as the case of the Spanish borderlands (Bolton 1921), into a more loosely defined area of cultural contestation. Social scientists have jumped into the fray, and nowadays the term *borderlands* is used in connection to a plethora of transnational activities oftentimes taking place far away from international borders but that engage in various forms of "border crossing" (Hämäläinen and Truett 2011; Lytle Hernández 2011). This work sees Colorado (or parts of it) as borderlands that eventually became "bordered" in the traditional sense (e.g., the case of the San Luis Valley in the late nineteenth century) but also as a place where Latinxs and Anglos (and sometimes other ethnic groups) overlap in ways that give rise to cultural borderlands (e.g., the Eastern Plains and the Western Slope), locations with transnational connections. There, Latinxs resist, accommodate themselves, integrate into, and seek ways around the pressures, changes, and continuities that the Anglo world and the forces of capitalism throw at them (Gutiérrez and Young 2010).

10. The concept of "the West" is an arbitrary but powerful Anglo-American creation. For Native Americans, there was no "West"; the West was home. For Spanish conquistadors and Mexican authorities, it was El Norte—the end of the mainland empire, and later, of the Mexican Republic. For Latinxs in the West, it is the borderlands—the place where Hispanic and Anglo cultural realms converge, and Mexico and the United States grind against each other at a political border.
11. As of 2021, 88% of the students in Adams County's fourteen School Districts are Hispanic. The percentage of Hispanic students in neighboring school districts around the Denver metro area (e.g., Brighton, Denver, Thornton, and Westminster) ranges from 40% to 75% (Annie E. Casey Foundation 2024).
12. "Mexican origin" may mean several things: from first-generation immigrants who are Mexican nationals, all the way to old Latinx families who have been in the United States for several generations but can trace their roots to the period when Mexico owned this part of the continent.
13. Colorado has historically attracted young adults (ages twenty-three to thirty-five), mainly Baby Boomers who relocated to Colorado starting in the 1970s. They are now entering retirement and are poised to rapidly expand the sixty-five-plus age category in the state over the next twenty years (State Demography Office 2016).

Chapter 1: The San Luis Valley

1. In colonial New Mexico, the informal slave trade led to widespread raiding and trading by Indigenous tribes that then sold their captives to the Spanish. The practice of keeping Indigenous women and children as domestic servants in Hispanic households continued well into the nineteenth century, even after the US takeover, and it created a class of *genízaros* (i.e., detribalized Indian captives who became Hispanized) in most Spanish and Mexican settlements in what nowadays is the American West. See Reséndez 2016 for a comprehensive examination of the "other slavery."
2. *Hispano* (a Spanish-language term) refers specifically to the original settlers of Mexico's northern frontier. Nowadays, their descendants in Colorado and New Mexico still use the term to refer to themselves. "Hispanic," on the other hand, is an umbrella term used by the US Census Bureau to describe the nation's Latinx population. So, whereas Hispanos are Hispanics, not all Hispanics are Hispanos.
3. The term *Anglo* is short for "Anglo Americans" (and before that, "Anglo Saxons"), the name given to those English-speaking whites (including immigrants like the German and the Irish) that settled in the formerly Mexican territory of the American Southwest. The term not only serves to denote their race and color but also points to the fact that these were newcomers from a different culture and a different place (i.e., outsiders from the East) from lands settled long ago by Indigenous peoples and Spanish colonists (Meeks 2020, 13; Montgomery 2002, 58). This outsider/insider dynamic is very much alive in New Mexico to this day, where it is not uncommon for even a non-Hispanic Black to be seen as an Anglo.

4. Anti-Mexican sentiments among Anglos throughout the US Southwest did not evolve solely because of the US-Mexican War and the unequal treatment of these new subjects by US authorities. They also stemmed from long-held racial stereotypes dating back to the arrival of Anglo settlers in Mexican Tejas and the eventual founding of the Republic of Texas (in 1836) and US statehood (in 1846) (Horsman 1981, chap. 11). "Mexican" became an inferior racial category in Anglo eyes, and Hispanic Texans would experience discrimination and violence designed to keep them "in their place" well into the twentieth century (De León 1983; Montejano 1987; D. Sandoval 2011, 241).
5. To this day, the term *Hispano* is still widely used and celebrated among Hispanic New Mexicans (though not without controversy given the oppressive nature of the Spanish colonial administration that killed and enslaved thousands of Indigenous peoples). See hispanonewmexico.com for a good example of the former.
6. According to Nieto-Phillips (2004, 53), Anglo statehood boosters even boasted about the Spanish race and culture (i.e., "whiteness") of New Mexico's Hispanos in an effort to convince Congress to grant statehood to the territory.
7. Predating the founding of San Luis by decades are trading posts on what became US territory after the 1803 Louisiana Purchase, such as Bent's Fort (founded in 1833, and located near La Junta) and Fort Vasquez (founded in 1835, and located near Platteville), but these were all eventually abandoned (Flores 2019).
8. The San Luis People's Ditch, dating to 1852, for example, is still in use today. It received the first water rights adjudication in the new US territory of Colorado.
9. A handful of Hispanos were part of the convention that wrote the first constitution of the state of Colorado. Notably among them was Casimiro Barela (representing Las Animas County), who successfully lobbied for the printing of the state constitution in English, Spanish, and German (State of Colorado 1876). Barela—a regional political *patrón*—would go on to serve as a Colorado State senator for forty years (Taylor and West 1973, 352–353).
10. Even the renowned political activist Susan B. Anthony used the term *greasers* to refer to the Hispanos and Mexicans that she met in southern Colorado when she toured the state to gather support for female suffrage. She made an exception for "a representative Mexican, intelligent, cultivated" who was part of Colorado's constitutional convention (Daley 2008, 22–23).
11. Haverluk (1998, 466–467) classifies Hispanic communities in the United States as continuous (i.e., always majority Hispanic), discontinuous (i.e., founded by Hispanics but demographically overwhelmed by Anglos eventually), and new (i.e., originally settled by Anglos and with Hispanic migration). Most of the Hispano communities in Colorado's San Luis Valley are either continuous or discontinuous—with some of the latter recently experiencing a growth of their Hispanic population. As for the rest of the state, most Hispanic communities in Colorado are new—unlike those in northern New Mexico and south Texas.
12. *Manita/manito* (from the Spanish *hermanita/hermanito*, i.e., little sister/little brother) are terms of endearment used by working-class Hispanos from northern

New Mexico and southern Colorado to denote and reinforce their cultural bonds. See https://manitos.net/

13. Trinidad's diverse population (which included Italians and Eastern Europeans) opened up some spaces for Hispanos by the mid-twentieth century. Unlikely other highly segregated towns in Colorado, Trinidad had a greater degree of tolerance, meaning that Hispanos in Trinidad occupied civil service positions in the courts, and the fire and police departments. Schools, however, remained in Anglo hands much longer (Donato 2007, 99–100).

14. In its April 19, 1936, edition the *Denver Post* published a map of the border checkpoints suggestively entitled "Colorado's Southern Front Against Alien Entry" (A. Hernandez 2019).

15. To memorialize his legacy, the eastbound tunnel across the Continental Divide on highway I-70 is named after Governor Johnson.

16. This demographic disparity also explains why Hispanos in Colorado could not effectively leverage their Spanish claim to "whiteness" to the extent that the large population of Hispanos in New Mexico did (Nieto-Phillips 2004).

17. Technically, the Culebra Range of the Sangre de Cristo Mountains.

18. San Luis is the exception among towns in Colorado because of the political control that Hispanos still exert over it (including surrounding Costilla County). Due to the large percentage of Hispanos in its population, the locals were able to control public schools, giving Hispano children a much different—and empowering—experience relative to their peers in Anglo-dominated towns in the San Luis Valley (Donato 2007, chap. 6).

19. The case is *Lobato v. Taylor*, and it is examined in detail by Golten (2005).

20. Though it defines itself as a Chicano organization, the term is now conspicuously absent from its website (http://www.landrightscouncil.org/) and its latest newsletter available online (July 2008).

21. See López Tijerina (2000) for his firsthand account of the land rights struggle in northern New Mexico.

22. My interviewees included members from the three main ethnic groups in the San Luis Valley: Anglos, Hispanos, and Latin American immigrants. With some exceptions, respondents were either native to the San Luis Valley or longtime residents (with at least a decade of residence in the Valley). All interviews for this book were carried out in accordance with protocols approved by Colorado State University's Institutional Review Board. Interviews were conducted in English or in Spanish, following the respondents' wishes, and translated by the author. In some cases, pseudonyms were utilized to protect the respondents' privacy.

23. Rosa (pseudonym), June 12, 2012, Alamosa, Colorado.

24. Dawn (pseudonym), June 20, 2012, Alamosa, Colorado.

25. See Donato (2007, chap. 5) for a detailed examination of Anglo control of public education in the San Luis Valley and their discrimination toward Hispano students.

26. Noel and Maryanne Dunne, June 20, 2012, Alamosa, Colorado.

27. Daniel (pseudonym), June 20, 2012, Alamosa, Colorado.

28. For more on the Q'anjob'al Maya of the San Luis Valley and their traditions, see Ludwig et al. (2012) and O'Connor (2008).

Chapter 2: The Eastern Plains

1. Thus, the apt title of his biography: *The End of the Row*. I had the distinct pleasure of attending Mr. Solano's book release in Fort Collins in 2013, where besides talking about his storied life, he held a "show and tell" with agricultural tools to teach younger generations about the hard work regime of the Latinx sugar beet workers.
2. Also known as the High Plains, this dry region between the Rocky Mountains and the 100th meridian was considered by early explorers as a wasteland because of its lack of water and trees.
3. These were the ancestral lands of the Arapaho and the Cheyenne, as well as other Indigenous peoples who were forcibly displaced by the US military and Anglo settlers. See West (1998) for a detailed examination of how the Colorado gold rush transformed the territory's Eastern Plains, and Hoig (1961) for a scholarly account of the 1864 Sand Creek Massacre, the most infamous act of depredation committed against the Plains Indians of Colorado.
4. The term *Mexican* was generically used by employers and the public to label both Mexican nationals (i.e., immigrants from Mexico) and US-born Mexican Americans/Hispanos, as Anglos in the industry rarely differentiated them (Leonard 1993, 70). For Hispanos, eager to assert their rights as US citizens, the label was problematic, as it otherized them and made them "foreigners" in their own country. Still, Hispanos saw themselves culturally as Mexicans—though of a different kind and from a different country—in the same way that Mexican Americans nowadays have a cultural connection to things Mexican because of ongoing Mexican immigration and "replenished ethnicity" (Jiménez 2010).
5. See https://www.historycolorado.org/fort-vasquez.
6. Nowadays, Fort Collins is a thriving college town, and the neighborhoods where these *colonias* are located have become coveted (and pricey) real estate because of their proximity to Old Town, Colorado State University (CSU), and other locations. For example, the Holy Family neighborhood (just north of the CSU campus) is now made up mostly of student renters, whereas the other three *colonias* east of downtown are becoming gentrified as new businesses open around them (e.g., microbreweries) and real estate prices in Fort Collins keep rising, turning formerly marginalized neighborhoods into desirable locations for affluent buyers (Kyle 2014).
7. The "absence"—or rather, marginalization—of communities of color in Colorado was the product of a dominant white narrative, which placed the experiences of Anglo pioneers at the center of Colorado's history but seemed at odds with complex realities on the ground (see Aldama et al. 2011, editor's introduction). Also, see Junne et al. (2011) for a brief history of the African American farming enclave in Dearfield, Colorado, and Wei (2016) for a history of Asians in the Centennial State.
8. Ejidos consisted of communal lands in which individual farmers held parcels. The system dates back to the Aztec empire and medieval Spain.

9. Sundown towns had some spaces (e.g., downtown or main street) where non-whites were allowed to conduct business during the day, but they were expected to be gone by sunset and reside elsewhere (Loewen 2005, 76, 249–250). In most cases throughout the American West, there were no legal provisions dictating the separation of races, but custom and threats enforced the practice.
10. Lovato (2008), writing about the exploitation and persecution of undocumented Latinx immigrant laborers in Georgia and the Deep South in the early twenty-first century, coined the term *Juan Crow* to describe the various attrition laws created at the state level and the hostile racial climate designed to harass them. The term could also be used to accurately describe the various forms of historical oppression and intimidation of Mexican workers throughout the American West since the mid-nineteenth century.
11. Although Pueblo is considered a part of the Front Range urban corridor for statistical purposes, it is geographically located in the plains, a kind of "frontier" between the urban centers of the Front Range, the plains to its east, and the San Luis Valley. Actually, the Arkansas River that flows through Pueblo was the border between the United States and the Spanish empire (and later, Mexico) from 1819 until the 1846–1848 war with Mexico. Pueblo remains the gateway to southern Colorado, and the city has a marked Latinx/Chicanx vibe, unlike more Anglo (and conservative) Colorado Springs, less than an hour's drive north.
12. New Mexico—together with Arizona—were the last two territories in the Lower 48 to be admitted as states into the Union, in no small measure because of their proportionally large non-white populations of Mexican Americans and Indigenous peoples (Gómez 2018, 71–78). New Mexico was officially admitted as a US state on January 6, 1912, followed by Arizona on February 14, 1912, making of them the 47th and 48th states of the United States, respectively.
13. Throughout the 1960s–1980s, the Coors Brewing Company (Based in Golden, Colorado) was accused of discriminating against people of color and LGBTQIA+ (lesbian, gay, bisexual, transgender, queer/questioning, intersex, and asexual/aromantic/agender) individuals. Its discriminatory hiring practices were the target of official complaints, protests, product boycotts, and lawsuits (Baum 2000).
14. Literally "The Cockroach," the name comes from the eponymous Mexican song and the cockroach's hardiness to survive under adverse conditions (presumably even a nuclear holocaust).
15. There is an ongoing debate regarding whether Greeley is part of Colorado's Front Range or the Eastern Plains region. Although Greeley is a stone's throw away from significant Front Range urban centers, like Denver and Fort Collins, the city is geographically located in the Plains, its economy is based on agricultural and extractive industries (e.g., oil and gas), and despite being the location for the University of Northern Colorado and other urban attractions, it still retains a rural, plains character celebrated in its annual Greeley Stampede (2022).
16. Colorado was one of a handful of states to gain a congressional seat because of the 2020 US Census results.

17. As of 2022, Colorado had four "safe" Democratic congressional districts (the 1st, the 2nd, the 6th, and the 7th) and three "safe" Republican congressional districts (the 3rd, the 4th, and the 5th), as measured by the Cook Partisan Voting Index. The eighth was listed as "even" (Cook Political Report 2022).
18. "The Hand That Feeds" (figure 2.2), a 2021 bronze sculpture by Frank Garza, located at Sugar Beet Park in Fort Collins, is an attempt to rectify this partialized view of Colorado's rural history. See https://mujeresdecolores.org/monument for more information.

Chapter 3: The Front Range

1. The creation of the term *Chicanx* is a very recent, twenty-first-century development. It is an inclusive, gender-neutral term that seeks to move beyond the binary, cisgender *Chicana* or *Chicano* terms and include LGBTQIA+ individuals and groups. However, the term *Chicanx* did not exist in the 1960s–1970s. It was the "Chicano Movement," and participants referred to themselves as *Chicanas* and *Chicanos*. Thus, for the purposes of this book, and to honor historical accuracy as well as respecting contemporary usages, I use *Chicanx* (or *Chicanxs*) to generally describe groups of people whose gender identities were likely very diverse (e.g., Chicanx activists or Chicanx workers). But whenever I am referring to individuals, I will employ the terms that they used back then to describe themselves: *Chicanas* and *Chicanos* (utilized as nouns). The same goes for the historical name of the movement (i.e., the Chicano Movement) or its multiple social manifestations (e.g., Chicana literature or Chicano politics).
2. Young makes a compelling case for the recognition of the Indigenous identity of Chicanos (2011, 47).
3. Dr. Charles Truxillo—a native New Mexican, Chicanx activist, and college professor—gained instant notoriety when he suggested that the borderlands states of the United States and Mexico would unite and become a sovereign nation in the near future as Hispanics in the Western United States increased their share of the population and these states had more in common with Mexico's northern states (Truxillo 2000). His suggestion would become very controversial at a time of heightened anxiety over immigration and fears of a *Reconquista* due to growing Hispanic populations in places like California (Jacobson 2008).
4. See Girón (2011) for an examination of the connections between Indigenous people (Apache, in her case) and Chicanxs.
5. The term *La Raza* (literally "the race" but usually translated as "the people") refers to the idea that all Chicanxs, Hispanics, and Latinxs—despite their differences—represent but one people, the product of the Spanish empire and centuries of racial mixing between Indigenous peoples, Europeans, Africans, and others. The concept originated in Latin America and provided a common label for the mestizo societies that emerged in the nineteenth century. For example, Mexican Secretary of Education José Vasconcelos argued in *La raza cósmica* ([1925] 1997) that Latin America potentially represented an agglomeration of all the world's

races (a "fifth" race of sorts). For Chicanxs, the term also implied that all Mexicans, Hispanics, and Latinxs were united by common experiences in the United States (including discrimination at the hands of Anglos) and were different in their racial makeup to Anglo Americans (Lampe 1981).

The concept of *Aztlán* was introduced by Chicanx poet Alurista during the Denver Youth Conference held in 1969 ("Alurista" 2019). According to their lore, the Aztec people migrated from some place north before settling in the Central Valley of Mexico, where they established their empire. For Chicanx activists, the term *Aztlán* referred to the lands seized by the United States after the 1846–1848 war with Mexico, and it conveyed a sense of autochthony for Chicanxs, who could rightly claim to be "native" to the American West (unlike the Anglo newcomers) (De León and Griswold del Castillo 2006, 1–4). In the words of Chicana activist Deborah Espinosa: "We have a bloodline to this land" (Freedom Archives 2017).

6. Following the Spanish naming custom of using both paternal and maternal surnames, Reies was born as "López Tijerina." However, his followers and the press referred to him simply as "Tijerina."
7. For actual footage of Chicano Movement protests in Colorado (and its leaders), see the PBS documentary *La Raza de Colorado: El Movimiento* (Rocky Mountain PBS 2006).
8. The growing presence of other Latinxs from Central and South America in the American West has complicated claims of a Chicano homeland by rendering ethnic neighborhoods more heterogenous than in the 1960s–1970s, making it more likely for the second generation to identify as Latinxs, and making it less likely that these newcomers will support a separate ethnic nation within the United States (Alaniz and Cornish 2008, 16–17).
9. For example, the Auraria Higher Education Center was built in the early 1970s in what used to be a "Mexican" neighborhood just southwest of downtown Denver. The Hispanic residents tried to stop the bulldozing of their neighborhood, "but lacked the money and the clout to resist renewal developers" (Leonard and Noel 2016, 97). As a long-overdue measure of compensation, scholarships were offered to the children and grandchildren of displaced residents in the 1990s and, after 2021, to all direct descendants of those who lived there from 1955 to 1973 ("Expansion of the Displaced Aurarian Scholarship Program" 2021).
10. To this day, LULAC remains the oldest and largest Latinx civil rights organization in the United States. It won several legal cases of school segregation against Mexican American children, setting precedents that influenced the US Supreme Court on its landmark decision in the 1954 *Brown v. Board of Education* school desegregation case (League of United Latin American Citizens 2024).
11. From 1928 to 1929, a young Johnson taught impoverished Mexican American children at a rural elementary school near the Mexican border in south Texas. The experience of working with children "lashed by prejudice . . . [and] buried half alive in illiteracy" (Dallek 2004, 16) helped define Johnson's political priorities (LBJ Presidential Library 2024).
12. Mexican Americans (who were 10% of the US Southwest's population) were overrepresented among casualties in the Vietnam War—at 23% (Rosales 1997, 198).

13. More recent demographic developments in Front Range counties are examined in the introduction.
14. To put the figures into perspective, the number of "Mexicans" living in Denver in 1940 was greater than the total population of the city of Alamosa as of 2020.
15. The Front Range's economic dominance over the rest of the state has only been increasing over time, "attracting nearly all the growth the state has mustered" and "creating even more concentration of economic activity" by the early twenty-first century (Svaldi 2018).
16. Even the use of the term *Chicano* was problematic for conservative Mexican Americans, who viewed it as derogatory and politically divisive (Conan 2011).
17. Boulder is (in)famous for its progressive politics and alternative lifestyles, to the extent that Coloradans have nicknamed it (tongue-in-cheek) the "People's Republic of Boulder" (Leland 2021; Sheely 2003).
18. Colorado Springs—a major conservative enclave in the Front Range—is perhaps the most notable exception. Its big military presence and large number of evangelicals result in a very interesting conservative mix (Dunn 2014).
19. In the cases of Chavez and Tijerina, there is disagreement among Chicanx scholars regarding their level of identification with the goals of Chicanismo and, thus, whether they were really leaders of El Movimiento or just inspiring leaders who emerged during the Chicano Movement. For example, Chavez never embraced Chicano nationalism, limiting his goals to the improvement of labor conditions for Mexican American farmworkers (Muñoz 1989, 7–8). His commitment to peaceful, nonviolent social change clashed with the more militant ethos of Chicanx activists—and made him the darling of Anglo progressives who saw in Chavez a nonthreatening leader of the Chicano Movement (Kennedy 1968). On the other hand, Reies López Tijerina was a firebrand, but his radical struggle for the recognition of Mexican land grants was mostly limited to the Hispano farmers of northern New Mexico, whom he referred to as Indo-Hispanos (R. Gutiérrez 2022, 154–156).
20. Deutsch (1994, 3) pointedly reminds us "that men have families and that women have histories."
21. Unofficial, de facto school segregation in Denver was finally addressed by the *Keyes v. School District No. 1, Denver* court case. In 1973, the US Supreme Court ruled against the school district. Mexican American/Chicanx students, whom the school district argued were not being discriminated by virtue of being "white," were deemed "an identifiable class" by the Supreme Court, thus deserving of legal protection (Olden 2017, 62–64).
22. The Cuban Revolution was a political and cultural referent for the Chicano Movement and other US radical movements of the 1960s. Chicanxs and other radical militants like the Black Panthers even emulated the revolutionary fashion styles of the Cuban rebels: long beards, olive green fatigues, and Che Guevara's ubiquitous beret (Espinosa 2015). See Mariscal (2005) for an examination of the connections between the Chicano Movement, the Vietnam War, and Third World national liberation movements (particularly the Cuban Revolution).

23. Ernesto Vigil's *The Crusade for Justice* (1999) provides a thorough examination of the FBI's surveillance of Corky Gonzales and other Chicanx militants, based on documents obtained through the Freedom of Information Act. It is clear from the evidence presented by Vigil that the FBI and other agencies of the US federal government considered the Chicano Movement a major threat when seen through the lens of the specter of communism rising throughout the world.
24. The radicalization of the Chicano Movement led some of its adherents to assume extreme ideological positions at odds with democratic ideals and to engage in an ethnic counternarrative that mirrored dehumanizing Anglo racial rhetoric (D. Gutiérrez 1993, 529). Thus, it comes as no surprise that many Anglos and Mexican Americans rejected it as too radical and out of step with American values.
25. Some Chicanxs denounced the crude attempts by communists to influence the Chicano Movement and how a Marxist interpretation of their struggle that ignored the role that race played in their historic subordination missed the mark. According to an article penned by a Chicanx activist, Chicanxs are united by more than a class struggle; they are also "unified in language, culture and in a Spiritual way" (AZTLAN 1977). An untitled article in *Papel del Barrio* argued: "The Chicano movement is not just a movement for class liberation—it goes much further, it is a movement to regain stolen lands, stolen tongues, stolen identity, stolen unity" ("No title" 1977, 2).
26. Gonzales even claimed that as far back as the 1969 Chicano Youth Liberation Conference he alone had brought up the idea of a Chicanx political party (I. García 1989, 103). In 1970, the Second Youth Liberation Conference formally called for the creation of "an independent local, regional, and national political party" (Navarro 2000, 89).
27. Unlike in Texas, where it (briefly) achieved some success (Márquez and Espino 2010).
28. Escuela Tlatelolco (named after the location of a massacre carried out by the Mexican military against student protesters in 1968) opened its doors in 1970, and it was an instant success. Chicanx students who had not fared well in Denver's public schools felt inspired and empowered by a curriculum that included Spanish language instruction, history of Mexico, and folkloric music and dance, taught by instructors hired in Mexico (E. Vigil 1999, 160–162). At a time when public schools across the state insisted on the rapid assimilation of students of color, Escuela Tlatelolco's focus on culturally appropriate instruction was daring and innovative.
29. The Black Lives Matter movement is a poignant reminder of how white supremacy and structural racism still endanger Black and Brown lives in twenty-first century America. Even after dozens of documented cases of police brutality and the racism-fueled murders of people of color, promises to retrain officers to deescalate encounters, and the widespread use of vehicle and body cameras by law enforcement, hardly a month goes by without a Black man getting killed by the authorities in an unwarranted use of deadly force. For more information, see https://blacklivesmatter.com/.
30. Despite the lack of evidence, local Anglo newspapers stated that "it was assumed that they [the dead Chicanx activists] were assembling a bomb" (Crusade for

Justice 1974), reproducing the main theory of Boulder Police that "the six were victims of their own haphazard work" ("Car Bombings Claim 6 Lives" 1974).

31. Nowadays, a beautiful sculpture stands in front of TB-1 to honor Los Seis de Boulder (Juan Espinosa 2019b).
32. September 16 is Mexico's Independence Day. The date rememorates the 1810 Grito de Dolores (i.e., cry for independence at Dolores), when Father Miguel Hidalgo y Costilla called Mexicans to arms and launched what would become Mexico's war of independence against Spain (Meier and Ribera 1993, 28–29). Mexico finally achieved its independence in 1821.
33. Mrs. Falcón, the widow of slain Chicano activist Ricardo Falcón, went on to earn a PhD from the University of Denver and teach for decades at the University of Northern Colorado in Greeley.

Chapter 4: The Western Slope

1. *Beaner* is an ethnic slur used to refer to Mexicans, Mexican Americans, and in some cases, other Latinxs (D. Romero 2019). The term comes from the use of beans in various forms in traditional Mexican and Mesoamerican cuisine. It was such a common epithet at the time (1990s–2000s) that the Mexican rock band Molotov (2003) even wrote a caustic retort to its use, which became an instant hit among Latinx youth.
2. *Maquiladoras* are factories established by foreign companies throughout the Global South (in this case, Mexico). They take advantage of cheap labor and low tariffs to assemble or manufacture products that are exported to the Global North.
3. The use of the term *Mexican* in this chapter obviously refers to citizens of Mexico who migrated to the United States, eventually settling in Colorado. Let us not forget that *Mexican* is also a racialized term commonly employed by Anglos throughout the American West to derisively refer to Latinxs and people of color, regardless of their citizenship status.
4. Both cities have regional airports; large malls; and dozens of stores, restaurants, and offices that cater to local and regional growing populations. See the websites of their respective chambers of commerce at https://gjchamber.org/ and https://www.durangobusiness.org/.
5. Research for this chapter was made possible by grants from the Charles Redd Center for Western Studies at Brigham Young University and the College of Liberal Arts at Colorado State University.
6. Since the 1990s, the state of Colorado has issued a special "Pioneer" license plate for those who want to display their pioneer heritage, and there is also an "Italian American" license plate available since 2007 (Division of Motor Vehicles 2023), but no similar license plate existed for Latinx heritage until the approval of the "Chicana/o Power!" license plate in 2024 (Wilson 2024).
7. As related in an oral history interview by retired teacher and school Principal Mr. Larry Archibeque (interviewed on June 1, 2015, in Cortez, Colorado). As a Hispanic in an Anglo-dominated world, Mr. Archibeque had to face numerous

instances of racial prejudice on his way toward becoming a successful school administrator in Montezuma County.
8. Interviewed on June 11, 2014, in Loma, Colorado.
9. According to Mr. José Chavez, who grew up in Las Colonias, Latinx residents nicknamed their neighborhood "La Gara" (i.e., the rag), after the bandana used by *betabeleros* to protect themselves from the sun while working in the fields. Mr. Chávez (interviewed on June 16, 2014, in Grand Junction, Colorado) grew up to become a bilingual parole officer for Mesa County.
10. Most of my sources in the Western Slope recounted how Latinxs were forced to speak only English in school and were punished by their teachers if they used their maternal Spanish tongue—even outside of class.
11. José Chavez's mother was a Hispana that came to the Grand Valley from Del Norte, Colorado, whereas his father was a Mexican immigrant of Tarahumara Indigenous ancestry. He grew up in Las Colonias and was bullied in school by both teachers and Anglo classmates for being "Mexican." He identified as "Mexican" as a child, then as a *cholo* (i.e., an Americanized Mexican American of mixed heritage) growing up, and finally as a militant Chicano once he entered college and joined El Movimiento.
12. Interviewed on June 9, 2014, in Palisade, Colorado.
13. The H-2A visa program allows for the importation of seasonal or temporary agricultural workers into the United States, particularly to places and for occupations where there is a shortage of available local labor. For more information see Farmworker Justice 2023.
14. Interviewed on June 9, 2014, in Palisade, Colorado.
15. See the Migration Data Portal for data on migrant deaths and disappearances. Available at https://migrationdataportal.org/themes/migrant-deaths-and-disappearances.
16. Interviewed on June 5, 2014, in Telluride, Colorado.
17. It must be kept in mind that it is particularly difficult to count poor, immigrant populations—particularly unauthorized immigrants—so these numbers very likely represent an undercount of the state's total Latinx immigrant population (see Colorado Department of Local Affairs 2022a).
18. In Sergio Arau's 2004 comedy-fantasy film *A Day Without a Mexican* the economy of California comes to a grinding halt when all Mexicans suddenly (and mysteriously) vanish, underscoring the vital role that Mexican immigrant labor plays in the state's economy.
19. Interviewed on August 2, 2013, in Vail, Colorado.
20. More recently, refugees from Latin America have been the latest cohort of migrants to the region. In November 2023, dozens of mostly Venezuelan refugees were found living under a bridge in Carbondale (just thirty miles from Aspen), attracted by word-of-mouth news about jobs in the area. City authorities are struggling to shelter them in pricey towns notorious for their lack of services for the unhoused (Brulliard 2023).
21. Interviewed on June 13, 2014, in Telluride, Colorado.

22. Interviewed on June 4, 2014, in Montrose, Colorado.
23. Interviewed on June 13, 2014, in Telluride, Colorado.
24. Interviewed on June 29, 2014, in Gunnison, Colorado.
25. Interviewed on June 29, 2014, in Crested Butte, Colorado.
26. Interviewed on June 11, 2014, in Fruita, Colorado.
27. Interviewed on June 1, 2015, in Cortez, Colorado.
28. Interviewed on June 4, 2015, in rural La Plata County, Colorado.
29. On June 25, 2021, Colorado Governor Jared Polis signed into law Senate Bill 87, guaranteeing the state's minimum wage to farmworkers, as well as overtime pay, meal breaks and rest periods, the right to organize, protection from retaliation by employers, and a ban on the infamous short-handled hoe (Vasquez 2021). The new law is expected to be a game changer for agricultural laborers, most of whom are Latinxs.
30. Interviewed on June 5, 2014, in Telluride, Colorado.
31. Interviewed on June 4, 2014, in Montrose, Colorado.
32. Interviewed on June 10, 2014, in Grand Junction, Colorado.
33. Interviewed on June 5, 2015, in Durango, Colorado.
34. The Fourth Congressional District, which covers the Eastern Plains and wealthy suburbs south of Denver, is the most conservative district in Colorado, with a Partisan Voting Index of R+13 which heavily favors Republican candidates (Cook Political Report 2022).
35. Mr. Martín Valdez, a longtime resident of Montrose, argued that "Anglos are resentful of Chicano culture; they don't give them [Chicanxs] any space. There is a fear that they [Chicanxs] will dominate." In this context, Mr. Valdez felt that relations between Anglos and Mexican immigrants were better than between Anglos and Chicanxs. Obviously, educated, upwardly mobile, US-born Chicanxs are a greater threat to Anglo dominance than non-English-speaking immigrants with little education and knowledge of American society—not to mention a history of decades of hostile relations between Anglos and Chicanxs (Acuña 2000).
36. It is quite obvious that the forging and sustaining of these transnational social relations are much easier for today's (trans)migrants than, for example, for the great wave of immigration that arrived in the United States during the late nineteenth century and early twentieth. Still, transnationalism is not a new phenomenon but "a novel perspective" on common practices carried out (mainly) by the first generation of migrants (Portes 2003, 874).
37. Interviewed on June 4, 2014, in Montrose, Colorado.
38. Interviewed on June 29, 2014, in Crested Butte, Colorado.
39. Interviewed on June 10, 2014, in Grand Junction, Colorado.
40. Interviewed on June 13, 2014, in Telluride, Colorado.
41. Interviewed on June 15, 2014, in Delta, Colorado.
42. Mr. Lucero (who passed away in 2020), made significant contributions to Grand Junction during his lifetime and was honored with the naming of a dorm building (Lucero Hall) on the campus of Colorado Mesa University. Interviewed on June 16, 2014, in Grand Junction, Colorado.

43. Mrs. Enos-Martinez is a third-generation Latina from Grand Junction, whose mother immigrated from Italy and grandparents came from Brazil. She attended CU Boulder, where she joined UMAS, and later married a Mexican immigrant from San Luis Potosí. Her unlikely path to politics began in 1993, when she decided to run for City Council (which was all Anglo at the time) and was defeated. Interviewed on June 25, 2014, in Grand Junction.
44. Interviewed on June 9, 2014, in Grand Junction, Colorado.

Conclusion: Colorado's Latinxs and the New American West

1. For example, as of 2023, the Denver City Council had five Latinas among its thirteen members (City and County of Denver 2023).
2. A massive international airport so far removed from Denver's city center was considered by some a boondoggle, and the project was nicknamed "Federico's Folly" by Peña's political detractors.
3. In a matter of just a few decades, Colorado has gone from being a "red state" (i.e., controlled by the Republicans) in the late twentieth century, to becoming a competitive "purple" state around the turn of the century (i.e., a toss-up state), to eventually becoming the reliable Democratic (i.e., "blue state") bastion that it is nowadays, where Democrats control the governorship, the state legislature, most statewide elective offices, and a majority of its congressional delegation. Moreover, the state is famous for its progressive policies, such as the early legalization of marijuana and ample protections for abortion rights. Demographic changes and partisan realignment around the turn of the century lie behind the state's political transformation: Colorado's population has become "younger, more urban, and more diverse" (which largely favors the Democrats), and while local Democrats have moved to the center of the political spectrum, some Republicans have moved to the fringe—a trend exacerbated after Donald Trump's election in 2016 (Ball 2016; Elliott 2022). Moderate Republicans, like former Congressman Ken Buck (who represented Colorado's Fourth Congressional District from 2015 until he resigned in 2024) have been heading for the exits (Coltrain 2024).
4. Mexican food is nowadays hugely popular among Anglos, particularly in the American West (Widjaya and Shah 2024).
5. The recently reopened Casa Bonita Mexican restaurant is a Colorado institution visited by throngs of locals and out-of-towners, particularly after it was featured in an episode of the popular cartoon series *South Park* (season 7, episode 11). Trey Parker and Matt Stone, the creators of *South Park*, acquired Casa Bonita in 2021, after it was forced to shut its doors due to the COVID-19 pandemic (Richtel 2023). It has reopened to great acclaim.
6. The state of Colorado also issues a "Pueblo Chile" license plate (Division of Motor Vehicles 2023), an implicit recognition of the heightened role of Latinx culture in the state.

REFERENCES

Collections

David Marquez Papers, 1983–2001 (CSUP-EDMQ), Colorado Chicano Movement Archives, Colorado State University Pueblo.

Garcia Family Papers (CSUP-EGAR), Colorado Chicano Movement Archives, Colorado State University Pueblo.

Jose Esteban Ortega Papers (CSUP-EJEO), Colorado Chicano Movement Archives, Colorado State University Pueblo.

Juan Federico "Freddie Freak" Arguello Trujillo Chicano Movement Collection (CSUP-EFFT), Colorado Chicano Movement Archives, Colorado State University Pueblo.

Rodolfo ("Corky") Gonzales Papers, WH1971, Western History Collection, Denver Public Library.

United Mexican American Students Papers (CSUP-UMAS), Colorado Chicano Movement Archives, Colorado State University Pueblo.

Other Sources

Abbott, Carl, Stephen J. Leonard, and Thomas J. Noel. 2005. *Colorado: A History of the Centennial State*. 4th ed. University Press of Colorado.

https://doi.org/10.5876/9781646427260.c006

Acuña, Rodolfo. 2000. *Occupied America: A History of Chicanos*. 4th ed. Longman.
Adams State College, and San Luis Valley Historical Society. 1980a. *Entradas al Norte*. The Society.
Adams State College, and San Luis Valley Historical Society. 1980b. *Primeras placitas del Valle de San Luis*. The Society.
Adelman, Jeremy, and Stephen Aron. 1999. "From Borderlands to Borders: Empires, Nation-States, and the Peoples in Between in North American History." *American Historical Review* 104 (3): 814–841.
Aguayo, José. 1998. "*Los Betabeleros* (The Beetworkers)." In *La Gente: Hispano History and Life in Colorado*, edited by Vincent C. de Baca. Colorado Historical Society.
Aguilar, John. 2022. "Latino Voters Were Critical to Yadira Caraveo's Victory in Colorado's 8th U.S. House District, Exit Poll Finds." *Denver Post*, November 10.
Aguilar Rangel, Jazmin. 2022. "Infographic: Remittances in Mexico Reach a Historic High." Wilson Center, March 15. https://www.wilsoncenter.org/article/infographic-remittances-mexico-reach-historic-high.
"Alamosa Activist Settles U.S. Suit over Traffic Stops." 2007. *Denver Post*, July 4.
Alaniz, Yolanda, and Megan Cornish. 2008. *Viva la Raza: A History of Chicano Identity and Resistance*. Red Letter Press.
Aldama, Arturo J., Elisa Facio, Daryl Maeda, and Reiland Rabaka. 2011. *Enduring Legacies: Ethnic Histories and Cultures of Colorado*. University Press of Colorado.
Alire, Jay. 1972. "La Raza Unida: 'A Way of Life.'" *Rocky Mountain Collegian* 81, no. 41 (November 7): 1.
Allyn, Noah. 2019a. "Chicana Power: Female Leaders in el Movimiento and the Search for Identity." History Colorado, June 12. https://www.historycolorado.org/story/colorado-voices/2019/06/12/chicana-power-female-leaders-el-movimiento-and-search-identity.
Allyn, Noah. 2019b. "Guadalupe Briseño and the Female-Led Strike in Brighton, Colorado." History Colorado, March 14. https://www.historycolorado.org/story/colorado-voices/2019/03/14/guadalupe-briseno-and-female-led-strike-brighton-colorado.
Almaguer, Tomás. 1971. "Toward the Study of Chicano Colonialism." *Aztlán: A Journal of Chicano Studies* 2 (1): 7–21.
Almaguer, Tomás. 1974. "Historical Notes on Chicano Oppression: The Dialectics of Racial and Class Domination in North América." *Aztlán: A Journal of Chicano Studies* 5 (1–2): 27–56.
"Alurista." 2019. UC Santa Barbara Library, Special Research Collections. https://www.library.ucsb.edu/special-collections/cema/alurista.
Alvarez, Alayna. 2021. "Colorado's Latino Population Boom Will Shape Local Politics." Axios Denver, September 29. https://www.axios.com/local/denver/2021/09/29/colorado-latino-population-boom-local-politics.
Anderson, Benedict. 2006. *Imagined Communities: Reflections on the Origin and Spread of Nationalism*. Verso.
Anderson, James. 2016. "Assimilation Is Long Road for Somalis in Colorado Town." *Santa Fe New Mexican*, March 19.
Andreas, Carol. 1994. *Meatpackers and Beef Barons: Company Town in a Global Economy*. University Press of Colorado.

Andrews, Thomas G. 2008. *Killing for Coal: America's Deadliest Labor War*. Harvard University Press.

Annie E. Casey Foundation. 2024. "KIDS COUNT Data Center," Baltimore. https://datacenter.aecf.org/.

Anthony, Carmen. 1969. "Denver Peaceful Demonstration Turns into Rock Throwing Melee." *Golden Transcript* 103, no. 41 (March 20): 3.

Aparicio, Frances R. 2019. *Negotiating Latinidad: Intralatina/o Lives in Chicago*. University of Illinois Press.

Arce, Carlos H. 1976. "Chicanos in Higher Education." *Equity and Excellence in Education* 14 (3): 14–18.

Arellano, Anselmo. 2000. "The People's Movement: Las Gorras Blancas." In *The Contested Homeland: A Chicano History of New Mexico*, edited by Erlinda Gonzales-Berry and David R. Maciel. University of New Mexico Press.

"AZTLAN." 1977. *Papel del Barrio* 1 (8): 1–3. CSUP-UMAS.

Baca, Herman. 2021. "Commentary: The History Behind the Debate over 'Chicano' and Other Labels Goes as Far Back as 1848." *San Diego Union-Tribune*, January 4.

Balderrama, Francisco E., and Raymond Rodríguez. 2006. *Decade of Betrayal: Mexican Repatriation in the 1930s*. Rev. ed. University of New Mexico Press.

Ball, Molly. 2016. "The State That Fell off the Electoral Map." *Atlantic*, September 14. https://www.theatlantic.com/politics/archive/2016/09/the-state-that-fell-off-the-map/499529/.

Bardacke, Frank. 2011. *Trampling out the Vintage: Cesar Chavez and the Two Souls of the United Farm Workers*. Verso.

Barrera, James. 2004. "The Political Repression of a Chicano Movement Activist: The Plight of Francisco E. 'Kiko' Martínez." *NACCS Annual Conference Proceedings*, no. 9, 117–142.

Basch, Linda, Nina Glick Schiller, and Cristina Szanton Blanc. 1994. *Nations Unbound: Transnational Projects, Postcolonial Predicaments, and Deterritorialized Nation-States*. Gordon and Breach.

Baum, Dan. 2000. *Citizen Coors: A Grand Family Saga of Business, Politics, and Beer*. HarperCollins.

Beckford, George L. 1999. *Persistent Poverty: Underdevelopment in Plantation Economies of the Third World*. University of the West Indies Press.

Beeton, Jared M., Charles N. Saenz, and Benjamin J. Waddell, eds. 2020. *The Geology, Ecology, and Human History of the San Luis Valley*. University Press of Colorado.

The Bell Policy Center. 2018. "Demographics: A Changing Colorado." https://www.bellpolicy.org/wp-content/uploads/2018/01/Demographics-Guide-to-Economic-Mobility.pdf.

Biller, Ryan. 2024. "'We Don't Want to Be a National Laughingstock': How Lauren Boebert Blew Her Safe Seat." *Politico*, January 7. https://www.politico.com/news/magazine/2024/01/07/lauren-boebert-colorado-district-00134137?cid=apn.

Bills, Garland D., and Neddy A. Vigil. 2008. *The Spanish Language of New Mexico and Southern Colorado: A Linguistic Atlas*. University of New Mexico Press.

Black, Gordon. 2011. "The More a Problem Is Fed, the Bigger It Gets." *Cortez Journal*, March 3.

Blackwell, Maylei. 2011. *¡Chicana Power! Contested Histories of Feminism in the Chicano Movement*. University of Texas Press.
Bolton, Herbert E. 1921. *The Spanish Borderlands: A Chronicle of Old Florida and the Southwest*. Yale University Press.
Borowsky, Larry. 2020. "For Undocumented Workers, More Risk and Little Safety Net." *Collective Colorado*, April 7. https://collective.coloradotrust.org/stories/for-undocumented-workers-more-risk-and-little-safety-net/.
Boskin, Michael J., ed. 2014. *NAFTA at 20: The North American Free Trade Agreement's Achievements and Challenges*. Hoover Institution Press.
"Boulder Anti-War Protest May 1972." 2015. YouTube video. https://www.youtube.com/watch?v=-YETuxUoJqA.
Brosnan, Kathleen A. 2002. *Uniting Mountain and Plain: Cities, Law, and Environmental Change Along the Front Range*. University of New Mexico Press.
Brulliard, Karin. 2023. "Migrant Crisis Spreads to a Remote Mountain Town as Winter Descends." *Washington Post*, December 22.
Bulmer-Thomas, Victor. 2003. *The Economic History of Latin America since Independence*. 2nd ed. Cambridge University Press.
Bunch, Joey. 2021. "Colorado Poll Shows COVID-19's Economic Toll on Latinos." *Colorado Politics*, November 14. https://www.coloradopolitics.com/legislature/colorado-poll-shows-covid-19s-economic-toll-on-latinos/article_25b25a34-3067-11ec-ba1c-8713e96ea791.html.
Burness, Alex. 2020. "Colorado's 3rd Congressional District: Lauren Boebert Defeats Diane Mitsch Bush." *Denver Post*, November 3.
Camacho Liu, Michelle. 2011. "Trends in Latino College Access and Success." National Conference of State Legislatures. https://ahed.assembly.ca.gov/sites/ahed.assembly.ca.gov/files/hearings/NCSL%20TrendsInLatinoSuccess.pdf.
"Car Bombings Claim 6 Lives." 1974. *El Diario de la Gente* 3, no. 1 (June 11): 1.
Cardoso, Lawrence A. 1980. *Mexican Emigration to the United States, 1897–1931: Socio-Economic Patterns*. University of Arizona Press.
Carlson, Alvar W. 1973. "Seasonal Farm Labor in the San Luis Valley." *Annals of the Association of American Geographers* 63 (1): 97–108.
Carlyle, Thomas. 1841. *On Heroes, Hero-worship, and the Heroic in History: Six Lectures*. London.
Carr, Jonathan, and Claire Kempa. 2015. "The History of Las Colonias Park: Historic Crossroads Along the Riverfront of Grand Junction, Colorado." City of Grand Junction Parks and Recreation Department. https://www.gjcity.org/DocumentCenter/View/5887/Las-Colonias-CMU-Historical-Project---The-History-of-Las-Colonias-Park---2015---April?bidId=.
Carrigan, William D., and Clive Webb. 2013. *Forgotten Dead: Mob Violence Against Mexicans in the United States, 1848–1928*. Oxford University Press.
Castro, Fidel. 2016. "Palabras a los intelectuales." *Tareas* 154:77–110.
CDI Mx [Comisión Nacional para el Desarrollo de los Pueblos Indígenas, México]. 2016. "El Renacer de una Cultura Milenaria Semana Santa Cora Dolores, Nayarit." https://www.youtube.com/watch?v=vdqfUx46MFE.

"CF&I, Unions Charged with Race/Sex Discrimination." 1976. *La Cucaracha* 1 (4): 1, 3. CSUP-EJEO.

Chicano Law Students, University of Colorado. 1974. "Student Organizations Protest Coverage of Boulder Bombings." *El Diario de la Gente* 3, no. 1 (June 11): 3.

Childers, Michael W. 2012. *Colorado Powder Keg: Ski Resorts and the Environmental Movement*. University Press of Kansas.

Church Committee [United States Senate Select Committee to Study Governmental Operations with Respect to Intelligence Activities]. 1976. "Church Committee Reports." Mary Ferrell Foundation. https://www.maryferrell.org/php/showlist.php?docset=1014.

"Cinco de Mayo Celebration in Denver Among Nation's Largest." 2023. *9News*, May 5. https://www.9news.com/video/news/local/9news-mornings/cinco-de-mayo-denver/73-59bdf188-4cc1-4db2-82c0-fe79f16a13a6.

City and County of Denver. 2023. "Meet the Council Members." Denver City Council. https://www.denvergov.org/Government/Agencies-Departments-Offices/Agencies-Departments-Offices-Directory/Denver-City-Council/Meet-the-Council-Members.

Clyne, Rick J. 1999. *Coal People: Life in Southern Colorado's Company Towns, 1890–1930*. Colorado Historical Society.

Coates, James. 1989. "'English Only' Law Becomes a Matter of Interpretation." *Chicago Tribune*, January 15.

Cogan, Brian, and Thom Gencarelli, eds. 2015. *Baby Boomers and Popular Culture: An Inquiry into America's Most Powerful Generation*. Praeger.

Coleman, Caitlin. 2020. "Hundreds of San Luis Valley Farm Wells at Risk as State Shortens Deadline to Repair Rio Grande River." Water Education Colorado. https://www.watereducationcolorado.org/fresh-water-news/hundreds-of-san-luis-valley-farm-wells-at-risk-as-state-shortens-deadline-to-repair-rio-grande-river/.

Colin Powell School for Civic and Global Leadership. 2021. "From Academia to Public Policy." YouTube video. https://www.youtube.com/watch?v=Zf1p--1G_Rs.

"Colo. Man Wins Watch List Suit." 2007. *Denver Post*, July 31.

Colorado Department of Local Affairs, State Demography Office. 2022a. "Race and Hispanic Origin." https://demography.dola.colorado.gov/assets/lookups/region_sya_race_lookup.html.

Colorado Department of Local Affairs, State Demography Office. 2022b. "SDO County Data Resource Page." https://demography.dola.colorado.gov/assets/html/county.html.

Colorado Hispanic Chamber of Commerce. 2018. Denver. https://www.hispanicchamberdenver.com/.

Colorado Organization for Latina Opportunity and Reproductive Rights (COLOR), COLOR Action Fund, Voces Unidas de las Montañas and Voces Unidas Action Fund. 2022. "Colorado Latino Policy Agenda 2022." https://coloradolatinopolicyagenda.org/.

Colorado State Archives. 2023. "Symbols and Emblems." Denver: State of Colorado. https://archives.colorado.gov/collections/symbols-emblems.

Colorado Tourism Office. 2023. "Celebrate Colorado's Hispanic and Latinx History." State of Colorado. https://www.colorado.com/articles/celebrate-colorados-hispanic-latinx-history.

Coltrain, Nick. 2024. "Ken Buck Resigns from Congress, Setting Stage for Special Election—and Potentially Scrambling Race Again." *Denver Post*, March 12.
Conan, Neal. 2011. "Chicano Movement's Denver Roots Run Deep." *CPR News*, June 30. https://www.npr.org/2011/06/30/137529484/the-chicano-movements-denver-roots-run-deep.
Cook Political Report. 2022. "2022 Cook PVI: District Map and List." July 12. https://www.cookpolitical.com/cook-pvi/2022-partisan-voting-index/district-map-and-list.
Counihan, Carole M. 2009. *A Tortilla Is Like Life: Food and Culture in the San Luis Valley of Colorado*. University of Texas Press.
Cronin, Tom, and Bob Loevy. 2021a. "Front Range Owns CO's Growth." *Colorado Politics*, September 3. https://www.coloradopolitics.com/opinion/cronin-loevy-front-range-owns-cos-growth/article_e69c31d4-0c68-11ec-b4e7-bbaa3e47da35.html.
Cronin, Tom, and Bob Loevy. 2021b. "Rural Counties Reveal Inequality in Colorado." *Gazette*, November 27.
Crusade for Justice. 1974. "Crusade Says 'Third Party' to Blame in Bombings." *El Diario de la Gente* 3, no. 1 (June 11): 3.
Curry, William Nye. 1977. "The Death of a Colo. Sugar Beet Crop." *Washington Post*, April 4.
"DA Said Lax on Police Beatings." 1976. *La Cucaracha* 1, no. 1 (May 5): 3.
Daley, James, ed. 2008. *Great Speeches by American Women*. Dover Publications.
Dallek, Robert. 1999. *Ronald Reagan: The Politics of Symbolism*. Harvard University Press.
Dallek, Robert. 2004. *Lyndon B. Johnson: Portrait of a President*. Oxford University Press.
Daum, Courtenay W., Robert J. Duffy, Kyle Saunders, and John A. Straayer. 2011. "Introduction—State of Change: Colorado Politics in the Twenty-First Century." In *State of Change: Colorado Politics in the Twenty-First Century*, edited by Courtenay W. Daum, Robert J. Duffy, and John A. Straayer. University Press of Colorado.
Dávila, Arlene. 2001. *Latinos, Inc.: The Marketing and Making of a People*. University of California Press.
De Baca, Vincent C., ed. 1998. *La Gente: Hispano History and Life in Colorado*. Colorado Historical Society.
De Genova, Nicholas, and Ana Y. Ramos-Zayas. 2003. *Latino Crossings: Mexicans, Puerto Ricans, and the Politics of Race and Citizenship*. Routledge.
De la Garza, Rodolfo O. 1979. "Chicano Political Power: An Increasingly Important Role." *Denver Post*, November 25.
De León, Arnoldo. 1983. *They Called Them Greasers: Anglo Attitudes Toward Mexicans in Texas, 1821–1900*. University of Texas Press.
De León, Arnoldo, and Richard Griswold del Castillo. 2006. *North to Aztlán: A History of Mexican Americans in the United States*. 2nd ed. John Wiley and Sons.
Delgado, Richard, and Jean Stefancic. 1999. "Home-Grown Racism: Colorado's Historic Embrace—and Denial—of Equal Opportunity in Higher Education." *University of Colorado Law Review* 70 (3): 703–811.
Democratic Party of Denver. 2023. "Going for It: The Groundbreaking Career of Polly Baca." https://www.denverdemocrats.org/post/going-for-it-the-groundbreaking-career-of-polly-baca-1.

Denver Public Library. 2009. "Rodolfo 'Corky' Gonzales." Genealogy, African American and Western History Resources, WH1971. https://history.denverlibrary.org/rodolfo-corky-gonzales.

DeSipio, Louis. 1996. *Counting on the Latino Vote: Latinos as a New Electorate*. University Press of Virginia.

Deutsch, Sarah. 1987. *No Separate Refuge: Culture, Class, and Gender on an Anglo-Hispanic Frontier in the American Southwest, 1880–1940*. Oxford University Press.

Deutsch, Sarah. 1994. "Gender, Labor History, and Chicano/a Ethnic Identity." *Frontiers: A Journal of Women Studies* 14 (2): 1–22.

DiPrince, Dawn. 2023. "Remarks on Opening the Display of the Treaty of Guadalupe Hidalgo." History Colorado, February 3. https://www.historycolorado.org/story/2023/02/03/remarks-opening-display-treaty-guadalupe-hidalgo.

Division of Motor Vehicles. 2023. "Group Special License Plates." Colorado Department of Revenue. https://dmv.colorado.gov/group-special-license-plates.

Dokson, Katie. 2022. "An Almost-Forgotten Fight for School Desegregation." History Colorado, September 13. https://www.historycolorado.org/story/2022/09/13/almost-forgotten-fight-school-desegregation.

Donato, Rubén. 2007. *Mexicans and Hispanos in Colorado Schools and Communities, 1920–1960*. State University of New York Press.

Donato, Rubén, Gonzalo Guzmán, and Jarrod Hanson. 2017. "*Francisco Maestas et al. v. George H. Shone et al.*: Mexican American Resistance to School Segregation in the Hispano Homeland, 1912–1914." *Journal of Latinos and Education* 16 (1): 3–17.

Dorsett, Lyle W. 1977. *The Queen City: A History of Denver*. Pruett Pub. Co.

Dowling, Julie A. 2014. *Mexican Americans and the Question of Race*. Austin: University of Texas Press.

Duncan, Oli Olivas, ed. 1988. *We, Too, Came to Stay: A History of the Longmont Hispanic Community*. Longmont Hispanic Study and El Comité.

Dunn, Joshua M. 2014. "The Paradoxes of Politics in Colorado Springs." *Forum* 12 (2): 329–342.

Eagles, Charles W., ed. 1986. *The Civil Rights Movement in America*. University Press of Mississippi.

El Gallo. 1974. "COLORADO'S La Raza Unida Party Position Statement." *El Gallo* 6 (1): 5–8. January.

"El Plan Espiritual de Aztlán." 1969. *El Gallo* 2, no. 5 (April 1): 16.

Elliott, Philip. 2022. "Trumpism Has Hijacked Colorado's Shrinking GOP: That Has National Implications." *Time*, June 28. https://time.com/6191924/colorado-primary-trump-republicans/.

"English-Only Means Genocide for Mexicans in U.S." 1989. *¡Ya Basta!* (Fall): 1. CSUP-EGAR.

Ennis, Sharon R., Merarys Ríos-Vargas, and Nora G. Albert. 2011. "The Hispanic Population: 2010." Washington, DC: US Census Bureau.

"Erroneous Enlistment or Induction." 1973. *¡Ahora!* 4 (13): 8–9. CSUP-EFFT.

Espinosa, John L., and Pat Moore. 1972. "Opinion: Viva La Raza." *Colorado Daily* 21, no. 68 (December 8): 10.

Espinosa, Juan. 2015. "Photographing the Front Lines of El Movimiento." *Colorado Heritage*, March/April: 22–25.

Espinosa, Juan. 2019a. "History, Overview of El Diario—'72–83." *El Diario de la Gente*, September 6.

Espinosa, Juan. 2019b. "Sculpture Honors Six Killed by 1974 Bombings." *El Diario de la Gente*, September 6.

Esquibel, Antonio. 2015. "El Movimiento Chicano de Colorado, 1960–1980." *Colorado Heritage*, March/April, 16–21.

Everett, Derek R. 2014. *Creating the American West: Boundaries and Borderlands*. University of Oklahoma Press.

"Expansion of the Displaced Aurarian Scholarship Program." 2021. Auraria Higher Education Center, November 4. https://www.ahec.edu/campus-announcements/expansion-of-the-displaced-aurarian-scholarship-program.

Facio, Elisa. 2011. "(Re)constructing Chicana *Movimiento* Narratives at CU Boulder, 1968–1974." In *Enduring Legacies: Ethnic Histories and Cultures of Colorado*, edited by Arturo Aldama, Elisa Facio, Daryl Maeda, and Reiland Rabaka. University Press of Colorado.

"Falcon Gave His Life For La Gente." 1977. *La Cucaracha* 2, no. 7 (August 1): 13.

Falcón, Priscilla. 2003. "Only Strong Women Stayed: Women Workers and the National Floral Workers Strike, 1968–1969." *Frontiers: A Journal of Women Studies* 24 (2/3): 140–154.

Falcón, Priscilla. 2015. "Soldiers of the Field: Mexican Labor in Northern Colorado." *Colorado Heritage*, March/April, 30–31.

Farer, Paola. 2004. "John Salazar Carries 3rd District." *9News*, November 3. https://www.9news.com/article/news/local/john-salazar-carries-3rd-district/73-344842034.

Farmworker Justice. 2023. "H-2A Guestworker Program." https://www.farmworkerjustice.org/advocacy_program/h-2a-guestworker-program/.

Federal Bureau of Investigation. 1968. "Cover Letter Re: Rodolfo 'Corky' Gonzales." Internal memo. WH1971.

"Felony Assault Charges Filed Against 4 in Police Shootout." 1973. Newspaper clipping. WH1971.

FitzGerald, David. 2008. "Colonies of the Little Motherland: Membership, Space, and Time in Mexican Migrant Hometown Associations." *Comparative Studies in Society and History* 50 (1): 145–169.

Flores, Devin. 2019. "Where Is the Oldest Town in Colorado?" History Colorado, October 15. https://www.historycolorado.org/story/do-you-know-place/2019/10/15/where-oldest-town-colorado.

Flowers, Tatiana. 2022. "After 50 Years, Homeownership Gap Between White and Latino Coloradans Narrows. But for Black Coloradans, It's Widened." *The Colorado Sun*, June 8. https://coloradosun.com/2022/06/08/colorado-homeownership-racial-gap/.

Fort Morgan Museum. 2015. "Major Morgan County Crops." Museum exhibit. Fort Morgan, Colorado.

Foster-Frau, Silvia. 2021. "A Colorado County Offers a Glimpse of America's Future." *Washington Post*, August 13.

Fox, Lauren. 2014. "For Colorado GOP, Outreach to Latinos Isn't an Option, It's Essential." *U.S. News and World Report*, September 11. http://www.usnews.com/news/articles/2014/09/11/for-colorado-gop-outreach-to-latinos-isnt-an-option-its-essential.

Francis-Fallon, Benjamin. 2019. *The Rise of the Latino Vote: A History*. Harvard University Press.

Frank, John. 2019. "Crisanta Duran, Once a Rising Democratic Star, Abandons Bid to Unseat Diana DeGette." *Colorado Sun*, October 11. https://coloradosun.com/2019/10/11/crisanta-duran-withdraw-congress-diana-degette/.

Frank, John. 2021. "How Colorado's Population Grew and Why It Matters." *Axios Denver*, August 16. https://www.axios.com/local/denver/2021/08/16/census-2020-colorado-population-redistricting.

Freedom Archives. 2017. *Symbols of Resistance: A Tribute to the Martyrs of the Chican@ Movement*. PM Press.

Fulcher, Michelle P. 2018. "A Menace, a Scapegoat, an Emblem: What 'California' Really Means to Colorado," *Colorado Public Radio*, August 27. https://www.cpr.org/news/story/a-menace-a-scapegoat-an-emblem-what-california-really-means-to-colorado.

Gabriel Jose [no last name]. 1972. "An Analysis." *El Gallo* 4, no. 1 (January).

Gallegos, Phillip. 2011. "Religious Architecture in Colorado's San Luis Valley." In *Enduring Legacies: Ethnic Histories and Cultures of Colorado*, edited by Arturo Aldama, Elisa Facio, Daryl Maeda, and Reiland Rabaka. University Press of Colorado.

Gamio, Manuel. 1930. *Mexican Immigration to the United States: A Study of Human Migration and Adjustment*. University of Chicago Press.

García, Ignacio M. 1989. *United We Win: The Rise and Fall of La Raza Unida Party*. University of Arizona Press.

García, Ignacio M. 1997. *Chicanismo: The Forging of a Militant Ethos Among Mexican Americans*. University of Arizona Press.

García, Ignacio M. 2000. *Viva Kennedy: Mexican Americans in Search of Camelot*. Texas A&M University Press.

García, Mario T. 1989. *Mexican Americans: Leadership, Ideology, and Identity, 1930–1960*. Yale University Press.

García, Mario T. 2021. "Introduction: The Chicano Movement, Chicano History, and the New American Narrative." In *Rewriting the Chicano Movement: New Histories of Mexican American Activism in the Civil Rights Era*, edited by Mario T. García and Ellen McCracken. University of Arizona Press.

García, Mario T., and Sal Castro. 2011. *Blowout! Sal Castro and the Chicano Struggle for Educational Justice*. University of North Carolina Press.

Gibson, Campbell, and Kay Jung. 2002. "Historical Census Statistics on Population Totals by Race, 1790 to 1990, and by Hispanic Origin, 1970 to 1990, for the United States, Regions, Divisions, and States." Working Paper No. 56. Washington, DC: US Census Bureau.

Gill, Hannah. 2018. *The Latino Migration Experience in North Carolina: New Roots in the Old North State*. 2nd ed. University of North Carolina Press.

Girón, Helen. 2011. "When Geronimo Was Asked Who He Was, He Replied, I am an Apache." In *Enduring Legacies: Ethnic Histories and Cultures of Colorado*, edited by Arturo Aldama, Elisa Facio, Daryl Maeda, and Reiland Rabaka. University Press of Colorado.

Goetz, Andrew R., and E. Eric Boschmann. 2018. *Metropolitan Denver: Growth and Change in the Mile High City*. University of Pennsylvania Press.

Goldberg, Robert A. 1981. *Hooded Empire: The Ku Klux Klan in Colorado*. University of Illinois Press.

Golden, Allen. 2004. "'We Were Never the Same': The Story of the San Luis Valley During World War II." *San Luis Valley Historian* 36 (3): 5–49.

Golten, Ryan. 2005. "*Lobato v. Taylor*: How the Villages of the Rio Culebra, the Colorado Supreme Court, and the *Restatement of Servitudes* Bailed Out the Treaty of Guadalupe Hidalgo." *Natural Resources Journal* 45:457–494.

Gómez, Laura E. 2018. *Manifest Destinies: The Making of the Mexican American Race*. 2nd ed. New York University Press.

Gómez, Laura E. 2022. *Inventing Latinos: A New Story of American Racism*. New Press.

Gómez-Quiñones, Juan. 1990. *Chicano Politics: Reality and Promise, 1940–1990*. University of New Mexico Press.

Gómez-Quiñones, Juan. 1994. *Mexican American Labor, 1790–1990*. University of New Mexico Press.

Gómez-Quiñones, Juan, and Irene Vásquez. 2014. *Making Aztlán: Ideology and Culture of the Chicana and Chicano Movement, 1966–1977*. University of New Mexico Press.

Gonzales, Phillip B., and Virginia Sánchez. 2018. "Displaced in Place: Nuevomexicanos on the Northern Side of the New Mexico–Colorado Boundary, 1850–1875." *New Mexico Historical Review* 93 (3): 263–301.

Gonzales, Rodolfo. 1967. *I Am Joaquín: An Epic Poem*. El Gallo.

Gonzalez-Barrera, Ana. 2015. "More Mexicans Leaving than Coming to the U.S." Washington: Pew Research Center. https://www.pewhispanic.org/wp-content/uploads/sites/5/2015/11/2015-11-19_mexican-immigration__FINAL.pdf.

Goodland, Marianne. 2018. "Colorado Senate Dems Choose Garcia as President: House Dems Tap Becker as speaker." *Colorado Politics*, November 8. https://www.coloradopolitics.com/news/colorado-senate-dems-choose-garcia-as-president-house-dems-tap-becker-as-speaker/article_c6539f4e-5aa5-56a7-a36a-6a4eb41c08ff.html.

Gouveia, Lourdes. 2005. "Latinos in Rural America and U.S. Agriculture: From Pioneers to New Arrivals." *Journal of Latino/Latin American Studies* 1 (4): 1–24.

Great Western Sugar Company. 1924(?). "Beet Labor Film." Records of the Great Western Sugar Company, Agricultural and Natural Resources Archive, Colorado State University. https://archives.mountainscholar.org/digital/collection/p17393coll85/id/8/rec/2.

Greater Pueblo Chamber of Commerce, The. 2023. "The Greater Pueblo Chamber: We Mean Business." https://pueblochamber.org/.

Greeley Stampede. 2022. "Greely Stampede." https://www.greeleystampede.org/.

Griego, Tina. 2019. "Parked: Eagle County Mobile-Home Parks Become Immigrants' Home Away from Home." *Colorado Sun*, September 15. https://coloradosun.com/2019/09/15/parked-mobile-home-parks-become-immigrants-home-away-from-home/.

Guardino, Peter. 2017. *The Dead March: A History of the Mexican-American War*. Harvard University Press.

Gurr, Ted. 1970. *Why Men Rebel*. Princeton University Press.

Gustin, Georgina. 2004. "A Valley from the Past." *New York Times*, October 10.
Gutiérrez, David G. 1993. "Significant to Whom? Mexican Americans and the History of the American West." *Western Historical Quarterly* 24 (4): 519–539.
Gutiérrez, David G. 1995. *Walls and Mirrors: Mexican Americans, Mexican Immigrants, and the Politics of Ethnicity*. University of California Press.
Gutiérrez, David G. 1998. "Ethnic Mexicans and the Transformation of 'American' Social Space: Reflections on Recent History." In *Crossings: Mexican Immigration in Interdisciplinary Perspectives*, edited by Marcelo M. Suárez-Orozco. Harvard University Press.
Gutiérrez, Ramón A. 2000. "Chicano History: Paradigm Shifts and Shifting Boundaries." In *Voice of a New Chicana/o History*, edited by Refugio I. Rochín and Dennis N. Valdés. Michigan State University Press.
Gutiérrez, Ramón A. 2022. *New Mexico's Moses: Reies López Tijerina and the Religious Origins of the Mexican American Civil Rights Movement*. University of New Mexico Press.
Gutiérrez, Ramón A., and Elliott Young. 2010. "Transnationalizing Borderlands History." *Western Historical Quarterly* 41 (1): 27–53.
Hämäläinen, Pekka, and Samuel Truett. 2011. "On Borderlands." *Journal of American History* 98 (2): 338–361.
Hamilton, Candy. 2009. *Footprints in the Sugar: A History of the Great Western Sugar Company*. Hamilton Bates Publishers.
Haverluk, Terrence W. 1998. "Hispanic Community Types and Assimilation in Mex-America." *Professional Geographer* 50 (4): 465–480.
Haverluk, Terrence W. 2002. "Chile Peppers and Identity Construction in Pueblo, Colorado." *Journal for the Study of Food and Society* 6 (1): 45–59.
Haverluk, Terrence W. 2003. "Mex-America: From Margin to Mainstream." In *Western Places, American Myths: How We Think About the West*, edited by Gary J. Hausladen. University of Nevada Press.
Henderson, Timothy J. 2011. *Beyond Borders: A History of Mexican Migration to the United States*. Wiley-Blackwell.
Hernandez, Alejandro. 2019. "When Colorado Closed the Door on the Poor." Denver Public Library, August 19. https://history.denverlibrary.org/news/when-colorado-closed-door-poor.
Hernández, José. 1997. *Conquered Peoples in America*. 5th ed. Kendall Hunt Publishing Company.
Hernández, Roberto D. 2020. "Commentary: To Be a Chicano Is to Inherit Generations of Resistance, Defiance, Resilience and Dignity." *San Diego Union-Tribune*, December 31.
Herrera, Carlos R. 2000. "New Mexico Resistance to U.S. Occupation During the Mexican-American War of 1846–1848." In *The Contested Homeland: A Chicano History of New Mexico*, edited by Erlinda Gonzales-Berry and David R. Maciel. University of New Mexico Press.
Herrera, Liz. 1991. "Hispanic People of Grand Junction." *Journal of the Western Slope* 6 (3): 4–18.
Hindi, Saja, and Tina Griego. 2023. "Colorado Latino and Black Poverty Rates near Historic Lows, but Economic Stability Remains Elusive." *Denver Post*, February 16.
Hispanic Affairs Project. 2022. "About Us." https://hapgj.org/about-us/.

Hoig, Stan. 1961. *The Sand Creek Massacre*. University of Oklahoma Press.
Holley, George. 2006. "A Divided Campus: Tensions at Adams State in the 1970s." *San Luis Valley Historian* 38 (3): 5–23.
Holmes, Samuel. 1926. "An Argument Against the Mexican Immigration." *Transactions of the Commonwealth Club of California* 21:27.
Hordes, Stanley M. 2005. *To the End of the Earth: A History of the Crypto-Jews of New Mexico*. Columbia University Press.
Horsman, Reginald. 1981. *Race and Manifest Destiny: The Origins of American Racial Anglo-Saxonism*. Harvard University Press.
Hubbard, Burt, and Ann Carnahan. 2013. "Losing Ground, Part 1: Equality Gap Grows for Minorities." *The Gazette*, January 18. https://gazette.com/news/losing-ground-part-1-equality-gap-grows-for-minorities/article_ffc05228-931e-516a-a2a1-1514ac41a199.html.
Hubbard, Burt, and Tina Griego. 2022. "Key Gaps Between Black, Latino and White Coloradans Have Narrowed, but Equity Is 'a Dream Unrealized.'" *Colorado Sun*, June 2. https://coloradosun.com/2022/06/02/economic-equity-black-latino-white-colorado-census/.
Huntington, Samuel P. 2004. *Who Are We? The Challenges to America's National Identity*. Simon and Schuster.
Hutchinson, John, and Anthony D. Smith, eds. 1996. *Ethnicity*. Oxford University Press.
Iber, Jorge, and Arnoldo De León. 2006. *Hispanics in the American West*. ABC-CLIO.
Immigration Reform and Control Act of 1986, Pub. L. No. 99-603, 100 Stat. 3359 (1986).
Irwin, Douglas A. 2017. *Clashing over Commerce: A History of US Trade Policy*. University of Chicago Press.
Isenberg, Sydney, and Robert Garrison. 2023. "Rep. Lauren Boebert Announced Congressional District Switch." *Denver7*, December 27. https://www.denver7.com/news/politics/rep-lauren-boebert-announces-congressional-district-switch.
Jacobson, Robin D. 2008. *The New Nativism: Proposition 187 and the Debate over Immigration*. University of Minnesota Press.
Jessen, Kenneth. 2019. "Mariano Medina—Loveland Area's First Settler." *Loveland Reporter Herald*, January 12. https://www.reporterherald.com/2019/01/12/mariano-medina-loveland-areas-first-settler/.
Jiménez, Tomás R. 2010. *Replenished Ethnicity: Mexican Americans, Immigration, and Identity*. University of California Press.
Jiménez, Tomás R. 2017. *The Other Side of Assimilation: How Immigrants Are Changing American Life*. University of California Press.
Jimenez Sifuentez, Mario. 2016. *Of Forests and Fields: Mexican Labor in the Pacific Northwest*. Rutgers University Press.
Jobin, Bill. 2014. "Lambert Offers Chance to Discuss Race." *Cortez Journal*, October 16.
Johnson, Kirk. 2006. "At Fore on Immigration, Senator Has a Story to Tell." *New York Times*, June 11.
Jones, Jennifer. 2019. *The Browning of the New South*. University of Chicago Press.
Jones, Kristin. 2016. "The Shepherd." *Collective Colorado*, December 8. https://collective.coloradotrust.org/stories/the-shepherd/.

Jordan, Miriam. 2022. "Alone in a New World with Vast Open Space, and Sheep." *New York Times*, September 23.

Junne, George H., Jr., Osita Ofoaku, Rhonda Corman, and Rob Reinsvold. "Dearfield, Colorado: Black Farming Success in the Jim Crow Era." In *Enduring Legacies: Ethnic Histories and Cultures of Colorado*, edited by Arturo Aldama, Elisa Facio, Daryl Maeda, and Reiland Rabaka. University Press of Colorado.

Kandel, William, and Emilio A. Parrado. 2005. "Restructuring of the US Meat Processing Industry and New Hispanic Migrant Destinations." *Population and Development Review* 31 (3): 447–471.

Kazin, Michael. 2022. *What It Took to Win: A History of the Democratic Party*. Farrar, Straus and Giroux.

Keller Montez, Gloria, and Nita Aleman. 1973. "La Raza Unida Party 1973 State Convention." *El Gallo* 5 (3): 6–7. July.

Kennedy, Robert F. 1968. "Robert F. Kennedy Statement on César Chávez; 3/10/1968." Robert F. Kennedy Papers, Senate Papers, Speeches and Press Releases, 1965–1968. John F. Kennedy Library, Boston.

Kim, Joon K. 2012. "California's Agribusiness and the Farm Labor Question: The Transition from Asian to Mexican Labor, 1919–1939." *Aztlán: A Journal of Chicano Studies* 37 (2): 43–72.

Konishi, Bessie, and Lorrie Crawford. 2020. "The Thread of *Gaman*: Japanese American Settlement in the San Luis Valley." In *The Geology, Ecology, and Human History of the San Luis Valley*, edited by Jared M. Beeton, Charles N. Saenz, and Benjamin J. Waddell. University Press of Colorado.

Korecki, Natasha. 2022. "Republicans Struggle in the Southwest as Latino Voters Stick with Democrats." *NBC News*, December 11. https://www.nbcnews.com/politics/2022-election/latino-voters-stuck-democrats-southwest-2022-rcna58260.

Krainz, Thomas A. 2005. *Delivering Aid: Implementing Progressive Era Welfare in the American West*. University of New Mexico Press.

Krogstad, Jens M. 2020. "Most Cuban American Voters Identify as Republican in 2020." Pew Research Center, October 2. https://www.pewresearch.org/short-reads/2020/10/02/most-cuban-american-voters-identify-as-republican-in-2020/.

Kuang, Brian. 2018. "John Tanton, the Nativist Next Door." *Michigan Daily*, September 18.

Kwak-Hefferan, Elisabeth. 2021. "COVID-19 Created the Hottest Real Estate Market Denver Has Ever Seen." *5280*, May 2021. https://www.5280.com/covid-19-created-the-hottest-real-estate-market-denver-has-ever-seen/.

Kyle, Sarah J. 2014. "Tres Colonias Neighborhoods Work Through Growing Pains." *Coloradoan*, August 31. https://www.coloradoan.com/story/news/local/2014/08/31/tres-colonias-neighborhoods-work-growing-pains/14912955/.

"La Chicana: Recognize Her for What She Is." 1975. *El Diario de la Gente* 3, no. 7 (March 6): 7. CSUP-EFFT.

Lahiri, Tripti. 2004. "A Hometown Away from Home: Mexican Migrants in New York Unite to Give Back." *New York Times*, June 30.

Lampe, Philip E. 1981. "'Viva La Raza': A Possible Chicano Dilemma." *Social Science* 56 (3): 158–163.

Landis, David W. 1988. "Early Spanish Settlement in the San Luis Valley." *San Luis Valley Historian* 20 (3): 5–32.

Lang, Robert, and Mark Muro. 2008. "A Profile of Colorado's Front Range." Metropolitan Policy Program at Brookings. https://www.brookings.edu/wp-content/uploads/2016/07/front_range.pdf.

Lawrence, Mike. 2010. "Republican Tipton Unseats Salazar for 3rd Congressional District." *Steamboat Pilot and Today*, November 3.

Lawson, Megan. 2017. "Youth Migration in the West." Bozeman, MT: Headwaters Economics. https://headwaterseconomics.org/economic-development/trends-performance/youth-migration-west/.

LBJ Presidential Library. 2024. "Biography: Lyndon B. Johnson." LBJ Presidential Library. https://www.lbjlibrary.org/life-and-legacy/the-man-himself/biography.

League of United Latin American Citizens. 2024. "LULAC's Milestones." Washington, DC https://lulac.org/about/history/milestones/.

Legg, Kathleen. 2005. "'That Young Girl Should Be in School, Not Out Drilling Wheat!': The Germans from Russia, Race, and Americanization in Northeastern Colorado." http://hdl.handle.net/10217/6574.

Leland, Halie. 2021. "Boulder Is Too Liberal." *Owl*, May 18.

LeMay, Michael C. 2000. *The Perennial Struggle: Race, Ethnicity, and Minority Group Politics in the United States*. Prentice-Hall.

Leonard, Stephen J. 1993. *Trials and Triumphs: A Colorado Portrait of the Great Depression with FSA Photographs*. University Press of Colorado.

Leonard, Stephen J. 2002. *Lynching in Colorado, 1859–1919*. University Press of Colorado.

Leonard, Stephen J., and Thomas J. Noel. 1990. *Denver: Mining Camp to Metropolis*. University Press of Colorado.

Leonard, Stephen J., and Thomas J. Noel. 2016. *A Short History of Denver*. University of Nevada Press.

"A Letter from a Very Unhappy 'White'" Personal correspondence, April 14, 1972. CSUP-EGAR.

Lewis, Shanna. 2023. "Pueblo's Chicano Newspaper, La Cucaracha, Is Again Rolling Off the Presses Regularly after a 40-Year Hiatus." KRCC, *Colorado Public Radio*, June 9. https://www.cpr.org/2023/06/09/pueblo-chicano-newspaper-la-cucaracha-editor-interview/.

Limerick, Patricia Nelson. 1987. *The Legacy of Conquest: The Unbroken Past of the American West*. W. W. Norton.

Loewen, James W. 2005. *Sundown Towns: A Hidden Dimension of American Racism*. New Press.

Lofholm, Nancy. 2013. "Fear from Swift Plant Raid Resonates in Greeley Six Years Later." *Denver Post*, January 14.

Loosbrock, Richard D. 2020. "The Steel Curtain: Railroads and the Making of the San Luis Valley." In *The Geology, Ecology, and Human History of the San Luis Valley*, edited by Jared M. Beeton, Charles N. Saenz, and Benjamin J. Waddell. University Press of Colorado.

López, David E., and Ricardo D. Stanton-Salazar. 2001. "Mexican Americans: A Second Generation at Risk." In *Ethnicities: Children of Immigrants in America*, edited by Rubén G. Rumbaut and Alejandro Portes. University of California Press.

López, Fred A. 1992. "Reflections on the Chicano Movement." *Latin American Perspectives* 19 (4): 79–86.
Lopez, Jody L., and Gabriel A. Lopez (with Peggy A. Ford). 2007. *White Gold Laborers: The Spanish Colony of Greeley, Colorado*. AuthorHouse.
López Pulido, Alberto. 2000. *The Sacred World of the Penitentes*. Smithsonian Institution Press.
López Tijerina, Reies. 2000. Translated by José Angel Gutiérrez. *They Called Me "King Tiger": My Struggle for the Land and Our Rights*. Arte Público Press.
Lopez Tushar, Olibama. 2007. *The People of El Valle: A History of the Spanish Settlers in the San Luis Valley*. El Escritorio.
Lovato, Roberto. 2008. "Juan Crow in Georgia." *Nation*, May 26. https://www.thenation.com/article/archive/juan-crow-georgia/.
Ludwig, Sheryl A., Francisco Lucas, Lucia Nicolas, Flora Archuleta, Antonio Sandoval, and Ren Carbutt. 2012. "Supporting Respect: Community Partnership in Alamosa, Colorado." *Practicing Anthropology* 34 (1): 32–36.
Lukens, Patrick D. 2012. *A Quiet Victory for Latino Rights: FDR and the Controversy over "Whiteness."* University of Arizona Press.
Luning, Ernest. 2020. "Lauren Boebert Rockets to Fame—and Controversy—with Primary Upset in CD3." *Colorado Politics*, July 5. https://www.coloradopolitics.com/2020-election/lauren-boebert-rockets-to-fame-and-controversy-with-primary-upset-in-cd3/article_4487f388-be2b-11ea-a267-43e1ea2acf98.html.
Lutz, Catherine. 1999. "An Ancient Ditch Hits a Glitch." *High Country News*, October 11.
Lydersen, Kari. 2007. "Kiko Martinez: Watch Listed for Life." *In These Times*, January 19. https://inthesetimes.com/article/kiko-martinez-watch-listed-for-life.
Lytle Hernández, Kelly. 2006. "The Crimes and Consequences of Illegal Immigration: A Cross-Border Examination of Operation Wetback, 1943 to 1954." *Western Historical Quarterly* 37:421–444.
Lytle Hernández, Kelly. 2011. "Borderlands and the Future History of the American West." *Western Historical Quarterly* 42 (3): 325–330.
MacAulay, Suzanne P. 2011. "Pictorial Narratives of San Luis, Colorado: Legacy, Place, and Politics." In *Enduring Legacies: Ethnic Histories and Cultures of Colorado*, edited by Arturo Aldama, Elisa Facio, Daryl Maeda, and Reiland Rabaka. University Press of Colorado.
Maestas, Dana. 2015. *Images of America: San Luis*. Arcadia Publishing.
Mariscal, George. 2005. *Brown-Eyed Children of the Sun: Lessons from the Chicano Movement, 1965–1975*. University of New Mexico Press.
Markoff, Dena S. 1979. "A Bittersweet Saga: The Arkansas Valley Beet Sugar Industry, 1900–1979." *Colorado Magazine* 56 (Summer/Fall): 161–178.
Márquez, Benjamin, and Rodolfo Espino. 2010. "Mexican American Support for Third Parties: The Case of La Raza Unida." *Ethnic and Racial Studies* 33 (2): 290–312.
Marquez, David. 1983. "'The Chicano Wars': The Advent of the Chicano Movement in Pueblo, Colorado." Unpublished paper. University of Southern Colorado, CSUP-EDMQ.
Marrin, Albert. 2016. *Uprooted: The Japanese American Experience During World War II*. Alfred A. Knopf.

Martinez, Becky. 1970. "La Raza Party Chooses Candidates to Fill Slate." *Rocky Mountain Collegian* 68 (146): 1. July 1.

Martínez, Elizabeth. 1982. "The 'Kiko' Martinez Case: A Sign of Our Times." *Crime and Social Justice* 17:92–95.

Martinez, Orlando. 1980. "Kiko Martinez, The Last Reminder of an Era." *La Voz Hispana de Colorado* 6, no. 23 (December 1): 5.

Massey, Douglas S., Jorge Durand, and Nolan J. Malone. 2002. *Beyond Smoke and Mirrors: Mexican Immigration in an Era of Economic Integration.* Russell Sage Foundation.

May, William J., Jr. 1989. *The Great Western Sugarlands: The History of the Great Western Sugar Company and the Economic Development of the Great Plains.* Garland Publishing.

McBride, Peter. 1997. "Chaos Comes to Costilla County." *High Country News*, June 9.

McConnell, Eileen D., and Edward A. Delgado-Romero. 2004. "Latino Panethnicity: Reality or Methodological Construction?" *Sociological Focus* 37 (4): 297–312.

McCoy, Jenny. 2021. "What Allowed Greeley to Become One of the Fastest-Growing Metro Areas in the Country?" *5280*, September 7.

McIntosh, Marjorie K. 2016. *Latinos of Boulder County, Colorado, 1900–1980.* Vol. 1, *History and Contributions.* Old John Publishing.

McKelvey, Carole Ann. 2016. "Tuxedo's Owner One of Festival Founders." *Montrose Daily Press*, August 6.

McNeill, Mac. 2017a. "Protesters of the Vietnam War Period." Fort Collins Images, October 1. https://fortcollinsimages.wordpress.com/2017/10/01/protesters-of-the-vietnam-war-period/.

McNeill, Mac. 2017b. "Vietnam Protesters and the Burning of Old Main." Fort Collins Images, October 8. https://fortcollinsimages.wordpress.com/2017/10/08/vietnam-protesters-and-the-burning-of-old-main/.

Meeks, Eric V. 2020. *Border Citizens: The Making of Indians, Mexicans, and Anglos in Arizona.* University of Texas Press.

Meier, Matt S., and Feliciano Ribera. 1993. *Mexican Americans / American Mexicans: From Conquistadors to Chicanos.* Farrar, Straus and Giroux.

Meredith, Jennifer A. 2012. "Colorado Governor Edwin Johnson: Politics and Race." *Historia: The Alpha Rho Papers* 2:29–54.

Merleaux, April. 2015. *Sugar and Civilization: American Empire and the Cultural Politics of Sweetness.* University of North Carolina Press.

"Mexican-American or Chicano." 1969. *Transition* 2 (9): 9. November 20.

Milner, Clyde A., ed. 1996. *A New Significance: Re-Envisioning the History of the American West.* Oxford University Press.

Minor, Nathaniel. 2018. "The Crusade for Center." *Colorado Public Radio*, July 10. https://center.cpr.org/.

Mitchell, Mark D., and Angie Krall. 2020. "Indigenous Lifeways in the San Luis Valley." In *The Geology, Ecology, and Human History of the San Luis Valley*, edited by Jared M. Beeton, Charles N. Saenz, and Benjamin J. Waddell. University Press of Colorado.

Mize, Ronald L., and Alicia C. S. Swords. 2011. *Consuming Mexican Labor: From the Bracero Program to NAFTA.* University of Toronto Press.

Mohammadi, Kristen. 2022. "Pitkin County Real Estate Sees Record Low Inventory and Sky High Prices." *Aspen Times*, December 30.

Molotov. 2003. "Frijolero." YouTube video. https://www.youtube.com/watch?v=8iJMOBcPQyg.

Montejano, David. 1987. *Anglos and Mexicans in the Making of Texas, 1836–1986*. University of Texas Press.

Montgomery, Charles. 2001. "Becoming 'Spanish-American': Race and Rhetoric in New Mexico Politics, 1880–1928." *Journal of American Ethnic History* 20 (4): 59–84.

Montgomery, Charles. 2002. *The Spanish Redemption: Heritage, Power, and Loss on New Mexico's Upper Rio Grande*. University of California Press.

Montoya, Fawn-Amber. 2006. "From Mexicans to Citizens: Colorado Fuel and Iron's Representation of Nuevo Mexicans, 1901–1919." *Journal of the West* 45 (4): 29–35.

Montoya, Maceo. 2016. *Chicano Movement for Beginners*. For Beginners LLC.

Moreno-Brid, Juan C., and Jaime Ros. 2009. *Development and Growth in the Mexican Economy: A Historical Perspective*. New York: Oxford University Press.

Mulkern, Anne C. 2005. "Firebrand Tancredo Puts Policy over Party Line." *Denver Post*, November 26.

Muñoz, Carlos, Jr. 1989. *Youth, Identity, Power: The Chicano Movement*. Verso.

Muñoz Martinez, Monica. 2018. *The Injustice Never Leaves You: Anti-Mexican Violence in Texas*. Harvard University Press.

Murphy, Arthur D., Colleen Blanchard, and Jennifer A. Hill, eds. 2001. *Latino Workers in the Contemporary South*. University of Georgia Press.

Nash, Gerald D. 1985. *The American West Transformed: The Impact of the Second World War*. Indiana University Press.

Navarro, Armando. 2000. *La Raza Unida Party: A Chicano Challenge to The U.S. Two-Party Dictatorship*. Temple University Press.

Nevins, Joseph. 2010. *Operation Gatekeeper and Beyond: The War on "Illegals" and the Remaking of the U.S.-Mexico Boundary*. 2nd ed. London: Routledge.

New-York Historical Society. 2020. "Presidential Ad: 'It's Morning Again in America' Ronald Reagan (R) v Walter Mondale (D)." YouTube video. June 8. https://www.youtube.com/watch?v=pUMqic2IcWA.

Ngai, Mai. 2004. *Impossible Subjects: Illegal Aliens and the Making of Modern America*. Princeton University Press.

Nieto, Adriana. 2011. "Running the Gauntlet: Francisco 'Kiko' Martínez and the Colorado Martyrs." In *Enduring Legacies: Ethnic Histories and Cultures of Colorado*, edited by Arturo Aldama, Elisa Facio, Daryl Maeda, and Reiland Rabaka. University Press of Colorado.

Nieto-Phillips, John M. 2004. *The Language of Blood: The Making of Spanish-American Identity in New Mexico, 1880s–1930s*. University of New Mexico Press.

"No title." 1977. *Papel del Barrio* 1 (9): 1–4. CSUP-UMAS.

Nostrand, Richard L. 1992. *The Hispano Homeland*. University of Oklahoma Press.

Obmascik, Mark. 2021. "The Water Supply of the San Luis Valley Faces Pressure as Never Before." *Colorado Sun*, August 29.

"Occupation at TB-1." 1974. *¡Ahora!* 5 (5): 20–25. CSUP-EFFT.

O'Connor, Colleen. 2008. "Mayans Retain Their Culture." *Denver Post*, February 24.

Odem, Mary E., and Elaine Lacy, eds. 2009. *Latino Immigrants and the Transformation of the U.S. South*. University of Georgia Press.

Ogburn, Stephanie P. 2011. "Cattlemen Struggle Against Giant Meatpackers and Economic Squeezes." *High Country News*, March 21.

Olden, Danielle R. 2017. "Becoming Minority: Mexican Americans, Race, and the Legal Struggle for Educational Equity in Denver, Colorado." *Western Historical Quarterly* 48 (1): 43–66.

Omi, Michael, and Howard Winant. 2015. *Racial Formation in the United States*. 3rd ed. Routledge.

Orme, William A., Jr. 1996. *Understanding NAFTA: Mexico, Free Trade, and the New North America*. University of Texas Press.

Osgood, Carrie, and John Frank. 2020. "Colorado Continues to Shift Blue: The 2020 Election, Explained in Graphics." *Colorado Sun*, November 10. https://coloradosun.com/2020/11/10/colorado-2020-election-explained/.

Padilla, Fernando V., and Carlos B. Ramírez. 1974. "Patterns of Chicano Representation in California, Colorado and Nuevo México." *Aztlán: A Journal of Chicano Studies* 5 (1–2): 189–234.

Park, Lisa Sun-Hee, and David N. Pellow. 2011. *The Slums of Aspen: Immigrants vs. the Environment in America's Eden*. New York University Press.

Paul, Jesse. 2021. "A Deep Dive into the Electorate in Colorado's Super Competitive New 8th Congressional District." *Colorado Sun*, November 22.

Paul, Jesse. 2024. "Gabe Evans Unseats Yadira Caraveo in Colorado's 8th Congressional District." *Colorado Sun*, November 10.

Peña, Devon G. 1998a. "A Gold Mine, an Orchard, and an Eleventh Commandment." In *Chicano Culture, Ecology, Politics: Subversive Kin*, edited by Devon G. Peña. University of Arizona Press.

Peña, Devon G. 1998b. "Los Animalitos: Culture, Ecology, and the Politics of Place in the Upper Rio Grande." In *Chicano Culture, Ecology, Politics: Subversive Kin*, edited by Devon G. Peña. University of Arizona Press.

Peña, Devon G. 2005. *Mexican Americans and the Environment: Tierra y Vida*. University of Arizona Press.

Peña, Devon G., and Rubén O. Martínez. 1998. "The Capitalist Tool, the Lawless, and the Violent: A Critique of Recent Southwestern Environmental History." In *Chicano Culture, Ecology, Politics: Subversive Kin*, edited by Devon G. Peña. University of Arizona Press.

Peña, Federico. 2021. *"Not Bad for a South Texas Boy": A Story of Perseverance*. Lighting Source.

Pew Hispanic Center. 2011. "Demographic Profile of Hispanics in Colorado, 2011." Copy in author's possession.

Pew Research Center. 2016. "Latinos in the 2016 Election: Colorado." Pew Research Center, https://www.pewresearch.org/hispanic/fact-sheet/latinos-in-the-2016-election-colorado/.

Pierce, Jason E. 2016. *Making the White Man's West: Whiteness and the Creation of the American West*. University Press of Colorado.

Piore, Michael J. 1979. *Birds of Passage: Migrant Labor and Industrial Societies.* Cambridge University Press.
Pitt, Leonard. 1998. *The Decline of the Californios: A Social History of the Spanish-Speaking Californians, 1846–1890.* University of California Press.
Pohl, Kelly. 2017a. "The Growth of Hispanic Populations Across the West." Headwaters Economics. https://headwaterseconomics.org/economic-development/trends-performance/hispanic-populations/.
Pohl, Kelly. 2017b. "Minority Populations Driving County Growth in the Rural West." Headwaters Economics. https://headwaterseconomics.org/economic-development/trends-performance/minority-populations-driving-county-growth/.
Portes, Alejandro. 2003. "Conclusion: Theoretical Convergencies and Empirical Evidence in the Study of Immigrant Transnationalism." *International Migration Review* 37 (3): 874–892.
Portes, Alejandro, and Rubén G. Rumbaut. 2001. *Legacies: The Story of the Immigrant Second Generation.* University of California Press.
Power, Thomas M., and Richard N. Barrett. 2001. *Post-Cowboy Economics: Pay and Prosperity in The New American West.* Island Press.
"Press Release: History Colorado Opens El Movimiento: The Chicano Movement in Colorado." 2015. History Colorado, February 2. https://www.historycolorado.org/press-release/2015/02/02/history-colorado-opens-el-movimiento-chicano-movement-colorado.
"Professor Predicts 'Hispanic Homeland.'" 2000. *Kingman Daily Miner*, January 21.
"The Public Domain." 1975. *¡Ahora!* Winter, 4–7. CSUP-EFFT.
Publications Committee, San Luis Valley Historical Society. 1969a. "Time-Event Chart of the San Luis Valley." *San Luis Valley Historian* 1 (2): 1–30.
Publications Committee, San Luis Valley Historical Society. 1969b. "Time-Event Chart of the San Luis Valley." *San Luis Valley Historian* 1 (3): 1–30.
Pueblo Board of Trade. 1883. *Sketch of the Pueblos and Pueblo County, Colorado.* Chieftain Steam Print.
Quinton, Sophie. 2019. "As Farmers Retire, Their Families Face Difficult Choices." *Stateline*, Pew Charitable Trusts, March 27. https://www.pewtrusts.org/en/research-and-analysis/blogs/stateline/2019/03/27/as-farmers-retire-their-families-face-difficult-choices.
Ramos, Manuel. 1969. "Editorial." *Transition* 2, no. 2 (October 1): 5.
Rayes, Adam. 2021. "'We Were Here First': Native American, Mexican Residents Reflect on Life in Loveland: A Former Sundown Town." *KUNC*. https://www.kunc.org/culture-identity/2021-09-30/we-were-here-first-native-american-mexican-residents-reflect-on-life-in-loveland-a-former-sundown-town.
Rees, Jonathan H. 2010. *Representation and Rebellion: The Rockefeller Plan at the Colorado Fuel and Iron Company, 1914–1942.* University Press of Colorado.
Reisler, Mark. 1976. *By the Sweat of Their Brow: Mexican Immigrant Labor in the United States, 1900–1940.* Greenwood Press.
Rensink, Brenden W., ed. 2022. *The North American West in the Twenty-First Century.* University of Nebraska Press.

Reséndez, Andrés. 2016. *The Other Slavery: The Uncovered Story of Indian Enslavement in America*. Houghton Mifflin Harcourt.

"Ricardo Falcon Presented by Priscilla Falcon." 2022. NEWSED CDC. YouTube video. https://www.youtube.com/@newsedcdc1164/videos.

Rice, Jeff. 2021. "Census Bureau Report Shows Continued Declines in Rural Colorado Populations." *Sterling Journal-Advocate*, August 13.

Richardson, Chad. 1999. *Batos, Bolillos, Pochos, and Pelados: Class and Culture on the South Texas Border*. University of Texas Press.

Richtel, Matt. 2023. "The Refries That Bind: A Cavernous Cantina Returns, Cliff Divers and All." *New York Times*, June 6.

Rivas-Rodriguez, Maggie, ed. 2005. *Mexican Americans and World War II*. University of Texas Press.

Rivera, José A. 2010. *La Sociedad: Guardians of Hispanic Culture Along the Río Grande*. University of New Mexico Press.

Rivera, José A. 2016. "The Roots of Community in the Historic Rio Arriba: Mutualism, Cultural Endurance and Resilience." Albuquerque: Center for Regional Studies, University of New Mexico.

Rivera, Juan M., Scott Whiteford, and Manuel Chávez, eds. 2009. *NAFTA and the Campesinos: The Impact of NAFTA on Small-Scale Agricultural Producers in Mexico and the Prospects for Change*. University of Scranton Press.

Rivera, Stephanie, and Kevin Beaty. 2022. "Migrants in Denver Faced Horror on Their Journeys to the U.S., but Despite Their Desperate Risks, Many Will Be Forced to Leave." *Denverite*, December 27. https://denverite.com/2022/12/27/migrants-in-denver-faced-horror-on-their-journeys-to-the-u-s-despite-their-desperate-risks-many-will-be-forced-to-leave/.

Roberts, Michael. 2011. "Immigration: 89% of Workers at Wildcat Dairy Not Authorized to Work in United States." *Westword*, June 1.

Robles, Yesenia. 2022. "Driving a Decade of Progress, Hispanic Students Made Huge Gains in High School Graduation." *Colorado Sun*, June 4. https://coloradosun.com/2022/06/04/hispanic-high-school-graduation-colorado/.

Rocky Mountain PBS. 2006. *La Raza de Colorado: El Movimiento*. Rocky Mountain Public Media. https://www.pbs.org/video/rmpbs-specials-la-raza-de-colorado-el-movimiento/.

Rodó, José E. 1988. *Ariel*. Translated by Margaret Sayers Peden. University of Texas Press.

Rodríguez, Clara E. 2000. *Changing Race: Latinos, the Census, and the History of Ethnicity in the United States*. New York University Press.

Rodriguez, Marc S. 2015. *Rethinking the Chicano Movement*. Routledge.

Rodríguez, Sylvia. 1987. "Land, Water, and Ethnic Identity in Taos." In *Land, Water, and Culture: New Perspectives on Hispanic Land Grants*, edited by Charles L. Briggs and John R. Van Ness. University of New Mexico Press.

Rodríguez, Sylvia. 1992. "The Hispano Homeland Debate Revisited." *Perspectives in Mexican American Studies* 3:95–114.

Román, Ediberto. 2013. *Those Damned Immigrants: America's Hysteria over Undocumented Immigration*. New York University Press.

Romero, Dennis. 2019. "The Worst Slur for Mexican-Americans Is Still a Mystery for Some." *NBC News*, February 1. https://www.nbcnews.com/news/latino/worst-slur-mexican-americans-still-mystery-some-n959616.

Romero, Levi. 2020. "Following the Manito Trail: A Tale of Two Querencias." In *Querencia: Reflections on the New Mexico Homeland*, edited by Vanessa Fonseca-Chávez, Levi Romero, and Spencer R. Herrera. University of New Mexico Press.

Romero, Tom I. 2004a. "Of Race and Rights: Legal Culture, Social Change, and the Making of a Multiracial Metropolis, Denver, 1940–1975." PhD diss., University of Michigan.

Romero, Tom I. 2004b. "Wearing the Red, White, and Blue Trunks of Aztlán: Rodolfo 'Corky' Gonzales and the Convergence of American and Chicano Nationalism." *Aztlán: A Journal of Chicano Studies* 29 (1): 83–117.

Rosales, F. Arturo. 1997. *Chicano! The History of the Mexican American Civil Rights Movement*. 2nd ed. Arte Público Press.

Rouse, Roger. 1992. "Making Sense of Settlement: Class Transformation, Cultural Struggle, and Transnationalism Among Mexican Migrants in the United States." *Annals of the New York Academy of Sciences* 645 (1): 25–52.

Rumbaut, Rubén G., and Alejandro Portes, eds. 2001. *Ethnicities: Children of Immigrants in America*. University of California Press.

Sabin, Dena M. 1986. *How Sweet It Was! The Beet Sugar Industry in Microcosm: The National Sugar Manufacturing Company, 1899 to 1967*. Garland Publishing.

Saenz, Charles N. 2020. "Colorado's Hispanic Frontier: Spanish Exploration and the Early Settlement of the Conejos and Sangre de Cristo Land Grants." In *The Geology, Ecology, and Human History of the San Luis Valley*, edited by Jared M. Beeton, Charles N. Saenz, and Benjamin J. Waddell. University Press of Colorado.

Sahagun, Louis. 1993. "Column One: This Land 'Belonged to All of Us': A Timber Baron Shut Out Descendants of Colorado's Mexican Settlers from the Mountains They Loved. Now, the State Is Trying to Turn the Area into a Park and Preserve an Endangered Heritage." *Los Angeles Times*, November 17.

Sálaz Márquez, Rubén. 2004. *Epic of the Greater Southwest: New Mexico, Texas, California, Arizona, Oklahoma, Colorado, Utah, Nevada*. Cosmic House.

Salazar, Secundino. 2004. 2017.45.0001A-C. Permanent Collection, City of Greeley Museums.

San Luis Valley Community Action Agency. 2020. "San Luis Valley Community Needs Assessment, 2021–2023." https://www.slvdrg.org/wp-content/uploads/2020/11/SLVCAA-Needs-Assessment-2020-08.12.20-PDF.pdf.

Sánchez, George J. 1993. *Becoming Mexican American: Ethnicity, Culture, and Identity in Chicano Los Angeles, 1900–1945*. Oxford University Press.

Sanchez, Hayley. 2019. "1969 Denver School Walkout Helped Launch Chicano Movement." Colorado Public Radio, March 24. https://www.coloradopolitics.com/news/1969-denver-school-walkout-helped-launch-chicano-movement/article_6440a4da-4ce5-11e9-bb09-2f7cc5da9b0d.html.

Sánchez, Virginia. 2010. *Forgotten Cuchareños of the Lower Valley*. History Press.

Sánchez, Virginia. 2020. *Pleas and Petitions: Hispano Culture and Legislative Conflict in Territorial Colorado*. University Press of Colorado.

Sandoval, David A. 2011. "Recruitment, Rejection, and Reaction: Colorado Chicanos in the Twentieth Century." In *Enduring Legacies: Ethnic Histories and Cultures of Colorado*, edited by Arturo Aldama, Elisa Facio, Daryl Maeda, and Reiland Rabaka. University Press of Colorado.

Sandoval, Robert. 1979. "The People Who Paved the Way." *Empire Magazine (The Denver Post)*, November 25, 26–31.

Sangre de Cristo National Heritage Area. 2019a. "Early Hispano Settlement." Sangre de Cristo National Heritage Area. https://www.sangreheritage.org/early-hispano-settlement/.

Sangre de Cristo National Heritage Area. 2019b. "Los Caminos Antiguos Scenic and Historic Byway." Sangre de Cristo National Heritage Area. https://www.sangreheritage.org/los-caminos/.

Sarathy, Brinda. 2012. *Pineros: Latino Labour and the Changing Face of Forestry in the Pacific Northwest*. UBC Press.

Sassen, Saskia. 1988. *The Mobility of Labor and Capital: A Study in International Investment and Labor Flow*. Cambridge University Press.

Scamehorn, Howard L. 1992. *Mill and Mine: The CF&I in the Twentieth Century*. University of Nebraska Press.

Schlosser, Eric. 2001. *Fast Food Nation: The Dark Side of the All-American Meal*. Houghton Mifflin.

Schulten, Susan. 2013. "The Civil War and the Origins of the Colorado Territory." *Western Historical Quarterly* 44:21–46.

Scott, James C. 1985. *Weapons of the Weak: Everyday Forms of Peasant Resistance*. Yale University Press.

Sheely, Rob. 2003. *The People's Republic: Stories of Boulder, Colorado*. Boulder Weekly Press.

Sheflin, Douglas. 2019. *Legacies of Dust: Land Use and Labor on the Colorado Plains*. University of Nebraska Press.

Shumway, J. Matthew. 2015. "The Spatial Distribution of Hispanics in the Mountain West: 1970–2010." In *Immigrants in the Far West: Historical Identities and Experiences*, edited by Jessie L. Embry and Brian Q. Cannon. University of Utah Press.

Sigman, Mike. 2010a. "Anti-Americanism Colors Border Debate." *Durango Herald*, May 24.

Sigman, Mike. 2010b. "Series Ignored Effects on U.S. Citizens." *Durango Herald*, September 3.

Sigman, Mike. 2012. "Dems, Media Hide Illegal Immigrants' Crimes." *Durango Herald*, July 26.

Silverman, Craig. 2021. "Former Mayor Federico Peña Still Makes Denver Proud." *Colorado Sun*, November 22. https://coloradosun.com/2021/11/22/federico-pena-denver-politics-opinion/.

Simmons, Virginia McConnell. 1999. *The San Luis Valley: Land of the Six-Armed Cross*. 2nd ed. University Press of Colorado.

Simpson, Kevin. 2017. "Rural Colorado's White Population Is Declining, and Minorities Are Transforming the Region's Culture and Economy." *Denver Post*, November 9.

Sinclair, Upton. 1906. *The Jungle*. Doubleday.

Slack, Jeremy, Daniel E. Martínez, and Scott Whiteford, eds. 2018. *The Shadow of the Wall: Violence and Migration on the U.S.-Mexico Border*. University of Arizona Press.

Smith, Duane A. 1992. *Rocky Mountain Boom Town: A History of Durango, Colorado*. University Press of Colorado.

Smith, Robert C. 2006. *Mexican New York: Transnational Lives of New Immigrants*. University of California Press.

Smith, Heather A., and Owen J. Furuseth, eds. 2006. *Latinos in the New South: Transformations of Place*. Routledge.

Solano, Carmel C. 2013. *The End of the Row*. Xlibris Corporation.

Sorensen, Greg. 1969. "Chicanoes, Panthers Hit 'Racist' Denver Schools." *Colorado Daily-University of Colorado Boulder* 17, no. 105 (March 21): 1.

Sowards, Stacey K. 2019. *¡Sí, Ella Puede! The Rhetorical Legacy of Dolores Huerta and the United Farm Workers*. University of Texas Press.

Spaulding, Trey. 2020. "SLV Counties Among the Most Impoverished in the State." *Conejos County Citizen*, September 9.

State Demography Office. 2016. "Aging in Colorado Part 1: Why Is Colorado Aging So Quickly?" Denver: Department of Local Affairs, State of Colorado. https://gis.dola.colorado.gov/crosstabs/aging-part-1/.

State Demography Office. 2020. "Hispanic Percent of Population by County." Department of Local Affairs, State of Colorado. Chart. https://storage.googleapis.com/maps-static/Hispanic_County.pdf.

State of Colorado. 1876. *La Constitución del Estado de Colorado, adoptada en convención general, marzo 14, de 1876; junto con la dedicatoria de la convención al pueblo de Colorado*. Imprenta del Tribune.

State of Colorado. 2022. "Constitution of the State of Colorado." https://www.sos.state.co.us/pubs/info_center/laws/COConstitution/ColoradoConstitution.pdf.

Stebbins, Samuel. 2019. "What Counties in Each State Have the Most Expensive Housing Market? Check this List." *USA Today*, April 5.

Stewart, Samantha. 2009. "DU's 'Woodstock of the West.'" *University of Denver Magazine*, June 1. https://magazine-archive.du.edu/campus-community/dus-woodstock-of-the-west/.

Straayer, John A. 2011. "One Thing After Another: Layers of Policy and Colorado's Fiscal Train Wreck." In *State of Change: Colorado Politics in the Twenty-First Century*, edited by Courtenay W. Daum, Robert J. Duffy, and John A. Straayer. University Press of Colorado.

Stuesse, Angela. 2016. *Scratching Out a Living: Latinos, Race, and Work in the Deep South*. University of California Press.

Suarez, Ray. 2013. "How the Civil Rights Movement Launched the Fight for LGBT, Women's Equality." *PBS News Hour*, September 2. https://www.pbs.org/newshour/show/civil-rights-launched-the-fight-for-lgbt-women-s-equality.

Sullivan, Sharon. 2020. "Devastated by Weather and the Pandemic, Western Slope Farmworkers Try to Hold On." *Collective Colorado*, May 26. https://collective.coloradotrust.org/stories/devastated-by-weather-and-the-pandemic-western-slope-farmworkers-try-to-hold-on/.

"Summer in March." 1969. *Denver Blade* 9, no. 24 (March 25): 1–2.

Svaldi, Aldo. 2018. "Front Range a GDP force." *Denver Post*, December 20.

Svitek, Patrick, and Matthew Choi. 2022. "No Red Wave, but Republicans Continue Inroads into Long-Democratic South Texas." *Texas Tribune*, Nov. 10.

Tancredo, Tom. 2006. *In Mortal Danger: The Battle for America's Border and Security*. WND Books.

Taylor, Paul S. 1930. *Mexican Labor in the United States*. Vol. 1. University of California Press.

Taylor, William B., and Elliott West. 1973. "Patrón Leadership at the Crossroads: Southern Colorado in the Late Nineteenth Century." *Pacific Historical Review* 42 (3): 335–357.

Teixeira, Ruy, and Karlyn Bowman. 2010. "The Intermountain West Today: A Regional Survey." Brookings Mountain West. https://digitalscholarship.unlv.edu/cgi/viewcontent.cgi?article=1008&context=brookings_pubs.

Telles, Edward E. 2014. *Pigmentocracies: Ethnicity, Race, and Color in Latin America*. University of North Carolina Press.

"These Our Their Leaders: Who Do You Believe Ours or Theirs??" 1976. *El Gallo* 8, no. 3 (June 1): 5.

Thomas, Adam. 2003. "Hang Your Wagon to a Star: Hispanics in Fort Collins, 1900–2000." SWCA Environmental Consultants. https://www.fcgov.com/historicpreservation/pdf/hispanics-doc.pdf.

Tracey, Caroline E. 2020. "Gentrification and Denver's Hispanic Past." In *The Rocky Mountain West: A Compendium of Geographic Perspectives*, edited by Michael J. Keables. American Association of Geographers.

Travis, William R. 2007. *New Geographies of the American West: Land Use and the Changing Patterns of Place*. Island Press.

Treviño, Jesús S. 2017. "Boricuas and Chicanos—A Common Bond." Latinopia, June 4. http://latinopia.com/blogs/boricuas-and-chicanos-a-common-bond/.

Truxillo, Charles. 2000. "Dr. Charles Truxillo on Nationalism in the 21st Century." Lecture at University of New Mexico School of Law, February 28. https://nmdigital.unm.edu/digital/collection/videos/id/225/.

Turner, Frederick J. 1894. "The Significance of the Frontier in American History." In *Annual Report of the American Historical Association for the Year 1893*. Government Printing Office.

Twitty, Eric. 2003. "Silver Wedge: The Sugar Beet Industry in Fort Collins." http://www.fcgov.com/historicpreservation/pdf/sugar-beet-industry-doc.pdf.

UCLA Latino Policy & Politics Institute. 2023. "15 Facts About Latino Well-Being in Colorado." Data brief. https://latino.ucla.edu/research/15-facts-latinos-colorado/.

United States Congress. n.d. "SALAZAR, Kenneth Lee." *Biographical Directory of the United States Congress*. https://bioguide.congress.gov/search/bio/s001163.

Upson, J. E. 1939. "Physiographic Subdivisions of the San Luis Valley, Southern Colorado." *Journal of Geology* 47 (7): 721–736.

US Census Bureau. 1990–2020. "Decennial Census of Population and Housing." US Department of Commerce. https://www.census.gov/programs-surveys/decennial-census.html.

US Census Bureau. 2022. "Quick Facts: Colorado." https://www.census.gov/quickfacts/CO.

Valdés, Dennis N. 1990. "Settlers, Sojourners, and Proletarians: Social Formation in the Great Plains Sugar Beet Industry, 1890–1940." *Great Plains Quarterly* 10:110–123.

Valdez, Arnold, and María Mondragón-Valdez. 2000. "Costilla County, Colorado: Contested Landscapes." *ReVista: Harvard Review of Latin America* 3 (1): 25–27.

Valdez, Donald. 2021. "Valdez: Instead of Vilifying Immigrants, Boebert Should Focus on Meaningful Reform." *Denver Post*, May 20.

Valdez, Maria. 2001. "La Sociedad Protección Mutua de Trabajadores Unidos." *The San Luis Valley Historian* 33 (2): 5–25.

Vallejo, M. Edmund. 1998. "Recollections of the Colorado Coal Strike, 1913–1914." In *La Gente: Hispano History and Life in Colorado*, edited by Vincent C. de Baca. Colorado Historical Society.

"Valley Low in County Health Rankings." 2018. *Valley Courier*, March 16.

Van Nuys, Frank. 2002. *Americanizing the West: Race, Immigrants, and Citizenship, 1890–1930*. University Press of Kansas.

Vargas, Zaragoza. 2005. *Labor Rights Are Civil Rights: Mexican American Workers in Twentieth-Century America*. Princeton University Press.

Vargas, Zaragoza. 2017. *Crucible of Struggle: A History of Mexican Americans from Colonial Times to the Present Era*. 2nd ed. Oxford University Press.

Varsanyi, Monica W. 2020. "Hispanic Racialization, Citizenship, and the Colorado Border Blockade of 1936." *Journal of American Ethnic History* 40 (1): 5–39.

Vasconcelos, José. [1925] 1997. *The Cosmic Race: A Bilingual Edition*. Translated by Didier T. Jaén. Johns Hopkins University Press.

Vasquez, Tina. 2021. "Update: Colorado Gov. Jared Polis Signs Bill Enacting Some of the Strongest Farmworker Protections in the Nation." *Counter*, June 16. https://thecounter.org/colorado-farmworker-bill-of-rights-goveror-polis/.

Vergara Wilson, Damián, and Devin Jenkins. 2020. "Estas palabras están conmigo: The Spanish Language of the San Luis Valley." In *The Geology, Ecology, and Human History of the San Luis Valley*, edited by Jared M. Beeton, Charles N. Saenz, and Benjamin J. Waddell. University Press of Colorado.

Vigil, Ernesto B. 1998. "Rodolfo Gonzales and the Advent of the Crusade for Justice." In *La Gente: Hispano History and Life in Colorado*, edited by Vincent C. de Baca. Colorado Historical Society.

Vigil, Ernesto B. 1999. *The Crusade for Justice: Chicano Militancy and the Government's War on Dissent*. University of Wisconsin Press.

Vigil, James D. 2012. *From Indians to Chicanos: The Dynamics of Mexican-American Culture*. 3rd ed. Waveland Press.

Vigil, Jess. 1974. "Agreement Reached at TB-1." *El Diario de la Gente* 3, no. 1 (June 11): 1, 6–7. June 11. CSUP-EFFT.

Vigil, Maurilio E. 1987. *Hispanics in American Politics: The Search for Political Power*. University Press of America.

Vigil, Rick. 2006. "Spirituality and Its People: El Valle De San Luis." OpenMind Media. https://www.cultureunplugged.com/documentary/watch-online/play/8153/-spirituality-and-its-people-el-valle-de-san-luis.

Waddell, Benjamin J., and Victoria Martinez. 2020. "The Political Economy of Discriminatory Lending in the San Luis Valley." In *The Geology, Ecology, and Human History of the San Luis Valley*, edited by Jared M. Beeton, Charles N. Saenz, and Benjamin J. Waddell. University Press of Colorado.

Wei, William. 2016. *Asians in Colorado: A History of Persecution and Perseverance in the Centennial State*. University of Washington Press.

West, Elliott. 1998. *The Contested Plains: Indians, Goldseekers, and the Rush to Colorado*. University Press of Kansas.

Western Sugar Cooperative. 2022. "History." https://www.westernsugar.com/who-we-are/history/.

White, Richard. 1991. *"It's Your Misfortune and None of My Own": A History of the American West*. University of Oklahoma Press.

Widener, Jeffrey M. 2022. "Agritourism as Land-Saving Action in the New West." In *The North American West in the Twenty-First Century*, edited by Brenden W. Rensink. University of Nebraska Press.

Widjaya, Regina, and Sono Shah. 2024. "About 1 in 10 Restaurants in the U.S. Serve Mexican Food." Pew Research Center, January 11. https://www.pewresearch.org/short-reads/2024/01/11/about-1-in-10-restaurants-in-the-us-serve-mexican-food/.

Wilmot, Frank. 2006. "A Look at Race and Ethnicity in Colorado (1860–2005): Census Definitions and Data." *Colorado Libraries* 32 (4): 10–18.

Wilson, Sara. 2024. "Bill to Create Chicano License Plates Clears Colorado Legislature." *Colorado Newsline*, April 30. https://coloradonewsline.com/briefs/bill-to-create-chicano-license-plate-clears-colorado-legislature/.

Wingerter, Meg. 2024. "Colorado Is One of Just Three States Where Latinos Don't Outlive White Residents. Why?" *Denver Post*, August 25.

Wittevrongel, Shelley, and Jennie Sanchez. 2017. *Center, Colorado: Su Voto Cuenta!* Old John Publishing.

Woodcock, Claire, and Phelan Bowie. 2019. "Remembering Los Seis: Criticism and Analysis of a 1974 News Cycle." December 23. https://storymaps.arcgis.com/stories/9b50970b344f435eb0747774b0ece7ef.

Woods, Lucas B. 2022. "Colorado Latinos Overwhelmingly Voted for Democrats Despite Republican Hopes to Win Them Over." *KUNC*, November 11. https://www.kunc.org/2022-11-11/colorado-latinos-overwhelmingly-voted-for-democrats-despite-republican-hopes-to-win-them-over.

Wyckoff, William. 1999. *Creating Colorado: The Making of a Western American Landscape, 1860–1940*. Yale University Press.

Wyckoff, William. 2014. *How to Read the American West: A Field Guide*. University of Washington Press.

Young, David Byron (Atekpatzin). 2011. "Chicanismo, Indigenous Identity and Lateral Violence: A Qualitative Study of Indigenous Identified Individuals in Colorado." MA thesis, Department of Ethnic Studies, Colorado State University.

Young, David Byron (Atekpatzin). 2013. "Oral History Interview with David B. Young, 2013." Boulder Public Library, Carnegie Library for Local History, OH1898-V. https://

localhistory.boulderlibrary.org/islandora/object/islandora%3A40594?solr_nav%5Bid%5D=1588bff8d9b7332215ff&solr_nav%5Bpage%5D=0&solr_nav%5Boffset%5D=1&solr_nav%5Bquery%5D=OH1898-V.

Young, David Byron (Atekpatzin). 2015. "Forty-One Years Ago, Bombings Shook Boulder." KGNU Community Radio, May 29. https://kgnu.org/forty-one-years-ago-bombings-shook-boulder/.

Zinn, Howard. 2010. *A People's History of the United States: 1492–Present*. HarperCollins Publishers.

Zorrilla-Velazquez, Daniel, Berenice Alfaro Ponce, and Joaquín García-Hernández. 2021. "Political Transnationalism in Mexico: The Importance of Mexican Communities in the United States and the External Vote." *International Journal of Interdisciplinary Civic and Political Studies* 16 (1): 1–15.

INDEX

Page numbers followed by f indicate figures, and page numbers followed by n indicate notes.

acequias, 37, 53
Acosta, Paul (UMAS-EOP Assistant Director), 144
Adams County (Colorado), 18, 20, 192, 215n11
Adams State College (Adams State University), 54–55; racial conflicts in, 54–55
Africa, 8, 220n5
African Americans, 10, 13, 47–48, 75, 83, 112, 116, 118, 136, 191, 196, 214n6, 218n7
agropastoralists, 52
Aguascalientes (Mexico), 161
Aguilar (Colorado), 44
Alamosa (city and county in Colorado), 21, 38, 44–45, 54, 56, 58, 62–65, 117, 141, 222n14
Alamosa School Board of Education, 44
Alcantar, Antonio, 144

alien citizens, 36
Alta Vista neighborhood (Fort Collins, Colorado), 75
"Alurista." *See* Urista, Alberto
American Beet Sugar Company, 71
American Dream, the, 98, 106, 108, 119, 124–125, 143, 186–187
American GI Forum, 115, 140
American Heartland, 14
American Indian Movement (AIM), 136
American West. *See* West, the
Americas, the, 8, 34
Amerindians, 7. *See also* Indigenous persons
Andersonville neighborhood (Fort Collins, Colorado), 75
Anglo America. *See* Anglo(s)
Anglo Coloradans, 23–26, 41, 73, 190, 199, 205, 214n9. *See also* Anglo(s)

Anglo Texans, 216*n4*
Anglo(s), 13, 32, 36, 50, 66, 112, 114, 116, 130, 132–133, 148, 178, 185–186, 191–192, 195–196, 203, 212, 214*n6*, 218*n3*, 222*n19*; cattle ranchers, 41, 172, 185; control of schools, 124–126, 217*n13*, 217*n18*, 217*n25*, 221*n5*, 221*n10*, 222*n21*; definition of, 215*n3*; establishment, 128–131, 133, 138, 141, 146–151, 156, 160, 188, 191, 201, 203, 205, 208, 211–212; farmers, 81, 84–85, 88, 90, 95, 104, 185; interethnic marriages, 58–59, 61, 184; pioneers, 156–157, 189, 199, 203–204, 218*n7*, 224*n6*; racial prejudices, 42–46, 49, 53–54, 56, 59–61, 64–66, 75, 78–89, 91, 93–94, 98–99, 101, 104, 106–107, 109–112, 114–116, 119–120, 122–125, 129–130, 138–140, 142, 145, 147–153, 153*f*, 158–160, 170–172, 177–181, 183–188, 190, 192–199, 201–203, 206, 216*n4*, 218*n4*, 218*n7*, 219*n9*, 219*n13*, 221*n5*, 222*n21*, 223*n24*, 223*n29*, 223*n30*, 224*n1*, 224*n3*, 225*n7*, 225*n10*, 225*n11*, 226*n35*
Anglo-Saxon race, 66, 214*n4*, 215*n3*
Animas River, 157
Anthony, Susan B., 216*n10*
Antonito (Colorado), 39, 44, 58
Arapaho(s), 218*n3*
Arapahoe County (Colorado), 18, 20
Arau, Sergio, 225*n18*
Archibeque family, 157
Archuleta County (Colorado), 176
Arizona (US state), 29, 36, 48, 62, 74, 161, 192, 204, 219*n12*
Arkansas River, 14, 90, 219*n11*
Arkansas River Valley, 21, 71, 89, 99
Asia, 8
Asian Americans, 48, 97, 112, 191, 214*n6*
Asians, 13, 75, 202, 218*n7*
Aspen (Colorado), 21, 22, 28, 161, 166–169, 174, 176, 178, 225*n20*
Auraria neighborhood (Denver, Colorado), 192
Auraria Higher Education Center (Denver, Colorado), 221*n9*
Aurora (Colorado), 18, 19, 29, 113, 154, 191
Aztec(s), 111, 218*n8*, 221*n5*
Aztlán, 111, 149–150, 221*n5*

Baby Boomers, 13, 23–24, 116, 102, 138, 143, 148, 154–155, 162, 196, 215*n13*
Baca, Pauline "Polly" (Colorado State Representative and Senator), 192–194
Baker Junior High (Denver, Colorado), 125
Ballesteros, Marisela (Gunnison City Councilmember), 171
Barela, Casimiro (Colorado State Senator), 216*n4*
Basalt (Colorado), 22
Battle Mountain Gold, 52
Battlement Mesa (Colorado), 22
beaner, 224*n1*
Beaubien, Charles (father), 51
Beaubien, Narciso (son), 51
Bent, Charles, 34
Bent County (Colorado), 103
Bent's Fort, 216*n7*
Bernal family, 158
betabeleros, 76, 85, 158, 225*n9*
Black Beret Creed, 93
Black Berets, 93
Black Lives Matter movement, 223*n29*
Black Panthers, 222*n22*
Black persons, 8, 54, 118, 124, 215*n3*, 223*n29*. *See also* African Americans
Bloomfield (New Mexico), 157
Boebert, Lauren (US Representative), 179, 197
Bolivia, 171–172, 202
borderlands, 12, 27, 67, 70, 105, 111, 163, 188, 202–204, 214*n9*, 215*n10*, 220*n3*
Boulder (city and county in Colorado), 20, 78, 86, 92, 113, 120, 222*n17*
Bracero Program, 10, 50, 70, 88–89, 159, 164
braceros, 88, 90, 98, 105, 159, 188. *See also* Bracero Program
Brazil, 96, 227*n43*
Breckenridge (Colorado), 167
Brighton (Colorado), 44, 72, 123, 215*n11*
Briseño, Guadalupe, 122–123
Brown Berets, 93–94
Brown v. Board of Education, 221*n10*
Brunson, Perry, 139–141
Brush (Colorado), 71

Buck, Kenneth "Ken" (US Representative), 227*n3*
Buckingham neighborhood (Fort Collins, Colorado), 75
Bureau of Land Management, 40, 51

California (US state), 24, 35, 36, 48, 55, 111, 121–122, 127, 131, 149, 178, 181, 189, 192, 203–205, 211, 220*n3*, 225*n18*
Californians, 13
Californios, 9, 35
Canada, 98, 154, 163
Caraveo, Dr. Yadira (US Representative), 102, 198
Carbondale (Colorado), 22, 176, 225*n20*
Cargill company, 96, 98
Casa Bonita, 205, 227*n4*
Castro, Richard, 138
Catholic Church, Roman, 42–43, 75, 79, 181; Catholic faith, 38–39, 43, 116, 181–182
Centennial High School (Pueblo, Colorado), 94
Centennial State, 22, 29, 68, 147, 190, 214*n3*, 218*n7*. *See also* Colorado
Center (Colorado), 54
Center Consolidated School District, 54
Central America, 25, 28, 97–98, 103, 105, 164, 169, 198, 202, 209, 221*n8*
central Mexico, 31, 60, 76, 99, 163–164, 168–170, 202, 209, 221*n5*. *See also* Mexico
Chafin, Chief Henry, 53
Chautauqua Park (Boulder, Colorado), 144
Chavez, Cesar, 54, 93, 112, 121–122, 127–129, 131, 222*n19*
Cheyenne(s), 218*n3*
Chicago (Illinois), 96
Chicana(s). *See* Chicanx(s)
Chicanismo, 110–112, 134, 222*n19*
Chicano(s). *See* Chicanx(s)
Chicano Homeland, 13, 133, 203, 221*n8*
Chicano Movement, 6, 11, 13, 26, 28, 46, 53–55, 67, 93–95, 106–107, 117–118, 120, 126–127, 130–131, 135, 137–138, 142–143, 145, 147, 149–150, 153, 159–160, 190–192, 208, 210, 220*n1*, 221*n7*, 222*n19*, 222*n22*; Chicana Power, 122, 124; Chicanas, 121–124; and connections with communism, 107, 129, 133, 141, 222*n22*, 223*n23*, 223*n25*; decline of, 138, 153, 205; demands, 54, 93–94, 110, 116, 120, 121–126, 143, 147–150, 223*n25*; electoral strategies, 54, 134–136; ideology, 127, 130–133, 147, 149, 199, 222*n22*, 223*n24*, 223*n25*; labor struggles, 112, 122–123, 148, 206, 222*n19*; leadership, 121–123, 127, 129, 134–139, 143, 150, 221*n7*, 222*n19*; legal strategies, 54; machismo, 122–124, 138; militant ethos, 54, 93, 95, 108, 110–113, 117, 120, 123–124, 126, 129–130, 132, 134–136, 138–139, 141, 144–150, 222*n19*, 222*n22*; nationalism, 132–133, 138–139, 149–150, 200, 221*n8*, 222*n19*; and police brutality, 123, 125–129, 137, 141–142, 145–146, 150; politics, 112, 127, 132–136, 223*n26*; press coverage of, 107–108, 126, 128, 135, 137–138, 141–142, 145, 223*n30*; publications, 95; radicalization of, 107, 120, 121–123, 126, 128–129, 132, 136–138, 147–149, 191, 223*n24*; student movement, 54–55, 93–94, 112, 120, 125–126, 143–147; women in, 121–124, 138, 222*n20*
Chicano Youth Liberation Conference, 131, 136, 149, 221*n5*, 223*n26*
Chicanx(s), 11, 53, 59, 94, 106–107, 117, 119–120, 126, 132, 148, 174, 188, 203, 206, 214*n7*, 220*n1*, 226*n35*; definition of, 109–110, 220*n1*, 222*n16*, 225*n11*; identity, 53, 67, 109–112, 118, 130–131, 136, 147, 150–151, 199, 220*n2*, 221*n5*, 223*n25*, 224*n6*; Indigenous roots of, 109–112, 130–131, 199, 220*n2*, 220*n4*; and workplace discrimination, 91, 108, 115, 120, 127, 226*n35*
Chihuahua (Mexico), 163–164, 170
Child & Migrant Services, 161, 180
Chile, 171, 202
cholo, 225*n11*
Cinco de Mayo Festival (Denver), 204
circum-Mediterranean, 33
City Hall, Denver, 125
Ciudad Juárez (Mexico), 163
Civil Rights era, 11, 116, 191
Civil War (US), 9, 38

260 | INDEX

Clinton, William "Bill" (US President), 193
Coffman, Mike (US Representative), 29
Cold War, 107, 129, 154
colonias, 74–76, 78, 81, 218n6
Colorado (US state), 13, 25–26, 35, 63, 66–68, 77, 85, 118, 126, 210, 214n3, 215n13, 224n6, 227n6; Anglo-Hispanic relations, 9, 12, 66, 68, 77–78, 80, 114, 124, 126, 130, 139, 141, 146–151, 153, 156, 172–173, 177–178, 180, 185, 187–191, 193–196, 198, 202–211, 214n9, 221n9, 226n35; as a "border" state, 12, 67, 204, 214n9; borders, 3, 33, 49, 86, 217n14; colorfulness, 3–4; constitution, 44, 60, 216n9; demographic growth, 154–155, 161–162, 164–167, 170, 173–176, 190–191, 204; economy, 90, 95, 103–104, 113–114, 153–154, 161–162, 167–169, 176–177, 185–186, 188, 190, 193, 196–197, 204, 206, 208–209, 211, 222n15, 227n3; etymology of, 4, 204; geography, 26–27, 32, 112–113, 118; housing segregation, 114, 158, 206; Latinx demographics, 11, 17–18, 19f, 20f, 22–26, 23f, 50, 77, 88, 99, 102–103, 114–115, 117, 119, 154–155, 161–162, 164–167, 170, 173–176, 186, 189–192, 195–197, 203–204, 208–209, 211, 215n11, 217n16, 222n13, 222n14, 225n17; Latinx electorate, 11, 193, 197; Latinx political views, 197–198; lifestyle, 154, 196, 210; lynchings, 41; martial law, 49; mining, 47, 90–92, 113; politics, 29–30, 94, 102, 118, 135–136, 149, 190–198, 204, 211, 214n8, 217n16, 219n16, 220n17, 222n17, 222n18, 226n34, 227n3; racial diversity, 3–4, 6, 190–191, 202, 205, 208–211, 227n3; school segregation, 44, 79, 108, 114–115, 124–125, 127, 222n21; Spanish roots, 5; statehood, 38, 203; sugar beet industry, 69–73, 72f, 77, 85, 90, 157–158; tourism industry, 21, 162, 190, 205–206, 210. *See also* eastern Colorado; southern Colorado; western Colorado
Colorado (US territory), 9, 10, 12–13, 26, 35–36, 38, 41, 66, 113, 204, 210, 216n8, 218n7; gold rush, 218n3; martial law, 41; race riots, 41, 87
Colorado Coalfield War, 48

Colorado Constitutional Convention, 216n10
Colorado Convention Center, 193
Colorado Fuel and Iron Company (CF&I), 47–48, 90–92; workplace discrimination, 91–92
Colorado General Assembly, 45–46, 195
Colorado House of Representatives, 45–46, 192–195; Democratic Caucus, 192
Colorado Independent Redistricting Commission, 102
Colorado Mesa University, 160, 185, 226n42
Colorado Mounted Rangers, 53
Colorado National Guard, 48–49, 86
Colorado Rapid Response Network, 101
Colorado River, 4, 14
Colorado Rockies (baseball team), 193
Colorado Senate, 45–46, 192, 195, 216n9; Democratic Caucus, 192
Colorado Springs (Colorado), 18, 20, 22, 113, 154, 159, 209, 219n11, 222n18
Colorado State University (CSU), 146, 192, 218n6
Colorado State University Pueblo, 93, 214n8
Colorado State Vigilantes, 87
Colorado Supreme Court, 52
Colorado Territorial Legislature (Legislative Assembly of the Territory of Colorado), 45–46
commons, the, 40–41
compadre, 37
Compañeros: Four Corners Immigrant Resource Center, 178, 180
Conejos (city and county in Colorado), 21, 39, 45, 63, 65
Conejos Grant, 40
Constitution of Colorado, 44, 60, 216n9
Continental Divide, 113, 154, 217n15
Cook Partisan Voting Index, 220n17, 226n34
Coors Brewing Company (Coors beer), 93, 219n13
Coors, Peter "Pete," 194
Cora people, 170–171, 182, 202
Cortez (Colorado), 157, 178–179
Cortez Journal, The, 177

Costigan, Edward P. (US Senator), 85
Costilla County (Colorado), 21, 45, 63, 65, 217n18
COVID-19 pandemic, 25, 168, 179, 196, 211, 227n5
Craig (Colorado), 171
Crested Butte (Colorado), 170
Crowley County (Colorado), 103
Crusade for Justice, the, 121, 126–129, 131, 133, 136–141, 223n23
"crypto-Jews," 34
Cuba, 141
Cuban(s), 209
Cuban Americans, 198
Cuban Revolution, 129, 222n22
Culebra Range, 217n17
Culebra watershed, 52
Currigan, Tom (Denver Mayor), 127–128

Dakotas, the, 14
Dearfield (Colorado), 218n7
Declaration of Independence, US, 214n3
Del Norte (Colorado), 225n11
Delta (city and county in Colorado), 72, 176
Democratic Party, 29, 46, 94, 102, 129, 135–136, 179, 191–195, 197–198, 220n17, 227n3
Denver (city and county in Colorado), 5, 13, 15, 18, 19, 20, 22, 27–29, 38–39, 44, 50, 54, 60, 63, 83, 89, 93, 102, 113–114, 117–118, 120, 124, 126–129, 131, 136, 138–139, 141, 147, 149, 153–154, 159, 188, 190–193, 195, 200, 204–205, 208–209, 214n8, 215n11, 219n15, 221n9, 222n14, 222n21, 223n28, 226n34, 227n2; socioeconomic indicators, 119–120, 124
Denver and Rio Grande Railroad (D&RG), 38–39, 47, 63
Denver City Council, 227n1
Denver International Airport, 193, 227n2
Denver Post, The, 142, 217n14
Denver Public Schools, 126
Department of Homeland Security, 100
Díaz, Porfirio, 76
Dingley Tariff Act, 71
Dougherty, Francisco, 144
Douglas County (Colorado), 20

DREAM Act, 29, 185
dual labor market theory, 98
Duran, Crisanta (Colorado State Representative), 195
Durango (Colorado), 44, 155, 157, 161, 166–167, 172, 178, 224n4
Durango Herald, The, 178
Dust Bowl, 85

Eagle County (Colorado), 22, 167, 174–176, 181
Eagle County RE-50J School District, 176
East, the (US region), 58, 90–91, 113–114, 154, 178, 199, 202, 215n3
East Africa(n), 97–98
East Coast. *See* the East
East Otero R-1 School District, 103
eastern Colorado, 27, 69–70, 75, 90. *See also* Eastern Plains
eastern Europe, 47, 91, 217n13. *See also* Europe
Eastern Plains, the, 14, 48, 69–70, 80, 85, 90, 92, 95, 97–99, 101–106, 119–120, 188, 203, 209, 214n9, 218n3, 219n15, 226n34; communities, 84–85, 90, 99, 101–103, 105, 109, 113; demographics, 95, 97, 102–104, 103f, 209; meatpacking industry, 95–98, 100, 103, 105, 209. *See also* eastern Colorado
Easterner(s), 58
Eaton (Colorado), 71
Edwards (Colorado), 22
Eight Congressional District (Colorado), 102, 198
Eisenhower, Dwight D. (US President), 89
ejido system, 76, 218n8
El Diario de la Gente (The People's Daily), 144
El Movimiento. *See* Chicano Movement
El Norte, 13, 99, 112, 163, 202–203, 206, 215n10
El Paso (Texas), 77, 135, 139
El Paso County (Colorado), 20
"El Plan Espiritual de Aztlán," 131–133, 136, 149
El Pueblo, 73
El Salvador, 164
Ellis Island, 200–201

England, 178
Engle Mine, 43
English colonies, 8
English-Only movement, 60
Enos-Martinez, Cindy (Grand Junction Mayor), 185, 227n43
Entérate Latino, 180
entradas, 33
Equal Employment Opportunity Commission, 91
Escuela Tlatelolco, 137, 223n28
Española Subdivision (the Spanish colony), 75
Espinosa, Juan and Deborah, 95
ethnicity, 111, 135, 200
Europe, 72, 158, 199
Europeans, 13, 47–48, 70, 97, 186, 217n13, 220n5
European Union, 154
Evans, Gabe (US Representative), 102

Falcón, Ricardo, 139–141, 224n33
Federal Bureau of Investigation (FBI), 129, 133, 136–137, 140, 142, 145, 223n23
Federal Emergency Relief Administration (FERA), 86
First World, the, 97, 201
Flagstaff Mountain (Boulder, Colorado), 78
Fort Collins (Colorado), 15, 18, 71, 75, 99, 113–114, 120, 218n1, 218n6, 219n15; ethnic neighborhoods, 75, 218n6; Sugar Beet Park, 220n18
Fort Garland, 37, 40
Fort Lupton (Colorado), 72
Fort Massachusetts, 37
Fort Morgan (Colorado), 13, 71, 75, 89, 98–100, 102, 209
Fort Morgan RE-3 School District, 103
Fort Pueblo. *See* El Pueblo
Fort Vasquez, 216n7, 218n4
Fort Worth (Texas), 77
Fountain Sand and Gravel Company, 92
Fourth Congressional District (Colorado), 179, 226n34, 227n3
Francisco Maestas et al. v. George H. Shone et al., 44–45
Franco, Joe (UMAS-EOP Director), 144

Freedom of Information Act, 223n23
French Basque(s), 157
frijoles, 206
Frisco (Colorado), 167
Front Range, 13, 14, 19–20, 28, 47, 53, 63–65, 71, 78–79, 90, 95, 99, 102, 106, 109, 112–114, 117–119, 146, 149, 154, 157, 159–161, 165, 173, 186, 191–192, 209, 211, 219n11, 219n15, 222n13, 222n15, 222n18
fur trappers, 73

Gallegos, Bert A. (Colorado State Representative), 117
Garcia (Colorado), 37
García, Joseph "Joe" (Lieutenant Governor), 214n8
Garcia, Leroy (Colorado State Senator), 195
Garcia, Louis "Lugs," 94
Gardner, Cory (US Senator), 29
Garfield County (Colorado), 22, 167, 174–176, 181
Garfield RE-2 School District, 176
Generation X (Gen Xers), 23, 139, 148
Generation Z (Gen Z), 23, 196
gender, 8
genízaros, 215n1
Gentlemen's Agreement of 1907, 72
Georgia (US state), 219n10
German Russians, 72–74, 76, 79, 81–82, 104
German(s), 215n3
Gilberts, Robert D. (Denver Public Schools Superintendent), 126
G.I. Bill, 50
Glenwood Canyon, 152
Glenwood Springs (Colorado), 22, 152, 153f, 161, 168, 176
Global North, 187, 201–202, 224n2
Global South, 173, 201–203, 224n2
Golden (Colorado), 86, 219n13
Gonzales, Rodolfo "Corky," 54, 94, 121–123, 126–127, 131–132, 134–139, 143, 147, 149–150, 223n23, 223n26; biography, 127–129; charisma, 134–136, 150; ideology, 130–134, 136, 149–150
Government Highline Canal, 158
Granado, Florencio "Freddy," 144

Grand Junction (Colorado), 14, 22, 70, 117, 155, 157–161, 166–167, 174, 177–178, 180, 185, 224n4, 226n42, 227n43
Grand Junction City Council, 227n43
Grand Valley, 71, 157–159, 161–162, 225n11
Grand Valley Diversion Dam, 158
greaser(s), 45, 81, 216n10
Great American Desert, 70–71. *See also* Eastern Plains
Great Depression, 49–50, 81, 85, 87, 113, 115–116, 159
Great Plains, 13, 85, 90, 104, 219n15
Great Sand Dunes National Park and Preserve, 63
Great Western Sugar Company, 71–72, 74–75, 77, 81, 88–90, 92
Greeley (Colorado), 18, 71, 75, 87, 95, 98–100, 102, 192, 209, 219n15, 224n33; Greeley Stampede, 219n15
Greeley 6 School District, 103
gringo, 93
Grito de Dolores, 224n32
Guanajuato (Mexico), 163, 182
Guatemalan(s), 37, 56, 60–62, 68, 164, 202
Guerrero (Mexico), 163
Guevara, Ernesto "Che," 222n22
Gunnison (city and county in Colorado), 170–171, 182
Gunnison City Council, 171
Gurule, Alberto "Al," 93, 135
Gutiérrez, José Angel, 112, 121–122, 134–135
Guzmán, Lucía (Colorado State Senator), 195
Gypsum (Colorado), 22, 168

Haro, John, 137
Harold, John, 185
Hatch (New Mexico), 206
Hidalgo y Costilla, Father Miguel, 224n32
High Plains, 218n2. *See also* Great Plains
Highland neighborhood (Denver, Colorado), 192
Hinsdale County (Colorado), 166, 175
Hispanic Affairs Project, 169–170, 173, 177, 180, 185
Hispanic Caribbean, 205

Hispanic paradox, 25
Hispanic(s), 11, 17, 32; census term, 11, 215n2; classification of communities, 216n11; definition, 213n1, 215n2; "Hispanic origin" category, 17; identity, 67, 99, 204; "Mexican" category, 17; "Spanish language" category, 17; "Spanish mother tongue" category, 17; "Spanish surname" category, 17, 117. *See also* Latinx(s)
Hispanidad, 31
Hispano-Americans, 45. *See* Hispano(s)
Hispano(s), 12, 13, 22, 27, 35–36, 38–43, 45, 63, 74, 77, 81, 83, 87, 91–92, 104–105, 121, 135, 188, 199, 203–204, 206, 208, 213n1, 216n5, 218n4; assimilation, 57–58, 185; definition of, 35, 215n2; Hispano Homeland, 36, 39, 48, 55, 62, 65, 67, 203; identity, 53, 55, 57–58, 65, 67, 94, 110, 216n12, 222n19; military service, 50, 115; politics, 45–46, 117, 217n16, 217n18; prejudices, 45, 49, 55–56, 58, 60–61, 77, 80; relations with Mexican immigrants, 56–61, 77, 80–81, 159, 184–185; resistance, 42, 46–48, 51–52, 54, 66, 81, 109, 111–113, 119, 222n19; settlements, 41, 48–51, 66–68, 99, 112, 114, 156–158, 194, 198, 216n11, 217n13; sheepherders, 41; Spanish language, 57–60, 91; traditions, 43, 51–53, 57–58, 65; upper classes, 36, 46
History Colorado, 210
Hoene (Colorado), 158
Holly Sugar Company, 71, 158
Holy Family neighborhood (Fort Collins, Colorado), 75, 218n6
Holy Week, 182
Homestead Act of 1862, 40
Hoover, J. Edgar (FBI Director), 129
H-2A visas, 161, 171, 173, 225n13
Huehuetenango Department (Guatemala), 61
Huerfano County (Colorado), 45, 47
Huerta, Dolores, 112, 122, 127

I-70 highway, 18, 21, 152, 155, 167–168, 174
Iberian Peninsula, 33
imagined community, 110–112, 132

264 | INDEX

Immigration and Customs Enforcement (ICE), 59, 100–101
Immigration and Naturalization Service (INS), 89, 99–100
Immigration Reform and Control Act of 1986, 62
Indian(s). *See* Indigenous persons
Indigenous persons, 8, 32, 33, 34, 35, 38, 41, 55, 60, 66–67, 109, 111, 130, 137, 156, 170–171, 189, 202, 206, 210, 215n1, 215n3, 218n3, 219n12, 220n5
Indo-Hispanos, 222n19
Industrial Revolution, the, 71
Inquisition, Spanish, 34
Intermountain West (region). *See* West, the
International Monetary Fund (IMF), 162
Italian(s), 192, 200, 217n13
Italian American(s), 199, 224n6
Italy, 227n43
Irish, 215n3
Irish Americans, 116

Jaakola, Una, 144
Jackson County (Colorado), 175
Jalisco (Mexico), 163, 182
Japanese Americans, 47, 55, 74, 76, 81, 87; immigration, 72
JBS Foods, 96, 100
Jefferson County (Colorado), 20
Jews, 33–34; Sephardic, 34. *See also* crypto-Jews
Jicarilla Apache(s), 73
Jim Crow segregation, 80, 116, 118, 124
Johnson, Edwin "Big Ed" (Governor), 49–50, 86, 217n15
Johnson, Lyndon B. (US Senator and President), 116, 192, 221n11
Johnstown (Colorado), 72
Jones-Costigan Amendment of the Agricultural Adjustment Act (the Sugar Act of 1934), 85, 89
Juan Crow, 219n10

Kansas: US state, 3, 35; US territory, 38
Kearny, Stephen W. (Brigadier General), 34
Kennedy, John F. (US Senator), 116

Kennedy, Robert F. (US Senator), 139
Keyes v. School District No. 1, Denver, 222n21
King, Jr., Dr. Martin Luther, 128, 139
Kit Carson County (Colorado), 18
Kitayama Corporation, 122–123
Ku Klux Klan (KKK), 78, 157, 159

La Capilla de Todos Los Santos (The Chapel of All Saints), 31, 32*f*
La Cucaracha, 95, 219n14
La Hermandad (the Brotherhood). *See* Los Hermanos Penitentes
La Gara. *See* Las Colonias neighborhood
la gente, 57
"La Judea," 182
La Junta (Colorado), 102–103, 209, 216n7
La Plata County (Colorado), 166
La Paz (Bolivia), 172
la raza, 57, 111, 220n5
la raza cósmica, 132, 220n5
La Raza Unida Party (LRUP), 112, 121, 133–136, 139
La Sierra, 51–53
La Sociedad (Sociedad de Protección Mutua de Trabajadores Unidos), 42–45, 55
La Veta Pass, 38
La Voz del Pueblo, 180, 184
Lake County (Colorado), 22
Lake County R-1 School District, 176
Lakewood (Colorado), 205
Lamar (Colorado), 102, 209
land grants, 9, 27, 37, 40, 67, 222n19. *See also* mercedes
Land Rights Council (San Luis), 52, 54
Larimer County (Colorado), 20
Las Animas (city and county in Colorado), 21, 45, 47, 102, 216n9
Las Colonias neighborhood (Grand Junction, Colorado), 158–159, 225n9, 225n11
Las Gorras Blancas, 10
Latin America, 15, 131–132, 186, 188, 199, 202, 208, 220n5, 225n20; lost decade, 97, 162
latinidad, 209
Latina(s). *See* Latinx(s)

Latinization, 205
Latino(s). *See* Latinx(s)
Latino Movement, 212
Latinx(s), 13, 112, 126, 132, 198, 206, 224n1; assimilation, 9–10, 184, 187, 200, 204, 211; definition of, 213n1; immigration trends, 4, 37, 63, 68, 149, 156, 180, 198, 205, 207–209, 221n8; as a labor force, 8, 60, 97–98, 101, 153, 158, 164, 179, 185–186, 201, 219n13; middle class, 5, 12, 148, 208; numbers, 16, 18, 203; politics, 11, 102, 192–194, 196–198; as racialized Others, 12, 46, 66, 83, 87, 98, 104, 107, 112, 153, 184, 188, 190–191, 199–203, 219n10; recognition of, 11, 211; as relics of the past, 4, 210
Leadville (Colorado), 176
League of United Latin American Citizens (LULAC), 10, 115, 221n10
Lee, Stephen Luis, 51
LGBTQIA+, 220n1
Lobato v. Taylor, 217n19
Logan County (Colorado), 18
Loma (Colorado), 158
Longmont (Colorado), 71, 78–79, 99, 113
López Tijerina, Reies, 54, 112, 121–122, 127–128, 131, 221n6, 222n19
los americanos, 203. *See* Anglo(s)
Los Caminos Antiguos Scenic & Historic Byway, 5
Los Hermanos Penitentes (La Fraternidad Piadosa de Nuestro Padre Jesús Nazareno), 42–43
Los Seis de Boulder, 145, 224n30, 224n31
Los Voluntarios, 128
Louisiana Purchase, 216n7
Louisville (Colorado), 79
Loveland (Colorado), 71, 73, 78, 99
Lower 48 (US), 219n12
Lower Rio Grande Valley, 77, 112
Lucero, Levi, 226n42
Lucero family, 158
Ludlow Massacre, 48

Maestas, Francisco (father), 44
Maestas, Miguel (son), 44
Mancos (Colorado), 157

Manifest Destiny, 8, 40–41, 66, 214n4
manita(o), 47, 67, 80, 216n12
maquiladoras, 154, 163, 224n2
Mares, Alberto, 137
Martinez, David, 95
Martínez, Francisco E. "Kiko," 141–142
Martinez, Levi, 94
Martinez, Luis "Junior," 137
Martínez, Reyes, 144
McInnis, Scott (US Representative), 179
McNichols, William "Bill" (Denver Mayor), 193
meatpacking industry, 95–101, 105, 209; labor practices, 96–98, 101
Medina, Mariano, 73
mejicanos, 54
mercedes, 37. *See also* land grants
Mesa College. *See* Colorado Mesa University
Mesa County (Colorado), 166, 179, 225n9
Mesa State College. *See* Colorado Mesa University
Mesoamerica, 224n1
Mexican-American Committee for Equality (MACE), 146
Mexican American Legal Defense and Education Fund (MALDEF), 141
Mexican Americans, 10, 48–49, 67–69, 74, 79, 87, 91, 105–106, 109, 112, 114, 117, 119–120, 127–128, 133, 135, 148–150, 159, 174, 183, 203, 214n7, 218n4, 221n11, 221n12, 223n24, 224n1, 225n11; assimilation strategies, 110, 115, 120, 133, 138, 160, 183–185, 200; identity, 99, 130, 183–184; labor, 70, 87, 101, 108, 114–115, 119, 121–122, 124, 184, 201, 206, 222n16, 222n19; organizations, 115, 193, 221n10; politics, 94, 116–117, 133, 138, 192, 198. *See also* Chicanx(s)
Mexican Farm Labor Agreement. *See* Bracero Program
Mexican Republic. *See* Mexico
Mexican Tejanos, 8–9
Mexican Revolution, 77, 158
Mexicano(s), Mexicana(s), 35, 57, 110, 184
"Mexican(s)" (generic label), 9, 11, 17*f*, 36, 41, 44–45, 47, 49–50, 66, 73, 79, 81, 89,

91, 93–94, 98, 105, 109, 114–115, 124–125, 140–141, 147–148, 157, 181, 183, 185, 189, 194, 199, 201–202, 205, 210, 214*n5*, 222*n14*, 221*n9*, 222*n14*, 224*n3*, 225*n11*; definition of, 9, 216*n4*, 218*n4*, 224*n2*; deportations, 85–87, 89, 101, 184; labor, 69, 72–74, 81–84, 87–88, 90, 92, 97–99, 101, 104, 106–107, 119, 201, 222*n19*

Mexico, 8, 12, 28, 31, 34, 41, 48, 53, 57, 86, 88, 98–100, 110–111, 130, 132, 141, 154, 158–159, 176, 178, 180, 186, 194, 202, 215*n1*, 215*n3*, 215*n10*, 215*n12*, 220*n3*, 223*n28*, 224*n32*, 224*n1*; borderlands, 12, 28, 111, 163, 202–203, 220*n3*; citizens of, 34, 45, 55, 81, 83, 86–87, 94, 156, 206, 214*n5*, 218*n4*, 224*n1*, 224*n3*; consuls, 83; economy, 76, 99, 154, 162–163, 176, 182, 186, 224*n2*; government, 40, 50–51, 67, 83, 162–163, 223*n28*; Mexican Revolution, 77, 130; migrants from, 49–50, 55, 58, 60, 62–63, 66–70, 74, 77, 80, 88, 90–92, 97–99, 101–103, 105, 111–112, 114, 119, 133–134, 154–156, 158–159, 161–165, 167–170, 173–178, 180–182, 185–188, 198–203, 209, 218*n4*; modernization, 76; northern frontier, 109, 215*n2*, 219*n11*; US-Mexican War, 8–9, 12, 34, 66, 109, 133, 150, 156, 189, 200, 210, 216*n4*, 219*n11*, 221*n5*; US-Mexico border, 12–13, 62, 67, 86–87, 99, 111, 141, 154, 163, 198, 201–202, 205, 219*n11*, 221*n11*; wages, 76

Mexico City, 35, 99, 154, 163, 209
Michoacán (Mexico), 161, 163, 182
Midwest (US region), 77, 96, 113–114, 154, 191
Midwestern, Midwesterners, 13
Millennial(s), 23, 196
Mineral County (Colorado), 63
Minnequa Steelworks steel mill, 90, 95
Misioneras Guadalupanas del Espíritu Santo, 181
Mississippi River, 90
Monfort family companies, 98, 100
Montana (US state), 3
Monte Vista (Colorado), 53
Monterrey (Mexico), 99, 163

Montezuma County, 178, 225*n7*
Montrose (city and county in Colorado), 22, 44, 161, 169–171, 176, 226*n35*
Montrose County RE-1J School District, 176
Moors, 33
Mora, Pablo, 95
Morgan County (Colorado), 18, 103
Morley, Clarence (Governor), 78
Mormons, 206
Mountain States' labor stream, 77
Mountain Village (Colorado), 169
Mountain West, the (US), 150, 188, 191. *See also* West, the
Movimiento Estudiantil Chicano de Aztlán (MEChA), 93
mutualista(s), 10, 43

National Beef Packing, 96
National Conference to Combat the English-Only Movement, 60
National Floral Workers Organization (NFWO), 122–123
National Park Service, 40
Native Americans, 13, 35, 37, 48, 66–67, 75, 109, 111–112, 117, 156, 191, 199, 214*n5*, 214*n6*, 215*n10*. *See also* Indigenous persons
Naturita (Colorado), 169
Navajo(s), 111, 156–157
Nayarit (Mexico), 170, 182
Nebraska: US state, 3; US territory, 38
neolocalism, 206
Nevada (US state), 35
New Castle (Colorado), 22
New Deal, 86
New Englanders, 13
New Hispano Party, 94
New Mexico, 31–33, 44, 50, 67, 74, 111–112, 141, 189, 203–205, 211, 215*n3*; colonial, 215*n1*; Hispano identity, 216*n5*, 217*n16*, 222*n19*; land grants, 9, 112, 222*n19*; Spanish colony, 215*n1*; statehood, 36, 38, 66, 216*n6*, 219*n12*; US state, 3, 4, 27, 31–33, 35, 37, 44, 48–51, 69, 73–75, 80, 86, 90, 109, 111–112, 114, 121, 127–128, 139, 141, 158, 203–206, 211, 213*n1*, 215*n2*,

215*n3*, 216*n11*, 217*n12*, 217*n21*, 219*n12*, 222*n19*; US territory, 9–10, 13, 21, 33–38, 41–43, 51, 53, 66–67, 91, 157–158, 189, 194, 198, 204, 216*n6*, 217*n16*, 219*n12*, 219*n12*; violence, 42
New South, 208. *See also* the South
New West, 7, 13, 79, 114, 154–155, 161–162, 169, 188, 201, 207, 210, 212. *See also* West, the
New World, 57, 204
Newlands Reclamation Act of 1902, 71
Nixon, Richard (US President), 116
Nogales (Arizona), 141
North Africa, 33
North American Free Trade Agreement (NAFTA), 28, 98–99, 154, 163, 165, 173–174, 176, 186–188, 209
North Carolina (US state), 51
North Platte River Valley, 90
northern Colorado, 74
North Side School (Alamosa, Colorado), 44
Northeast, the (US region), 191
northern Europe, 47, 91, 178. *See also* Europe
northern Mexico, 27, 34–35, 60, 76–77, 161, 163–164, 169, 202, 220*n3*. *See also* Mexico
northern New Mexico, 32–39, 42–43, 48, 51, 53, 74, 128, 157–158, 194, 216*n11*, 216*n12*, 222*n19*; land rights struggle, 121, 128, 217*n21*, 222*n19*. *See also* New Mexico
Norwood (Colorado), 169
Nuevo México territory, 34, 57
Nuevomexicano(s), 9, 35, 66. *See also* Hispano(s); New Mexico

Obama, Barack (US President), 29, 194
Ocate (New Mexico), 158
Oglala Lakota, 136
Oklahoma (US state), 3, 35
Olathe (Colorado), 169–170
Olathe's Sweet Corn, 185
Old Town Fort Collins, 75, 218*n6*
Old West, 13, 114, 154, 161–162, 188, 201, 207. *See also* West, the

Oñate, Don Juan de, 33
100th Meridian, 218*n2*
Operation Wetback, 89
Order of Sons of America, 10, 115
Orogrande (New Mexico), 139
Otero County (Colorado), 21, 80, 103
Ovid (Colorado), 72

Pacific coast, 9
Pacific Northwest, the (US region), 208
Pagosa Springs (Colorado), 44, 161, 176
Palisade (Colorado), 161–162
pan-ethnic identity, 22, 209
Parachute (Colorado), 22, 168, 176
Parker, Trey, 227*n5*
patrón, 37, 216*n9*; system, 37
Pearl Harbor (Hawaii), 87
Peña, Federico (Denver Mayor), 60, 190, 193–194, 214*n8*, 227*n2*
Peru, 171, 202
Phillips County (Colorado), 18, 103
Pike, Zebulon, 14
Pitkin County (Colorado), 168
Plains Indians, 218*n3*. *See also* Indigenous persons
Platteville (Colorado), 73, 216*n7*
Plaza de los Leones, 47. *See* Walsenburg
Plaza de los Manzanares, 37
plazas, 37
pochos, 109
Polis, Jared (Governor), 226*n29*
Poor People's March, 128
Poudre River, 75
Protestants, 43
Prowers County (Colorado), 103
Pueblo (city and county in Colorado), 20, 21, 28, 38, 47, 90, 93–95, 159, 114, 178–179, 194–195, 206, 219*n11*, 227*n6*
Pueblo Chile & Frijoles Festival, 206, 207*f*
Pueblo School District, 94
Pueblo United, 93
Puebloans, 33, 34, 67, 157
Pueblo's District 60, 93
Puerto Montt, 171
Puerto Ricans, 22, 209

Q'anjob'al Maya, 61–62, 218*n28*

race, 46, 189, 202; and class, 8; racialization process, 8, 84, 112, 147, 188, 199–202; racialized Others, 66, 83, 87, 104, 107, 110–111, 190, 199, 203, 214n6; as a social construct, 7–8, 111
Rael, Apolinar, 52
Rakhra Mushroom Farm, 62
Reagan, Ronald (US President), 138–139, 154
Reconquista, 220n3
reggaeton, 205
replenished ethnicity, 99, 105, 133–134, 184, 200, 218n4
Republic of Texas, 216n4
Republican Party, 29, 46, 102, 129, 179, 191, 194, 197, 220n17, 226n34, 227n3
Rifle (Colorado), 22, 168, 176
Rio Blanco County (Colorado), 175
Rio Grande, 32, 33, 55, 67; Rio Arriba region, 55; Upper Rio Grande, 36, 55; watershed, 14, 33
Rio Grande County (Colorado), 21, 63–65
ristras, 206
Rito Seco Creek, 52
Roaring Fork RE-1 School District, 176
Rockefeller family, 47, 90
Rocky Ford (Colorado), 71, 84, 87
Rocky Ford R-2 School District, 103
Rocky Mountains, 13, 14, 113, 154, 169, 218n2
Romer, Roy (Governor), 60
Romero, Neva, 144
Romero, Ricardo, 60
Routt County (Colorado), 175
rural proletarians, 42, 76, 84
Russian Revolution, 72

Safeway supermarkets, 93
Saguache County (Colorado), 21, 63, 65
Salazar, John (US Representative), 179, 194
Salazar, Ken (US Senator), 194
Salt Creek neighborhood (Pueblo, Colorado), 94
San Antonio (Texas), 77
San Juan County (Colorado), 166, 175–176
San Juan mountains, 32, 38

San Luis (Colorado), 31, 32, 33, 52, 217n18; founding, 37, 216n7
San Luis People's Ditch, 52, 216n8
San Luis Potosí (Mexico), 227n43
San Luis Valley (the Valley), 5, 9, 12, 14, 21, 27, 31–35, 37–40, 44–68, 104–105, 113, 119–120, 141, 156–160, 178–179, 192, 194, 204, 208, 214n9, 217n18, 219n11; agricultural production, 33, 37–38, 48, 50–53, 61, 65; demographics, 63–64, 64f, 117, 188, 222n14; environmental challenges, 65; geography, 32; health indicators, 65; migration patterns, 46–52, 60–63, 188; mining, 52–53; settlement of, 35, 37–39, 47, 51, 53, 66–67, 216n11; socioeconomic indicators, 63–65
San Miguel County (Colorado), 170, 175
San Miguel Resource Center, 177
Sanchez, Jennie, 54
Sand Creek Massacre, 218n3
Sangre de Cristo Land Grant, 51
Sangre de Cristo mountain range, 21, 31, 32, 47, 217n17
Santa Eulalia (Guatemala), 61
Santa Fe (New Mexico), 33, 34, 194
Santa Fe Ring, 9
September 11, 2001, terrorist attacks (9/11 terrorist attacks), 142, 163
Serna, Martín, 93
Shone, George H. (Superintendent), 44
Silt (Colorado), 22, 168, 176
Silverthorne (Colorado), 167
Sixth Congressional District (Colorado), 29
slavery, 8; in colonial New Mexico, 215n1; in the United States, 8
Smelter Mountain (Durango, Colorado), 157
Sonora (Mexico), 161, 163
South, the (US region), 119, 191, 219n10
South Africa, 80
South America, 25, 171, 173, 202, 209, 221n8
South Coloradan, The, 54
south Florida, 198
South Park, 227n5
South Platte River, 14, 113

South Platte River Valley, 71, 90, 191
south Texas, 135, 193, 198, 216n11, 221n11. *See also* Texas
Southeast Asia, 116
southern Colorado, 14, 18, 21, 27, 32, 35–37, 39, 41, 43, 45, 47–48, 50, 53, 63, 67, 73–74, 90, 114, 157–158, 198, 216n10, 216n12, 219n11. *See also* Colorado
Southern Colorado Junior College. *See* Colorado State University Pueblo
southern Europe, 47, 91. *See also* Europe
southern Mexico, 163, 202, 209 . *See also* Mexico
Southwest, the (US region), 5, 9, 10, 11, 12, 13, 14, 17, 33, 35, 37, 40, 57, 77, 117, 156, 215n3, 216n4. *See also* West, the
southwestern Colorado, 38, 157, 172, 178. *See also* Colorado; Western Slope, the
Spain, 31, 57, 218n8, 224n32
Spanish American(s), 35–36, 45, 57, 73–74, 117, 119, 148. *See also* Hispano(s)
Spanish-American War, 45, 71
Spanish Crown, 34
Spanish empire, 7, 12, 33–35, 67, 110, 130, 156, 204, 214n9, 215n1, 215n10, 219n11, 220n5; colonists, 215n3
Spanish language, 205
Stapleton, Benjamin "Ben" (Denver Mayor), 78
Stations of the Cross sculptures, 31. *See also* La Capilla de Todos Los Santos
Statue of Liberty, 200
Steamboat Springs (Colorado), 175
Sterling (Colorado), 71, 209
Stone, Matt, 227n5
sugar beet industry, 27, 50, 69–73, 85, 101, 157, 160, 164; child labor in, 73, 82–83; factories, 71–72, 72f, 89, 158; history, 70–72, 85, 89–90, 103–105, 113, 115, 220n18; housing, 74–77, 88, 158; labor practices, 76, 81–83, 85, 88, 90, 92, 101, 119, 218n1; labor recruitment strategies, 74–77, 85, 92, 158; "Mexican labor," 73–74, 77, 80, 84, 90, 92, 101, 104, 106, 192, 210, 220n18; segregation, 75–76, 78–80, 83–84; wages, 81, 83, 85
Summit County (Colorado), 167, 174, 181

Summit RE-1 School District, 176
sundown towns, 78, 219n9
Sunken Gardens Park (Denver, Colorado), 125
surumatos, 80
Sweetheart City. *See* Loveland
Swift plant (Greeley, Colorado), 100
Swing, Joseph May (General), 89

Tabasco (Mexico), 170
Tancredo, Tom (US Representative), 29–30, 153, 197, 200
Taos (New Mexico), 33, 34, 73; 1847 uprising, 34, 51
taquerías, 167
Tarahumara, 60, 225n11
Taylor, Jack, 51–52
Tejanos, 35
Tejas, Mexican, 8, 204, 216n4
Telluride (Colorado), 22, 28, 64, 161, 164, 166–167, 169–170, 175–178
Temporary Building #1 (TB-1), 144, 224n31
Tepic (Mexico), 170
Terán, Heriberto, 144
Texas (US state), 8–9, 14, 35, 36, 50, 74, 111–112, 116, 121, 127, 134, 149, 189, 203–205, 211, 223n27; Anglo Texans, 8, 58, 178, 216n4; Mexican Tejanos, 8–9; statehood, 216n4
Texas, Republic of, 8
Texas Panhandle, 50. *See* Texas
Texas Rangers, 140
Thieme, Frederick P. (CU Boulder President), 140
Third Congressional District (Colorado), 178–179, 194
Third World, the, 150, 201, 222n22
Thirty-seventh parallel, 33
Thornton (Colorado), 215n11
Tierra Amarilla (New Mexico) courthouse, 128
Tijuana (Mexico), 163
Time magazine, 11
Tipton, Scott (US Representative), 179
transnationalism, 181–183, 186–188, 203–204, 226n36; remittances, 182

Treaty of Guadalupe Hidalgo, 34, 35, 67, 91, 156, 198, 214n3
Trinidad (Colorado), 41, 43, 47, 91, 217n13
Trump, Donald (US President), 179, 197, 227n3
2008 recession, 164, 176, 196, 211
Tyson Foods, 96

United Farm Workers (UFW), 140
United Mexican American Students (UMAS), 54, 140, 143–144, 144f, 146–147, 160, 227n43
United Mexican American Students Equal Opportunity Program (UMAS-EOP), 140, 144
United Mine Workers of America, 48
United States of America, 8, 10, 26, 31, 41, 50, 62, 67, 94, 98, 100, 106, 110, 112, 154, 159, 163, 176–177, 182, 186, 214n3, 215n10, 215n12, 219n11, 219n12, 220n3, 221n8, 225n13; Civil War, 9, 38; Great Depression, 49–50, 81, 85, 87, 113, 115–116; immigration, 37, 50, 62, 66, 97, 163–164, 205, 226n36; imperialism, 67; national politics, 138–139, 153, 191, 194–195, 198; race, 8, 94; US-Mexican war, 8–9, 34, 66, 133, 150, 156, 189, 200, 210, 216n4, 219n11, 221n5; wages, 76, 88
University of Colorado Boulder (CU Boulder), 78, 80, 140, 143–144, 146, 160, 227n43
University of Denver, 224n33
University of Northern Colorado, 219n15, 224n33
Univisión, 29
Urista, Alberto "Alurista," 131, 221n5
US Army of the West, 34, 55, 156
US Census Bureau, 11, 15, 16, 17, 165, 213n1; categories, 17, 215n12; decennial census, 11, 16, 18
US Congress, 38, 89, 153, 179
US courts, 40
US federal government, 40, 85, 87–88, 100, 107, 112, 121, 128, 136, 141–142, 146, 163, 172, 177, 179, 216n4, 223n23
US Forest Service, 40, 51

US-Mexican war, 8–9, 12, 27, 34–35, 66, 109, 133, 150, 156, 189, 200, 210, 216n4, 219n11, 221n5
US-Mexico border, 12–13, 62, 67, 86–87, 99, 111, 141, 154, 163, 198, 201–202, 205, 219n11, 221n11
US military governors, 40
US Senate, 49, 194
US Supreme Court, 221n10, 222n21
Utah: US state, 3, 14, 35, 44, 47; US territory, 38
Ute(s), 34, 38, 73, 111, 156–157, 189

Vail (Colorado), 14, 22, 28, 64, 161, 166–168, 174, 176
Vasconcelos, José, 132, 220n5
Vasquez, Louis, 73
Venezuela(n), 209, 225n20
Viceroyalty of New Spain, 34, 35, 202. See also Spanish empire
Vietnam War, 10, 116, 128, 138–139, 221n12, 222n22; protests, 116, 120, 125, 143, 154
Violent Gang and Terrorist Organization File, 142
Viva Kennedy clubs, 116
Virginia colony, 7–8

Wall Street, 128
Walsenburg (Colorado), 44, 47
War on Poverty, 128
Washington, DC, 128, 192
Washington, George (US President), 130
Welcome to Colorful Colorado road signs, 2f, 3
Weld County (Colorado), 18, 79, 103, 140
West, the (US region), 7, 10, 13, 26, 28, 38–40, 49, 53, 63, 65–67, 73, 76, 91, 99, 109, 111–112, 149, 169, 173, 191, 199, 203, 214n6, 214n9, 215n1, 219n9, 220n3, 221n8; Anglo-Hispanic relations, 9, 12, 60, 66, 79, 81, 83–84, 86–87, 96, 107, 111, 114, 116, 121, 124, 127, 130, 134, 140, 143, 149–150, 153, 156, 158, 177–178, 180, 183–184, 186, 191, 194, 198–202, 204–207, 210, 216n4, 219n10, 221n5, 222n19, 224n3; definition of, 201–203, 215n10; ethnic division of labor, 84,

87–88, 93, 99, 115, 124, 153, 164, 167, 171–173, 179, 185–186, 189, 201; as a frontier, 201, 207, 214n9; fur trappers, 73; Hispanicization, 204–206, 227n3; Intermountain West, 5, 177; race riots, 87; railroads, 71
West Coast, 87, 119
West High School (Denver, Colorado), 125–126
Western I-70 corridor. *See* I-70 highway
western Europeans, 192
western Colorado, 14, 169. *See also* Western Slope, the
Western Colorado Latino Chamber of Commerce, 180
Western Slope, the, 5, 27, 28, 71, 113, 120, 152, 154–156, 159–160, 167, 172–173, 176, 178–179, 181, 184–187, 194, 199, 202–203, 208, 214n9; demographics, 154–155, 159–162, 164–167, 165f, 166f, 170–171, 173–176, 174f, 175f, 186–188; economy, 155, 157, 160–162, 164, 167–171, 177, 180, 185–187, 208–209; geography, 154, 166; history, 156–157; Mexican labor, 155, 158–162, 164–165, 167–170, 173, 175–176, 179–180, 185–187, 202, 208, 225n18, 226n29; sheepherding, 171–173, 202; sugar beet industry, 71, 89, 157–158
Western Sugar Cooperative. *See* Great Western Sugar Company
Western United States. *See* West, the
Westminster (Colorado), 215n11
Westwood neighborhood (Denver, Colorado), 114
Wheeler, George, 40
"White American West," 75
white persons, 8. *See* Anglo(s)
Wildcat Dairy, 100
Wolf Creek ski area, 176
women of color, 8, 123
World War I, 45, 50, 71–72, 91, 115, 158
World War II, 10, 50, 79, 87, 100, 113–116, 143, 159, 181
Wounded Knee (South Dakota), 136
Wyoming (US state), 3, 14, 35, 47, 90

Yuma County (Colorado), 18, 103
Yo soy Joaquín (I am Joaquín), 130–131

ABOUT THE AUTHOR

Ernesto Sagás is professor of ethnic studies at Colorado State University. He has a PhD in political science from the University of Florida with a concentration in Latin American studies. His research focuses on the politics of the Hispanic Caribbean (particularly on issues of race, elections, and democratization), democracy and authoritarianism in Latin America and the Caribbean, transnational politics, Latinx politics, Latinxs in Colorado, US immigration policies, and race/ethnicity/identity in the American West.